BLOODSPORT

BLOODSPORT

When Ruthless Dealmakers,
Shrewd Ideologues, *and*
Brawling Lawyers Toppled *the*
Corporate Establishment

ROBERT TEITELMAN

PUBLICAFFAIRS

New York

PublicAffairs books are available at special discounts for bulk purchases in the US by corporations, institutions, and other organizations. For more information, please contact the Special Markets Department at the Perseus Books Group, 2300 Chestnut Street, Suite 200, Philadelphia, PA 19103, call (800) 810-4145, ext. 5000, or e-mail special.markets@perseusbooks.com.

A CIP catalog record is available from the Library of Congress
ISBN 978-1-61039-413-0 (HC)
ISBN 978-1-61039-436-9 (EB)

First Edition

10 9 8 7 6 5 4 3 2 1

The world is not the way they tell you it is.
—ADAM SMITH, *The Money Game,* 1967

Now what's going to happen to us without barbarians?
They were, those people, a kind of solution.
—C. P. CAVAFY, "Waiting for the Barbarians"

CONTENTS

Introduction

A REVOLUTIONARY EXPERIMENT

E. I. DU PONT de Nemours and Company was hardly the sort of corporation, and Edward Garland Jefferson hardly the kind of chief executive, we would expect to find in one of the messiest takeover brawls in US history. DuPont was the oldest big corporation in America, founded in 1802 to manufacture gunpowder along the banks of Brandywine Creek outside Wilmington, Delaware, by the son of a French *physiocrat*—an early economist—fleeing the French Revolution. DuPont had, through war and peace, crisis and prosperity, grown into one of America's preeminent R&D-driven companies—a pioneer of industrial science on par with AT&T and General Electric—developing and selling everything from plastics to paints to space-age textiles to myriad other advanced chemically based products. The company had long been family controlled and operated; the countryside around Wilmington was thick with "cousins" living as *rentiers* off the stock. Pierre du Pont and his two cousins, all MIT-trained, had acquired the then–munitions maker in 1902 from family members who were, as a history of DuPont research notes, "tired, leaderless and ready to sell out to businessmen who were not du Ponts."[1] The cousins undertook a series of acquisitions of chemical rivals (stirring the company's first antitrust woes) and transformed management with innovative techniques and investments in science-based product development. In 1914, Pierre acquired a stake in then-foundering General Motors, joined its board, became its president, and DuPont eventually took control. DuPont also designed, built, and operated the Hanford works

1

in Washington State that produced plutonium for atomic weaponry. Its legacy as a munitions maker was an ambiguous and increasingly troublesome one—profitable yet also hazardous (plants occasionally blew up) and controversial. DuPont psychologically (if a company can have a psychology) never really recovered from being a target of the congressional Nye Committee in the 1920s, which investigated wartime business practices and hung the label "merchant of death" around its metaphorical neck.

The 1970s had been hard on DuPont, as it had for many US corporations. Key raw material costs—notably oil—spiked, and competition, mostly in its massive textiles business, mounted. The stock sank. The federal government had awakened to environmental degradation, and it hit chemical makers (not to say builders of plutonium-producing reactors) hard. DuPont's old nemesis, antitrust, loomed. In 1971, the last du Pont CEO and chairman, Lammot "Mots" du Pont Copeland, retired. (The history of DuPont research notes dryly that Copeland "would not turn out to be a propitious choice" to run the company.[2]) After a two-year interregnum by a family retainer, the board—still dominated by the family—handed the reins over to a lawyer named Irving Shapiro, the son of a Jewish Lithuanian immigrant tailor and dry cleaner, and a graduate of the University of Minnesota Law School during the Great Depression. Shapiro had made his name, and won the family trust, during DuPont's long antitrust struggle with the government over GM and the forced sale of its stake in 1962.[3] For the first time in decades, Shapiro made modest cuts to the all-but-sacrosanct research budget and raised questions about R&D. He took the initial steps to reduce dependence on textiles. In 1973, DuPont quietly shuttered the last black gunpowder facility, in Moosic, Pennsylvania. Unlike a long line of DuPont executives, Shapiro made himself a spokesman for corporate America, was active at the Business Roundtable, and was heretically close to Jimmy Carter (the du Pont family was, in the main, cloth-coat Republican). He retired in 1981, at age sixty-four, and accepted a partnership with an up-and-coming New York law firm, Skadden Arps Meagher & Flom, run by a diminutive, combative mergers-and-acquisitions attorney named Joe

Flom, and opened a Skadden outpost in Wilmington, where the nation's preeminent state corporate-law courts operated.

Ed Jefferson, fifty-nine, succeeded Shapiro. The lanky Jefferson was not a du Pont, although his ascension returned DuPont to its tradition, dating back to the cousins, of placing a technical man at the helm. Jefferson was British, raised in London, with a soft English accent and a predilection for amateur singing.[4] His father had been a director of Hawker Siddely, which made some of the fighter planes that helped win the Battle of Britain, and he had served in the Royal Artillery during the war and participated in the Normandy invasion. DuPont recruited him after he earned a first-class degree in chemistry at King's College, University of London, offering him a job at one of its West Virginia factories; he met his wife there and took US citizenship in 1957. Jefferson's talents were quickly recognized in Wilmington. DuPont put him on the "skimmer" list as a manager who was deliberately moved from one area to the next, mastering the intricacies of a remarkably complex company; eventually, he found himself running all of DuPont's Central Research, one of the summits of industrial science. When he was named Shapiro's successor in May 1981, he was already talking about the need for DuPont to move in a radical new direction from maturing chemicals to youthful life sciences. Genetic engineering had emerged in the '70s, and Jefferson recognized the potential of what he called "living polymers," as if proteins were plastics. "Even though the molecules are admittedly large, they have chemical symbols," said Jefferson. "It's a heck of a lot closer to chemistry than particle physics."[5] What Jefferson may not have recognized is what a leap molecular biology was from traditional chemistry, and how the newly emerging biotechnology industry—Genentech went public in a spectacular initial public offering in October 1980—was already undermining the hegemony of large, stable, centralized, industrial-style corporate research efforts.

And yet for all the talk of life sciences, Jefferson made a move weeks after assuming leadership that drove DuPont in a totally different direction. On June 7 he announced an offer for an oil company, Conoco, the ninth-largest corporation in America, and one slightly larger, by revenue, than DuPont. Conoco provided a solution to DuPont's thirst for oil—a strategic need that looked back to the crises of the '70s rather than forward to the nascent wonders of life sciences. The plan emerged out of DuPont's strategic planning bureaucracy, and it decisively shaped Jefferson's tenure at the top of DuPont: defense, not offense. It also represented, at $7.57 billion in cash and stock, the largest mergers-and-acquisitions transaction in history. DuPont, which had not engaged in many acquisitions under Mots Copeland and had a balance sheet with little debt, could afford it.

What Jefferson may not have fully comprehended was the maelstrom he was entering, so different from the coolly deliberative processes of the DuPont bureaucracy. DuPont was a fortress, and high-corporate life had its hierarchies, its rituals, its sense of propriety, even its romance. DuPont in particular believed its history and achievements insulated it from a rapidly changing corporate world, though the '70s had breached some outer walls. Shapiro, a lawyer, a Jew, an outsider throughout all his years of loyal service, had sensed the magnitude of change. Takeover battles, like the one for Conoco, featuring unrestrained financial forces, legalism gone mad, a profound market relativism, and an ethos of victory at all costs, was just the most visible sign. The corporation was losing control over its destiny; the CEO was a potentate dragged into a democratic marketplace. Attitudes toward shareholders, workers, customers, toward pay, toward a rooted past and any sense of legacy, would now be put under vise-like pressures. Outsiders were re-imagining the very governance of the corporation—the legal and ethical code that structured its operations, the mechanisms of control and participation.

In fact, the corporate world Jefferson would discover in the summer of 1981, and struggle to master throughout his tenure as CEO, was far more similar to our own current one than to that of Mots Copeland. It is demonstrably the environment that everyone from workers to senior executives to shareholders to directors cope with every day: fluid, uncertain, changeable, with its activists, free agents, mobility, suspicions, and uncertain loyalties. With one exception: This corporate world was just emerging in 1981. There is far more of it today—more M&A, more money, more insecurity, instability, inequality, complexity, ambiguity, and change. We're just more accustomed to it.

DuPont had bid for Conoco at the oil company's request, as a so-called white knight, which fit DuPont's self-regarding self-image. Despite its size, Conoco was under siege by Seagram, the New York liquor giant run by the handsome scion of the founding Bronfman family, Edgar Bronfman Sr., who had sold some high-priced oil and gas properties and chose not to reinvest the money into booze. He wanted Conoco, and he went hostile when the company rebuffed him. But he wasn't alone. Canadian oil producer Dome Petroleum craved Conoco's sizable position in another Canadian oil company, Hudson's Bay Oil & Gas, and stalked the US oil giant. Conoco, in turn, had engaged in quiet talks with yet another US oil company, Cities Service, which was under attack by a third Canadian company, NuWest Group. And there was talk that other bidders—including one of the largest oil companies in the world, Mobil Oil—were sniffing around.

In making the decision to bid for Conoco, Jefferson and DuPont found themselves mired in the surreal counterreality of a takeover struggle. On announcing the merger, DuPont stock immediately thudded 8 percent. Despite DuPont's prestige, history, and size, the company not only found itself engaged in a multiparty bidding contest that escalated faster than the Vietnam War but also was besieged by a breed of Wall Street advisors, friend and foe, wise men and hustlers, who spoke a vaguely violent, opaque language of struggle, coercion, and control—two-pool bid structures, pro-rated shares, bear hugs, lockups, scorched-earth tactics—and were harbingers of a strange short-term, market-driven mentality. They played M&A as if it were a bloodsport. DuPont didn't view business as a *game*; many in the Wall Street crowd did. The two lawyers who had all but invented the modern takeover game, Wachtell Lipton Rosen & Katz's Martin Lipton and Skadden's Joe Flom, quickly appeared on the scene: Lipton counseling Conoco, Flom DuPont. (Shapiro, an articulate champion of director-driven governance, orchestrated some of this despite his layers of loyalties: he remained a DuPont board member, and head of the

executive committee, while running Skadden's Wilmington office.)
DuPont also hired the two most aggressive merger groups on the
Street, its traditional advisor, starchy Morgan Stanley, whose unit was
run by intense Robert Greenhill, and First Boston, whose freewheeling
team was headed by Joseph Perella and his larger-than-life partner, the
already notorious savant of takeover tactics, Bruce Wasserstein. In fact,
advisors swarmed all over the deal, which quickly got so complicated
that Perella and Wasserstein dubbed it the double-barreled two-step
or, more colloquially, Big Rube, like a Rube Goldberg mechanism.[6]

After a long summer of struggle, lawsuits, and desperate maneuvering, DuPont emerged victorious—not because anyone thought it
was the best fit for Conoco (except Conoco) but, rather, simply because it could. In the end, DuPont won on a technicality: with Cities
Service and Seagram tapped out, the last rival bidder, Mobil, got
snarled in a government request for antitrust data and had to delay its
bid. (Mobil had a $120-a-share bid out, well over DuPont's $98.) That
left DuPont, whose bid for Conoco convinced enough shareholders
to "tender"—that is, to sell their shares to the company rather than
take the risk of waiting for Mobil to get clear. But that wasn't all. Seagram received a consolation prize: its stake in Conoco translated into
24.3 percent of DuPont once the deal closed. Seagram was now the
largest shareholder of DuPont, surpassing du Pont family interests;
and Seagram, a company founded on bootlegging during Prohibi-
tion, took two seats on the board. All this posed considerable challenges to Jefferson. The oil crisis was over but a recession was
beginning, and DuPont bought Conoco just as the markets were recognizing that an oil glut, not a shortage, was the order of the day.
Meanwhile, the move into life sciences was constrained by the need
to pay down debt accumulated in the deal—as the *New York Times*
noted after the deal closed, interest rates were rising while oil prices
were falling[7]—and by the executive time and attention required to
integrate the new folks from Conoco.

Jefferson did press plans for a life sciences push, forming a splashy
joint venture with pharmaceutical company Merck & Co., but while
the effort generated some products and profits (though never enough
to make a big difference at a company the size of DuPont), life

sciences required enormous patience and capital and faced the kind of competition, from academic labs, venture-backed start-ups and Big Pharma, that DuPont had not experienced before. The market demanded results. Jefferson already sounded defensive in the *New York Times* in 1984: DuPont's "long experience in launching not just new products but new ventures and new areas" had given it "a grasp of the things that lead to success." Words would not produce blockbusters, however. DuPont struggled on, after Jefferson retired in 1988. In 1998, Merck called it quits and sold its stake in the venture back to DuPont. Around that time, DuPont, in need of capital, spun off Conoco; Wall Street had been calling for that move for years. Three years later, DuPont unloaded the pharma venture entirely to Bristol-Myers Squibb. By then the Bronfmans were also long gone. In 1995, Seagram sold its stake back to the company for $10 billion; Seagram had done well in its DuPont dalliance, but it was time to move on. Bronfman's eldest son (and namesake) then plowed that money into Vivendi, a go-go French would-be media conglomerate. Vivendi crashed, burned, and almost failed when the dot-com bubble burst. A bonfire of the legacy.

Today, DuPont remains a large, even older company recently run by its first female CEO, Ellen Kullman, who grew up in Wilmington, studied mechanical engineering at Tufts and business at Northwestern, started at GE, and worked her way up through various managerial posts. Under Kullman, the company still talked about its post-chemical transformation, now focused on seeds and agricultural chemicals. In May 2015, Kullman battled an attempt by shareholder activist Nelson Peltz (a former member of Michael Milken's 1980s junk-bond-network) to install four nominees on the DuPont board. Peltz was unhappy with DuPont's earnings and demanded a breakup of the company. Though he lost the proxy contest, it was a narrow defeat, and shareholders were left with high expectations, which Kullman failed to quickly satisfy. Earnings slid, the stock plummeted, and Kullman announced her retirement in early October 2015. In early December came the denouement. Dow Chemical approached Kullman's replacement with a proposition: a $130 billion merger following by serious cost cutting, mostly in people, setting up the breakup of the company into three tax-free spinoffs—chemicals, agriculture, and material sciences, mostly plastics. The name, at least for the interim, was DowDuPont. So much for the oldest large corporation in America.

In these last days for the old DuPont, the Conoco deal still hung over DuPont, raising the intriguing counterfactual: What might Jefferson have accomplished in the life sciences if he had never made the fateful decision to buy Conoco? Perhaps most galling to DuPont loyalists, Wall Street insisted on comparing the company to Monsanto, a once-second-tier chemical rival that had aggressively made the transformation to agricultural biotech and was now being rewarded with a more highly valued share price than DuPont.

The reality of a counterfactual, of course, is that we will never know the answer.

Takeovers, as DuPont discovered, were never a certainty, despite the jargon and the promises of the Wall Street crowd. They represented enormous risk, an experiment at both the microeconomic and macroeconomic level that, unlike a true scientific investigation, could rarely be tested, judged, or quantified, either prospectively or retroactively. Takeovers, as we shall see, were swaddled in theory; but facts were rare: even the most prevalent rationale for takeovers, shareholders strolling away with a premium, was flawed. (Conoco shareholders got a 70 percent premium.) Takeovers are among the most disruptive activities a corporation can engage in—often quite literally a game changer. As part of a larger wave of mergers-and-acquisitions activity, they can—for good or bad—sweep through the economy, reordering arrangements, tearing up roots, planting new seeds. DuPont was hardly alone in discovering this. M&A had long been a feature of corporate life, at least since corporations in their modern form, fed by deep and sophisticated US financial markets and owned by public shareholders, developed in the late nineteenth century. Mergers, like most financial phenomena, tend toward cyclicality. DuPont itself had participated in a takeover wave at the turn of the twentieth century, using it to remake itself from munitions maker to chemical colossus. But its success had been so great that it rarely needed to buy anything large again, with the exception of GM—at least until 1981. Takeovers generally had not been a major feature of corporate life since the '20s.

Companies were bought and sold—the large routinely gobbled up the small—but until the emergence of conglomerates in the late '60s, mergers-and-acquisitions activity had been desultory, hostile deals unheard-of, and large companies safe by virtue of their size. Even conglomerates posed little threat to the largest companies. They were an experiment in portfolio diversification applied to the corporation, one that was first celebrated, then condemned as a failure.

Many viewed the takeover wave that erupted in the mid-'70s as unprecedented, sinister, even vulgar, a sign of strange and disordered times, a world out of kilter. By later measures, the number of deals was tiny—they would multiply many times over in the next four decades—but the hostility was new and striking. The hostile takeover hammered against the prevailing corporate order. Managers and boards resisted the notion that just anyone, a "raider" or even another large company, could simply demand that a company surrender and sell itself. *Who were these people?* They were strangers, outsiders, who did not understand (or care) how their companies worked or what a corporation's responsibility to workers was, whether they were white collar or blue. (In 1980 DuPont had 140,000 employees, Conoco 41,500—many of whom expected to work for "the company" for their entire careers, as Jefferson had, then retire with a decent pension.) These outsiders did not see how deeply the corporation was tied into the *real* economy, with relationships extending beyond the legal boundaries of the firm. A hostile takeover, like a war, threatened to blow up those relationships. Acquisitions were expensive and risky and put these often long-term, even familial relationships at risk. Takeovers led to layoffs, broken contracts, shuttered factories, relocated corporate headquarters, stunted careers, dislocated lives. Takeovers affected local real estate, schools, charities, even the tax base. Takeovers were an attack upon an often multigenerational past: a shared legacy. And less direct, if still vital relationships were put at risk: networks of suppliers and subcontractors. Even if a merger in the long run produced renewed growth and prosperity, the process of adjustment was often painful, and the disruption far wider than just within the company itself. Takeovers were *transactional,* short-term rewards for shareholders who came and went as they pleased, were rarely involved in running the company, and had little interest in true proprietorship—that is, ownership.

That was, for many, the perception on the ground—and it was a perspective often offered up by besieged managers when a takeover threat developed and by workers faced with takeover-induced restructurings. The conflict in a takeover often came down to two simple questions: Who knows best what a corporation needs—the managers who built it and run it, or the market that values it every single day? And who do you trust?

In fact, under the zero-sum pressure of a takeover attack, with control in play, judgment quickly became poisoned by self-interest, or the suspicion of personal gain. These managers, went the charge, did not really care about workers, customers, suppliers, or local schools. They cared about themselves. Jefferson pushed DuPont to act as a white knight because he was entrenching himself or the family or his team. Indeed, the age of hostile takeovers can be seen as one long sermon on the stain of self-interest, of *amour propre* or self-regard, in the governance of corporations. The 1980s were a decade of mounting suspicion. Stakes were high. Doubt was contagious. The duties of fiduciaries were suddenly open to question. Raising the issue of self-interest, or conflict, or agency costs in regard to managers led to the same suspicion over the motives of shareholders, workers, bankers, lawyers, the media, politicians, and policymakers—nearly everyone with a hand in the game. But the pursuit of self-interest turned out to be an endless chase through a dark forest after an elusive quarry.

This debate, often formulated simplistically as shareholders versus managers, was brought to life by new ideas that attacked the prevailing self-image of the corporation as a patriarchal, organic, and essential entity that conducted its affairs through reciprocal relationships, which were interwoven with the national fabric: the stakeholder model. The turmoil of the '60s, the successive and wrenching crises of the '70s, the rise of institutional investors, the deregulation of Wall Street and globalization, effectively undermined those ideas, and in their place arose a new way of looking at corporations and what came to be called their "governance." This involved a more abstract and narrow version of the corporation. Companies may have seemed impressively tangible, with their products, office buildings, and factories—with their monetary resources and employee bases—but that was an illusion. Companies could be theoretically deconstructed. Most relationships could be redefined as mere legal contracts—with workers or unions, with suppliers and subcontractors, even with bondholders—thus allowing these stakeholders to be erased from the governance equation. Only one relationship mattered: with shareholders, defined as the corporation's true owner or principal, to which boards and managers had the responsibility to solely serve. This shareholder model, which gained traction in the '70s, was developed, elaborated, and promoted by—strangely enough, given the traditional American distrust of intellectuals—academics, initially from the University of Chicago. These scholars from economics, finance, and the law swept away the long-held stakeholder view and provoked a fierce debate, echoes of which still sound.

Right or wrong, this shift, as profound as any in the postwar period, took place without a vote, without a national debate, without the vast majority of Americans, many of whom worked at corporations, able to even summon up an opinion on a matter that implicitly tapped one group—shareholders—as a proxy for the national interest, as the embodiment of the People, and raised up one goal above all others: efficiency attained through competition. This wasn't a decision secretly made and executed by politicians or regulators but, rather, that rarest of revolutions: a *zeitgeistian* shift conceived and driven by a small band of professors. So profound has been that revolution that memories of an earlier corporate identity—the patriarchal company managed for stakeholders, the Platonic corporation—have grown dim, as if it had never existed or had arisen, like castles and knights, in an impossibly naive and distant age.

Takeovers played a key role in the triumph of shareholder-centric ideas. Takeovers were conceptualized as the hand of the markets—Adam Smith's invisible-hand analogy lurks—ensuring that companies fulfill their duty to shareholders. Takeovers afflict companies that have wandered afield, lost their way, engaged in improper, self-interested, self-defeating behavior. Takeovers, despite the disruption they left in their wake and the appearance of spiraling bidding contests like the one for Conoco, were characterized as omniscient, rational, disciplinary responses to distress or failure, a kind of cleansing re-ordering, the veritable bony finger of an economic God. The old stakeholder model, in turn, was depicted as a way for managers to entrench themselves, playing off various interests like a small country in a tough neighborhood, insulating the company from the efficient market, *which knows best.* Stakeholder companies were too deeply invested in the past, in stability, in resistance to change. American corporations needed to be disrupted, restructured, re-imagined, remade. The challenges of a new age loomed. There was no choice. Shareholder governance was a kind of Jeffersonian (the US president, not the CEO) revolutionary, or transformative, *process.* And thus the wave of takeovers that began in the mid-'70s represented the very edge of a necessary revolution.

BLOODSPORT REVISITS THE debates that took place in the '70s and '80s over these different ideas—each of which claimed to be a rational and beneficent remedy for corporate malaise, testable as a math problem. As we shall see, this particular math problem was a lot more difficult to solve than anyone thought. In fact, from the perspective of four decades later, even with the help of up-to-date computers and big data, there remains the same stubbornly resistant problem that bedeviled DuPont's decision to buy Conoco: we know what DuPont decided to do, but once that choice was made, we have no idea how a different future might have unfolded. Ed Jefferson did not know the future, though given DuPont's past, he may have overestimated the company's ability to shape it. A similar situation exists with respect to mergers generally, whereas human agency is more difficult to pin down. What if regulators had defused the takeover wave? What if Boone Pickens had flamed out as a wildcatter or Milken had gotten bored with finance or Lipton had become a full-time law professor rather than a practitioner? History happened, and we can't go back and edit the tape in a way that allows us to demonstrate that one view, one approach, was necessarily better than another.

And so, unable to prove the case, we're left with politics and its bubbling stew-pot of opinion, argument, and belief, with its inconsistencies and gaps of logic. Takeover politics are far more complex than a simple difference of views about corporations, markets, and takeovers. True, advocates of one position or the other—say, Lipton as a defender of management prerogatives and Harvard's Michael Jensen as a proponent of market power and takeovers—assumed opposed and clearly defined positions. But once overlaid upon conventional political divisions—liberal and conservative, Democrat and Republican, state and federal, even regulatory rules and principals—the landscape grows increasingly ambiguous, paradoxical, *strange,* like a cubist painting with a nose abutting a neck. This begins with conservatives taking the anti-Burkean stance that corporations need to be radically deconstructed and with liberals making the case for stasis. Conservatives prop up shareholders as owners, while acknowledging that most are not accountable for corporate performance, and, maddeningly, mindlessly support managers. The liberal impulse to rein in managers as symbols of entrenched corporate power, and to enshrine investors as embodiments of shareholder democracy, founders when raiders attack and corporations and their employees find their only defense in, well, entrenched managers and boards, or in Lipton's oft-repeated plea: "Just say no." Lipton and Jensen battled for years over managers and shareholders but found themselves defending the power of the states to shape corporate law (meaning mostly the Delaware courts) over that of the federal government. Unions defended jobs against raiders, who in turn may have been quietly aided by *worker* pension funds. And then there's the inevitable evolution of ideas and attitudes over time. The very fact that DuPont was willing to edge onto a fractious, dangerous battleground to rescue an oil company suggests that even by 1981 the management view of hostile takeovers was changing. A similar evolution took place among shareholders that resulted in the '90s in a new, if uneasy, consensus with management, though producing little underlying improvement in corporate behavior or performance.

We will explore all of this. Many books have been written about the '80s takeover wars, but this book offers a view of the modern era of hostile takeovers that goes beyond the conventional imagery of Pickens and Carl Icahn riding the corporate range or Milken as Disney's sorcerer's apprentice, or whether greed was a plague upon the land, as Felix Rohatyn argued, or whether Henry Kravis was a barbarian, with a horned helmet and muddy shoes. Toward this end, *Bloodsport* returns to the original arguments about the nature and governance of corporations when tested by hostile takeovers. There are deals here and dealmakers, the pursuit of self-interest and the exercise of judicial judgment, but what's unique about this story is how much of it is shaped by ideas and ideologies. Much of this debate resides in aging piles of law reviews, business school papers, judicial opinions, client letters, and books. Within corporate law, a number of essays, such as Lipton's seminal "Takeover Bids in the Target's Boardroom" or Jensen and William Meckling's "Agency Cost Theory," are regularly cited, if less regularly read (which also applies to Adolf Berle and Gardiner Means's 1930s Ur-text, *The Modern Corporation and Private Property*). But there are many more, including essays and opinions by the chancellor of Delaware Chancery Court during this era, William Allen, who struggled to reconcile often violently diverging interests unleashed by takeovers. And there is the interaction of that body of work—or the lack of interaction—with financial journalism and its own mass audience. Returning to this literature, reading it critically and placing it in historical context, provides a new coherence to a period that has often seemed baffling in its timing, scale, and violent, disruptive, unleashed energies. Did these crazy Rube Goldbergian deals really occur? How did that great governance shift occur? What role, if any, did the federal government play? How do we parse the politics of governance? How American is the hostile takeover?

This rereading of the 1980s may not answer the question of whether the bold experiment in economic change was worth it, but it does reveal a lot about how we view this powerful, diverse, and omnipresent latter-day institution—the corporation—and how we should govern it and, like barbarians of old, divide its spoils.

Chapter One

ADOLF BERLE AND THE DEBATE OVER TAKEOVERS

Manhattan, 1956. The trip uptown wasn't long but it was heavy with meaning. Newly minted New York University law grad Martin "Marty" Lipton clattered north on the IRT to meet—to work with—Columbia University Law School's Adolf A. Berle, Jr. This was a big moment for the then-lanky Lipton.[1] At twenty-five he was bright, ambitious, if unknown—the son of a garment-factory manager from Jersey City and a graduate of that "Jewish" law school, New York University, with hopes of an academic legal career. Berle, on the other hand, at sixty-three, was an intimate of presidents, a commanding figure of the Protestant and liberal establishment: short, slim, fast-talking, dapper in a double-breasted suit. The son of a Congregationalist minister, he had been a legendary prodigy who went off to Harvard College at the age of fourteen in 1913 and received his law degree from Harvard Law School at twenty-one—the youngest in the school's history. He had been at ivied Columbia since the late '20s. He struck many as too smart, too arrogant, for his own good; in law school, he made a lifelong enemy of Harvard law professor and later Supreme Court justice Felix Frankfurter when he took his class and muttered sarcastic comments from the back row.[2]

Nonetheless, Berle had long been considered a master—the master—of corporate law, the field Lipton was interested in entering. Berle, remarkably, saw himself as a kind of Karl Marx of capitalism.[3] There was something elusive about him, a refusal to be pinned down,

15

to subordinate himself to mere mortals or to one activity; or perhaps he was just too glib, too self-regarding, for his own good. For three decades, he had taught at Columbia, all the while operating a law office downtown, on Wall Street. A registered Republican, he had been an original member of Franklin Roosevelt's Brains Trust, with fellow-Columbians Rexford Tugwell and Raymond Moley. He and his wife had written Roosevelt's New Individualism speech, which led to the National Industrial Recovery Act, considered by many to be the high tide of the New Deal's impulse to manage a corporate economy. Typically, he refused to leave Columbia or his law practice for a Washington job, choosing to try to influence Roosevelt directly without actually joining the administration. In the years since the New Deal, Berle had moved into the higher realms of the establishment: consulting on New Deal projects like the Reconstruction Finance Corp. and the International Civil Aviation Board and serving as ambassador to Brazil, as a member of a Kennedy task force on Latin America, and as chairman of the 20th Century Fund. He wrote regularly, prolifically: law articles, speeches, book after book.

Lipton never took a class from Berle, but he spent a lot of time talking to him. "He was a storyteller," Lipton recalls. "He was as interesting as could be."[4] Berle wanted Lipton to write a dissertation on the impact of institutional investors on corporate law, but Lipton, who left Columbia for a clerkship, then a job at a firm, never got around to it. "He was prescient," Lipton admits. "At this time, only about 5 percent to 6 percent of shares of public companies were held by institutions. Not much in the way of mutual funds. Pension funds were just getting started. But he saw that the institutions would come to dominate."

Little did either man realize it at the time, but Berle had met a disciple who, for the next half-century or so, would labor to revive key aspects of the Columbia professor's vision of how corporations fit into the great American commonwealth.

BERLE WAS, IN many ways, everything Lipton dreamed about as a lawyer who could do, as he later said, "great things."

Still, for all his accomplishments, Berle was best known in 1956—as he is today—for one book he co-authored with Columbia economist Gardiner Means: *The Modern Corporation and Public Property,* which the pair began in the late 1920s but published at the height of the Great Depression, 1932.[5] The book, an uneasy blend of Berle's theories and commentary on the nature and role of the public corporation and Means's statistics—with page after page of tables exploring the increasingly concentrated structure of the American corporate economy—is not an easy read, and was probably mostly unread, but it was a book that literate Americans felt responsible to buy and retain in their libraries. It was, everyone said, generationally important, like Keynes's *General Theory* or, more recently, Thomas Picketty's *Capital in the Twenty-First Century.* (At the time of publication, Means's facts about corporate concentration—that 180 companies owned 47 percent of US corporate assets—was considered the sexy takeaway, not Berle's musing on the separation of ownership and control.) And so it became a best seller and an iconic text. Today, Means is frequently passed over; the book is about Berle and his views, although it remains a text more often referred to than carefully read. At a minimum, the book embodied a partnership between law and economics that would later play a major role in rationalizing an unrestrained merger regime. Few books in American history have had a more winding path, or produced more argument about meaning and context, than *The Modern Corporation and Private Property.*

Why is this book important? Both the book and Berle's long career were focused on control of the single greatest source of American wealth: the corporation. By the time he came of age, the American economy, dominated by a relatively small number of large, sophisticated corporations, was the world's largest. But who really owned the corporation? Who controlled its massive cash flows and accumulated capital? Was it Wall Street and the bankers, such as the formidable J. P. Morgan and his powerful House of Morgan? Was it executives, overseen by boards of directors? Was it shareholders? Or, most provocatively, was it the government, acting as an instrument of a broader public, what Berle called "the community"? These were fascinating questions, even in the 1920s; but they became compelling in the chaos and uncertainties of the next decade with its devastating economic breakdown that exposed so much of the underlying skeleton of the system. By the '50s and '60s—decades of enormous growth and prosperity—these issues submerged again in the warm glow of consensus, at least on corporate matters. By the time Lipton met the by-now sage-like Berle, there was a general consensus that corporations were run for stakeholders—workers, shareholders, customers, communities—which effectively put managers, overseen by the government, in control. Berle championed this approach.

But the concept of stakeholders and government oversight had not always been quite so universally accepted, even by Berle himself. *The Modern Corporation and Private Property,* for all its fame, is an elusive and ambiguous text. Berle's clearest message—that as American companies grew larger and more complex, they needed to sell shares to larger numbers of investors—did not actually originate with him. Inevitably, the founder-owners surrendered control to a broader diversified shareholder base. The result was a separation of ownership and control, a kind of original sin of the public corporation. The primary movers within corporations shifted from "owners," the shareholders, to managers, those most deeply involved in operations. As a result, managers developed a degree of independence from shareholders; they felt that the company was theirs, and they acted autonomously, even plutocratically—in a later popular phrase, they entrenched themselves.

This is the message that has sifted down through the decades. Over the years it gradually dovetailed with other, often contentious ideas, many coming from law and business schools, but nearly all of them beginning with the snake in the garden: the separation of ownership and control. Over the last forty years or so, the separation of ownership and control has emerged as the central message of *The Modern Corporation and Private Property,* particularly for those who never actually read the book, and Berle has been elevated posthumously to the status of "the father of shareholder governance." This is, at best, half right. Advocates of shareholder governance argue that the managerial assumption of autonomy is both illegitimate and inefficient; that shareholders are the sole "owners" of corporations and the source of their power; and that "governance" implies that the primary end of the corporation is not to generate jobs, or to help customers, or to provide concert halls for local communities, or even to create prosperity for the masses: it is to maximize the value of shareholders' investment. Shareholders thus become a kind of proxy for the common good. And good corporate governance shifted from a form of republicanism (the political system, not the party), in which managers juggle a variety of interests or stakeholders, to democracy, in which shareholders rule absolutely.

Berle, who died in 1976, did not live to see this transition, but he would almost certainly have been surprised by how quickly and abruptly it occurred. However, he had never been a slave to consistency. His mind was supple, his instincts pragmatic and political. And so his ideas about the one set of preoccupations that he dwelled upon for most of his adult life—the role of the corporation in American life—shifted with the times.[6] His treatment of the separation of ownership and control both in *The Modern Corporation and Private Property* and in later years reflected a deeper ambiguity in how Americans broadly viewed corporations. In the late '20s, when times were good and he was beginning to work on the book, Berle did focus on the separation of ownership and control, and he argued for the idea of managers as "trustees" for shareholder interests and for greater "market regulation" that would empower shareholders. But by the time the book was nearing publication, the global economy had crashed and Berle was angling for a spot as an adviser to the Roosevelt campaign. His views changed. More drastic measures were necessary. Despite the self-evident concentration, large corporations needed to be more aggressively regulated for the larger good by the government. Managers were still trustees, but for a shifting constellation of interests that reflected the larger community. That point of view found its way into the pro-planning mentality of Roosevelt's New Individualism speech.

Berle, in short, had become a *stakeholder* advocate. This issue became confusing when in 1932 Berle found himself tangled up in a debate with Harvard Law School professor E. Merrick Dodd that reverberated around the legal community for decades.[7] Dodd believed that corporations had responsibilities to many constituencies or stakeholders. He was not aware that Berle had changed his views. Berle, feeling constrained by his campaign responsibilities, chose to defend his old position, one that made him to this day the patriarch of shareholder governance, despite the fact that he was already recanting that position in the soon-to-be-published *The Modern Corporation and Private Property*. Even as he was debating Dodd, Berle was growing more committed to an approach that featured heavy state regulation—even planning and administration—of large, powerful, technologically sophisticated and, in his view, necessary industrial corporations. In 1968, he revisited the debate, which had taken on legendary proportions, in a law article and declared Dodd, who died in 1951 in a car crash, the winner. "The late Professor E. Merrick Dodd of Harvard insisted, and history seems to have vindicated him, that they [large corporations] are also stewards for employed personnel, for customers and suppliers, and indeed for that section of the community affected by their operation," he wrote.[8]

By then, the issue had grown obscured, like the motivations of characters in a particularly tangled spy novel. Dodd, repulsed by the activism of the New Deal, had long since abandoned his old views and embraced Berle's early shareholder-centric stance, even as Berle had moved to assume Dodd's old stakeholder position. Once the Great Depression passed and new federal regulations appeared, Dodd turned to markets to resolve the problem of separation of ownership and control, while Berle embraced managers and regulation.

By the mid-'50s, however, Berle appeared triumphant, and the stakeholder approach carried the day. There were critics, but they were marginal. A new, free-market *zeitgeist* associated with Friedrich Hayek and Ludwig von Mises, Austrian economists who had both made their way to the United States, was percolating at the University of Chicago where Hayek taught. In the mid-'60s, Berle tangled over the matter with Henry Manne, forty-eight, a University of Chicago Law School graduate then teaching at George Washington

University Law School. Manne believed that separation of ownership and control was a major problem and challenged Berle by focusing on "the market for corporate control"—that is, the ability of companies to freely buy and sell each other and thus establish accountability through the market, not ultimately through the government.[9] Given high industrial concentrations, antitrust laws were tight, and after the chaos of depression and war, and the anxieties of the Cold War, the powers-that-be saw no reason to encourage the disruption brought by large-scale dealmaking. In fact, there were relatively few mergers, particularly among the largest companies, which resembled autonomous kingdoms. As Manne acknowledged, "Mergers among competitors would seem to have no important saving grace. The position has gained considerable legal currency that any merger between competing firms is at best suspect and perhaps per se illegal. The latter result seems especially likely when one of the combining firms already occupies a substantial portion in the relevant market."[10] Manne identified managerial efficiency with a high share price and argued that the best way to discipline managers in a world where ownership and management were separate is the threat of a takeover, with buyers hungrily drawn to a bargain share price.

Berle swatted Manne away. In an arch reply, he suggested that the younger Manne hadn't been around for World War I, the 1920s, or the Great Depression, or "experienced a world without the safeguards of the Securities and Exchange Commission," systematized accounting, aggressive regulation of conflicts of interest, or a Federal Reserve.[11] In other words, Manne was a babe in the woods. He accused Manne of taking refuge in a nineteenth-century set of ideas that did not fit the "industrial system" with its technologically sophisticated corporations. Berle defended that system in a long, stem-winding paean of praise (he had a weakness for rhetorical overkill): "The American industrial system, under guidance and control, has done more for more people, has made possible a higher standard of living for the vast majority of a huge population in a huge country, has preserved more liberty for self-development, and now affords more tools (however unused or badly used) from which a good society can be forged so far as economics can do so,

than any system in recorded history." He added, "It is eons from per-
fection. It has, nevertheless, empirically arrived at results that relegate
both the communist economics of Karl Marx and the classic economics
of his contemporary, John Stuart Mill, and of the modern expositor,
Ludwig von Mises, to a museum of 19th-century thought."[12]

Berle was no more impressed with the wisdom of shareholders and
markets. "In practice," he wrote, "the rise and fall [of stock] has a
vague relation to the success or failure of the corporation in its operations (a sweepstakes ticket has a similar unpredictable relation to the
speed of the horse)."[13] Most shares, he argued, were traded on secondary markets, between individuals or firms, transactions that had nothing to do with the company in question. This stock, he wrote, is not
an "investment" in a company at all. The stock market is less an allocator of capital than of wealth, mostly to the financial crowd. And even
if the market closed, as it had in 1914 during World War I, large corporations could easily get by on their own internally generated capital.
In Berle's worldview, which he shared with Harvard economist John
Kenneth Galbraith, only large corporations really mattered; entrepreneurs and start-ups were far too small and far too weak to matter very
much. America's large corporations were thus too important, too central to capitalism, to leave to the speculative forces of chaotic markets.

The very definition of property was in flux, declared Berle, and
"classical economic logic did not apply."[14] The notion that shareholders owned companies no longer applied: "For the fact is that purely
passive property—that is, property divorced from any responsibilities
of ownership, whose value grows or shrinks in the owner's hands without any relationship to his risk-taking, work, or effort—has outlived
most of the economic justifications that gave it birth."[15] Remarkably,
Berle blithely ignored Manne's emphasis on the disciplinary benefits
of change of control. Instead, he viewed the large company as a kind
of public utility, with a self-legitimating importance not to the market
but to the community and to itself. "Not that 'control' or the managements have become thieves; quite the contrary," he wrote. "Rather
they have come to recognize (perhaps as 'business statesmen') that first
claim in accumulated profits *is the claim of the enterprise itself*—that,

for example, the first duty of a steel company is to make steel, and have it there in sufficient quantity to meet the existing or foreseeable future requirements of the community. These needs take precedence over the dividend desires of any body of passive shareholders—as indeed they should."[16]

In the years ahead, nothing would take precedence over Berle's "dividend desires." Berle's reply to Manne sums up an entire worldview forged in the New Deal and World War II that within a decade would crumble and wash away. Berle's Olympian attitude was partly a product of his personality and partly the liberal articulation of a by-now long-established set of ideas, made all the more potent by American economic preeminence and power. But by the early 1970s that prosperity would crash, undermining the ideas that underpinned it. Manne would prove far more prescient than Berle gave him credit for. As new free-market ideas increasingly became orthodoxy, the markets grew to supersede concerns about community. And the most contentious arena of struggle for control turned out to be exactly what Manne had predicted: mergers and acquisitions.

All this occurred a decade after Lipton briefly studied with Berle. Lipton went on to clerk for a federal judge in 1956, then took a job as an associate at a ten-person firm, Seligson, Morris & Neuberger. (Seligson was a longtime New York University law professor and bankruptcy specialist.) There he worked with two other recent NYU grads, Leonard Rosen and George Katz, while lecturing at NYU in corporate law. In 1965, around the time Manne and Berle were going at it, Lipton, Rosen, and Katz teamed up with Herbert Wachtell, another former NYU law review editor, to open their own firm, Wachtell, Lipton Rosen, Katz & Kern. (Kern was a friend of Wachtell and left to become an investment banker, taking his name with him.) One of the firm's specialties was bankruptcy, a field that top firms avoided—a "Jewish" field. Another was mergers and acquisitions, Lipton's interest, which in those years was also viewed as "beneath" the grand calling of the established firms.

Over the next five decades the firm, run by Lipton, would go on to become a remarkable success: elite, small, immensely influential, and far more profitable than any of the old white-shoe firms. More importantly, in the years ahead, as Berle's notion of a corporate community came under attack (particularly after the explosion in M&A), Lipton became the most rigorous and effective defender of Berle's mature vision of stakeholders and the prerogatives of managers. He became, in a sense, a figure as large, and certainly as controversial, as Berle himself.

BY THE TIME Berle died, his world had changed in ways large and small. The hegemony of the White Anglo-Saxon Protestant was ending. The American dominance in the world economy began to wane, not only as a result of reviving economies in Europe and Japan but also because oil-rich countries were banding together to hold the rest of the world hostage. Unions struggled as industrialization peaked and began a long decline. The American economy staggered under Lyndon Johnson's attempt to fund the Vietnam War and the Great Society without raising taxes—pushing Keynesian policies into the realm of dysfunction. Inflation merged with stagnation. Liberal pieties shattered. The government seemed feckless, corrupt, and stifling. The large corporations that Berle had celebrated appeared sclerotic and risk-averse, their CEOs bureaucratic and self-interested. Wall Street itself was a sleepy den of cartels, inbred, ethnically divided and technologically anachronistic.

In 1975, the first hostile bid for a New York Stock Exchange company occurred—a shock that reverberated throughout corporate America after Morgan Stanley, the epitome of the white-shoe investment bank, helped engineer the attack for an NYSE member. This marked the rise of what would become a bloodsport of American business—hostile M&A—and of a new, harsher, and much more powerful financial economy.

The deal ushered a new reality into corporate life that was more Manne and less Berle, more about the discipline of market power and, year by year, less about the needs of the community or the wisdom of "business statesmen." Giant companies fell to unknown raiders. Uncertainty spiked. The liberal Berle died, replaced by selective memories of a dusty old book and an ancient cliché: separation of ownership and control. Corporations were now viewed not as organic entities but as conglomerations of self-interested agents and nexuses of contracts, monitored by shareholding proprietors. Results were measured by the daily "rational" judgment of share prices. Markets were "efficient" and replaced communities as standards of good and bad. Measurement and calculation swept away the balancing of qualitative interests. A new world dawned.

What emerged were new ways of viewing corporations, fueled by collisions of Hobbesian forces: managers and directors, shareholders, traders and bankers, and, of course, policymakers, politicians, regulators, judges, and that great protean beast, the public. All made their play: lawyers such as Joe Flom and Lipton; academics like Michael Jensen, Daniel Fischel, and Frank Easterbrook; Wall Street uber-advisors such as Felix Rohatyn, Michael Milken, and Bruce Wasserstein; Delaware judges like William Allen and Andrew G. T. Moore, economists like Frederic Scherer who dug deeply into the empirical reality (an elusive concept) of mergers; and many others. They were all swept up in a struggle for control—not just of corporate wealth in the heat of a takeover battle but of ideas that explain and interpret exactly what such a struggle was supposed to be all about. Berle understood that corporations were embedded in a democratic context of popular opinion, rules, regulations, and laws: politics. (He may, in fact, have discounted the market by overestimating the power of the political community.) The evolution of modern M&A proceeded in waves of excess and retrenchment, innovation and restraint, like markets themselves. Year by year, with the exception of recessions, M&A grew in frequency and size, buoyed by what in retrospect was a remarkable post-'70s bull market. Sunny economic times and M&A were self-reinforcing, in much the same way that the postwar boom justified stakeholder governance. After 1975, despite doubts, failures, and controversy, the ascendancy of the shareholder—the shareholder as owner—spread and congealed into popular belief, a kind of orthodoxy. This set of ideas eventually came to appropriate the phrase *corporate governance,* as if there were but one way to govern companies, with shareholders as owners. Like any ideology, corporate governance defined alternatives out of existence.

This is not to suggest that, as two prominent law professors declared in a 2000 paper, all the issues had been resolved and shareholder primacy was as inevitable as death and taxes.[17] In fact, nothing is inevitable, the world keeps changing, and the future—as Keynes once noted—is irremediably uncertain. Views shift. There are no history-ending truths, which is why both markets and democracies work. Berle understood that the large public corporation is a relatively new phenomenon. The Founding Fathers were not omniscient. Even Alexander Hamilton, a promoter of manufacturers, never imagined a United States in which the most powerful, ubiquitous, and pervasive organizational form would be something called the corporation. They could not have imagined either the complexity of a mature corporate system or the deep, global markets that financed it. They never foresaw the challenge that corporations would pose to federal and state governments, to individual rights. They could not have seen the rise of byzantine administrative and regulatory functions within the government, the power of industrial and post-industrial technologies. Most importantly, they never paused to consider how these organizations would be controlled and governed, who would profit from them, and how they would fit into the American community.

Berle himself, who liked to speak prophetically, did not anticipate a global, post-industrial economy, with its decentralizing whirlwinds of information technologies, empowered entrepreneurs, consumers, dealmakers, and fierce global competition.

Today, after crises, recessions, and mounting inequality, questions proliferate more than ever. Who really matters when it comes to the fate of corporations: workers, shareholders, managers, communities? Who really owns corporations, and what rights and responsibilities does ownership entail? Are corporations republics or democracies, or are they something else—autocracies or bureaucracies, military units or sports teams—that operate under different rules? Should corporate oversight occur on a state or federal level, or should it be left to the markets? How should executives and directors behave in takeover battles? How rational, wise, and prescient are markets and shareholders? How does M&A affect the ability of corporations to grow, prosper, generate jobs, spur innovation? Is M&A good, bad, or a complex amalgam of good and bad? And if it's both, how do we ensure the most optimal results? Where does the corporation fit in a democracy? How do we manage and master change?

This is not "science," as Harvard's Michael Jensen often said while arguing for unrestrained M&A in the '80s. None of these questions has an easy black-or-white answer.

AND WHY SHOULD ordinary Americans care about seemingly abstruse debates conducted by lawyers, bankers, academics, and policymakers? As Berle wrote, Americans might see themselves as individuals but they spend their lives within organizations, some bewilderingly large, mostly corporations. (Typically, Berle recognized this reality but missed the underlying tensions it engendered.) Americans earn their livings there. Their friends and colleagues are there. Their retirement plans are stuffed with corporate shares. "The company"—even in an age of free agents, job mobility, and high unemployment—absorbs the bulk of their time and energy. Who controls "the company" is no abstract academic matter. M&A every year touches millions: a husband laid off, a friend receiving a buyout, a town devastated by a shuttered factory, or, for that matter, a banker wheeling past in a shiny new Porsche or a small group of unimaginably wealthy individuals. M&A is one of a handful of steps companies can take to cope with a ceaselessly changing environment and markets that demand results. When we debate competitiveness, jobs, inequality, deindustrialization, or Mitt Romney's tenure at Bain Capital or tax policy, we're arguing about M&A. When we complain about CEO pay, decry golden parachutes, or unrestrained greed, we're also talking about M&A.

Corporations are here to stay and so is dealmaking. M&A, for good or evil, is a key ingredient in that great imperative of modern life: economic growth. M&A is, however, a profoundly disruptive force—the embodiment, ritualistically offered up as a defense of the practice, of Joseph Schumpeter's notion of creative-destruction. M&A in the popular culture is conflated with capitalism and Wall Street, and shares in the historical American ambivalence toward financial power and markets. And M&A these days is ubiquitous. Even in less-than-stellar years—M&A activity lagged after the financial crisis of 2008, only to reemerge in 2014—tens of thousands of deals were made annually, large and small, far more than anyone could imagine in, say, 1965. Indeed, as Manne reminded us, it's difficult to recall an age when deals were relatively rare. Today, many of these transactions are vast, global, involving the largest companies and hundreds of thousands of people. But most are middling to small. No matter. Disruption is inescapable, through restructuring, layoffs, new ways of doing things, new bosses, new technologies, the potential for failure, bankruptcy—or, yes, even success, profits, and riches. M&A is one sign of a dynamic economy; it's also an activity that, like hitting a baseball, fails more often than it succeeds.

Corporations and M&A are key aspects of the environment we live in. And yet subjects such as M&A, apart from views that tend to mirror popular political stereotypes, remain too often wreathed in mystery, opaque, like so many other aspects of modern finance. That can't be a good thing. Let us explore how we got here.

Chapter Two

JOE FLOM: BE VERY AFRAID

MODERN M&A BEGINS with Joe Flom. He was never a principal or a financier. He was never more than an advisor, a lawyer, an intermediary, an agent, though in Flom's skillful hands those roles made him the essential, central figure. This was paradoxical: in an age that believed that authenticity and accountability arose only from having money in the game, Flom never did, at least not directly. In normal circumstances, this would have opened him up to suspicions of double-dealing. But he negotiated those currents—building one of the world's most successful law firms around himself like a carapace in the process—with surpassing skill. He might have been occasionally harsh, ruthless, devious, ambitious, cagey, even vulgar, certainly prone to the off-color joke or the perfectly targeted insult, but he generally managed to convince clients that his self-interest was identical to theirs.

There were predecessors to Flom in the rough-edged world of the '50s and '60s where companies were fought over, but there weren't many of them, and most were operators who did their best work outside the limelight. M&A involved small investors, obscure or fallen companies, and murky, bare-knuckled practices; it was a marginal, "pocket" business, like selling used cars. Wall Street had still not recovered from the Great Depression: financial firms were small, private, thinly capitalized, ethnically homogenous. There were Wasp firms, Jewish firms, Irish firms, Italian firms. The economy was highly concentrated and a relatively small number of large industrial corporations dominated, feeding off the postwar boom; little had changed since Berle and Means wrote about corporate concentration in *The Modern Corporation and Private Property,* except that an air of corporate self-satisfaction had swelled. Chief executives and boards of the largest companies were potentates and statesman. As Berle admitted, "Managements of the major giants are, for practical purposes, impregnable."[1] It was, as one commentator later called it, "the age of heroic managerialism."[2] Large corporations were so grand that they transcended mere economics and had grown into essential social institutions. They were paragons of stability. They viewed their prosperity as identical to the success of the country; they basked in the warm glow of consensus. Because shareholding was consigned mostly to individual investors, any thought of taking over a major corporation— AT&T, DuPont, General Electric, IBM, General Motors, U.S. Steel—or even changing management or policy, smacked of lunacy. No "major" Wall Street firm or law firm would mastermind a hostile raid of one large company for another; if they did, all their other clients would flee. And even if someone made the leap, federal regulators, still energized by a New Deal liberalism that viewed size as a threat to democracy, would almost certainly bring antitrust actions against the resulting entity. Takeovers were a throwback to a less respectable, more barbarous, more reckless age. The *realpolitik* of the business judgment rule—executives and boards know best—produced a practical ethics that sank deeply into the financial consciousness. Certain steps were never taken, at least among respectable corporations. Hostility, in short, was bad form, not to say socially improper.

The period also experienced a stifling consensus that shaped corporate law. In 1958, a young Yale law professor noted that in the modern industrial system "it is the corporation as an institution which is permanent and the shareholders who are transitory."[3] He added, in what smacked of economic realism, that the "purpose clause in the charters of these companies reads simply 'to make money.'" The author had the impeccably establishment name of Bayless "Bay" Manning; he was one of those marvelously bred young men that law schools used to produce. Manning had graduated from Yale College; as one of his law school friends observed, "He brought with him . . . the special assurance of the man who had made it at Yale as an undergraduate"[4]—going off to the war, graduating first in his law school class in 1949, and serving as editor in chief of the *Yale Law Review.* After clerking with Supreme Court justice Stanley Reed, he returned to the law school in 1955, as part of a wave of postwar recruitment. Manning had it all: he was smooth, articulate, trim, with a strong chin and a head of thick hair. Reed called him "one of the most able men with whom I have had close contact. He was a hard worker: interested, but with a sense of proportion; sociable, but not a waster of time."[5] He was deeply interested in corporate law but he worked in the government, was actively involved in Latin American affairs, served as dean of Stanford Law School, and became the first president of the Council on Foreign Relations; he was even a partner at Paul Weiss later in life. He was a shining figure of the mid-century American establishment.

And yet, Manning struggled against the consensus. He was never prolific; but when he wrote, his prose sparkled (he was actually witty, mildly subversive in law review circles), and others, at least in the rarefied world of elite law schools, took notice. He wrote as if he were a white-clad amateur tennis player of that era: effortless grace with a wooden racket and a white ball. In 1958, he established his reputation with a review in the *Yale Law Review* keying off a book about the New York Stock Exchange's PR campaign for People's Capitalism—that is, the marketing notion that everyone should own shares.[6] In 1962—three years before Berle and Manne's skirmish over corporate control—he followed up with a long examination of shareholder appraisals, which entail the right of shareholders to demand compensation from companies in the event of a sale or merger.[7] Manning recognized how deeply tied shareholder rights like appraisal were to legal concepts about the corporation that had dominated the nineteenth century, the heroic age of big business. He argued that in "lucid moments" (meaning *rare* lucid moments) most people saw General Motors—which Peter Drucker had celebrated as the harmonious essence of the modern firm in *Concept of the Corporation* in 1946—as a social organization designed to attain economic ends. This, Manning added, was not how the nineteenth century envisioned the corporation. Back

then, the corporation as a legal construct was "something quite separate from the economic enterprise, three dimensional, virtually alive, a
little bit sacred because of its 'immortality' and the connection with
the 'sovereign,' and withal terribly important."[8]

Manning's contention was not just some historical diversion. He
argued that many of the concepts that shaped corporate law in the
mid-century stemmed from an approach that had grown anachronistic by the 1920s: "The 19th century obsession with corporate 'powers,'
'franchises,' and *ultra vires* [acts beyond the powers of law] was
grounded upon the insistence that corporation law was about corporate ideology, not economic policy. If the legislature created a particular corporation in the shape of a horse, the horse 'could not' moo. It
was not that the enterprise should not violate a legislative prescription; it was that the corporation could not do so as a matter of inherent incapacity."[9] This attitude made mergers a problematic exercise.
Manning then offered a litany of questions, hedged in ironic quotation marks, which lawyers continued to ask about corporations despite their irreverence. "Is a corporation a 'person'? 'Is' a corporation
'really' an 'entity'?" This produced the conclusion that Manning came
to be most famous for, a chill breeze in the warm, self-regarding air:
"In the last sixty years of business laws in the United States, point by
point, topic by topic, issue by issue, the commercial image of the
business organization has emerged to overshadow the concept of the
'corporation.'"[10] In a footnote, like a voice from the underground,
Manning unloaded on what he *really* meant: "Corporate law, as a
field of intellectual effort, is dead in the United States. When American law ceased to take the 'corporation' seriously, the entire body of
law that had been built upon that intellectual construct slowly perfo-
rated and rotted away. We have nothing left but our great empty corporation statutes—towering skyscrapers of rusted girders, internally
welded together and containing nothing but wind. . . . There is still a
good bit of work to be done to persuade someone to give a decent
burial to the shivering skeletons." Academics, he added, who specialize in corporate law "face technological unemployment, or at least
substantial retooling."[11]

Still that empty edifice stood. Beneath it, in the shadows, mergers and acquisitions—sometimes hostile—did occasionally occur, but mostly among companies well below the top drawer that Manning, Berle, and Drucker thought about. The numbers were tiny: twenty-one mergers and acquisitions occurred in 1954, seventeen in 1957.[12] (No one was really counting.) In fact, many of the aspects of what we've come to think of as the modern age of M&A existed, just in smaller quantities in the '50s. Companies and corporate assets were bought and sold regularly. Poor performance brought retribution in the form of takeover attempts. The decade had its raiders, its activists, its hostile deals, its struggles for control. But while lively, all this was a relatively small game, played by marginal characters, few of whom resembled corporate statesmen. The M&A game had its coterie of take-over artistes: Thomas Mellon Evans, Art Landa, Charles Green, Robert R. Young, Victor Muscat, and, a little later, the indefatigable Victor Posner. There were few rules to this game. Throughout the '50s and into the '60s, most struggles for control occurred through the mechanism of the proxy contest. This involved a highly political struggle in which the two parties solicited shareholders to give them their vote. The winner got to control the board of directors. The contest often occurred through advertisements in newspapers or press releases, the two sides verbally attacking each other, much like a political campaign, albeit in a compressed time frame. There was an element of flimflam to it all, subterfuge, underhanded dealings, bullying, bluffing, occasionally fibbing. Lawyers were particularly important—notably, as one commentator put it, for their ability "to maneuver within the rules" with "devilishly clever schemes."[13] Then the votes—proxies submitted by shareholders—had to be counted in what was officially called the counting room, or what was delicately and evocatively dubbed the snake pit, and a victor declared.

Proxy contests required a particular set of skills: ingenuity, quick thinking, a talent for demagoguery, a sharp and practical mastery of what was legally possible. Proxy contests resembled mud wrestling: no one came out spotless. Moreover, the business was difficult enough

and the risks high enough that it hardly represented a viable way to
wealth except for a very small number—a handful—of specialists.
The lawyers were mostly lone practitioners, well below the "big" New
York City corporate law firms, which made their livings by catering
to large corporations and large banks. ("Big" was relative: the largest
law firm in New York was Shearman & Sterling with 125 lawyers,
mostly doing work for First National City Bank, later Citibank.)
Takeovers, raids, proxy contests, and hostile M&A were thus consigned to a small, shadowy corner of a financial world, separate from
large, industrial companies and their captive, white-shoe law firms,
nearly (but not completely) out of sight. Part of the reason Wall
Street firms were so small was that their best clients—large, industrial
companies—didn't need them very often to underwrite offerings,
round up financing, or advise on transactions. Big business was so
flush in the '50s that companies rarely had to access financial markets,
which, as a result, were thin on volume and on what traders call liquidity—that is, easily sellable financial assets. The other reason was
that stocks were still viewed as dangerously risky, and the behemoths
of the investing world—such as insurance and trust companies—
bought and held mostly "safe" bonds. Memories of 1929 and the
Great Depression were sharp.

Proxy contests, while legal, did little to enhance one's reputation
with the uptown swells. There was something untoward, threatening,
even repellent about the game. As one legal survey of the business
noted in 1969, "The proxy insurgent has been the recipient of much
abuse at the hands of smugly ensconced management. 'Raider' is one
of the more printable epithets hurled at him. Name calling is typical
when the corporate mighty are challenged, whether in a proxy fight or
in a stockholder suit, where the fashionable insult is 'strike suitor.' But
the truth is that the proxy contest is therapeutic for the body corporate, and in the best traditions of corporate democracy."[14]

IN THE '50s, the intersection of law and finance appeared deceptively
placid. For over a half-century, the most prominent firms in the New
York bar—those white-shoe firms (after the white bucks worn with

summer seersucker suits by Ivy-League-trained lawyers) such as Cravath Swaine & Moore, Sullivan & Cromwell, Davis Polk & Wardwell, Dewey Ballantine, and Milbank Tweed—had been pursuing a paradoxical, double mission: first to professionalize themselves by adhering to increasingly areligious and meritocratic standards; second, to embody a Wasp social identity. This was a little like trying to blend oil and water. The former effort was captured in what became known as "the Cravath System," named for Paul Cravath's meritocratic reforms at the eponymous New York firm after the turn of the century.[15] Cravath built a firm that claimed to be all about competence and professionalism. Cultural, social, and religious standing was deemed irrelevant. The Cravath System became gospel at the largest, most powerful corporate law firms. (Despite his academic roots, Manning embodied it in spades, but characteristically resisted the pull of the firm until later in life, in a different era, when he joined Paul Weiss.) Oddly enough, however, while these firms pursued elite professionalism, they were also overwhelmingly Protestant in makeup. For a while that made sense: everybody knew Protestant root stock was simply superior. In the '60s, the New York City bar was 60 percent Jewish, but none of the large, elite firms was Jewish, and they employed very few Jews as partners. As Eli Wald wrote in a study of Wasp and Jewish law firms in New York, "Nor was the religious identity of the large firms superficial. While the merit-based firing and promotion criteria of the Cravath System purported to ignore irrelevant considerations such as social standing and religious affiliation, its carefully prescribed path was never based on merit alone." Rather, "[i]n addition to academic credentials [the young men] were expected to possess 'warmth and force of personality' and 'physical stamina.' These hard-to-quantify and difficult-to-assess qualities were a cover for, or at least directly correlated with, certain religious, socioeconomic and cultural characteristics."[16] In short, only sporty, social Wasps need apply.

As a result, a division of legal labor opened up. The Wasp firms catered to the large corporations and adhered to Paul Cravath's phrase that "great lawyering was done in the conference room, not the courtroom."[17] Litigation, once the bedrock of legal practice, lost favor at the Wasp firms. As Wald wrote, "Litigation was thought of as necessary only as a result of a failed transaction, not as yet another strategic tool at the hands of corporate clients. Litigation, bankruptcy, takeover law were needed only when the corporate attorney failed to successfully reorganize and restructure the affairs of his clients. Because the need to practice in these areas of law were perceived to result from attorneys' failure, they were deemed unbecoming practice areas for the elite corporate attorney."[18] Note the moral opprobrium heaped on a notion of "failed transaction."

But, of course, transactions failed every day. Was it the failure or the transaction itself that was the problem? Who would take ownership of those ghetto-like specialties? Increasingly, the answer to the latter question was the swelling ranks of Jewish lawyers.

JOE FLOM CAME upon the scene in the waning days of the Wasp ascendancy. He was Jewish, from Bensonhurst in Brooklyn. His father had been a labor organizer, a maker of shoulder pads for ladies' dresses, and probably, at times, a Communist, or at least a sympathizer; Flom himself said he had "charisma." Flom's story, buffed to a high sheen by everyone from Steven Brill to Malcolm Gladwell to Flom himself, resembles a Jewish Horatio Alger tale, a rise so vertiginous that it resembles fiction, not to say a refutation of class determinism. The Floms, Russian immigrants, were poor; in the '30s the family restlessly moved from apartment to apartment when the rent came due. Flom was bright. He attended an academically rigorous high school, but could only afford to go to City College at night. He thought he might want to be a lawyer. By day he worked as a messenger at a Jewish law firm, Cooke, Nathan & Lehman. Then World War II came and he was drafted into the Army before he could graduate. As the war was ending, and in the midst of a bridge game, he pounded out letters to Harvard, Columbia, and Yale seeking admittance under a special wartime dispensation for veterans who had not been able to get an undergraduate degree. Remarkably, Harvard at the last minute offered him a spot.[19]

Flom did so well at Harvard that he made the law review. It was true: he did not resemble a Cravath attorney in any way. He was short, thick, and spoke with a Brooklyn accent; his last name sounded a lot like *phlegm*. He did have "warmth and force of personality" in spades, but it was not evident at the time, and no one would ever mistake him for an Episcopalian. Like most Harvard Law third-years he traveled to New York to interview for associate jobs, including at Cravath. But despite his good grades and law review experience, he struck out. The effort undoubtedly failed from both sides: the white-shoe firms did not view Flom as partner material, and he, in turn, saw them as rigid, uptight, and not much fun at all; he also painfully recognized that he was overweight and lacked the requisite social graces. But now he posed a problem for Harvard Law, which couldn't let one of their better students go jobless. So once again Flom took the train to New York, this time to meet with three partners of a new firm, founded on April Fool's Day 1948: Marshall Skadden, Leslie Arps, and John Slate. None of them was Jewish. Flom didn't care. Each of them had suffered career setbacks at larger firms. He didn't care about that either. He did care that they seemed more informal and fun than the stiffs at the white-shoe firms. Indeed, early on Skadden Arps & Meagher developed a reputation for "anti-pomposity and pro-kook." Still, they recognized how whiplike-smart Flom was and offered him an associate's job—he was the firm's first—and even paid him, $3,500 for the first year. (They were not yet taking pay.) Flom accepted.

In six years he became a partner and *Flom* was appended to the firm letterhead: Skadden Arps Meagher & Flom. By then Flom had begun to imbue the small firm with some of his own deep reserves of ambition, workaholism, and genius for blunt realism. The firm was still scrambling for billings and he did a little of everything. Except for some regulatory work for Pan American, Skadden Arps had no large corporate clients. The firm had to scuffle to make a living. It needed an angle. It had Flom.

IN THE EARLY '50s, the preeminent lawyer in the proxy business was a man named George Demas, a tall, heavy-set, cigar-smoking, Hell's

Kitchen–born Columbia Law School attorney who ran his practice out of a green-walled office off Wall Street. Demas had been drafted into the Navy, then found himself in the Office of Strategic Services—the predecessor to the CIA—during World War II, and served as an investigating attorney at the Nuremberg trials.[20] This training clearly made him suitable for managing the subterranean currents of proxy contests. He was not a figure of any establishment. He once admitted that he was unknown in the larger world except to boards and executives. He affected a pugilistic air. "I do nothing but company fights," he said. "I'm at home where the next fella isn't."[21]

In 1967, the *Los Angeles Times* called Demas "The Superman of Wall Street." This was undoubtedly an exaggeration. He was affable and liked to talk, particularly with the press. "It used to be I'd have a busy season," he told a reporter. "Now there's no slack season. It's almost like a Dick Tracy cartoon. You finish one chapter and another comes along." Demas tried to boil down what he did to a mastery of the mechanics of the shareholder letter. "Mechanical things are terrifically important in a close vote. You need to send out 'thank you' letters. 'Dear stockholder, thank you for your proxy. The other side may make every effort to change your vote. If there are any questions, call me.' Then there are corrective letters. I've made up 31 forms. A joint tenant comes in with one signature. You don't have time to dictate a letter. You just send out form 11."[22]

Demas admitted he was good at dictating "pretty poisonous" letters about the opposition. "You've got to get the pitch in your material. You don't treat all stockholders alike. I wouldn't write to an AT&T stockholder like the owner of a $2 stock. A $2 stock, you can shout at them." This was a little duplicitous. Persuasion was essential, but the real value of legal advice in proxy contests came from knowing how to stagger a board in order to extend the struggle and hike often-backbreaking costs; how to force the company to pick up those costs; how to delay a meeting if you're behind, attain or withhold shareholder lists, find the leverage on a key investor, or convince the Securities and Exchange Commission to allow near-libelous charges against an opponent.[23] This wasn't material that a nice newspaper like the *LA Times* needed to know.

By the time Flom stumbled into the proxy game, Demas was a dominant figure, having participated by the early '60s in what he estimated to be "125 fights." Skadden had recruited a high-profile lawyer who had spent two years as general counsel of the SEC, William Timbers, and he suggested Flom talk to executives at a company called United Industrial, a former maker of auto bodies that had become a financial holding company; Timbers knew the management. United Industrial had bought a stake in a missile company that was prospering, stirring suspicions of a group of shareholders—at least publicly—that United Industrial was being run for insiders; less publicly, the shareholders were probably interested in grabbing those missile profits themselves. A proxy contest began. Flom, after having read everything available on proxy contests, found himself across a table from an even younger associate on his first deal—Martin Lipton from Seligson, Morris & Neuberger—representing the insurgents. (The significance of this is retrospective: Lipton would not appear in another M&A deal for fifteen years, by which time Flom had become the go-to M&A lawyer.) After the usual charges and countercharges—Flom wrote the flyers attacking the attackers—the contest ended in a stalemate: the insurgents won four seats on the United Industrial board but not control. "It was a great deal of fun," Flom said. " I just took to it."[24]

In 1960, Flom came up against Demas in one of the most spectacular proxy contests of the era. How he ended up there tells you how intimate this world was; the details are still known today at Skadden as the "dead-body" story. Skadden had advised a client on a tangled personal matter: a disagreement between his family members over the care of his sister, who had suffered a stroke. In a display of legal acumen, Skadden suggested that the man take the sister to the hospital while the others were out. He did; she recovered. Now the client, who had once worked for a ruthless early-twentieth-century accumulator of corporate assets (transit, tobacco, insurance, typewriters, the Thompson submachine gun) named Thomas Fortune Ryan, had a son,

Arthur "Artie" Long, who was a senior executive for the major proxy solicitor D. F. King, which did the hard work of actually squeezing signed proxies from shareholders. (A common tactic in the game was to hire all the major proxy solicitors, leaving your opponent, as one observer put it, "like a diver without oxygen." Flom would learn this lesson well and apply it to Skadden's M&A business.) Long and Flom became buddies: "I'd fought a couple of fights," Long said, "and Joe was interested. We started having dinner together three nights a week—at Manny Wolf's or the Assembly. We were *kids!*"[25] Long recommended Skadden to management of the Alleghany Corp., which had come under attack by aggrieved shareholders and needed to assemble a defense team. Demas was already advising the insurgents.

Alleghany, a sizable company, was the former railroad holding company of the Van Swearingen brothers, who had once been backed by J. P. Morgan & Co., which was about as respectable as you could get. As with so many proxy contests, the struggle for control took place among former friends and allies. During World War II, a rising broker named Robert Young—a protégé of John Jacob Raskob, who had been instrumental in affairs at General Motors and DuPont—and his partner Allan Kirby, the son of a co-founder of five-and-dime chain F. W. Woolworth's, acquired Alleghany. In 1954, after a long struggle, Young and Kirby managed to buy the nation's No. 2 railroad and Van Swearingen property, the New York Central. Young began to streamline New York Central operations, but in 1957 the railroad began to fail and the Alleghany board rejected a proposal for a shareholder dividend. A few days later Young killed himself, leaving Kirby in charge. Alleghany also owned a financial company, Investors Diversified Services, which it had bought from the Murchison brothers, John D. and Clint W., scions of a Texas oil fortune. (Clint was the first owner of the Dallas Cowboys.) Alleghany not only acquired IDS but sold it back to them, then purchased it again. This made them almost family. Now, in a fratricidal spasm, the Murchisons turned on Kirby and launched a proxy contest for control of Alleghany. Their argument, amplified by Demas's letters: Kirby had been the late Young's puppet and was running Alleghany into the ground.

Alleghany management fired back that the Murchisons were just a couple of rich kids set up by their oil-drilling papa, as if Kirby was not. Proxy contests got personal fast.

Flom ran the counting of the votes for Alleghany in the snake pit, with the bow-tied Demas right across the table. There's a grainy newspaper photograph of the scene, with a Pinkerton guard looming behind Flom, who, husky with big glasses, in his shiny suit, seems to be hectoring Demas. The Murchisons won. They went on to sell the New York Central to the Pennsylvania Railroad, which ended up as part of the most spectacular bankruptcy of the '60s, Penn Central. A sign of what was to come.

No matter. As Flom said, just sitting across the table from Demas made him a player. "Not very heady or sophisticated stuff, but that put us at least one ahead of everyone else in New York City," he said. The business was growing, but the deals were generally small. As Long, who bought D. F. King in 1967 and was one of the great Damon Runyonesque characters in M&A until his death, at sixty-one, in 1988, said: "Until 1968, you had the Securities Act of 1934, but there were no rules, no Williams Act, nothing. It was a shooting gallery. Every Saturday, I'd get a phone call from some company saying, 'I'm going to get hit in the ass,' and if I wasn't on the opposition, I'd be hired to defend. Every Monday you were playing in another city."[26] Other proxy contests followed; in many of them, Flom played defense, contrary to his later reputation for offense. In the years that followed, Flom (with Long) was asked to defend the American Firefighting Co. against Alphonse "Art" Landa, and American Hardware Corp. against Victor Muscat. In the latter case, Flom managed to win despite the fact that Muscat, advised by Demas, already held a third of the stock. *Barron's* mentioned Flom as an up-and-coming advisor and the phone began to ring. Flom kept busy through the early-'60s, representing brand names like Elgin Watch, Studebaker, and Metro-Goldwyn-Mayer. Flom was Skadden's rainmaker. He bought a racehorse with Long. ("A cheap little nag," said Long, "but we won three out of four races at Belmont and Aqueduct."[27]) He acquired a big car, which his wife, worried about his swelling head, promptly sold. The proxy business was booming and fueling the growth of Skadden, and Flom was personally engaged in stumping up business. As Lincoln Caplan writes in his history of Skadden Arps, "By 1965, the firm had more work than it could handle."[28] The level of takeovers kept rising and the business was growing more complex. Demas continued to advise in proxy situations, but Flom had a growing firm with which to extend his reach. The era of the lone practitioner in M&A was ending.

Another thing was growing apparent, not just to Skadden partners and associates but also to clients and opponents: Flom was a ferocious competitor. He played to win. He was not always gentle, nice, or classy. He was as blunt as a smack to the head. He did not confuse clients with what he couldn't do; he did not take refuge in legalistic sophistry; he offered answers. And, in a sign of his immersion in the proxy business, he won by edging as close to the line as possible. He did what had to be done—this side of the rules. He lived for the fight—not just for his clients but for the larger struggle for supremacy in the legal and financial world. He was brilliant legally, but unlike Berle he was not a theoretical thinker; his biggest ideas had to do with tactics: how to win. He also harbored a grudge. For all their color and excitement, the years of struggle did not leave Flom unmarked. In the late '80s, Flom spoke in a debate celebrating the hundredth anniversary of the *Harvard Law Review,* scoffing at "those creeps who keep talking about their gentlemanly practice." He gleefully exposed the contradictions of the Wasp ascendancy. He didn't care about being classy, posh, or elite; he wasn't competing in a popularity contest; he wanted to win. His contempt for nostalgia about a waning world came pouring out. Caplan quotes him:

> When law firms were run with their father's handing them down to their sons, what was so great about that? What was so great about the fact that certain people could get into clubs and others couldn't? Or that women or blacks couldn't work at those firms? Or that there were Jewish, gentile, and other separate firms? What was so great about the fact that you had to go to one of the four or five major law firms in order to get into one of the major firms?

What was so great then that it was more important what your family background was, in terms of whether you got into one of those firms, than what your academic background was? You say everything was lost when those practices disappeared. Every change involves some loss. The question is whether things are better off or worse off.[29]

By then they were clearly better for Joe Flom. And the world was full of striving Joe Floms, though none as shrewd as he was. The future had arrived.

Chapter Three

THE AMBIVALENCE OF FELIX ROHATYN

WALL STREET AFTER depression and war was sleepy, private, controlled by an imperial institution in that neoclassical pile on Broad Street, the New York Stock Exchange. Wall Street's stone towers and dark, mazelike streets remained, but the crowds had thinned and aged; the great engines of the economy roared elsewhere. New construction had stopped. Volume on the NYSE, the Big Board, was, by both earlier and later standards, low, though slowly growing as the postwar economy boomed. Individual investors traded stock, paying hefty fixed commissions to a flock of brokerage firms, large and small; many investors purchased stock for income in the form of dividends. Buying stocks for their appreciation was viewed as a practice not terribly different from proxy contests: marginal, shadowy, vaguely vulgar like betting on the ponies, speculating, and thus a widely accepted cause of the Crash; Saul Bellow in *Seize the Day* captured this disdain in his 1956 portrait of a brokerage firm's customer trading room on Manhattan's Upper West Side, with its cigar smoke and whiff of failure, fraud, and retail punters. Institutions and rich people, on the other hand, mostly stuffed portfolios with bonds, which were viewed as inherently secure, productive, and respectable.

Wall Street was divided into compartments, like an exclusive train. Some of this stemmed from New Deal financial legislation: Glass-Steagall split commercial from investment banking, sundering, most famously, the House of Morgan into J. P. Morgan & Co., the bank,

and Morgan Stanley, the investment bank, which imperiously controlled the all-important Wall Street underwriting syndicates. Both
were preeminent and true-blue Wasp, the financial analogue of Cravath, Sullivan & Cromwell, and Davis Polk. Some of this came from
embedded social attitudes: Jews dealt with Jews, Irish with Irish,
Wasps with Wasps. African-Americans were invisible; women were
secretaries. But a lot stemmed from the Big Board's dense thicket of
regulations, which determined everything from commissions to capital requirements, to how firms were structured and how business was
organized. The NYSE board of governors resembled that of a particularly fussy coop. As with law firms, partnerships reigned supreme; the
stock exchange allowed only private companies to join and severely
limited the number of new members. Public ownership was banned as
a potential conflict; the exchange argued that it was easier to regulate
private firms without shareholders, some of whom might be "undesir-
able unqualified persons." These partnerships were small and risk-
averse: partners sat at wooden desks in the partners' room watching
one another for signs of incipient imprudence, larceny, or senility.
Capital was dear; you didn't toss it around. The system was unabash-
edly monopolistic and anti-competitive. Wall Street might have been
fragmented, but it was also, in terms Chris Welles described so com-
prehensively in 1975, a club, or as he wrote, the Club.[1] You had to pass
muster to get into the Club—ethnic identification and family helped,
an insider patron was required—but then nearly everything was set.
This was a kind of post-Crash, postwar pact that much of America
shared, at least until the '60s: Wall Street traded risk and reward for
certainty, a guaranteed, if by later excesses, modest living. The world,
after all, was a dangerous place. Go with the bonds.

THIS WAS THE world Felix Rohatyn entered in 1950. Rohatyn was not
your typical American or Wall Streeter. In his later career, he often
seemed a reluctant investment banker, an ambivalent financier; he was
criticized (nearly always in a whisper) for his thin skin, his vanity, ambition, and overactive conscience, his sense that he was placed on earth
for higher ends than simply making money. Much of this response

was envy; some was valid. In the 1950s, life was simpler; he was not yet famous, though he was still a rare bird in a profoundly parochial Wall Street: bilingual, young, cosmopolitan. Rohatyn was European and Jewish—his father was a Viennese who had settled in France as a brewer—and young Felix arrived in the United States during the war with his mother (his parents had divorced), one step ahead of a train ride to Dachau.[2] The passage out of France had been harrowing. Rohatyn began his memoirs in 1940, when he, at the age of twelve, his mother, his grandmother, and the Polish cook fled south toward Spain with a mattress tied to the roof of the car, some gas coupons, and toothpaste tubes stuffed, on his mother's instructions, with gold coins. They had heard talk of the camps; the roads were jammed. Down narrow side roads they made their way to Biarritz, but the Spanish border was closed. Heading to Marseille, they hit a German checkpoint. The soldier asked for papers that would identify them as Jews. But rather than examine them, he reached into his pocket to light a cigarette, and waved them forward. As they drove on, they saw him stop the car behind them.

What is this story about? Ethnic identity, persecution, a world turned upside down. The necessity to be other than who you really are. The importance of luck, fate, and chance. History played its vicious games. The family, now including his stepfather, scored transit visas and made their way to New York, via Casablanca, Lisbon, and a year in Rio de Janeiro. The gold coins came in handy. Upon arrival, the family landed more softly than many refugees; Rohatyn has little to say about those details. We next hear of him at Middlebury College, a tiny picture-postcard liberal-arts school in Vermont, studying physics and skiing. Middlebury was no City College night school, and Rohatyn was no Joe Flom. For one thing Rohatyn flunked out of the physics program that would have sent him on to MIT; he ended up in the Army for a tour. For another, he had already learned how to negotiate the social worlds of a certain privileged part of postwar America. Socially, he was operating at a much higher level than Flom.

On a ship returning from a failed attempt to learn the brewery trade of his father in Paris, Rohatyn—you can't make this up—met

Edith Piaf and ended up tutoring her in English. When that was over (Piaf ended a romance and, as in a sad song, departed), his stepfather offered to introduce him to "an acquaintance" named André Meyer at a small Franco-American investment bank known as Lazard Frères. Rohatyn agreed; he needed a summer job, though he had no particular interest in finance. He writes that a short time later, he had a breakfast conversation at a Hudson River house party with the patriarch of the estate, who advised him to do anything he could to get close to Meyer. To do so, he had to learn dealmaking, even if it involved a cut in pay. "The only thing André is interested in is doing deals," he declared.[3] Rohatyn called his host "Mr. Sam." It was Samuel Bronfman, the founder of Canadian distiller Seagram.

How many coins were in those tubes?

André Meyer is to Rohatyn's career what that cigarette-smoking soldier was to his life. Meyer is an extraordinary figure in the private, clubby environs of postwar Wall Street.[4] Lazard, founded in New Orleans in 1848 but with autonomous outposts in Paris and London, is an investment bank that still operates; Meyer turned the New York arm into something European and ahead of its time, a *banque d'affaires*. Meyer, too, was Jewish; he'd had a remarkable career in France at Lazard before the war. He fled to New York, set up shop at the Carlyle Hotel on Madison Avenue, and successfully plotted his takeover of New York's Lazard Frères. Meyer must have seemed remarkably strange and foreign, with his heavily accented English and his elaborate manners, in New York at that time. He was a kind of high-level financier, transcending the conventional banker, broker, trader designations; in his Meyer biography, Cary Reich calls him "The Picasso of banking."[5] Picasso, of course, broke the rules. So did Meyer. Writes Reich: "In many ways, André Meyer was not a very nice man. He was greedy, vindictive, domineering, and often quite sadistic. His constant browbeating and temper tantrums made life unbearable for his business associates and his family. No matter how wealthy he became—and he became very wealthy—he could not stop plotting and scheming to build an even bigger fortune. He would allow nothing and no one to get in his way."[6] He was also highly cultivated, an art collector, and supremely persuasive, particularly when advising the wealthy and powerful, who ranged from Jackie Kennedy to Katharine Graham to David Sarnoff. He was creative, a brilliant negotiator, and, as Reich notes, "Better than any man alive, he could strip a deal to its essence, to the underlying value that did or didn't make it worthwhile. Then . . . he would give that essence a form, a structure that enabled him to wring all he could out of the deal with a minimum amount of risk. This he called 'financial engineering,' and the term become the byword of Meyer's artistry."[7]

Rohatyn became first his employee, then his protégé, then something akin to his son. Meyer came to see him as the future of Lazard. It is worth pausing to wonder how this happened. Rohatyn is clearly very bright—though, up to that moment, of suspect motivation—and socially sophisticated. He does not initially seem particularly serious, but he finds he intellectually enjoys M&A; soon he's taking night classes at NYU and reading Graham and Dodd on value investing. He and Meyer shared Paris, the war, exile—a sense of loss, survival, and success. But in retrospect they also shared a deeper appreciation of what later became much more common than it was in the '50s: deal-making.[8] Soon Meyer is coming to dinner with Rohatyn and his new wife and doing the dishes. And yet he is still abusive, domineering, a man of secrets. Decades later, Rohatyn recalls Meyer telling him to go see a client who had not paid. "Be soft," he said, "and hard."[9] Just before Meyer is about to offer Rohatyn a Lazard partnership—he is now thirty-two, married, with two sons—Meyer recites a long list of his professional shortcomings. This is not to go to your head, he says. You must redouble your efforts. Rohatyn does.

ROHATYN FULLY ABSORBED the moral norms of Wall Street in those years; in later decades, much of his critique of what had grown wrong in M&A is based on his sense of the decline and fall of the role of the intermediary after the '60s. In that postwar period, the investment banker was strictly an intermediary—a guide, an advisor, in *Godfather* terms a consigliere—for a client engaged in buying or selling his company. This was broader than just mergers, which were just a small function in the '50s, a service to clients, hardly a business at all. Wall Street generally served as an intermediary for American business, a reality the New Deal reforms tried to enforce. Wall Street had two major businesses: brokerage and underwriting. They were tightly connected; Wall Street, like economics, often resembles plumbing. Individuals purchase stock from brokers who, in turn, buy them from investors who, in turn, have acquired them from underwriters hired by companies coming to Wall Street to trade pieces of their business—securities—for cash. There are a lot more steps in there, but that's the simple version. Wall Street firms stood in the middle of both transactions, collecting hefty fixed brokerage fees from investors and fixed underwriting fees from corporations. They risked nothing, as long as they were solvent and remained members of the Club. Fixed meant there was no competition on price. Competition was a concept for others, not for this utility called finance, popularly known as Wall Street.

In those postwar decades, Wall Street embraced the narrow, legalistic definition of the intermediary to justify its existence. It needed justifying; Wall Street had been blamed for everything that had gone wrong in the '30s this side of the Treaty of Versailles. Wall Street firms, through brokerage and underwriting, were, in theory, expert guides into the dark and tangled swamps of the market. This was not the creative, liberating, efficient, omniscient, heavenly market of later decades. Rather, this was the treacherous, seductively dangerous market of 1929 and the grim years that followed. This was a risky, scary, irrational, unpredictable, and uncertain market where there was no such thing as innocence and very little in the way of truth or beauty. Markets, like economics and the inside of TVs, were mysteries accessible only by experts. The market was necessary, of course, as a meeting ground to buy and sell participation in the larger economy belching smoke from factories in places like Detroit or Pittsburgh; markets existed to set prices, though whether they were accurate, predictive, or meaningful is another question. To enter those murky realms, you needed a guide who in theory knew the lay of the land. Corporations thus assembled slates of underwriters—in truth, Morgan Stanley determined the makeup of syndicates as a form of divine right—to help price, market, and peddle securities to customers. As a result, syndicates became as rigid as a European court. (Why did syndicates remain so rigid? A 1947 antitrust suit arguing that seventeen firms, led by Morgan Stanley, colluded—won by Wall Street in 1953—answered that question: success breeds success. The system worked, companies got financing, the jungle had been tamed, no problem here.[10]) Brokers, in theory, existed to provide investors with advice and execution. In the best of all possible worlds, these middlemen (they were all men) remained steadfastly loyal to clients. There were, of course, rules to prevent conflicts of interest. But while conflicts regularly occurred— sin does not disappear just because God publishes the Ten Commandments—the conventional wisdom was that the role of the Wall Street intermediary was sound. Success bred success. If these firms didn't act fair and square with clients, they would go out of business. This was, of course, a self-justifying recipe for hierarchy, and not unlike the later rationales for market omniscience.

The same logic applied to an even smaller number of merger advisors. They, too, brought expertise to the task at hand. They, in theory, had mastered the complexities of buying and selling corporate assets. They knew markets well enough to find buyers, set prices, structure deals. They were not sullied by a confusion of self-interests; their self-interest was identical with clients, from which they received a fee. They were wise, shrewd, servants to their clients. Mergers might have been relatively rare, but they were a high-level activity with access to CEOs and boards—and thus a job for the most senior figures on Wall Street: Lehman Brothers' Robert "Bobby" Lehman, Goldman Sachs's Sidney Weinberg, Morgan Stanley's Perry Hall, Lazard's Meyer. Mergers were, by definition, friendly affairs. Like brokers and underwriters, merger advisors reflexively referred to two ideas that emerged from a past defined appropriately by The Old Man, J. P. Morgan Sr.: the essential importance of character and reputation. Morgan, of course, was the very summit of Wasp financial rectitude, though he was always (like Meyer) more than just an intermediary. In 1912, during congressional hearings, lawyer Samuel Untermeyer asked him leadingly, "Is not commercial credit based primarily upon money or property?" He answered: "No sir. The first thing is character." And he continued: "Before money or property or anything else. Money cannot buy it . . . because a man I do not trust could not get money from me for all the bonds of Christendom."

Ah, Christendom. Nice place, though not for everyone. Character, of course, is elusive except for the all-seeing Almighty; and leaving the definition of it in the hands of one red-nosed man—even a rotund giant—not to say his less impressive descendants, would eventually look stranger and stranger. Like the white-shoe law firms that assumed that the best-and-the-brightest—the apotheosis of rationality and upright character—had to walk, talk, worship, and golf with Protestant uprightness, so too did the role of the intermediary harbor its own complexities and contradictions. You didn't necessarily have to be Protestant—Jewish firms like Lehman Brothers, Goldman Sachs, and Kuhn Loeb did a lot of business—but you certainly had to act that way. And part of that set of ideas, so similar to the nineteenth-century British ideal of the gentleman, was that the highest calling was that of the advisor; far lower on the scale was anyone engaged in the grubby business of transactions, with its implication of unwashed, unsublimated greed.

IN ALL OF THIS Meyer is a walking, talking contradiction. Not that he cared. He was neither Protestant nor true-blue American. He advised and he stealthily transacted. He was a big believer in a banker's irreproachable reputation, though his sense of financial morality went back not to Jack Morgan and a bunch of Wasp grandees but to prewar Paris. Meyer reshaped Lazard in New York into a firm that resembled Lazard in Paris. (With one exception: Lazard Paris also acted as a commercial bank, which was not allowed in New York because of Glass-Steagall.) Meyer envisioned a firm—and a firm that was an extension of himself—that advised large and wealthy clients, but also conducted dealmaking operations for itself: both an intermediary (advisor) and a principal (investor). Meyer saw nothing wrong in simultaneously pursuing his clients' interests and his own; he was not foolish enough to articulate such crass sentiments himself, but everyone close to him knew the goal was to make Mr. Meyer rich. (Meyer was also cheap: he didn't believe in spending money on fancy digs for Lazard, or overpaying. He hoarded capital. It was a survivor's strategy.) As a result, Meyer and Lazard often served both as advisor and as investor, respectively. Lazard often preferred to act as co-investor on deals with clients; this was an ethical juggling act that sometimes went awry. Sometimes he would buy the very asset he was selling for a client, as he did with Avis, the car-rental company. Meyer was secretive and Machiavellian; he was no devotee of that keystone of New Deal reforms, transparency. In fact, even when it came to dealmaking, Reich notes, Meyer favored deals that, if they went wrong, would never make the papers. He was secretive even with his closest partners.[11]

When Rohatyn set out to find clients, he was not dealing with the kind of characters Flom and Demas yelled at in proxy contests. Lazard had a corporate clientele, many of them stemming from Meyer's own extensive and elite connections. Meyer advised and did deals with William Zeckendorf, the real-estate magnate; David Sarnoff of RCA; Harold Geneen at ITT; and Ferdinand Eberstadt, an innovative investment banker at Dillon Read in the '20s, then at his own firm, F. Eberstadt & Co. in the '50s, and a pioneer of mutual funds with his Chemical Fund. Eberstadt was another man ahead of his time. He was, as Reich points out, a loner like Meyer. "He was constantly chided for not being a good sport in the syndicate game, for driving overly hard bargains, and for going to extraordinary lengths to protect himself when he brought an issue public. His response to these complaints was characteristically caustic: 'I don't want to stick anyone else, and I damn well don't want to get stuck myself'."[12]

Rohatyn profited from these relationships. Sarnoff—General Sarnoff, for his PR efforts in World War II—had two cousins, Steve Ross and Edward Rosenthal, who owned funeral homes and parking lots and wanted to get into the rental-car business by buying Avis. Sarnoff asked Meyer to look into it. As Rohatyn puts it in his memoirs, "A deal involving a funeral home company was not elegant enough to require Mr. Meyer's personal participation."[13] So Rohatyn was dispatched. While the deal never materialized, Rohatyn bonded with Ross, who would go on to build media conglomerate Warner Communications through dozens of acquisitions, including the Warner Brothers film studio; Rohatyn eventually joined the Warner board. When RCA launched a desperate attempt to expand through acquisition, Rohatyn did most of the deals, both for the general and for his son, Robert Sarnoff, who succeeded him. But no relationship proved as rich to Rohatyn as his ties to Geneen, which began when the executive, a former NYSE floor clerk with an accountant's mien, acquired the much-shopped Avis for ITT from Lazard in 1965 and Meyer introduced his young protégé to the budding conglomerateur. Meyer was too volatile for Geneen, but Rohatyn, who had mastered the art of dealing with an explosive ego, was perfect. "Geneen is a very difficult person," Rohatyn once said. "A very difficult person. But I always knew where Geneen was going."[14] Rohatyn would visit with Geneen nearly every night at six, and was always present for brainstorming dinners.[15] Thus began what Rohatyn called "a friendship—and a learning experience—that stretched over two decades. In the process I advised ITT on nearly a dozen takeovers, served on the board, and helped engineer what was at the time one of the largest acquisitions in U.S. history."[16]

Enter the conglomerates. Much has been written about the growth of conglomerates in the go-go '60s. The American economy was still growing fast, though both Europe and Japan were starting to revive, and the stock market was booming. The first signs of a fundamental shift in shareholding were emerging (as Berle had pointed out to Lipton): institutions, including aggressive mutual funds, were buying more and more stocks and performance was becoming the mantra. The dominance of small shareholders was ebbing away. Moreover, in hindsight, the triumph of industrial America, with its unions, factories, and mass middle class, was plateauing, though this was not obvious at the time. Overall, the federal government remained vigilant when it came to mergers that involved acquiring ever-greater market shares in specific businesses. But antitrust authorities were much more lenient when large companies acquired completely different businesses. Underpinning all this was a story that made sense in a decade infatuated with high technology: a belief in management science that could, through financial operations and quantitative metrics, manage anything, which in turn was buttressed by another, related metaphor: the corporation as a portfolio, with businesses that could be bought in their growth stages and sold as they matured, or with cash-cow units that could feed growing units. The corporation was less an organic entity and more a fluid collection of assets. By the mid-'60s, an M&A boom had begun, the first since the 1920s, with tinder provided by the aptly named conglomerates. As the incomparable John Brooks wrote in his history of Wall Street in the '60s, *The Go-Go-Years*, with that combination of wit and proportion that now feels lost:

Nobody seems to know who first applied the term "conglomerate"—which in earlier times had usually meant a kind of mineral popularly called pudding stone—to corporations given to diversifying their activities through mergers with other corporations in other lines of business. At any rate, the new usage made its popular appearance in 1964 or 1965, shortly before conglomerates became the darling of investors. Derived from the Latin word *glomus*, meaning wax, the word suggests a sort of apotheosis of the old Madison Avenue cliché, "a big ball of wax," and is no doubt apt enough; but right from the start, the heads of conglomerate companies objected to it. Each of them felt that his company was a mesh of corporate and managerial genius in which diversified lines of endeavor—producing, say, ice cream, cement and flagpoles—were subtly welded together by some abstruse metaphysical principle so refined as to be invisible to the vulgar eye. *Other* diversified companies, each such genius acknowledged, were conglomerates; but not his own.[17]

Rohatyn made his name doing conglomerate deals. He was a one-man merger machine, a supremely effective facilitator, a superb negotiator. He became the very image of the modern investment banker, at least before Hollywood re-imagined the job. By the end of the decade, having just passed forty years of age, he was the most important M&A banker in America and a pillar of Lazard. "Every week, or so it seemed, I was flying around the country, setting out to play a role in a potential financial marriage as one giant conglomerate after another became smitten with a new corporate conquest."[18] He was proud of himself. He was smart, methodical, mature, professional, and he had a way with older CEOs; he did not waste anyone's time. But at this point—and there may be some biographical revisionism at work here—Rohatyn's ambivalence begins to emerge. Looking back, he recognizes that the stock market loved conglomerates and that CEOs, laden with stock options, did too. He sees a Wall Street that "believed that bigger was always better—and more valuable." But he insists that he harbored doubts. "My contrarian view, however, was that a focused company tended in the long run to provide more value for its shareholders. And despite all the adoring attention the market focused on the galloping conglomerates of the 1960s, it seemed to me several of them were doomed from the start. For example, I was not surprised when James Ling's LTV, an aerospace and steel giant, eventually went bankrupt. To my conservative mind, it made little business sense for a company to grow simply for the sake of growth."[19]

This is all a little tricky: Rohatyn engineered many of those conglomerate deals—though not for LTV—some good, some bad. Rohatyn looked at all this subjectively. It's not just that advisors, like lawyers, can't necessarily be blamed for the actions of clients. It's that Rohatyn for decades to come regularly drew distinctions between M&A practices good and bad, and his deals, including for Geneen, often ended up in the good bucket. LTV was bad. Geneen's ITT, he judges, was mostly good—and ITT was one hell of a company, at least in theory. "I did appreciate," he writes, "that if a conglomerate was diverse enough, had a well thought-out, even expansive, business plan, and prudently rolled up its sleeves to do sufficient due diligence, so that it could make its acquisition at a reasonable price, then it could grow *and* prosper. And so, guided by this banker's philosophy and encouraged by the high-flying spirit of the times,"[20] he clambered aboard Geneen's merger bandwagon.

Rohatyn admired Geneen, this "hard-driving but colorless" man, as Brooks depicted him, who worked endless hours and was always prepared. (Brooks insightfully depicted ITT as a company that "embodied the old Protestant ethic in new conglomerate clothes. It was the Establishment's conglomerate." It was also, he adds, the most Republican of conglomerates.[21] Rohatyn was a Democrat, with liberal tendencies, which suggests that politics isn't everything.) Geneen demanded to know everything, and when he didn't succeed to his satisfaction, his rage, like Meyer's, could be volcanic. Rohatyn, having survived Meyer, found working for Geneen exhilarating. But even in Rohatyn's telling, there are flaws. The bespectacled, deceptively bland Geneen tried to control a vast, growing, and utterly diverse corporation from a center occupied by himself and his formidable calculating machine of a mind. The details of manufacturing or selling meant little to him. He was fixated on the numbers. There was an amazing arrogance to it, not unlike Robert McNamara's war-by-numbers with elements of Dr. Strangelove. "Hal" Geneen was an imperious and hard-driving autocrat in a Sears Roebuck suit, though he had an aversion to hostile deals. His monthly management meetings, where he interrogated eighty managers arrayed around a large table, were legendary; he kept the curtains shut so no one would know the time. He was also, for someone who claimed to be driven by rationality and empirical fact, surprisingly willing to make snap, intuitive decisions. Rohatyn admits that, in his first M&A deal for Geneen (and Geneen's first as CEO), "the careful strategy that was shaping ITT's growth . . . was more a product of intuition and happenstance than a banker's well-reasoned battle plan." The target was a small high-tech radio company in a nascent Silicon Valley. Geneen agreed and took it to the board, which rejected it. "Geneen realized at once that more was at stake than a simple acquisition of a small San Jose technology concern. The board was attempting to undermine his control—and all his large plans for the future growth of ITT."[22] Geneen laid down an ultimatum and the board folded. Rohatyn cheered—he was still cheering in 2010—what would later be characterized as a governance transgression.

In reality, ITT was not dramatically better designed or built than most other conglomerates, despite Geneen's mad-science genius and bland intensity; he never achieved his ambition of building the world's most profitable company. Rohatyn's close ties to Geneen also brought him much agony, after he was dragged in front of Congress to explain some ITT deals, including Continental Baking (later of Twinkies fame) and Hartford Insurance, which he had urged on Geneen and which had had to clear some difficult antitrust issues, and raised the first questions of influence peddling. Rohatyn was affronted, and appalled, that he would find himself attacked in public. But it got nightmarishly worse. ITT settled the Hartford antitrust case for $1.5 billion. Then ITT-Sheraton was accused of contributing $400,000 to the Republican National Committee to ensure the Hartford settlement. Rohatyn, who was advising a Democratic presidential candidate, Edmund Muskie, confronted Geneen: Was that a bribe? Geneen denied it, and Rohatyn choose to believe him. Then a memo surfaced from ITT lobbyist Dita Beard about behind-the-scenes machinations on the Hartford merger. Rohatyn again denied wrongdoing; he had personally negotiated the settlement, he said, with Nixon's attorney general, Richard Kleindeinst, later of Watergate fame. And so, what even he called his "fool's role" dragged on. To explain his work for ITT, he was again hauled before Congress, where he was humiliated by Democrats. Then ITT was accused of assassinating Chilean president Salvador Allende, an episode Brooks summed up by saying "here, naked and unashamed, was immense power without a sense of place, proportion or responsibility." Columnist Nicholas Von Hoffman dubbed Rohatyn "Felix the Fixer," which he despised. At one point, he testified before a grand jury. And perhaps the cruelest cut of all: He had to fight Securities and Exchange Commission charges about the murky sale for tax reasons of a Hartford stake to secretive Italian bank Mediobanca—suggested by Meyer himself. Rohatyn eventually wriggled free, but he remained loyal to both Meyer and Geneen, with just a grudging sense that the latter had somehow run afoul of politics. Meyer was just being Meyer.

Were Rohatyn's actions motivated by money? Was he fooling himself about Geneen and ITT? He made a good deal of money from ITT (at least for that era), but he never appeared driven by pay; he never was the inveterate investor like Meyer; and given his skills, he could easily have cashed out. Indeed, status, power, and the faith of a powerful older patron may have made more difference than money. He was an advisor who remained loyal to his client. But for all his focus on ITT's political woes, Geneen, and his own embarrassment, Rohatyn brushed past tougher questions about his role in the '60s. He built his remarkable career on the erection of massive, ramshackle, financially driven corporate structures piled to the sky by ITT, RCA, Warner, United Technologies, and others on inflated shares—all things that in later decades he would condemn others for. He was mostly blind to their weaknesses. He undoubtedly did not see the fall of the conglomerates coming—who did?—but their collapse in the '70s would help usher in a new era of M&A. It would be an era that would make Rohatyn ever more uncomfortable and ambivalent about the rising transactional tide. And ever more nostalgic for an age now past.

THERE ARE TWO episodes in the late '60s that reveal just how treacherous Rohatyn's pursuit of status and power had become. In 1966, Geneen decided he wanted Rohatyn, then thirty-eight, on the ITT board of directors. This was big stuff. The ITT board was a who's who of the American establishment, including John McCone, who had run the CIA, and Eugene Black, who had once headed the World Bank. Rohatyn, not surprisingly, viewed an ITT board seat as a "personal triumph." But Meyer killed the idea. It wasn't that Rohatyn was too young or not established enough, he relates: "Rather, he [Meyer] explained to me with some delicacy, a Jewish refugee like myself would never be fully accepted on the board of what was then a very Waspy, deliberately blue-blooded company." Instead, Meyer pushed forward a Lazard partner who had been a CEO and, notes Rohatyn, who "carried himself with a Protestant aristocratic grace shared by many of his fellow Brook Club members." Rohatyn glumly accepted the verdict.[23]

But Geneen wanted Rohatyn and overrode Meyer and his designated Wasp. Once on the board, Rohatyn discovered that the only voice that mattered there was Geneen's. "There would be five or six acquisitions before the board at a single meeting and all the overwhelmed board would do was bow deferentially to Geneen's betterinformed will." Eugene Black once left the room to use the bathroom and said, "Don't buy anything until I get back." He wasn't necessarily joking.

The second incident involved an even more prestigious board. In 1969, with the stock market still booming despite domestic disorders and the Vietnam War, Rohatyn was asked to join the NYSE board of governors. This was the inner sanctum of Wall Street, and a dizzying laying-on-of-hands for a still-young banker at a secondary firm, not to say a Jewish refugee. But times were uncertain; the NYSE was under siege; and Rohatyn had brains and youth. This time, Meyer approved the appointment. Meyer had his reasons: he was worried about the ability of smaller, thinly capitalized firms like Lazard to survive if markets crashed. More specifically, writes Rohatyn, "[h]e believed that I would be in a position to persuade the NYSE to rethink the members' unlimited bailout exposure"—that is, the promise that members of the club would protect each other forever. Maybe this wasn't such a swell idea.

That doubt was prescient on Meyer's part, but almost immediately, Rohatyn found himself confronted by developments that threatened to unleash more change on Wall Street. As institutions crowded into stocks, they made demands on members of the club, which was suddenly beginning to feel like an *ancien régime* at midnight: more competition, lower fees, greater efficiencies, more research, new technology, a new crowd with sideburns and bell-bottoms. Even M&A was changing in ways that felt like the world was accelerating. In 1968 Congress, agitated by the very conglomerate wave that had tossed Rohatyn so high, finally passed the Williams Act after three years of debate. The bill provided rules for tender offers, a long-obscure, increasingly popular acquisition technique that represented an alternative to the proxy contest; tender offers involved not a board election like a proxy fight but the outright seizure of control, often with lightning speed through a bidding contest. At first the bill, demanded by management, sought to "protect management." Sponsor New Jersey senator Harrison Williams branded tender offers as "industrial sabotage resulting from reckless corporate raids on proud old companies." The bill's final version was more subtle than just banning the practice, suggesting, in hindsight, that management was losing some respect and clout. Still happily envisioning shareholders as small investors, it featured disclosure as a mechanism to provide directors and investors time to respond to takeover bids. Congress fully expected the new rules to stifle tenders—not the first or last time it would be shocked by consequences of its own actions. Instead, in 1969 two outsiders, Victor Posner and Saul Steinberg, used tenders to launch surprise attacks on established, even iconic corporations: Posner, a secretive (and widely loathed) Baltimore-turned-Miami homebuilder, grabbed Sharon Steel; and Steinberg, a recent Wharton grad with a Long Island insurance company, tried, and failed, to acquire New York's Chemical Bank (Flom defended Chemical). Both were outsiders; both were Jewish; both used what an academic paper not long after termed "a deviant innovation,"[24] the tender offer, to threaten establishment institutions. The bank raid was a particularly shocking attack on proprieties. Regulated banks, particularly old and Waspy ones, were normally beyond reach, particularly by bumptious Jews from Long Island.

Behind it all was a reality that quickly dawned on Posner and Steinberg, and to the ever-alert Flom, who had been touring the United States with another early M&A attorney, Arthur Fleischer of Fried Frank, giving talks on the Williams Act:[25] institutions saw the Williams Act as *legitimizing* tender offers.[26] They were happy to unload blocks of shares at the right price. They were prepared to be transactional. They did not necessarily give a damn about proud old companies. They cared about performance—their performance.

On Wall Street itself, financial firms, small and undercapitalized, floundered in suddenly powerful riptides. Institutions wanted to trade bigger blocks of shares, a much riskier business for undercapitalized partnerships handling those trades. New firms offering new services emerged, banging on the club door. The old guaranteed living was threatened. Firms began to sell investment research to institutions, and funds increasingly viewed investing as a rational, quantitative endeavor. In 1959, three young Wall Streeters formed Donaldson, Lufkin & Jenrette, investment research house, and joined the Big Board. But DLJ promised to abandon the partnership structure for a modern publicly traded organization, install computer technology to handle larger blocks of stock, and raise capital. Each of these measures represented revolutionary change; the walls were coming down. In 1969 DLJ went public, selling shares worth $25 million to the public.

Going public was a direct challenge to the Club, as Rohatyn recognized. "The board of governors was, it is no exaggeration to say, thrown into a panic," he writes.[27] NYSE rules banned firms that had raised capital from the public. If they allowed DLJ in, the push for modernization would accelerate as firms scrambled to keep up. The NYSE faced a choice: expel DLJ or change the NYSE constitution. What did Rohatyn do? He recognized that much of Wall Street was antiquated. But, as he later wrote, with considerable candor, he also "exhibited a prideful conservatism of someone who has just been granted membership in an exclusive club. With my appointment, I became another of the insiders eager to preserve *our* historic and fraternal practices, regardless of how outdated—wrongheaded, really— these rules and traditions were."[28] He opposed DLJ's petition.

Rohatyn, who soon had to personally wade in to save an anachronistic Wall Street from its own debilities (and unlimited bailouts, as Meyer foresaw), thus launching his stellar public career, was quickly appalled by his own vote. In time, he wrote, "My common sense trumped my reluctance. I realized that if Wall Street was to survive as a profitable enterprise, the old boy club would need to be open to the public—and its capital."[29] He swung to support changes in the NYSE constitution allowing public companies. But here emerges the classic split between Rohatyn's head and heart. He had first reflexively supported a Wall Street he admired but knew was fated to crumble. He then agreed to usher in a new, in some ways repellent Wall Street, which had the merit that it would, like a weed, prosper. This was where Rohatyn's ambition and sentiments had brought him: to help birth a new age of finance that was faster, bigger, more transactional, more hostile, and a threat to old notions of the wise advisor and the responsible management.

In short, everything he disliked.

Chapter Four

MARTY LIPTON AND THE DARK ARTS OF DEFENSE

THERE ARE ASPECTS to Wall Street that the American public, in its best Sunday School outfit, traditionally rejects: greed, flashy wealth, hubris, black limos a-tumble with lovely ladies, an ethos of vulgar self-interest. And there are aspects of Wall Street that the same public, on Saturday night, embraces: greed, flashy wealth, hubris, wealth, those same ladies, and an All-American zeal for self-aggrandizement. Linked to this conflicted view, this ambiguity, is the belief that Wall Streeters, like economists, investors, and gypsy ladies in trailers, can read the future, which swirls around the bottom of a crystal ball—or a glass of Scotch. This atavistic belief justifies wealth, power, and their ever-present sidekick, sex; animates cries to forecast and predict; and explains their ubiquity on cable television. It's why people ask Wall Streeters over cocktails for stock tips. The belief in prescience, which in the '80s attached itself to the markets like moss on a rock, has survived episodes that would normally obliterate this faith. Instead, in periods of epic failure, belief in prescience ripens into conspiracy, *explains* failure, particularly when a Wall Street disaster careens like a monster truck down Main Street. It's comforting. This produces a common fallacy that philosophers refer to as teleology, the idea that history has a deeply inscribed design—a purpose and an end. This tendency has three corollaries. First, belief that history has a pattern, like a rug. Second, that a rare few among us can see this pattern and extrapolate it into the future. And third: The existence of such prescience, of which wealth is an easy proof (too easy), establishes certainty and meaning in a market world that often seems random and relativistic. In short, there are no errors, there are only conspiracies.

Marty Lipton has long been perceived as a sage-like figure, although he himself is a skeptic of prediction.[1] Perhaps these two facts are connected. In truth, Lipton, eighty years old as of this writing, is sage-like in his dismissal of seer status.[2] In the lore of modern M&A, Joe Flom and Marty Lipton are so tightly linked that they appear to have been attached since birth. They are founders: Adam and Eve, Marty and Joe. A mythological duality hangs over them: thesis and antithesis, offense and defense, Mars and Venus, shareholder and management, Skadden and Wachtell; the kind of opposition required for zero-sum transactions and cage fights, not to mention for journalists, an irresistible symmetry. In reality, Flom and Lipton recognized a deeper, more symbiotic reality; for years, they breakfasted together weekly at New York City's Regency Hotel, no matter the struggle *du jour,* civilized souls breaking bread. They invariably complimented each other, which normally wasn't Flom's nature or Lipton's instinct. As Flom once said, "In my relationship with Marty, we talk about a lot of different subjects, both socially and on the business level, and some that are just evanescent."[3] *Evanescent?* That's not to say they did not ferociously compete: one often-repeated anecdote has them publicly battling for the attentions of Lester Pollack, an important client, at a dinner one night, like two boys fighting over a prom queen; and the two snarled over Lipton's poison pill.[4] But mostly they dealt with each other, as if M&A came down just to them: in a long, fly-on-the-wall account of an early '80s T. Boone Pickens deal, Joe Nocera recounts how Flom would pad into a bedroom to take Lipton's calls privately—all other calls, even Pickens's, were listened to collectively.[5] The pair would share info, compare notes, settle matters. Was their pairing inevitable? Lipton and Flom did first meet on opposite sides of what was for both of them their first proxy fight, which is cosmically coincidental, if only in retrospect. But at the time, it meant nothing. Two nobodies in a nothing deal, neither with proxy experience, though Flom was a partner and Lipton a mere associate. And after that episode Lipton disappeared from the M&A scene, while Flom ruled. That situation prevailed until the early '70s.

WHERE WAS LIPTON? Well, he wasn't thinking big Berle-type thoughts. He was madly ambitious but the path ahead was obscure. When they first met, Lipton was a newish associate at Seligson, Morris & Neuberger, a firm with offices in the Empire State Building that had a better book of business than what Lipton still formally refers to as "the Skadden firm." Lipton was not your ordinary associate. He had credentials: a Root-Tilden scholarship to NYU, the Berle fellowship, the clerkship. A few weeks after classes started, NYU asked him to fill in and teach a securities-regulation class whose professor had inconveniently died. He spent the next two decades teaching at night.

Seligson, Morris was a respectable, if non-white-shoe firm, dependent on two senior partners, Charles Seligson and J. Lincoln Morris. "Professor" Seligson taught bankruptcy and corporate reorganization at NYU Law and he built a noted bankruptcy practice; in 1964, he served as trustee for bankrupt Ira Haupt & Co., a factoring operation that defrauded, among others, American Express, some big banks, and the NYSE, of millions in the then-spectacular, now amusingly quaint, salad-oil scandal. Morris, an Air Force captain in World War II and a Harvard Law grad, sat on a few big boards—Metropolitan Broadcasting (the remnant of the old DuMont Broadcasting, later renamed Metromedia), Schenley Industries, Pepsi Cola—and worked with Lehman Brothers on proxy fights and corporate control matters; he also represented Hollywood types, like Mike Todd and Joan Crawford. Most articles about him refer to his "photographic memory," suggesting he mentioned it fairly regularly. Lipton's initial plan was to get real-world experience and return to NYU to teach. He quickly became a bag carrier for Morris (it's pretty clear this rankled, perhaps because of Lipton, maybe because of Morris, probably because of both of them), while his classmate, Leonard Rosen, scurried after Seligson. Lipton worked on proxy contests for Detroit's Pfeiffer Brewing and Elgin Watch and acquisitions for Metropolitan Broadcasting, but, he admits, "We were not major players."[6] That undoubtedly rankled, too.

In 1960, Lipton became a partner, albeit a junior one; he was joined by two NYU pals who had worked on the law review with him—Rosen, now a bankruptcy specialist, and George Katz. But the legal business was changing, particularly in scale, and tensions were rising at what was now Seligson & Morris, particularly between junior and senior partners. In 1964, Pepsi CEO Donald Kendall blew it all up. Kendall had developed a fondness for Richard Nixon, who had lost the 1960 presidential race to John Kennedy, then flopped in the California gubernatorial contest. Kendall helped Nixon set up a New York law firm and handed him the Pepsi account—Seligson & Morris's account. Morris quit the Pepsi board in a huff, then quarreled with Lipton, who resigned; Morris, as Lipton later said, "decided he didn't want to practice law anymore and retired," making it look as if the firm would dissolve. Lipton and the law review boys decided to go out on their own and recruited Herbert Wachtell, Lipton's immediate predecessor as NYU's law review editor, who had worked as a federal prosecutor in New York before setting up his own shop. Wachtell brought in Jerome Kern (a lawyer, not the songwriter), but he left a few years later to become an investment banker. At that point the firm's name froze like a bug in amber: Wachtell Lipton Rosen & Katz.

What is most remarkable about this tale is the sheer talent packed into the offices of this small law firm, particularly among junior partners. Nearly all of them pursued practices that were, at the time, stereotypically Jewish: litigation, bankruptcy, M&A. (Nearly all had family roots in the garment industry.) But unlike a Flom, they were starting with a base of business; they had corporate relationships, some of which followed them to the new firm, including Metromedia; and Wachtell was a successful litigator. As the economy and Wall Street changed, each of these practices—none more dramatically than M&A—exploded like a shaken can of Pepsi. Among this group, however, Lipton was always first among equals, even if Wachtell, another Root-Tilden recipient, got his name first on the door. Wachtell Lipton from the start had a philosophy that had links to its law school origins: slightly academic, collegial, small, elite. This would not have worked if the principals weren't supremely talented. They established not only an equitable arrangement, at least in pay, among seniority levels but also, more importantly, a way of working that deemphasized individual practices for firm-wide efforts; this worked effectively in M&A and other transactional situations. Some of this was clearly Lipton himself, who saw himself in those terms. But some of this was a reaction to Seligson & Morris. "We tried to avoid the bad things," said a nameless partner (not Lipton) in a later study of the firm. "We didn't like imperious senior partners using people instead of developing a firm. We wanted to have a different relationship with our [junior] colleagues than we'd had with people we had worked for."[7] All four name partners had long, successful careers at Wachtell Lipton. And they all got quite wealthy doing it.

LIPTON WAS BUSY building the firm, but he had been paying close attention to M&A. The new firm participated in proxy contests between 1965 and 1970 and got, he said later, "Wall Street exposure." Metromedia dominated billings until someone there demanded something Lipton did not want to give; and the firm walked, putting two-thirds of its billings at risk. Wachtell Lipton survived, proof of concept. The firm successfully defended Pepsi-Cola General Bottlers from four takeover attempts in the late '60s, fending off "bear hugs" and "Chinese paper"—stock of shell companies that, Lipton quips, "had not yet reached junk bond status."[8] Lipton also wrote for the law reviews and was still teaching. For Lipton, writing was a way of seizing turf, defining the terms of battle, establishing credentials. Lipton fought over ideas; Flom waged war on the ground. Lipton was acutely aware of Flom's preeminence in M&A. In 1973, he reviewed a newly published book on the developing field of tender offers, *Tender Offers for Corporate Control,* by two New York City lawyers. (The pair had first published the authoritative text on proxy contests, *Proxy Contests for Corporate Control,* in 1957, just in time for Flom to pore over it before plunging into United Industrial.) Lipton noted that by 1966 corporations were making more than a hundred bids a year, which seemed like a lot. "Management was threatened," he noted in three prescient words. But what the review is best remembered for is Lipton's admission that, as he says, "[w]hen a hostile deal was announced, the first question to ask is, 'Which side has Flom?'"[9] In the review, Lipton never actually mentioned Flom's name, creating a kind of mystique: "Indeed, one member of the New York Bar has become so renowned for his successful defense against takeovers that the first question on Wall Street is which side is he on."[10] If you had to ask, 'Who's he?' you were out of it.

What's also striking is how fluid his views on these hostile takeovers still were. Lipton took for granted the fact that lawyers were key players. He depicted Flom primarily as a defender. Lipton's own views on M&A had not yet gelled. He criticized the book for failing to include court decisions that "have made the Williams Act an almost impossible barrier to contested takeovers. The courts have now done what Congress refused to do; they have made the Williams Act a shield for entrenched management against 'reckless corporate raids on proud old companies.'"[11] Clearly, Lipton has not yet articulated a view on the propriety of hostile takeovers, offering uneasy equivocation enlivened by a phrase, "entrenched management," that would become a rallying cry for the forces of unrestrained takeovers a decade later.

In fact, the Williams Act did not stifle hostile takeovers; it seemed to encourage them. As the economy tanked, tender offers rumbled down the runway like corporate jets. Most of them came from conglomerates that wanted to own shares—that is, own the company and its profits, not just control the board. Chris Welles in *The Last Days of the Club* writes about complex maneuverings in 1973 behind a tender offer by Eli Black, and his firm AMK, to acquire United Fruit, the world's largest banana producer—El Pulpo, "the octopus"—and form a conglomerate.[12] Black gathered his forces: Donaldson, Lufkin & Jenrette, a United Fruit supporter unhappy about its falling stock, backed him; Goldman Sachs advised (and gave Black cover at the New York Stock Exchange); and Morgan Guaranty, which ran United Fruit's pension plan, provided financing and prestige. Black recognized the new power of the institutions. He won the bidding contest by systematically "warehousing" big blocks of institutional shares, then springing the offer.

Black met a horrific end in 1975, following business reverses at the resulting conglomerate, United Brands, and charges that he had bribed an official in Latin America. He leapt to his death from an office window in the Pan American building in New York. His son, Leon Black, one of the most talented corporate finance minds to come out of Drexel Burnham Lambert, went on to build Apollo Management into a publicly traded, alternative-asset colossus.

Tender offers meant there was money to be made on Wall Street in M&A—through hostile takeovers. The top line of blue-chip underwriters—Morgan Stanley, Dillon Read, Kuhn Loeb, Halsey Stuart—had long eschewed hostile deals. (Goldman was wary for many years, but was not, at that time, a top-drawer firm.) But under the financial stress of the early '70s some of these firms, notably imperial Morgan Stanley, began to waver and assemble M&A specialists; the era of senior bankers handling chummy, high-class advisory work as a service with a nominal fee was ending. These firms needed to make a living and M&A beckoned. Rohatyn, between saving Wall Street and bailing out New York City, would discover that M&A was getting crowded and complex. Building those M&A units created its own momentum: bankers had to justify their existence with deals. As Lipton said in the '80s: "Deals are not bought. They are sold by investment bankers." Wall Street is nothing if not lemming-like, and soon members of less-than-top-line outfits were scrambling to build M&A units, too. Soon certain shrewd bankers set out to wrap up certain even-shrewder lawyers. In particular, at Waspy incarnate and often arrogant-seeming Morgan Stanley (*Institutional Investor* once asked the firm's then-CEO Robert Baldwin: "How do you feel when people say the firm is arrogant?" He replied: "I have to say it did surprise me."[13]), a young, lean, driven banker with an impeccably Protestant name, Robert Greenhill, discovered Flom and wanted his talents. He pursued Flom, who was thrilled, like an ingénue, to be caught, and by such a blue-chipper.

This was a breakthrough. It was a great triumph for Flom, who only a few years earlier still saw his career as a tilt at Wall Street's haughty establishment. "In the early '60s," he said, "we were supposed

to do an underwriting for a client but when the client called his investment banker, he was told there were only seven firms—all old Wall
Street firms—qualified to do the underwritings for the bank. So I figured, shit, we gotta do something about that. We've gotta show the
bastards that we don't have to be born into it." He was showing them
now. In the summer of 1974, Flom took his wife and family on a rare
vacation to Sotogrande, Spain, near Gilbralter. Just after they arrived,
the phone rang. It was Greenhill. Five times in the next six weeks
Flom flew back to the United States on deals, once going to Paris to
catch a flight. Always Greenhill. Flom never unpacked. "It was hard to
get the family to go anywhere after that," he said.[14]

Wachtell Lipton nurtured its own relationships, closer to home,
notably with Laurence "Larry" Tisch, who ran Loews, a conglomerate
with hotel, movie theatre, and tobacco assets. This was a less uncon-
ventional pairing than Flom and Greenhill. Tisch's lawyer, Lester Pollack, had known Lipton in law school; Tisch himself was an NYU
alumnus. (Tisch also conveniently owned the Regency, where Lipton
and Flom would breakfast.) Wachtell worked on some Loews securities offerings and failed bids, including a hostile attempt on investment firm Talcott National that Lipton shepherded. Loews had
invested in CNA Financial, an insurance and real-estate firm, which
began to flounder. Tisch first offered to rescue it, was rejected, then
opted to go hostile. Lipton got the assignment, with Salomon Brothers as the financial advisor. It was a coup and he knew it. At the same
time, Winterthur, a Swiss insurer, also had a stake in CNA and decided it wanted control; management's preference was for the remote
Swiss. This produced a nine-month struggle that ended only after Lipton won an injunction against Winterthur in Delaware over Williams
Act violations. By then it was December 1974.

The CNA saga, with its complexity and drawn-out maneuverings,
foreshadowed many deals to come. It helped make Lipton's name—
ironically, through the vehicle of a hostile takeover. 1975 was a hinge
year. The recession, triggered by the first oil crisis in 1973, had begun
two years earlier and, worse, had evolved into a plague-like combination of inflation, rising unemployment, and stagnation: stagflation.

Oil prices refused to fall. Keynes, the reigning (if long-deceased) economic God, had no answers; neither did Washington. Vietnam and Watergate hung grimly in recent memory. Officially, the recession ended in March 1975, but unemployment continued to edge up. The stock market had crashed in 1973, cratering after Nixon abandoned the Bretton Woods arrangement of fixed currencies; the market shed nearly half its value to depression-like lows, and began to stabilize only in December 1974. In May the SEC eliminated fixed commissions on stocks, knocking the tent pole from under Wall Street's guaranteed living. Competition now stalked the gloomy streets. "People don't seem to be having fun around here anymore," Chris Welles began *The Last Days of the Club* in 1975, quoting Isaac Wolf "Tubby" Burnham II, the "bearlike founder" through acquisition of Drexel Burnham & Co. at 60 Broad, a block south of the stock exchange, and the grandson of the founder of I. W. Harper Gin. "Wall Street is a very unpleasant place to exist and work in these days. We're trying to keep a sense of humor. But every day we're laying off people. We're saying good-by to people we've known and liked for years. We like to treat our people well. We like to pay them bonuses every year. But we can't do that anymore."[15]

In that environment, with its apocalyptic cloud cover, a truly shocking and historically significant lightning bolt didn't attract the attention it deserved: Morgan Stanley was suddenly in the market fronting a hostile bid against NYSE member-company ESB Storage, a Philadelphia maker of Rayovac batteries, on behalf of another NYSE corporation, Canada's Inco, the world's largest nickel miner. Inco (in the lethal blade-like person of Greenhill) sprang the bid on ESB on July 18, 1974—a Flom move from proxy days—just as the battery-maker's chief executive was about to go on vacation. This was not viewed as nice. More than that, this was a mind-bending rupture of propriety. This was like one member of a gentleman's club robbing another in the coatroom—while shrewd Joe Flom sat outside gunning the getaway car. This sent old-timers into wheezing fits of outrage, exacerbated by the hard times. Trickery. Hostility. Disloyalty. Bad form. Obviously, it was that man Flom's fault. Corporate managements had

to pause: What's the point of NYSE membership if we don't get protection? *Morgan Stanley?* Perhaps only Morgan Stanley could have
pulled this off and not suffered severe consequences; or perhaps the
time was simply poised for a shift in attitudes. Greenhill, thirty-eight,
an avid canoer, hiker, and skier who motorcycled to the Greenwich
train station and wore suspenders despite being lean as gristle, insisted
that the push toward a more aggressive stance came from clients who
had plenty of cash to pick up bargains in "a wrecked stock market," as
he told *Institutional Investor*.[16] Besides, he sniffed, "We do not call
them unfriendly takeovers—they are either opposed or unopposed."
Greenhill, muttered a former colleague, "has very little regard for human sensibilities."[17]

Lipton, in fact, may have summed up the change most concisely.
The hostile deal, he said, was "like spitting on the floor. It just wasn't
done."

Inco gobbled up ESB, after making multiple bids and offering a
more than 100 percent premium over the price of the stock on July 17.
ESB shareholders had no complaint, and Goldman, which defended,
could declare victory, too. Inco then successfully wrecked ESB. Dura-
cell ate its lunch in the batteries business, Rayovac disappeared, and
the remaining assets were unloaded at a loss: this was a sadly too-
common result of many M&A deals, though few people were paying
attention. Still, while a shudder raced through the corporate class, the
Inco takeover was hardly an epochal event in a year sunk in gloom and
distress. The rest of America, not attuned to niceties of Wall Street,
shrugged it off, if they ever heard of it in the first place, as just another
crazy deal, something about nickels and batteries. Few recognized that
now everything corporate was in play.

LIPTON KNEW. He did not see what was barreling at him, but the
phone was ringing like crazy. He had been working with a few clients
on deals, and he'd become a go-to instructor—a natural role—for
Salomon's arbitrage department when they were mulling whether to
invest in a deal. (This is a fascinating little detail: arbs often provided
leverage in hostile deals. Once a deal was announced, they'd jump in

to buy shares, speculating on the outcome. Knowing what arbs held and how they would vote was a major edge; and Lipton was instructing *them* on M&A.) Lipton had met Ira Harris defending the Pepsi bottlers years earlier, but it was through Solly's arbs that he established a relationship with the heavyweight (both literally and figuratively) Chicago-based Salomon banker and rainmaker, who began to regularly call him on "technicalities." After CNA, Billy Salomon, the scion of the Salomon partnership and Harris's boss, barged into Lipton's office and tried to hire him. Lipton refused him, then begged Harris to smooth Billy's ruffled feathers. CNA, in short, had flipped a switch. Lipton found himself awash in deals, a growing number of them hostile. He expanded his informal M&A pedagogy to young bankers at firms intent on M&A buildups. In 1976 he assembled materials for an early M&A primer in two volumes with a Wachtell partner who became his second wife, Erica Steinberger, and Flom: *Takeovers and Takeouts: Tender Offers and Going Private*; two years later he and Steinberger published *Takeovers and Freezeout*, also in two volumes (a review said the good parts were in volume two). Lipton continued to update and revise the latter with various up-and-coming Wachtell associates (Steinberger, no longer Lipton's wife, left the firm): the most recent edition in 2013 has five thousand loose-leaf pages in six fat volumes.

"Greenhill had a lock on Flom," says Lipton today. "Other firms sort of just came to us because there wasn't anyone else. Major Wall Street [law] firms were still not doing this. Through 1975, we must have been involved in a half-dozen or more hostile deals, half on offense and half on defense."[18]

In 1976, Steve Brill was twenty-five years old and had just completed Yale Law School. He plunged into magazine writing, which was then experiencing one of its last sustained spasms of brilliance and prosperity. Legal knowledge was exotic in journalism, in part because lawyers didn't often talk to journalists, caught up in their counselor-to-client rectitude, and Brill had an edge. (That was ending, too.) Brill was from the right side of the tracks: a graduate of Deerfield, Yale, Yale Law. He was aggressive, bombastic, and smart. He was already working on a big book about the Teamsters; Jimmy Hoffa had disappeared around the time Inco was sneak-attacking ESB. And he had begun to write for Clay Felker's *New York Magazine,* close to the red-hot center of what had become known as the New Journalism. On June 21, 1976, *New York Magazine* published Brill's "Two Tough Lawyers in the Tender-Offer Game," which canonized Flom and Lipton as the red-hot center of M&A—and M&A as the engine of Wall Street—while offering a knowing breakdown of how what the magazine called "the game" was played.[19] The magazine opened M&A to a glittering world beyond Wall Street. Oddly enough, a few months later Felker lost control of *New York Magazine* to ravenous media magnate Rupert Murdoch, who had recently bought the liberal *New York Post.* An aggrieved Felker characterized the episode as a hostile takeover, if not a tender offer. Brill himself went on to launch *The American Lawyer* magazine, which he eventually sold to an M&A magnate, Lipton acolyte and former college newspaper editor Bruce Wasserstein.

Brill plays a crucial role in establishing a public image for mergers. He took no stance on the rightness or wrongness of the business; neither did Lipton at that time. Brill circled two nuances: Jewish and lawyer. A more conventional thinker might have profiled Rohatyn, who plays a bit part in Brill's story—"He's constantly pushing targets on raiders," Brill offered dismissively—or a conglomerateur like Harry Gray of United Technologies, who doesn't. But Brill saw M&A as primarily a lawyer's game, a matter of manipulating rules and regulations. "Two Tough Lawyers" (and *tough* was a code word for *Jewish;* Brill mentions *Jewish* just a few times, but it's unmistakable what he's getting at) probably meant more to Lipton than to Flom; Brill raised Lipton to Flom's class. It was the rough draft of the Flom-Lipton mythology. As such, it missed some of the symmetries—offense and defense, shareholder and directors—that would become standard, mainly because they were still *in utero.* But Brill recognized an upheaval occurring. "Either because they're still snobby about the business or because Flom and Lipton have such a head start on them in terms of experience and reputation, the old-line law firms are still only rarely involved in tender offers," he wrote.[20] Still, this wasn't about the firms; this was about the two men. *New York Magazine* even managed to spell *Wachtell* as *Wachtel* throughout the piece.

Brill emphasized one more point that would cling to M&A like a rash: the money to be made. Both men—elfin Flom puffing a pipe with scuffed shoes, lanky Lipton behind "bottle-thick glasses"—were making lots of it. They charged higher rates than old-line firms—as much as $350 an hour, a hundred bucks over the next guy. Flom, who Brill calculated worked on 90 percent of tenders from 1973 to 1976, was so overbooked he began to ask clients to pay annual retainers, to guarantee his services in the event a hostile bidder materialized or, more practically, to keep him from the enemy: it became known as "The Joe Flom protection policy" or "sterilizing Joe." Flom piled up retainers, some over $50,000 a year. Brill guessed the pair were personally raking in as much as $600,000 a year, and that Flom was "perhaps the highest-paid lawyer in the country." They kept limousines on call. Brill gleefully trampled on a Wasp code in which wealth was rarely mentioned; Flom and Lipton were coy about profits, but can't have disliked the speculation. Money was a way of keeping score. These themes, including the limo, shaped the M&A story for decades. (Brill pioneered the ranking of top-flight law firms based on profits-per-partner at *The American Lawyer,* a very successful magazine strategy and a sign of changing legal times. Wachtell and Skadden were nearly always No. 1 and No. 2.)

Brill focused on a hostile deal that featured Flom on offense and Lipton on defense. Rohatyn represented Colt Industries, a conglomerate built by two ITT executives, best known for its Colt Firearms division. Colt wanted to unload consumer businesses and buy industrial assets, believing the economic slump was over. (That was a wrong call, particularly for industrial goods, whose heyday *was* passing in America.) Colt's president, Richard Margolis, served on New York's Emergency Financial Control Board, and was a friend of Rohatyn, who was simultaneously managing the Herculean effort to keep the city out of bankruptcy. Lipton had also gotten involved with saving the city. In the midst of all that, Rohatyn and Margolis targeted a Palmyra, (New York), maker of gaskets called Garlock. They hired Flom. He recommended, as usual, a quick strike; the Williams Act still allowed tenders that would expire in only seven days, and they often launched on Friday to use up a few days. In mid-November, Colt struck, laying down artillery of full-page ads in the *New York Times* and the *Wall Street Journal.*

Garlock, reeling, hired Lipton and Stephen Friedman, a Columbia Law grad-turned-banker who had put together Goldman Sachs & Co.'s M&A effort and who had defended ESB Storage. (Friedman was a former national American Athletic Union wrestling champ; M&A banking was sports crazy. Goldman under Friedman for a time had a touch football team that played in a league of facilities guys from Wall Street firms—not the usual opponents of a bunch of Ivied bankers. He himself liked to fall to the floor and do push-ups.) Friedman's team worked closely with Goldman's arb unit run by a tall, skinny Harvard Law grad named Robert Rubin. Goldman and Lipton had begun regularly working together, like Morgan Stanley and Flom. Still faithful to the sanctity of the client relationship, Goldman only played defense. "We feel our success in merger work depends on having the confidence of management," murmered the firm's patrician co-CEO John Whitehead. "Companies will deal more openly with us if they don't think we are going to appear with boxing gloves on behalf of someone else." (Some on Wall Street noted that Goldman had a large number of mid-sized clients that would be targets, not predators, but no matter: relationship matters are complicated.) On most corporate assignments, Goldman worked with Sullivan & Cromwell, the white-shoe law firm founded by Algernon Sidney Sullivan and William Nelson Cromwell in 1882, which advised J. P. Morgan on the creation of U.S. Steel, helped finance the Panama Canal, and wrote the 1933 securities law. John Foster Dulles, Eisenhower's unctuously moralistic secretary of state and a humorless Presbyterian, had once run S&C. Louis Auchincloss, the novelist, had been an unusually observant associate there. U.S. Steel or not, S&C knew, and cared, not a whit for the new M&A—at least not yet. And so Friedman turned to Lipton, who did.

Garlock had prepared itself, running down its cash, staggering its board (a strategy useful in a proxy contest), and putting together a file of friendly acquirers—"white knights." Lipton immediately sued to enjoin the tender on Williams Act grounds, a standard response and one that had worked for him at CNA Financial. Meanwhile, Garlock impugned Colt's motives. This was also standard. Impugning mostly involved newspaper ads aimed at shareholders. The ad copy was written by Richard Cheney, vice chairman of public relations firm Hill & Knowlton, and combined a shot at Flom's proxy-arena tactics with a slick reference to Colt's most famous, and most lethal, product. According to Brill, Cheney complained that Lipton reined in some of his best stuff, but allowed this one: "We don't think your rush 'Saturday Night Special' tender offer is a credit to American business and don't think it's in the best interest of shareholders," said the ad under the signature of Garlock's chairman, who never got credit for the words. Instead, sounding plaintive, the ad suggested it would be better to call and discuss the matter first.

For all its cleverness, the "Saturday Night Special" moniker made no difference except to journalists who recognized a potent phrase they could reuse. It was a theme that would echo. The arbs, however, were unfazed; perhaps they didn't read. Friedman went searching for a white knight, and found one in bowling-ball maker AMF. Colt raised its bid and Garlock's board began to worry that the bowling-ball guys were more threatening than the gunmaker, and lunged with alacrity to accept a revised Colt bid. Rohatyn and Flom won; Lipton and Friedman lost. Today, Lipton recalls Garlock mostly for a bizarre interlude. Negotiations over the fate of New York City had intensified, and Lipton found himself and Rohatyn in all-night sessions at city hall, sharing a couch in the hallway to catnap. At the same time, during the day, Lipton was deposing Rohatyn on Williams Act litigation for Garlock. Rohatyn, chuckles Lipton, was furious at him.[21] But Rohatyn took the prize, picking up a $750,000 fee, and New York, if not Garlock, was saved. Flom and Lipton, says Brill, split a million-dollar fee.

GARLOCK IS IMPORTANT mainly as a milestone on Lipton's road to Damascus. Defense was good for Wachtell Lipton, but odds of successful defenses were decreasing. The number of hostile offers mounted month by month. Both Lipton and Flom recognized that something fundamental had changed. As Flom offered, eschewing the hells and shits that seemed to accompany some of his most inspired soliloquies on M&A, in a sustained bout of realistic analysis of the looking-glass world of the late '70s:

> It was the size of the deals; the fact that major corporations were willing to treat this as a legitimate corporate tool and not say, "I'll be read out of the club if I get involved." They had gotten rid of fixed commission rates. The market was in the doldrums. This was the investment-banking house's big source of revenue and this encouraged them to go out and merchandise takeovers, which gave it additional life. Takeovers also provided almost the only liquidity in a very dormant market. [Earlier] we were able to identify the aggressors. And there were only one or two aggressors we represented. Everybody else was purely defensive. The acquisitions were totally different in the 1980s in that in the 1960s they were balance-sheet oriented, or financially oriented. People would take two and two and make it five because everybody was analyzing business based on historical earnings and you could distort that. The takeovers which started in 1974 were cash takeovers; they started primarily for business fit. The takeover movement in the 1980s is different again in the sense that the big deals have been fueled by the availability of money, huge amounts of money, both from the banks, high-yield bonds, and so forth. And you had people taking over companies that were worth more dead than alive; but more dead by a wide margin, or where by restructuring them after you took them over you could change the dynamics very significantly. In a lot of these takeovers, you buy it and sell off a lot of the divisions and you end up with a core business that's worth a heck of a lot more than what you had before.[22]

Flom extracted sense from an M&A process that seemed sheer lunacy. Increasingly, Lipton tended toward the lunacy view and he turned more to corporate defense. That meant, in the logic of the two-advisor scenario, that Flom did relatively more offense. By the '80s, as Flom said, M&A was a powerful engine, particularly when brokerage commissions were rapidly shrinking. As deals got larger, fees mushroomed. Size begat size; hostility bred hostility. For investment bankers, Greenhill and Morgan Stanley get credit for standardizing fees as a percentage of deal value. The percentage might be small—say, 2 percent—but as deal values added more zeroes, bankerly rewards exploded, so large that they transformed investment banking into a primo career for bright young things. Goldman at first chose a different scheme appropriate to its defense strategy: the firm charged a flat fee, and a percentage on any premium it extracted. Eventually, both the defense specialization and the flat fee went away: the money was too overwhelming. Lawyers racked up hourly fees—M&A was labor intensive, so bills mushroomed—and there came a point in that expanding universe when those Skadden retainers grew less important, even restricting, like Goldman's defense-only policy. Wachtell, for its part, imperiously charged by the deal, rather than by the hour; such was its prestige that it could get away with a bill with a single jaw-dropping number on it. But this was unusual. Flom and Lipton rode a wave of the common "mystique," as Nocera pointed out in the early '80s, that "at least part of the reason Joe Flom got hired in those deals was because he was supposed to be the man who could handle Marty Lipton . . . and part of the reason Lipton got hired was because he was supposed to be able to handle Flom. Whether that was in fact how it worked was something that corporate executives in those deals never got to find out; presumably that's the way Lipton and Flom preferred it."[23] Brill called this "the cyclical-spiral effect."[24]

And there was another factor at work: the business was rapidly growing not just larger but more complex, driven by a kind of evolutionary overdrive in technique, tactics, strategies, targets, financing. Big money was a stimulant, a catalyst, an aphrodisiac. Escalation was occurring deal by deal. Herbert Wachtell once wrote a guide on tender litigation tactics—just one aspect of many M&A deals—for *The Business Lawyer*. This was George Demas and his letters on steroids:

You are operating in a pressure atmosphere where you have constant surprise. You have very little turnaround time. The company goes running for counsel: help us. You have to commence litigation immediately. You have to get out your deposition notices. You have to make your motions for expedited discovery. You have to set up your teams for what could be two or three sets of simultaneous depositions, often in different cities. You have to be prepared to flow all the information you're getting from depositions and documents into affidavits and briefs almost simultaneously with the taking of depositions and the review of documents. You have to be scheduling your applications for temporary restraining orders, stays, preliminary injunctions and the like. You are essentially compressing into a span of four, five or six days what would normally be months and months, if not years, of typical big case litigation, including analysis of antitrust ramifications, industry studies, competitive lines of products and the like. It is unique.[25]

That was 1977, when the game was still getting going. This was a long way from Paul Cravath's notion of conference-room lawyering.

Meanwhile, Flom bounced from deal to deal, from tactic to tactic; he was immensely creative tactically, and he orchestrated his troops like a bandleader. He was, as he said, "having fun." Lipton was thinking not only how to engage a more effective defense but what it all meant.

IN 1979, BLUE-CHIP credit card provider American Express—under a chiseled, young, Atlanta-born, impeccably credentialed Wall Streeter, James Robinson III (famously known, to his regret, as Jimmy Three Sticks)—suddenly sprang a hostile bid on a New York blue-chip property, McGraw-Hill, the family-controlled publisher of *Business Week* and owner of Standard & Poor's. Robinson had a company with a hot product, credit cards (though apparently not hot enough for him), and a high share price. He hired Rohatyn and Flom to advise him. McGraw-Hill brought in Morgan Stanley and Lipton. "It became," says Lipton, "a cause-celebre in the press, probably because of *Business*

Week. It was the highest-profile takeover battle up to that point. By then, we were mostly on the defense side. But there were no clear legal theories in respect to defense. The McGraw-Hill board of directors really pressed us on the business judgment rule. When a client presses you on a legal opinion, you really want to research it carefully. And we had been researching this issue for years. But we had really failed to find a case directly on point. Most of the academic writing up to that point was that this was something the shareholders should decide, not management, not the board of directors. But we gave an opinion, an absolute opinion. And I used the opinion in that case to write an article called 'Takeover Bids in the Target's Boardroom.' That provoked a storm in academia. The people in Chicago, the economics department, went crazy. And they started to write articles that not only did the board not have the right to defend the company, but that it had to be passive, that it couldn't go out and solicit a higher price. It was the rule of passivity."

McGraw-Hill engaged in a drawn-out, scorched-earth defense that Lipton believed turned on Amex's fear that McGraw-Hill's employees, particularly its journalists, would walk in the event of an Amex victory, but that also focused on seamier charges that Amex president Roger Morley had used inside information as a McGraw-Hill director to launch the attack. (Lipton on the Morley affair: it—meaning Morley's "conflict"—was an "embarrassment.") It worked and McGraw-Hill was saved. But for Lipton, a larger war had begun. He wrote another article refuting the law of passivity. The academics fired back. He replied. They returned fire. This went on for some time. "And then I woke up to the fact that they were writing articles for a living, and I was writing articles on the side," he says. "And I stopped. But by this time it was 1982 and we weren't doing so well defending these companies. And around that time I got the idea for the poison pill."[26]

Chapter Five

CHICAGO'S UNFAITHFUL
SERVANTS

I N ADDITION TO hostile takeovers and chronic stagflation, the mid-1970s witnessed the discovery—or rediscovery—of corporate governance.[1] This was not as much fun as finding one's mojo, a popular '70s pastime, but it had more intellectual cachet. Adolf Berle died in 1976, just in time for the SEC to realize that corporate accountability might be part of its mission. Berle never used the term *corporate governance,* although it posthumously attached itself to his name. The term first turned up in the *New York Times* in December 1972, in an article about shareholder suits against directors provoked by the Penn Central bankruptcy.[2] It resurfaced five years later in association with a project from activists Ralph Nader, Mark Green, and Joel Seligman that applied the language of democratic politics to running large corporations.[3] That project resulted in a book, *The Taming of the Giant Corporation,* and urged federal regulation to reform board practices to curb corporate abuses—corporate bribery scandals (including ITT), at home and abroad, had broken out—mostly by empowering shareholders.[4] In December 1976, the term popped up in the Federal Register for the first time with the launch of a study on "shareholder democracy" by the SEC. In 1977, the SEC held hearings on corporate governance and the term crept into broader circulation, though the agency backed off reforms. Instead, in a 1978 speech to the American Society of Corporate Secretaries in beautiful pink-hued Boca Rotan, SEC chairman Harold Williams, a Jimmy Carter appointee, urged companies to embrace corporate governance to avoid federal legislation. Williams was an advocate of more accountable boards—he envisioned them as "countervailing forces" to management—but he resisted federal regulation, an odd stance for the chairman of the SEC. A year later, liberal Democratic Ohio senator Howard Metzenbaum appointed a blue-ribbon advisory committee on corporate governance to draw up reforms, but the panelists couldn't agree on what they should be.

A few points are worth noting. First, the target in this first wave of corporate governance was the American publicly traded, multidivisional, multinational industrial corporation, which only a few years and a nasty foreign war earlier had loomed Leviathan-like over the global economy. Now, not so much. Europe was back; Japan was coming in tiny cars. Vietnam was a rabbit punch to American confidence; Watergate a self-inflicted blow; recession and oil crises and charges of corporate malfeasance worked the belly. The big firm, managed by its cadres of William H. Whyte organization men, was unpopular in the '70s, and it wasn't just Nader's finger-pointing either. Stock prices were comatose, corporate life was viewed as conformist and soul-destroying, and companies were generally seen, at least among a certain advanced set, as corrupt, fusty, hide-bound producers of lousy cars, cancer-causing pollution, foreign bribes—and, hello ITT and Chile—occasional assassinations. (Not that government was much more popular. As Williams told the secretaries: "Some of you who have written to me regarding corporate accountability have argued that, whatever business' stature is in the public mind, government's is worse."[5] Both houses, according to the progressive critique, needed to be cleansed with participatory democracy.) Second, the criticism that rained down upon companies, under the guise of corporate governance, generally came from the left; hence the power of the phrase *shareholder democracy.* This critique demanded a redefinition of the corporation in American society, more specifically returning boards to their "historic" auditor role, in Nader, Green, and Seligman's formulation, what law professor Melvin Eisenberg in his 1976 book *The Structure of the Corporation* called the "monitoring model" or what early Merrick Dodd in the '30s referred to as the trustee model, which Berle eventually absconded with and Dodd abandoned. These governance critiques located the origin of the problem in the shift from private Adam Smithian proprietors of nineteenth-century capitalism to industrial magnates of the early twentieth century. Berle's separation of ownership and control was a deep flaw of the latter. Nonetheless, Berle's advocacy of corporations as trustees and boards as responsible to stakeholders of organic institutions faded as the left's version of corporate governance made its case.

Then Ronald Reagan shellacked Jimmy Carter in 1980, and pressure on corporations eased. The Reagan administration wanted, opined Reagan SEC chief John Shad (who had been a vice chairman of E. F. Hutton & Co.), "capital formation," not "corporate governance." The shift in sentiment was rapid and abrupt. Antitrust policy was rethought and loosened, taxes were cut, regulation culled or ignored. Talkative, elfin, regulation-skeptic and economist Milton Friedman emerged as a *Newsweek* columnist and Reagan advisor. The Business Roundtable, a lobbying group for CEOs founded in 1972, went on the offensive against the American Law Institute, a low-profile, high-minded, public-spirited New York legal group that had set out to codify, clarify, and modernize corporate governance and the law in 1978, when that was a liberal project built on Berlean stakeholders and federal oversight, and the corporate crowd was too spooked to complain. The Roundtable attacked, drawing in the free-market legal scholars who had their own anti-management, pro-shareholder point of view, and the melee was on. The response to the ALI's first draft in 1980 was so harsh, and the resulting civil war over what governance actually meant legally was so intense, that it took until 1994 for the ALI to publish guidelines, by which time much of what it promulgated had been hammered out in practice and in the courts.[6]

What Berle called "the princes of industry" undoubtedly thought they had sailed into a cozy harbor with Reagan, but they were wrong, which made the situation even more confused at the ALI. As Lipton and Flom were learning, hostile M&A was on the upswing. Corporate defenses crumbled against raiders of obscure provenance, and as inflation abated and recovery beckoned, biblical floods of financing fueled hostile takeovers. Henry Manne's vision had sprung to life: M&A increasingly was viewed as an accountability mechanism— a market mechanism—and one that pretty much obviated the need for Berlean corporate governance.

This posed a challenge to the White House, a clash between politics and ideology. "Yeah, it was very contentious, and one of the reasons it was contentious was it highlighted a split within the Republican party," recalled Joseph Grundfest, a young lawyer and economist who, despite being a Democrat (and a liberal on social issues), had generally free-market economic views and was brought into the White House Council on Economic Advisors to deal with two issues: the S&L crisis and takeovers. "Let's oversimplify it. Let's say that there is a market-oriented wing of the Republican Party and a corporatist wing of the Republican Party. The market-oriented wing would say, 'Let takeovers happen because if you structure them properly they can be very efficient means to redeploy capital, to discipline management, to rationally give voice to shareholders.' But then there's the corporatist wing of the Republican Party, which says, 'Hey, wait a minute, we're the CEOs, these takeovers threaten our ability to run the companies the way we want to and we're the ones that set corporate policy and we're major supporters so we are actually opposed to takeover activity.'"[7]

Grundfest, later an SEC commissioner and Stanford law professor, pointed to a similar split within the Democratic Party. "There you had large groups who said, "'We like takeovers.' Why? Because they can actually be threatening to management. And then you had groups that say, 'We hate takeovers.' Why? Because after a takeover, people tend to get laid off."[8]

One vital difference: The Republicans came to power as takeovers came of age. The intellectual rationale for a pro-takeover, free-market approach came from within academia, notably from the neo-gothic splendor of the University of Chicago, where potent ideas had been developing that, if anything, viewed managers even more skeptically than did Nader, Green, and Seligman. Designing and perfecting this market-oriented, shareholder-centric governance perspective—a model, in the jargon—was no mean feat and involved dozens of famous names, many eventual Nobelists. It began with fugitive ideas about fundamental finance and moved on to provocative theories about corporate organizations, with M&A as a primary force for remediation and repair. Two streams of thought converged in Chicago: first, a transformation of investing and corporate finance; second, the mixed marriage of free-market, "neoclassical" economics and the law. The result—arcane, abstract, seemingly remote from the human struggle of M&A—was declared a science, an inevitability, even the end of history.

THE FIGURE THAT came to serve as the point man for this rethinking in M&A was a tall, curly-blonde business school academician named Michael Jensen. He was brash, ambitious, and committed to the academy and to free-market economics. He would never become a celebrity like, say, Friedman, John Maynard Keynes, or, less deliberately, Friedrich Hayek; instead, he worked from within a tightly knit business school world, teaching, writing, sending students into business and academia, and developing, like many of his peers, a lucrative sideline in consulting. The business schools were latecomers to the traditional liberal arts academy—even later than the law schools. They were initially trade schools, slightly more exalted than academies of commerce that entrepreneurs like Roger Babson established. They were not havens from the quotidian world; in the effort to professionalize business management, they dragged that world, notably that of the burgeoning corporation, into academe. They produced research into commerce and business conditions, but they really existed to train business leaders. Their function was utilitarian, practical, engaged in the mastery of technique: management, marketing, finance, accounting. They were, to traditional scholars, even those in economics, tainted by the practical. There was a sense that their work was aimed at a market that wanted things fast, easy, and useful. But that secondary status, along with its accompanying insecurity, changed in a postwar America fueled, in part, by the revolution in financial theory percolating. This evolution had its ironies. During the era of unsurpassed corporate dominance, the business schools remained modest and vaguely vocational. Only with the transformation of Wall Street, and of finance as a powerful discipline, did they explode in size and power, and the Master's of Business Administration became an essential credential. Jensen's career tracked this evolution from theory to practice: from academic economics to financial economics to organizational theory to governance.

There was jockeying and friction as the business schools ascended. In particular, the cross-fertilization of business schools, law schools, and economic faculties that occurred in the '60s and '70s under the banner of "law and economics"—notice it wasn't law, economics, and *business*—was a complex sociological phenomenon and incubator of ideas: political power and financial power met the belief, certainly at Chicago, in deep scientific truth. The business schools were initially the junior partner. But they held a trump card: money. They brought vast amounts of money into academia, satisfying a deeply held American belief that education should be useful. As with investment bankers and traders on Wall Street, the success of the business schools threatened to overwhelm less "profitable," less "practical" endeavors, notably the humanities, which were increasingly viewed as ivory-tower exercises dominated by '60s leftists.

Jensen became a star of this world—he loved to cite how many times his papers were downloaded, as if academia was an exercise in democratic affirmation—and produced (or cited) the kind of research that mimicked the quantitative rigor of the physical sciences. Jensen viewed himself as a scientist and a synthetic thinker. He was unusual in that he had not only legitimate credentials in financial economics but a restless mind that wandered through other disciplines. His papers were a pastiche of law, philosophy, psychology, sociology, economics. He was the utilitarian as revolutionary, the apostle of—a favorite phrase—actionable access.

BORN AND RAISED in Rochester, Minnesota (home of the Mayo Clinic), Jensen was the son of a typesetter. He told the *New York Times* in 2007 that he had attended vocational school, then took a job

at a newspaper as a Linotype operator, but a teacher subsequently convinced him to enroll at Macalester College in St. Paul, a liberal arts
school, and he received an AB in economics in 1962.[9] He graduated at
the height of the consensus that Keynes—or, more significantly, the
formulation of the Great Economist's sometimes ambiguous thought
into equations and policies—was all that was necessary to manage a
modern economy efficiently. The triumph of a paradigm, of a conventional wisdom, is just about the best time for a young man of ambition and brains to buy a ticket for the counterrevolution. Jensen
acquired his at Chicago, where, quietly, if energetically, corporate finance was undergoing a rigorous rethinking.

Why Chicago? The university on Chicago's South Side, funded with
Rockefeller money and home to Thorstein Veblen (who had a few
things to say about the corporation), Jacob Viner, Frank Knight, Henry
Simons, and Paul Douglas, had a long tradition of independent, even
eccentric, economic thinking. The city of Chicago was built upon commerce and markets, the confluence of endless rivers of livestock, commodities, and grains—all of which, tangibly or intangibly, present or
future, discovered their value in the markets, or in that very-Chicago
lingo, the pits. But while Chicago economists expressed in varying degrees allegiance to free markets, catastrophic times—notably the Great
Depression—had spawned complex differences. Each balanced off theory and practice, free markets, and the reality of an economy dominated by large companies. Chicago was all about microeconomics: how
people and firms behaved economically. Compared to Cambridge's
MIT and Harvard, Chicago did not fall quite as hard for the macroeconomic ideas promulgated in Keynes's *The General Theory of Employment, Interest and Money*, published in 1936. The eastern schools
scrambled to "formalize" Keynes, taking his often recondite rhetoric
and turning it into equations and models. The greatest Keynesian in
America was Paul Samuelson, who entered Chicago as an undergrad at
sixteen (he survived Viner's Econ 301, famous for that crusty professor's
"ferocious manhandling" of students), received his PhD at Harvard,
then spent his glittering career at MIT, upon the banks of the Charles
River.[10]

Frank Knight was Chicago's most distinguished economic mind, a critic and skeptic of economic verities, though hardly an ideologue, whose greatest work, *Risk, Uncertainty and Profit*, which argued the necessity of risk-taking entrepreneurs in a world shot through with uncertainty, was, as he admitted himself, full of "contradictions and paradoxes," not unlike *The General Theory* that lurked out there in the future. Knight recognized markets as the most effective allocator of capital, but he also felt that faith in markets alone was morally destructive. (For his part, Viner, who spent much of the '30s advising FDR's Treasury, thought Knight spent too much time wrestling with "metaphysical" concepts.[11]) Knight saw himself as a conservative and as a radical, very Chicago style. As August Burgin wrote in his history of the free-market movement, "Knight's unsparing criticisms of the naiveté of social reformers made him a notorious opponent of progressive economists and left an indelible mark on his students' approach to political economy." Two of those students—members of the Knight affinity group who behaved, at times, says Burgin, like "Swiss Guards"—were Milton Friedman and George Stigler.[12]

Knight was a particular favorite of Lionel Robbins, who ran the London School of Economics' economics department, starting in 1929, as an institutional counterweight to Keynes's Cambridge University, in part by reaching out to American and Continental academics. Ronald Coase, a student at LSE in the '30s, recalls Robbins recommending *Risk, Uncertainty and Profit* as one of a handful of canonical texts.[13] Robbins leaned toward free markets in the '30s and away from state intervention (that changed with the war). In 1931, he recruited a young Austrian economist, deeply versed in business cycles, named Friedrich Hayek, to provide a contrarian perspective and to joust with Keynes. Hayek did debate Keynes and emerged bruised for it. During the war, Hayek wrote a tract decrying the kind of collectivization he saw in the totalitarian combatants of World War II, Nazi Germany and the Soviet Union. In the United States, however, conservative minds tended to apply Hayek's *The Road to Serfdom* not to Communism or Nazism but to the homegrown New Deal. Through the agency of Chicago economist Aaron Director, the book got picked up by the University of Chicago Press, took off (it was condensed in the *Reader's Digest*), and Hayek ended up settling at Chicago's Committee on Social Thought.

Hayek brought to Chicago a renewed appreciation for the virtues of the market, particularly for younger academics. Meanwhile, other currents were reshaping economics. Two related trends cross-fertilized to great effect: forecasting and statistics. Market forecasting blossomed with the explosion of US stock markets before World War I. Entrepreneurs and scholars like Roger Babson, George Moody (founder of Moody's, the credit-rating company), Yale economist Irving Fisher, and Harvard's Wesley Mitchell offered various statistical schemes that purported to predict the future course of stocks. Nearly all wiped out in the Crash of 1929 and the Great Depression.[14] (Babson was an exception: he called the market break, then ran out of luck.) Fisher sabotaged his own brilliant academic reputation by predicting that "stock prices have reached what looks like a permanently higher plateau" just before the Crash. He then made things worse by doubling down, and lost his fortune, most of which had come from his wife. Forecasting, in short, was mired in what appeared to be a terminal bear market.

Around that time, Fisher was contacted by the heir to the great-grandson of a founder of the *Chicago Tribune* fortune, Alfred Cowles III, a Yale grad who had (like Fisher years earlier) come down with tuberculosis and moved to Colorado Springs to recover. In 1931, he folded his forecasting service because he no longer felt confident that he could predict the economic future. A year later he developed doubts that anyone else could, either, and started a society to study what was becoming known as econometrics—that is, the marriage of statistics and economics, which mostly meant forecasting. Cowles funded a journal, *Econometrica,* and set up a foundation, the Cowles Commission for Research in Economics, in Colorado Springs in 1932 with the slogan "Science Is Measurement."[15] He also offered to fund Fisher's strapped economic society. In 1939, after his father died, he moved the operation to Chicago, with offices in the Tribune Tower and the university on the South Side. Cowles himself completed a massive hand-calculated study of market forecasters—this was an age before real computing power—and found in one 1944 study that the results failed "to disclose evidence of the ability to predict successfully the future course of the stock market."[16]

The partnership of Cowles and the university created an incubator for ideas that transformed corporate finance, producing a new discipline between investing and economics: financial economics. The commission attracted high-powered economists—Tjalling Koopmans, Kenneth Arrow, Herbert Simon—but it was a young Chicago grad who wasn't particularly interested in the stock market who lit the match. That was Harry Markowitz, who in 1952, to no acclaim whatsoever, wrote a fourteen-page paper for the *Journal of Finance* that focused on how to build an efficient portfolio of stocks. Markowitz approached the problem mathematically. He was fascinated by diversification. As Peter Bernstein in his history of the finance revolution launched by Markowitz writes, "Markowitz's key insight was that risk is central to the whole process of investing." Diversification and portfolio selection were ways of managing risk and its lucrative, if elusive, *doppelganger:* reward. Markowitz aimed at building an efficient portfolio—"a portfolio," writes Bernstein, "that offers the highest expected return for any given degree of risk, or that has the lowest degree of risk for any given expected return."[17] This was, as Bernstein stresses, a radical set of ideas in an investment world focused on actively investing in individual stocks and on the hocus-pocus of technical trading. The idea took a decade to gestate.

By the early '60s, Chicago was the destination for those interested in wandering the frontiers of financial economics. Bill Sharpe joined Markowitz in 1962 from Stanford, developing ways to simplify the complex calculations required by Markowitz's portfolio approach. Merton Miller had arrived at Chicago's business school a year earlier, after a stint at the Carnegie Institute of Technology in Pittsburgh, where he worked on a path-breaking paper with Franco Modigliano that argued that companies should not be concerned with trying to develop an optimal ratio of debt and equity. The reason, which Miller went on to apply to a variety of situations, was the power of arbitrage (a more general process than merger arbitrage)—that is, the tendency of investors to detect and whittle away perceived discrepancies from true value, returning assets to equilibrium. The arbitrage mechanism could be applied to markets themselves, as an explanation for why stock-market forecasters, and stock-picking results, rarely beat the market's overall performance; it also had a moral fillip, with markets always drifting toward the true, virtuous price. Markets were empirically random walks; that is, they produced no discernible—or predictable—pattern. In 1969, Eugene Fama, a Harvard grad recently appointed a Chicago professor, produced a paper that summarized proofs for the theory that markets that processed all available information quickly were "efficient." This featured a key paradox of modern finance. The very evidence of that efficiency could be found in the difficulty investors had over a longer period beating the market, which study after study demonstrated, initially to a resistant asset-management community, then to a generally baffled public.

By then the Cowles Commission had left Chicago for Yale. As Bernstein notes, the neighborhood around the university had deteriorated and there were tensions between Cowles and Chicago's economics department run by Friedman, who was never fully convinced that financial economics was truly "economics" at all. (Markowitz was almost denied his PhD because of Friedman.)[18] Despite that, Chicago remained the hotbed of new thinking in financial economics, which produced conclusions that ended up in an unexpected place: work that began to improve forecasting came to undermine the very notion of prediction and of active management of stocks. Instead, the efficient market itself emerged as the best of all guides—the increasingly omnipotent, omniscient, efficient guide—to what Keynes referred to as "irreducible uncertainty"—that is, a future that he believed was not apprehensible through mathematics.[19] Knight, who died in 1972, agreed with Keynes: a key concept of *Risk, Uncertainty and Profit* is the reality of uncertainty, which he defined as risk that can't be rendered as a probability—risk that is not, in short, predictive. Knight's uncertainty is the unfathomable, unpredictable randomness of life, and thus for him, the precondition for the central role played by entrepreneurs, or risk takers.

THE COUNTERREVOLUTION would mostly be fought with equations. But there was another intellectual stew-pot bubbling at Chicago: law and economics. Like many research universities, Chicago had a law school, a business school, and an economics department. Traditionally, these three faculties coexisted as remote fiefdoms. But by both design and chance, the walls began to crumble at Chicago: economics and business shared financial economics; and law sat at the feet of the economists. The law and economics dance had begun slowly with Henry Calvert Simons, an ill-fitting junior colleague of Knight, who had followed him from the University of Iowa to Chicago in 1928. Knight was a stout defender of Simons in Chicago. Simons was often unhealthy and not terribly productive—Stigler wrote about him that "by external signs he was a desultory, aimless student (that is, well ahead of his time!)"[20]—generating only three book reviews by the time he came up for reappointment in 1932. He was opposed by Paul Douglas, later a longtime US senator from Illinois. Knight, however, dug in and Simons kept his job. A decade later, Simons was still under duress, and was only bailed out by support from the law school, where he had begun to teach economic theory in 1939. Simons became one of the first American professors with a joint economic-law appointment.

Stigler downplayed Simons's tie to the law school: "Although Simons initiated the practice of having an economist in the law school at Chicago, the relationship was somewhat didactic in his time: There was no visible impact of his law school associations upon his own work, although he became an extremely popular teacher and had a substantial influence upon several of the law faculty."[21] Ronald Coase was not so sure, though he agreed with Stigler that Simons was something of a "utopian." A successor to Simons, Coase, in a memoir, reflected on Simons's most famous work, a pamphlet titled "A Positive Program for Laissez Faire," from the mid-'30s. Simons at the time was in a gloomy, the-end-is-near mood that often seemed to be his everyday outlook. Coase described the paper as "a propagandist tract" and noted that "it was more an essay in political philosophy than economics."[22] Like Knight and—famously—Louis Brandeis, Simons believed in small commercial units that could preserve competition and personal freedom; he rejected Berle's faith in large, industrial, technologically advanced corporations. He thought that to preserve free-market competition the government needed to break up corporations and monopolies, restrict advertising, eliminate tariffs and most forms of debt, and maintain monetary stability. Simons wanted courts to actively attack size; he envisioned the Federal Trade Commission as one of the most powerful agencies in Washington. But at the heart of Simons's "utopian" vision, said Coase (who rejected Simons's brand of state intervention), was that "there still remains a real alternative to socialization, namely, the establishment and preservation of competition as a regulative agency."[23]

Still, as popular as he was—and Friedman called Simons his "teacher, friend and shaper of ideas" though he looked back at "A Positive Program" with horror[24]—he, like Knight, was elusive. He resisted categorization and he elicited affection but few disciples. His greatest contribution to Chicago may have been his departure. In 1944, Simons had developed a scheme for a free-market institute linking law and economics—he feared libertarian thinking was about to disappear—with a colleague, Aaron Director, as its head, and he turned to Hayek, whose activities were financed by the Volker Fund from Kansas City, for help. Then he suddenly died; it had been coming for years. Director took over the program in 1946. Backed by Volker, Friedman, Director, and Stigler were able to attend the first meeting of the Mount Pelerin Society in 1947 in Switzerland, Hayek's initial gathering of "neoliberal"—meaning post-nineteenth-century market-oriented, or neoclassical—economists from around the world; it was Friedman's first trip outside the United States. In 1958, Hayek arranged a contribution from Volker to launch the *Journal of Law & Economics,* with Director as founding editor.

Director was one very plugged-in colleague.[25] He was an economist who not only had worked with Knight and Douglas but was

Friedman's brother-in-law and Stigler's best friend. Director had wangled acceptance of Hayek's *Road to Serfdom* by the University of Chicago Press, and he had spent a year at the LSE. Born in today's Ukraine, he had begun on the left. By the time he got to Chicago he was heading right. Director lacked the fertile, creative mind of Knight, Friedman, Stigler, or Hayek. His publication record was relatively unimpressive compared to theirs, though he was often credited with formulating a Chicago school of antitrust thought.[26] He was smart, adept politically, a superb networker, teacher, and polemicist, regularly holding dinners and discussions at his home; it was at one of these gatherings in 1960 that outsider Coase beat back objections by Chicago economists, led by Friedman, of his paper "The Problem of Social Cost" and finished the evening in triumph. In a letter to Knight in the '50s, Robbins praised Director's "charm, his urbanity and his most extensive culture" and "his quite unique balance of qualities—a perfectly civilized man."[27]

In the '50s, Director ignored the specter of Simons and began a long campaign against antitrust—notably in a class he taught with Edward Levi, who would become the US attorney general during the Ford administration, in which Levi presented antitrust cases for four days and Director on the fifth would, as one student said, argue that "the preceding four days were nonsense"[28]—and helped prod both Friedman and Stigler to greater skepticism about regulation. He influenced later conservative jurists like Robert Bork, Antonin Scalia, and William Rehnquist.

In 1964, Coase succeeded Director and revived the journal, which hadn't appeared for several years. Coase also eludes categorization; Stigler described him as a man immune to fashions. He was English, raised outside London, educated at the LSE. Chicago law professor and federal judge Richard Posner wrote that the key to understanding Coase was his Englishness ("feline in its subtlety and sharpness"[29]), his wit, and his hostility to theory, the latter of which Coase in a famous rejoinder—"Coase on Posner on Coase"—firmly, and wittily, rejected. His finest work consisted of a relatively few tightly argued short essays. "The Problem of Social Cost," which is a hybrid of law and economics, made him a natural to replace Director. He disdained math, which he called "blackboard economics." But as Posner discovered, trying to pin down such a subtle mind was a difficult task.

The only child of a postal telegrapher, Coase pursued a degree in commerce at the LSE, not economics, with the thought that he might pursue commercial law. But he won a traveling scholarship in his junior year and in 1932 he sailed to America, a latter-day economic Tocquevillian, to study its factories and companies, visiting Ford and General Motors. He was, at the time, a socialist; he met Socialist Party presidential candidate Norman Thomas. He puzzled over a big question: Lenin had said that the Soviet economy could be run like one giant factory. Economists scoffed at that, but how different was that from the great vertically and horizontally organized American corporations? Why, he asked, do firms exist? His reflection on this produced "The Nature of the Firm," which wouldn't be published until 1937 (he said he was too busy), not coincidentally, perhaps, in Cowles's *Econometrica*. Coase engaged in a thought experiment: he realized firms would not exist if markets cost nothing to access and use. In that utopian scenario—a model—every individual could conduct arm's-length market transactions. But because there are "transaction costs" to using markets, it's often more efficient to perform some tasks through the hierarchy of a firm, without "the intervention of the price mechanism" and upon the "authority" or "fiat" of a Knightean "entrepreneur-coordinator." (Coase had read Knight closely.) Much of "The Nature of the Firm" attempts to discriminate between what optimally occurs within the firm and what is cost effective to do in the markets—that is, settling on a firm's boundaries. Quoting British economist D. H. Robertson, he compared firms to "islands of conscious power in this ocean of unconscious cooperation [that is, markets] like lumps of butter coagulating in a pail of buttermilk."[30] Despite the metaphoric overreach, the essay was a revelatory piece of out-of-the-box thinking and created the field of transaction costs from nothing. This took thirty years. As Coase himself quipped, "Much cited and little used."

That would change in the '70s, particularly in the wake of "The Problem of Social Cost," which extended the transaction-cost approach into the realm of so-called public goods. Coase did not view the firm as an organic whole, as a fiduciary trust, as a social or political entity, or as a vehicle for workers, managers, customers, even shareholders; he approached it as a kind of Platonic mechanism, shaped by a few determinative rules, including Adam Smith's invisible hand (he believed economics had gone downhill after *Wealth of Nations*) and the dictates of marginal utility and substitution. By characterizing the firm as a shifting balance of authority and contracts, he opened the door to later, more radical definitions of companies as mere bundles of reciprocal arrangements, though Coase always pursued his own path. Coasian transaction-cost economics was bracing and baffling at the same time—intellectually satisfying for some academics, if seemingly divorced from common usage and practice. In decades ahead, Coase's unique style of thinking would become, despite his resistance to equations and theorizing, part of an increasingly mathematized economics; in fact, his "costless markets"—an unreal premise designed to provoke a real insight—would persist in a world awash with frictionless markets, rational expectations, and complex derivatives. This impulse to abstract, decompose, and reorganize—to define, simplify, and manipulate various elements of an organization—would not only define financial economics, with its trade-offs of risk and reward, but conglomerate strategy, with its portfolios of disparate, disposable business units, and an unrestrained M&A regime, with all assets theoretically up for sale.

A twisting path runs from "The Nature of the Firm" to the work Jensen and his partners began on redefining the corporate organization in the mid-'70s. Coase went his own way, unfolding the implications of his own ideas into transaction-cost economics. Jensen's agency theory, which cites Coase as a key influence, would usher in a new rationale for M&A, mobilize the law professors, and send them into battle with a waiting Marty Lipton.

JENSEN FELL IN with the second generation of Chicago financial economists. The group was led by Fama, initially a grad student with Jensen, then a faculty member. Outside, the '60s were erupting; inside, different insurrections unfolded. Markowitz had published his portfolio work only a few years earlier, Sharpe was around, and Miller presided intellectually over the business school and advised Jensen. The talk was all of random walks, capital-asset pricing models, and, above all else, efficient markets. Jensen shared an office with Myron Scholes, who was part of the team that developed the Black-Scholes-Merton option-pricing model; Richard Roll; and a few others who, he dryly noted in a later interview, "have done quite well in the profession." In fact, a remarkable number won Nobels. Jensen began working on his PhD thesis on mutual-fund asset pricing just as the business school's Center for Research on Securities Prices, commonly known as CRSP or "crisp," was launching its first computerized database, running on an IBM 7049 using punch cards. If you dropped the cards, he noted, you were cooked.[31] Jensen used the database to study how to evaluate mutual-fund performance, wrote his thesis on the subject, and developed a way of calculating abnormal returns of a security or a portfolio. The measure, Jensen's alpha, remains in wide use. And he pioneered with his colleagues the technique of calculating the effect on stock prices of discrete "news"—so-called event studies. "It was an interesting and creative time," he said, severely understating the case.

Jensen got his MBA in 1964 and his PhD in 1968, a lively year in Chicago that culminated in the demonstrations and violence at the Democratic Convention. By then he had left Chicago to teach at the University of Rochester's graduate school of management. (In 1969 Manne, who had been a student of Director's in Chicago, also arrived in Rochester, where he planned a new law school, built on specialties, one of which was to be law and economics. In 1971 he started an economics summer camp for lawyers, which he took with him after Rochester decided that a new law school was too expensive. Manne trekked through a number of different universities before starting George Mason University's law-and economics-centric law school.) Several years later, Rochester's management-school dean, the cigar-smoking William Meckling, and Jensen decided to jointly teach a course on the application of economics to the organizational problems of large firms. The reason: Students didn't see the practical use for economics, which was funny since the lawyers couldn't get enough of the stuff. But as Jensen noted, without apparent irony, "We ended up getting captured by organizational problems and lost interest in teaching economics and the basics of price theory. So Ken [French, the graduate assistant, a later collaborator with Fama and longtime professor at Dartmouth's Tuck School of Business] had to teach it on the evenings and on weekends, for which we were very grateful."

Instead, Jensen and Meckling focused on the firm—Coase's firm. In 1974, the pair had been invited to a conference in Europe—the Conference on Analysis and Ideology in Interlaken, Switzerland—and decided to poke a finger in the eye of an audience they figured consisted of European socialists and Marxists by reprising a famous Friedman provocation in the *New York Times Magazine* in 1970 that argued "the social responsibility of business is to increase its profits."[32] Friedman was offering to the public a distillation of Chicago's neoclassical economic theory of the firm (*neoclassical* meaning an updated version of classical Adam Smithian economics): management develops and executes a number of production plans, by buying and selling in anonymous, competitive, and efficient markets. Price theory reigns supreme. Management's goal is to maximize profits for shareholders. But, says Jensen, as they worked on the paper they realized Friedman was wrong. The more they looked at it, Jensen said, "the more we became convinced that you couldn't say that as a positive description of what went on in business firms. That was the beginning of breaking open the black box of the firm thought of as an actor in the system. Obviously, firms don't act, people act." By the time they set off for Europe, he added, "[w]e had no confidence that what business firms really did was to maximize profits."

The paper they presented was the start of the pair's work on agency theory. Jensen and Meckling first identified various conflicts of interest within the firm: between stockholders and bondholders and managers. They tried to apply transaction-cost economics from Coase's "The Nature of the Firm," but found the essay problematic. Said Jensen: "The trouble with that was that it didn't provide any actionable access to anything. It was a name that described our ignorance of a whole lot of things." In short, it wasn't useful. Their argument stirred uproar, even at Rochester, where the pair confronted harsh criticism. They had trouble getting the paper "Theory of the Firm: Managerial Behavior, Agency Costs, and Ownership Structure" published. They submitted it to the *Bell Journal of Economics,* and the referees not only rejected it, Jensen recalled, "but were incensed anyone would submit such a paper to the *Bell Journal.* That was discouraging." But Jensen was a co-editor of the *Journal of Financial Economics* with Fama and another luminary, MIT's Robert Merton, who had worked with Scholes and Fischer Black on options pricing. Fama was in Belgium and got a copy of the paper and sent Jensen a note accepting it for the journal. "We applauded his taste," said Jensen, who made it the lead piece.

The "Agency Costs" paper appeared in the *Journal of Financial Economics* in October 1976.[33] Unlike Coase's "The Nature of the Firm," it had an immediate impact in academic circles. Besides its extensive citations, the paper opened up entire veins of inquiry, not least for Fama and Jensen. It provided a language to describe dysfunction and breakdown in the firm: agency costs themselves, the notion of alignment or misalignment of interests, and, more problematically, "proof" of the validity of shareholders as ultimate owners of firms and monitors of corporate performance—that is, the modern version of shareholder-centric corporate governance. Despite the difficulty in getting the paper published, "Agency Costs" was seized upon by a now-burgeoning law and economics movement, which quickly applied it to corporate governance and to Manne's accountability mechanism, hostile M&A, and notions of efficient markets. Soon Jensen could declare it "a revolution in the science of organizations," which was a welcome declaration in a decade that seemed defined by decay, defeat, and depression.

The paper reflected the kind of hammer-on-the-head prose style that would be Jensen's calling card. The paper opened with the statement that it developed "a theory of the ownership structure for the firm" and claimed that it has implications "for a variety of issues in the professional and popular literature including the definition of the firm, the 'separation of ownership and control,' the 'social responsibility' of business, the definition of 'corporate objective function,' the determination of an optimal capital structure, the specification of the content of credit agreements, the theory of organizations, and the supply side of the completeness of markets problems."[34] Then, without a pause, the pair enumerated ten things the theory helps explain, from why managers would choose suboptimal financial strategies to why anyone would issue preferred stock. There's everything here but a cure for inflation and a replacement for oil.

Jensen and Meckling started with the Coasian firm, but swept past it. Unlike Coase, they didn't posit a balance between authority and markets. Instead, they viewed the firm as little more than a tissue of various contractors: a market of contracts seeking equilibrium. They were not the first to explore this idea: In 1972, two Chicago school economists laid out the basic idea of a corporation as a nexus of contracts without hierarchy. But, as then–Cardozo Law School professor William Bratton wrote in 1989, "The appearance of Jensen and Meckling's well-known analysis of the firm made 1976 the watershed year."[35] Agency costs—a variety of transaction cost—arise as a natural part of the contracting process; they're also symptomatic of the separation of ownership and control, and, Jensen later argued, much greater than many assumed. (In many ways Manne was the progenitor of the concept of agency costs in his 1965 paper, though he never called it that. In a sense, agency costs were simply representations of self-interest.) Agency costs arise in relationships between shareholders, as principals or owners, and managerial agents. Agents tend to shirk, to trade work for leisure, to cheat, to protect their cozy positions; they spend principals' money. The difficulty comes in getting agents to maximize the welfare of principals, particularly if those agents' self-interest lies elsewhere, as Jensen and Meckling assume it does. This requires incentives, usually monetary in nature. The agency theory of the firm has implications: companies are just the sum of their contracts with employees, vendors, and customers. Firms are thus legal fictions. In contrast to the Coasian firm, there is no inside or outside of a company. The firm has no center, no objective, no social responsibilities, no culture. Jensen and Meckling reduce Knight's entrepreneur to a mere agent, a contract player, one among many. They dismiss the reality of hierarchy, bureaucracy, and authority. They abandon the traditional legal metaphor of the firm as a trust, with managers and directors as fiduciary trustees. They ruthlessly simplify.

They locate the engine of the firm in the maximization of the principal's welfare—that is, the shareholders. Perhaps the most forbidding aspect of the paper is how quickly Jensen and Meckling feel they have to erect a model they call "Sources of Agency Costs of Equity and Who Bears Them." What follows are pages of assumptions and definitions, equations, vectors, indifference curves, measures of wealth (pecuniary and nonpecuniary), theorems, proofs, graphs: it cries out science. And yet, after all that, they end up offering: "The magnitude of the agency costs discussed above will vary from firm to firm." Agency costs will depend on managers' tastes, the ease with which they exercise their preferences, the cost of monitoring, measuring, and evaluating their performance. The factors trot on, each a subjective, nonquantifiable matter forced into a Procrustean frame of quantitation. The foundation of this scheme is a rational impulse to maximize self-interest. But what exactly is rational in an environment with varying amounts of information about the future—what economist Herbert Simon had already dubbed "bounded rationality"—that is, making judgments based on imperfect information? How do you measure taste? How do you value what good or evil lurks in the human heart, or the capacity for self-delusion, or, for that matter, cooperative, even sacrificial, behavior? How do you cost-out human variability?

Jensen and Meckling were self-consciously providing yet another "theory of the firm," one they believed was based on science. In fact, agency theory was less a theory than a financial model driven by market and economic inputs. It was, in a general taxonomy offered up decades later by Emanuel Derman, a physicist-turned-Wall Street risk manager-turned-Columbia professor, an attempt to project regularities of a complex reality onto a smaller, more manageable space. Theories, Derman argues, are attempts to capture aspects of reality.[36] The differences are important: "Models are analogies; they always describe one thing relative to something else. Models need a defense or an explanation. Theories, in contrast, are the real thing. They need confirmation rather than explanation. A theory describes an essence. A successful theory can become fact."[37] Jensen and Meckling claimed to be offering a theory; in fact, they had produced a model, which, as Derman lays out, always runs the risk of extrapolating a little too far. "Models are simplifications," writes Derman. "And simplifications are dangerous."[38]

What were the salient simplifications of Jensen and Meckling's psychology of the corporate black box? Shareholders, as recipients of a firm's "residual claims," need to more closely hold conflicted, self-interested managers to account. Companies are contractual abstractions that can be assembled and dissembled at will, for the sake of efficiency or performance. Like some postmodern author, companies are fictions, to be re-imagined and restructured at will. Firms have no other purpose than to maximize the performance of shareholders, holders of the residual risk. You can trust no one; the agent-principal conflict is omnipresent, if unquantifiable; it borders on paranoia. Employees are mere atoms. True or false, agency theory, like original sin, reflects a pessimistic view of human nature. The grazing herd of white-collar managers, not to say unionized blue-collar workers, were no longer well-meaning conformists but dangerously unaligned, wayward, alienated—potentially greedy, conflicted, duplicitous. They were free—if self-interested—agents, tethered to a corporate identity and a paycheck by a mere contract, perhaps even an implicit one.

But agency theory did open up, as Cardoza's Bratton writes, "a new line of microeconomic inquiry—the analysis of the internal functions of firms within the assumptions and methodology of neoclassical economics"[39]—for Chicago microeconomics. This approach appeared to many to be an austere, bracing, and persuasive view of the corporation, particularly for legal scholars, and an alternative to the managerialist consensus and to Keynesian orthodoxies. Bratton is quite clear about the demarcation line: Before 1972, Chicago only "theorized" about markets. Price theory explained how resources were coordinated and used. The corporation was a black box—a "production function." Chicago-style neoclassical economists viewed "actions inside of firms as 'engineering' functions of hierarchical structures, and therefore unsuited to a discipline that studies markets." But the nexus of contracts made hierarchy irrelevant. "Under it, neoclassical microeconomists could discuss organizations while remaining within the traditions of their discipline and without sullying their hands with 'engineering.'" Bratton was critical of the nexus-of-contracts approach. The model's basic assumptions—"contract, rationality, the desire to maximize profits, competition, and survival of the fittest—state propositions as much political as empirical."[40] The theory, he argues, has tautological elements: if you define the rules, you define the outcome.

Agency theory was also principal-centric. Ownership held great sway. The theory featured cheating and shirking by agents, but not by principals, like shareholders. Agents, meaning workers and managers, cannot simply come and go effortlessly—relatively frictionlessly—as shareholders could. And while it seemed easy enough to herd agents and principals into their separate pens, psychologically it was more complex. Yale University sociologist Charles Perrow pointed out how insidiously easy it is to apply agency theory, particularly for anyone in a supervisory role, which in a bureaucracy is almost everyone, except those at the very bottom. Supervisors, in short, find it easy to adopt the mindset of ownership; they're encouraged to do so. "We are all agency theorists far more than we think!" he wrote. "The theory allows those of us fortunate enough to supervise to play the seductive role of long-suffering principals victimized by the duplicity of ne'er-do-well subordinates after the fashion of the Social Darwinists."[41]

In agency theory, the state of nature, constructed of law and neoclassical economics and a reductionist rational psychology, beckoned.

THE "DISCOVERY" OF agency theory seemed to empower Jensen. That same year he produced an essay on a topic that he had actually some experience with, albeit from the Linotype room: the press. Jensen called the paper "Toward a Theory of the Press,"[42] the *toward* being an

attempt at restraint. Jensen declared the press, presumably from reading it, to be hopelessly romantic, ignorant, inaccurate, emotional, simplistic, and liberal, adding (in the words of H. L. Mencken, whom he
quoted) that "[t]he average newspaper, especially of the so-called better sort, has the intelligence of a Baptist evangelist, the courage of a
rat, the fairness of a Prohibitionist boob-bumper, the information of a
high school janitor, the taste of a designer of celluloid valentines, and
the honor of a police-station lawyer."[43] Newspaperman Mencken's
irony seemed to elude Jensen, unless the paper is a parody, which does
not appear to be the case.

The press theory is comical in its naïveté. Jensen analyzed the press
as if it were an alien creature that landed on his lawn. He observed
that consumers want entertainment, not news. (He seemed incapable
of imagining a combination of the two, or a diversity of media content.) Not being scientists, ordinary people have little tolerance for
ambiguity. They demand answers to problems. They love gossip. He
speculated that journalists attack public figures only when "they lose
monopolistic access to information" and shed their popularity with
news consumers, which, he says, explains Woodward and Bernstein.
He interpreted much of this based on his theory of the family. Most
people grow up in families where relationships are based on altruism.
They "erroneously" imagine that the world outside is one big family.
It's not: self-interest rules the transactional ethos of the outside world.
The press confuses the two, trying to personify complex issues and
make every story a conflict between self-interest (bad) and altruism
(good.)

"Toward a Theory of the Press" is a farrago of ideas and observations, some obvious, some silly, seemingly remote from agency theory's
sophisticated thinking. But the press theory was more deeply tied to
agency theory than would first appear. Not long after, Jensen and
Meckling cobbled together a polemic in the vein of the press theory
that insisted that there was a fundamental conflict between political
democracy and a free-market, private-enterprise, or capitalist system,
and that the "political sector," led by the press, was destroying the

market sector.[44] This wouldn't matter much, except for one thing: bits and pieces of the press theory—notably the altruism of the family and the monolithic presence of agent self-interest—surfaced in Jensen's topical papers on takeovers. "Toward a Theory of the Press" suggested a tendency toward psychological reductionism and a distrust of democracy that would shape Jensen's view of evolving financial issues.

Chapter Six

THE DEBATE OVER DEFENSE

T HE CHASM BETWEEN abstractions like the Coasian firm, a nexus of contracts and agency costs, and thoughts emerging from the dark id of your average CEO, banker, shareholder, reporter, or citizen squinting at his morning paper was, well, unbridgeable without tortured simplifications. M&A was a complicated business. The theory of the corporation, or corporate governance, slid quickly into a swamp of Talmudic hairsplitting, which was not normally tolerated in family newspapers. Smears were allowed, particularly if they were paid for in cash. The innuendo (Lipton's sighing "embarrassment" at the behavior of Amex's Roger Morley or the clever tut-tutting of Cheney's "Saturday Night Special" in defending Garlock) that Flom and Lipton and their PR representatives perpetrated with such glee had little to do with the nuances of Jensen and Meckling, not to say the law. But the two sides—high and low, academic and practitioner—did find a narrow slice of common ground, and it was one that Lipton did not see coming. They shared a primal message: Don't trust *those* people! They are stealing your money! You are being screwed! The "you" in this case was the stockholder, who was rapidly evolving into a proxy for the vast victimized democratic public.

By the late '70s, bigger and more complex hostile raids were erupting regularly; offense and defense were advancing tactically. New weapons rumbled out. New ideas and arguments were taken for a spin. The question recurs: How did Berle's notion that managers had to balance an array of stakeholders fade away? How was public opinion of

M&A shaped? How did defense come to be viewed as a controversial act akin to treason? As M&A surged—rising, slipping, then exceeding previous levels, like salmon flopping upriver—the struggle for control reached for new levers beyond a few mud-slinging ads. It expanded and diffused, driven by its own internally competitive dynamics.

In 1978, a seamy board squabble broke out at a New Jersey–based manufacturer of healthcare supplies named Becton Dickinson (BD), an ample company if not a household name unless you were a connoisseur of syringes. In 1974, the CEO and founder's son, Fairleigh Dickinson Jr., had handed control over to professional management to become chairman of the board, widely viewed as a snoozy job with nifty perks. The seemingly mild, introspective Dickinson, however, couldn't let go: the family name had its privileges, despite a less-than-controlling stake. He sparred with management, which believed, with reason, that it ran the show. Dickinson, however, liked his autonomy, and quietly hired F. Eberstadt & Co. to find a willing buyer, first Kodak, then Avon Products, for Becton Dickinson—that is, a white knight; the rub, however, was that he didn't bother telling his director colleagues he was selling the joint. Meanwhile, management was in hot pursuit of a Boston dialysis company called National Medical Care (NMC), which, after word got out, effectively blew up Dickinson's nascent Avon deal. Dickinson then asked Eberstadt and Salomon Brothers to analyze the NMC deal—they each loyally wrote negative reports—and the board backed away from NMC. The knives came out, and much to Dickinson's shock, the board booted him as chairman. He then went to war, gathering his bankers as well as Lipton (technically the advisor to one of the bankers, Salomon), who suggested a cooling-off period. His advisors would come to view Dickinson as unpredictable to the point of lunacy.

Revenge was in the air. Dickinson's bankers searched for buyers and finally got a bite at Sun Oil, owned by the very private, very rich Pew family of Philadelphia, who were eager to diversify out of oil. Sun and Dickinson (really Salomon and Eberstadt) quietly amassed shares and launched a classic Flom gambit—a quick after-market strike that hauled in 34 percent of institutional shares at a 37 percent premium,

including the Dickinson family block and a major holding by Eberstadt's prestigious Chemical and Surveyor funds. (Sun held the shares
in a structure called L.H.I.W.—Let's Hope It Works.[1] It didn't.) Becton was blindsided. The Sun raid—journalist Richard Phalon accurately dubbed it the "midnight raid,"[2] Lipton more evocatively, with
overtones of Pearl Harbor, called it the "dawn raid"—also caught
Flom by surprise; he was about to go on vacation to St. Croix and had
tried to squeeze from Lipton whether anything was about to break.
Lipton, tortured, passed on hints to Flom that the latter had missed.
And so when Becton hired Flom, another Flom family vacation was
ruined.[3] Perhaps it was all cosmic payback for Inco.

There seemed little to this squalid dispute to agitate a larger public.
It was a struggle between family and management that was more late
nineteenth century than 1980s. That's not, however, how Flom chose
to present it. As Phalon notes in his book-length account of the episode, Flom and his team knew effective defense depended on reaching
two audiences: the public and the politicians. You had to go wide to
go deep. Moreover, the message did not need to reflect an excess of
truth about the deal itself. "Yes, the public had to be told," wrote Phalon, "but the ultimate audience was small and very select. It consisted
of Harold Williams, then chairman of the SEC, and the board of the
Sun Company."[4] Flom's plan: Claim that Sun had committed grave
securities violations, "discomfiting" Sun's board and a publicity-shy
family. Flom knew that winning a suit on Williams Act violations was
no sure thing. But maybe he didn't have to. The way to the SEC and
the family ran through Congress. Powerhouse Paul Weiss litigator
Arthur Liman, who Becton had brought in to deal with Dickinson,
then reeled in a major *macher:* Theodore Sorenson, John Kennedy's
bespectacled former advisor and speechwriter (and alleged ghost of
Kennedy's *Profiles in Courage*) and a lawyer of counsel at Paul Weiss—
to handle Congress. Sorenson conjured up a variety of reasons why an
oil company buying a healthcare supplier might spook Congress. He
quickly made Sun's bid about threats to "healthcare and cost contain-
ment," suggesting Sun might not care about either. Moreover, in
talking points studded with hot-button words, Sorenson asserted that

an "acquisition by *outsiders* [italics mine] with a different set of *values* might *strip* such purveyors of health-care items as BD of cash in a way that could mean *higher* prices, or *siphon off* profits that could be plowed back into *vitally important* spending on research and development."[5] This sounded bad and ignored that the ultimate insider and culture carrier, Dickinson, supported Sun.

Sorenson drafted a position paper. Forget about a grumpy scion and a diversifying energy company. Sorenson made this about public policy: healthcare, R&D, stockholder protection, antitrust, energy— the fate of the nation. Sorenson spun his argument to Democratic senators William Proxmire, Harrison Williams, Edward Kennedy, and their staffs. Kennedy chaired the antitrust subcommittee and held hearings that dragged in SEC staff, unhappy small investors (not the institutions that sold shares to Sun in the midnight raid), and an investment banker who declared the price too low. He pressed the Federal Trade Commission for an opinion on the deal. Sorenson organized Becton plant managers across the country to call and telegram. He wrote letters to key congressmen, copying the SEC chairman. He raised doubts about the raid's legality. "The legislators underlined their 'great concern' over Sun's 'sudden and surreptitious purchase' of a controlling position in BD in a fashion that deprived 13,000 stockholders of 'the most fundamental benefits' of the Williams Act." He even called for an investigation of energy companies raising prices. Phalon refers to this as "the sting in the tail."[6]

All this was cynical and effective. Flom's chosen PR reps, Hill & Knowlton's Cheney and Kekst & Co.'s Gershon Kekst, worked the financial reporters at the big papers (a fairly small group), pressed Sun's outside directors, and produced a report on "the menace of takeovers." (The latter was the acme of irony: the very men who invented and drove hostile M&A were bemoaning its sinister nature.) They even leaked without any evidence that Sun directors were unhappy, a self-fulfilling prophecy when the SEC announced it was charging the oil company with violations of the Williams Act. Now Sun directors *were* unhappy.

The case was heavily lawyered and closely fought with a lengthy *dramatis personae* turning on murky questions of intent and motivation. Sun and Dickinson lost: a federal judge declared that the midnight raid, for all its skill, violated the intent of the Williams Act. Sun, Dickinson, their bankers, had acted as a group, the judge said, referring in particular to Eberstadt's use of shares from its funds, with the intent of stampeding Becton into submission. This turned on a fine distinction. Sun violated Section 14(d) of the legislation, by failing to disclose a "single, integrated project" to buy Becton. Sun, chagrined, retreated, changing CEOs, settling the suits, unloading the shares (the price of which rose as the market realized that Becton was now, as Phalon wrote, "institutionalized"[7]—that is, no longer a family-controlled entity), and paying off the lawyers; without a deal, the bankers got little. Becton Dickinson's stock price rose, and Sun, with a new CEO, made other acquisitions—in energy. Dickinson himself appeared lost and old, invested in a biotech company, and turned his attentions to the family university, Fairleigh-Dickinson.

So not much changed, except for those souls pondering whether takeovers were a threat to life and limb. Becton Dickinson had survived through a wide-ranging, multipronged, backs-to-the-wall defense. Flom's defense, much of which had been pioneered by Lipton, accelerated the process of putting hostile tender offers on the public agenda and cross-examining every major hostile deal with standards inflicted on Sun. In taking the case to Congress, Becton Dickinson circulated ideas that would increasingly shape one public view of M&A: the predatory outsider, the belief that the target would be pillaged, plundered, and stripped of its finest assets; that stockholders were getting abused; and that mergers represented a return to cartels and trusts. That the nation would suffer for this transgression of the corporation, made worse because the attacker was a Dickinson. These were just words, of course, but they tapped a deep sense of propriety and limits. Of course, to Flom it was just tactics, simply a means to an end, but those notions did not die just because the deal did.

Lipton did not exactly cover himself in glory. He had, albeit grudgingly, approved the dubious aggressiveness of the midnight raid. So he owned it: this was part of being Marty Lipton. It didn't really matter that the judge's decision was later criticized for errors. A loss was a loss. It was one thing to lose on defense: the odds were stacked against you. But in a transaction shot through with Shakespearean doublings, Lipton on offense had been bested by Flom on *defense*. Lipton had been sensitive to the appearance of a buying "group," had sparred with Flom over it, quizzed the bankers about what they were pitching, and let it pass. Wachtell got paid handsomely, as usual, and he was aware that Flom had thrown everything he had at Sun and still barely won.

In January 1979, a year after the midnight raid but with the trial still to come, American Express launched its attack on McGraw-Hill. Lipton, on defense, faced Flom, Amex's advisor. Turnaround. Lipton and his team mashed all the PR buttons, culminating in a letter "written by" Harold McGraw accusing Amex of multiple sins: Morley's treachery, a "secret plan," a lack of integrity, vague charges that Amex was using the float on traveler's checks to avoid taxes, the threat to the First Amendment, the flight of the journalists. That was standard stuff, but cranked up to bitter heights. (James Robinson, the Amex CEO, was personally insulted.) More importantly, Lipton sent his troops trotting down a path that Sorenson had cleared to Washington. He got the House Banking Committee involved in Amex's banking "issues," stirred investigations by the Federal Communications Commission (McGraw-Hill owned TV stations), the SEC, and the New York State attorney general, filed suits. He dragged in the First Amendment. And he began to think more deeply about where all this was going. Amex walked away in September 1979. As one commentator noted, Robinson "had all the chips and still lost. If you were going to undertake a battle, you had better have tough skin needed to stick out a fight."[8] Robinson didn't.

Like most M&A, the Becton Dickinson defense was quickly forgotten, except by participants. But Flom's tactics foreshadowed the developing politics of M&A, reinforced by Lipton's ferocious defense of McGraw-Hill. There was something recklessly out of control about M&A: the resources, the lawsuits, the charges, the big money. What did this *game* really have to do with jobs, innovation, prosperity, and growth; with lives; with the public welfare? And once M&A was taken to the public or to Congress, the technical and legalistic debate was replaced by more prosaic concerns. The public was stirred by the plight, real or imagined, of small shareholders, laid-off workers, turned-off customers, or repelled by plutocratic buyers, crass speculators, imperial CEOs. This was quickly becoming a drama of stock characters; as in the Becton Dickinson case, public opinion turned on what was going through the minds of these vague figures behind the deal. Were they straight or crooked? Were they liars, cheats, or stout corporate defenders? Were they self-interested, conflicted, duplicitous? For their part, Congress and state legislatures reacted to constituencies, interest groups, voting blocs: stakeholders. Those political realities provided context for the debate that Lipton was about to incite over the merits, or demerits, of playing defense.

IN PERSON, LIPTON speaks in a raspy voice with an orotund gentility. In his legal broadsides, Mr. Defense does not mess around: He attacks. He goes on offense. "Takeover Bids in the Target's Boardroom," his full-throated defense of the stakeholder model and board prerogatives, appeared in *The Business Lawyer* in November 1979,[9] a few months after Sun sold down its Becton stake and immediately after Amex slunk away; it was a last echo of that desperate struggle. "Takeover Bids" is a polemic, a screed, a manifesto with footnotes, from the opening sentence: "The heightened level of takeover activity during the past five years has focused attention on the legal, moral and practical questions faced by the directors of companies that become a target of an unsolicited bid."[10] A literature on defending against takeovers already existed. But Lipton's essay was more than a recipe of tactics. He dealt with urgent generalities, a crisis in our time; this was typical of Lipton's mature style. He was staking out defense as his territory; he was *alarmed*. Right at the start, Lipton defined directors as key decision-makers in takeover attempts; he hardly mentioned the usual *bête noir*, management. (Neither did he discuss the widespread belief that CEOs control boards, rendering them vestigial, like an appendix.) He argued that boards represented the last line of defense. He raised the specter of shareholders suing directors in successful takeover defenses, though he admitted that cases had so far sustained "the right of the directors to target a takeover on the grounds of inadequacy of price, illegality of the offer, and concern with the impact of the take-over on the employees of the target and the community in which it operates."[11]

And yet, he wrote, "the debate continues to rage." For directors he had just frightened out of their wits, he offered twelve questions they should review in every takeover situation. (Self-interest hung over these questions: They're obviously ones Lipton himself pep-pered boards with when he was brought in on defense. He's making a case: I am with you. It was a brilliant rainmaking ploy, his answer to Flom's retainers.) These range from whether directors had to ac-cept a bid at a substantial premium or whether they should automat-ically resort to an open auction. Should directors "consider the impact of the takeover on employees, customers, suppliers, the com-munity; indeed is national policy a proper consideration?" Can shareholder desires supersede "what the directors believe to be the best interests of the target as a business enterprise?" Many directors ignored antitrust issues, rejected any overture, built an anti-takeover fence with "shark repellent" and local takeover laws, authorized a standstill agreement with another company—a "big brother"—that allowed a noncontrolling stake as well as protection against attack. Were these classic defensive moves kosher, fair, *legal*? Can boards justify rejection with a mere investment-bank opinion or even con-sult with advisors to prepare a defense before a bid is made? Or should boards wait passively for an offer and grab it?[12]

His final two questions were more philosophical and legalistic. The first acknowledged the impact Jensen and Meckling had had, though not by name. Lipton summed up their initial agency paper in a few lines: "Are the management directors of the target so infected with self-interest that they are disqualified from participating in the ulti-mate decision to accept or reject a takeover bid?" he asked. Second, and this took refuge in the ultimate defensive redoubt, the business judgment rule: "Is a takeover bid so significantly different from other major business questions that the usual rules governing directors must be displaced by rules unique to takeovers?"

Lipton followed up these questions with, of course, advice. First, directors shouldn't be forced to accept a bid with a premium—even a jumbo premium—as long as they acted on a reasonable basis and in "good faith." (Here, Lipton was nodding to traditional corporate law, which is based on fiduciaries like directors practicing various "duties," such as the duty of good faith.) Second, takeovers aren't so different from other business decisions that new rules—meaning "direct action" by shareholders—needed to be made.

Who is perpetrating such heresies? Lipton fingered two culprits: arbitrageurs and professional investors. This was a pair "whose short-term perspectives are not in accordance with the long-term interests of other shareholders and other constituencies of the corporation."[13] The fact that Lipton once instructed arbs in M&A was as beside the point as Flom arguing that "takeovers are menaces." He was making a case. As for professional investors, what did he really mean by that? Hedge funds had not yet emerged as potent speculative forces. Lipton was talking about institutional investors, such as pension funds, mutual funds, bank trust departments, which, as he noted, Berle had anticipated, and that represented "the tertiary stage of capitalism." Just as control passed from entrepreneur-shareholders to professional managers, now it had shifted to professional investment managers. Essentially, Lipton was saying to directors: the vast bulk of shareholding power has its missiles aimed directly at *you.*

Arbs were easy to demonize; they were unabashed speculators. But in pointing a quivering finger at institutions, Lipton was taking a stand against what conventional wisdom viewed as the party of progress. With their massive portfolios, institutions were *the* current, modern, *au courant* financial power. They were up-to-date, technically sophisticated, technologically advanced, quantitatively driven, and passive enough to appear disinterested. They were accountable only to a Platonic ideal of "performance." They were *financial.* They had, as Rohatyn discovered, pressed the breakdown and reform of Wall Street. They were (relatively) new—or at least their power was. And yet

Lipton cleverly framed the debate in a way that tapped popular moral dichotomies about money and power, to the detriment of the institutions: he was defending Main Street against Wall Street; investors versus speculators; long-term against short; the virtuous demos of amateurs versus self-interested professional elites. These weren't bloodless academic dichotomies; this was a Wagnerian drama of good and evil: a call to arms and to long-term investment. To equity.

For the punctilious, institutions dealt with Wall Street, but they were really not *of* Wall Street, a nuance the media have long ignored; most institutions were long-term investors, not gamblers or hotshot dealmakers; and they served ordinary Americans, notably pensioners: they were about as flashy as a Chevrolet. But subtleties are lost in struggle. In fact, Lipton recapitulated how one should think about the issue in the very next sentence, which opened with a slippery double negative, featured italics throughout (just in case you missed how important this was), and ended five lines later in a question mark. "It would not be unfair to pose the policy issue as: *Whether the long-term interests of the nation's corporate system and economy should be jeopardized in order to benefit speculators interested not in the vitality and continued existence of the business enterprise in which they have brought shares, but only in a quick profit on the sale of those shares?*"[14] Like Sorenson's talking points, this wasn't about a grubby deal or two, but about "the long-term interests of the nation's corporate system and economy." In short: Wake up people. The nation is at risk.

This was powerful stuff when fed to a suddenly insecure regime shivering in their towers. The dichotomies Lipton piled up, which would shape the "defense" rump of the M&A debate for decades, not to mention play a key role in takeover jurisprudence, had been present in episodes like Becton Dickinson and McGraw-Hill; but outside the furious charges and countercharges, they were difficult to pin down, or quantify. What are speculators anyway, and how exactly do they differ from investors? Where's the line between short-term and long-term? Are they embodiments of the invisible hand? Are they victims or victimizers? While volumes on stock exchanges and trading were rising in the '70s—meaning the average holding period of shares was falling, a process the Bank of England's Andrew Haldane once evocatively called "the race to zero"[15]—the real implosion would only begin with the Reagan bull market of the '80s and motor into our era of computerized, high-frequency trading. Long-term versus short was compelling political narrative but, like pornography, difficult to define. This was similar, if the polar opposite, to the broad-brush critique provided by agency theory. In agency theory, management (and directors) are inevitably conflicted. Stockholders, as principals, share a common self-interest. Theory doesn't distinguish between loyal CEOs, wayward stockholders, incompetent (as opposed to conflicted) managers, and honestly mistaken strategies. What *was* Dickinson up to? Was he an agent or a principal or simply off his nut? (In court, he had admitted to taking lots of medication for a "neurological" disorder that may have affected his memory.[16]) Both sides excised human complexity from their theories, banished ambiguity, presumed guilt. Every agent was a potential sinner; every principal spotless, or vice versa. As the debate heated up, even issues that one might think would be black and white—Are target shareholders better off in hostile takeover situations?—proved elusive when you took a longer perspective on these continually evolving, dauntingly complex input-output black boxes known as corporations. A continual skirmishing over numbers would begin with Lipton in "Takeover Bids" arguing, with rudimentary statistics, that investors have been better off when they rejected unwanted advances, even if that meant extracting a better price. The Chicago crowd, notably Jensen himself in a series of '80s studies citing the complex math of fashionable "event studies," declared that investors in targets nearly always fared better, and that the economy was significantly better off for undergoing M&A's rigors. Who did you believe? What were these studies really measuring?

Lipton did go further. He asked: What are directors for anyway? What are their powers? Where do they fit? That is, he tackled corporate governance issues raised by hostile takeovers. And just as he categorized moral predilections around terms like *investment* and *speculation,* so too did he claim that corporate governance somehow mirrors American constitutional structures. As a result, he helped popularize the argument over governance as a matter of Federalists versus Jeffersonians: the former arguing that populist impulses needed to be filtered through wiser representatives (the board); the latter insisting on direct democracy—elections, referendums, the voice of the people (shareholders). Lipton favored the former, thus leaving the same impression that Rohatyn often conveyed: an uneasy mix of liberal and conservative tendencies (in fact, Lipton would find himself attacked by liberals *and* conservatives) that Hamilton and Adams might have understood. Here's Lipton as Madison in his *Federalist Papers* phase:

> Our corporate governance system is structured similarly to our national government. Ultimate power resides with the shareholders who cannot act directly but only through their elected representatives—the directors. The directors are elected annually and both state and federal law provide mechanisms to enable shareholders either to change the composition of the board of directors or to instruct the directors to take action desired by shareholders. Directors are considered to owe a fiduciary duty to the shareholders—that is, they are supposed to act as prudent businessmen, in good faith and on a reasonable basis to assure that the business of the corporation is operated for the benefit of the shareholders.[17]

Obviously, constitutional government and corporate governance did not emerge at the same time; what's now known as corporate governance developed in fits and starts as the nature of companies and the economy evolved. Private companies had a rudimentary form of governance built on authority and autocracy, what Coase called "fiat." Problems began with size, public ownership, separation of ownership and control. Few outside academia ever thought that large corporations ran like democracies. But as corporations were viewed as essential, first by Berle, then by Nader, Green, and Seligman in the '70s, the demands for democratization, or at least federal oversight, began. (Berle, like Galbraith, lauded the big firms, but not as examples of democratic governance. Berle thought companies were essential bureaucracies, managed, again as Coase suggested, by authority. He believed, like Thorstein Veblen, in technocracy.) As markets deepened and diversified, they came to resemble the electorate, voting continually. And the term *corporate governance* edged into the limelight with this "rediscovery" of markets and shareholders. Lipton himself admitted that "in the early years of this [twentieth] century" shareholders were the sole focus of directors, and legally the precedential case where courts identified shareholders as true owners, *Dodge v. Ford* in 1919, has never been overturned, though it's still debated—in part because it came from the Michigan Supreme Court, never an authoritative arbiter of corporate law, with almost no related cases since. (The Michigan court said that Henry Ford, who did not suffer from separation of ownership and control issues, since he owned and controlled the place, owed a duty to shareholders to operate his business profitably and pass them the rewards. Minority shareholders, the Dodge brothers, sued Ford after he refused to pay out a dividend, saying "that he preferred to use the corporation's money to build cheaper, better cars, and pay higher wages."[18] Lipton accepted that boards have some responsibility to stockholders, but didn't cite the Ford case.) But, noted Lipton, efforts to broaden concerns to include a range of constituencies and issues— the environment, health and safety, employee pensions, product safety, community betterment, even political action—"have reached full fruition only during the last 20 years. It is now well-settled through legislation and court decisions."[19]

It wasn't settled enough that it couldn't be unsettled. The notion that stakeholder governance had become practice may have been Lipton's weakest argument, which he seemed to admit when he confessed that he and his colleagues had been researching cases on the business judgment rule, the essential platform for a stakeholder approach, for years. He was reaching; Jim Crow had been settled practice, too. When it came to governance, there was no founding document, no constitution, no tablets, no iron-chain of precedent. It existed in the *zeitgeist,* emerging from popular attitudes toward corporations and the state, the demands of efficiency, and a hundred other social and economic factors. The law tended to validate what had already taken root; perhaps it was as basic as interest-group politics, with managers trumping small shareholders. It was democratic in the sense that it was widely accepted, often unthinkingly; it worked, until it didn't. But the problem with the *zeitgeist* as validation for Lipton is what happens when it changes its mind. If Lipton accepted the stakeholder model because it was settled practice, would he embrace shareholder control if that became part of legislation and regulation? The Jeffersonians did supplant the Federalists.

And why not put shareholders in charge? After all, equity suggests ownership. Berle, in his exchange with Manne, dismissed shareholders as products of a secondary market in shares that had nothing to do with the value of the corporation itself. "The buyer's investment is in the stock market quotation," offered a Berle disciple dismissively in 1964. Lipton, perhaps realizing that this particular notion had had its day, did not repeat it. Instead, he focused on the malign role of arbs and professional investors. Why shouldn't shareholders be able to vote on takeover offers? Because, he said, stockholders are tangled in a briar patch of conflicts, not unlike agency costs. They are not free to make decisions; they are coerced by considerations that have nothing to do with corporate good. "The special dynamics of a tender offer," Lipton wrote, "are such that the decision of shareholders is almost always a foregone conclusion—they will tender, therefore, it is misleading to speak of a free shareholder choice at all."[20] The only group that retains independence, he insisted, is the board. Second, he noted the shift in stock ownership from individuals to institutions, which by 1979 was old news except to millions of voters who still believed that markets were moved by small investors, and for them. Professional investors, he added, are captured by short-term performance demands. They cannot escape. They feel they must tender, or they'll be trapped in a minority hell stuck with falling shares. Arbs were worse. Their only drive "is in a quick sale at a profit."[21] Lipton slammed the point home: "Rather than forcing directors to consider only the short-term interests of certain shareholders, national policy requires that directors also consider the long-term interests of the shareholders and the company as a business enterprise with all its constituencies in addition to the short-term and institutional shareholders." Even if experience showed that target shareholders uniformly profited from accepting tenders, he said, "There is no reason to remove the decision on a takeover from the reasonable business judgment of the directors."[22] A takeover bid, he concluded, is no different than any other business decision.

Lipton had a number of other things to say, mostly involving how to react when a hostile bid lands with a thump on a board table. Don't panic! Call in advisors, starting with the lawyers. Tackle issues sequentially. Be calm. He offered minutes of a fictional Board of Target Corporation under attack from Raider Inc. and involving lawyers Messrs. Joseph Lipton and Martin Flom of Skadden & Wachtell, with Cromwell & Polk as a special counsel to the board's banker, Sachs, Morgan & Co. This was a sly, if obvious, joke. No one in Chicago was laughing.

THE RELATIONSHIP BETWEEN law professors and legal practitioners has long been complicated, like a large, talky, disputatious family at Thanksgiving. They share some DNA, a language, a law school experience, but conflicts simmer. They are, like dog breeds, alike, yet different. They often see the world through different lenses and they are intensely ambitious at higher levels, though in different ways. They growl at each other. Legal academics indulge more readily in theory and write thick books and long articles bristling with footnotes, many unread; practitioners live with the reality of cases, deals, pushy clients, fees, briefs, cranky judges, and, in Louis Auchincloss, spare novels; they make more money but they have more ulcers. Academics care about obscure cases like *Dodge v. Ford,* the decades-long dustups over the American Law Institute's corporate governance guidelines, and the implications of a corporation as a nexus of contracts. They engage in the play of ideas, though it's true that in this era, many were convinced that economics gave them a profoundly accurate view of how the world worked, and were enthusiastic in prescribing remedies that involved vast disruption—for good or ill—for others, while being insulated from those very same forces of arbitrage and takeover themselves. (That mixed breed—judges—was often similarly insulated.)

Practitioners tend to be attracted to opinions they find useful, persuasive facts, precedent. They tend—there are no bright lines here—toward empiricism, a rough-and-ready utilitarianism, not toward theory. They adjust their beliefs, like their arguments, to those of their paying clients. They are both knowing and self-interested; it creates a residue of cynicism.

Lipton was a rarity; he had a foot in both camps, though less so in the classroom as M&A heated up. By 1979, he was forty-eight years old; he had stopped teaching a year earlier; he *knew* Berle, which was as if he'd been hanging out with Lincoln talking states' rights. In the 1970s, tensions between practicing corporate attorneys and academics rose, as the law and economics movement began to crank out books, theories, and judges, dropping talented disciples into law schools across America. Reagan embraced the Chicago gang, starting with the endlessly argumentative Friedman, and they rushed to serve him in Washington. Lipton's "Takeover Bids in the Target's Boardroom" was a jab at the law and economics academics, confident in their market-oriented, Chicago-style economic theories. And so one of the stranger skirmishes in the annals of intellectual combat erupted between the academics and the practitioners.

Chicago remained the epicenter. Frank Easterbrook and Daniel Fischel were two rising products of Chicago's law and economics movement. Both graduated from Chicago's law school: Easterbrook in 1973, Fischel in 1977. Easterbrook had been editor of the law review, clerked for a federal appeals judge, and served as a deputy solicitor general under Robert Bork during the Ford administration before returning to Chicago to teach in 1978. He edited the *Journal of Law & Economics* from 1982 to 1991 after Coase retired. Fischel was the comment editor of the law review, clerked for a federal judge, then for Potter Stewart on the Supreme Court. In 1980 he returned to Chicago to teach at Northwestern, then rejoined the University of Chicago Law School in 1984. Somewhere after 1980, Fischel and Easterbrook began to work together on M&A.

The result in April 1981 was "The Proper Role of a Target's Management in Responding to a Tender Offer" in that font of prestige, the *Harvard Law Review*.[23] This was not the first major application of new financial ideas to M&A: that probably belonged to a young law professor, Ronald Gilson, at Stanford Law a year earlier. But Easterbrook and Fischel's paper had the stamp of orthodoxy upon it. A few things are immediately apparent upon reading the forty-three-page article. First, Easterbrook and Fischel were responding to "Takeover Bids in the Target's Boardroom," and "The Proper Role" was, at the time, the official rejoinder from law and economics headquarters. The pair thanked twenty-five people, based in Chicago and Northwestern, including Richard Posner (soon to be a federal judge), Myron Scholes, David Ruder (eventually to replace John Shad as chairman of Reagan's SEC), and "participants" of law and economics workshops at Chicago and Harvard, mostly academics with a handful of practitioners. The Law and Economics Program at Chicago provided support. Then, there's the title: *proper*—a term last heard in dancing class. Easterbrook and Fischel are offering a corrective to deviance from "proper" norms of "scientific" fact. If Lipton has written a manifesto, Easterbrook and Fischel's tone is academic Olympian. Despite their utter certainty, the foundations of their argument—efficient markets and agency costs—were still damp. Theories loom, empirical facts were scarce, and qualifications—how efficient?—not yet present. Their truth broke with past norms and human nature. Where Lipton's arguments are tendentious, they're also familiar, anchored in history. Managers and boards run the show. Easterbrook and Fischel presented a view that even today seems iconoclastic and unsettling. They insisted that boards should accept the first takeover bid that appeared and immediately surrender. Companies, both managers and shareholders, were passive instruments in the powerfully shaping hands of the market. Struggle was irrational; in the long run, destructive. Defense was socially unworthy.

Even today, much of the paper has an unstable quality, as if the ground were heaving. Easterbrook and Fischel flung arguments at readers as if they were still in the workshop. They made declarations based on theory, which they supported with more theory. They piled up arguments, backed into key assumptions, dropped in phrases (then new) like "rational expectations" that cried out for further explanation; Chicago's use of the word *rational* in the early days took on a gnomic air. Their argument for efficient markets was a tissue of future and conditional tenses, and qualifying prepositional phrases:

> It is very unlikely that price and "value" will diverge in large markets for shares. If there were such divergences, investors would reap substantial gains by identifying and buying underpriced shares and selling overpriced shares. Since there are many sophisticated investors with ample capital, the arbitrage process would proceed quite quickly, and it would become impossible to make systematic gains by finding undervalued shares. As investors bought and sold on the basis of what they knew, their very activity would drive the price to the correct one. . . . Indeed, once information about a firm reached the market, prices would adjust quickly whether or not anyone traded, because no trader with rational expectations would sell for less than the price he expected the shares to reach once the news became widespread.[24]

They rhetorically tilted the table. Early on they wrote: "The ability of management to engage in defensive tactics in response to a cash tender offer is a relatively recent development in contests for corporate control."[25] The tricky part of that sentence is the insertion of "cash tender offers," as if that was, and had been, the only way to do M&A, and that playing defense—in, say, a proxy contest—had never occurred. They ignored the fact that the Williams Act had made tender offers viable on a large scale. They blamed the Williams Act for setting a deadline—the SEC doubled the time period to twenty days in late 1979—to respond to tender offers, putting would-be buyers at a disadvantage. Their counterintuitive implication: Tough defensive tactics represented a newfangled innovation that was somehow responsible for poor corporate performance. (This also ran contrary to what M&A

practitioners had been experiencing: defense was increasingly porous and weak. And that's without going as far as Lipton's belief that acceptance of a tender offer by shareholders "is a foregone conclusion.") Previous to 1968, Easterbrook and Fischel wrote, "offerors were free to structure offers in a manner designed to force shareholders to decide quickly whether to sell all or part of their shares at a premium." Of course, back then, there were relatively few tender offers. As they increased, both shareholders and managers complained that they were getting mugged; the bidder's "freedom" to force a bid hinged, as Lipton noted, on panicking boards and shareholders—coercion. But Easterbrook and Fischel saw any defense as retrograde, socially suboptimal, inefficient, money wasting, evidence of self-interest and agency costs; around that time, Stanford's Ronald Gilson declared that state courts that "facilitate such conduct, under the guise of deference to business judgment, do no more than sanction corporate treason."[26]

The Chicago pair painted a landscape radically different from Lipton's. They saw a world of ruthlessly efficient markets where rational traders arbitraged away mis-valuations and share prices mirrored available information. Managers could not logically argue that a premium bid was "too low"; markets *always* knew best, contrary to Lipton's belief that boards and managers possessed the best information on firm prospects, which gave them the freedom to reject a bid. Oddly, premium bids—that is, bids over the market price of the stock—weren't a violation of efficiency but proof that outsiders—certain outsiders— can discern agency costs that managers or shareholders cannot. Easterbrook and Fischel did not really explain how markets can be efficient but not in takeovers, failing to detect the presence of agency costs, which lurk like Dark Matter, allowing everything to net out. Managers are beset by self-interest; shareholders by passivity. Bidders are an odd category: a kind of wise investor, Platonic guardians that resemble robots with X-ray vision. "The most probable explanation for unfriendly takeovers emphasizes their role in monitoring the performance of corporate managers," they wrote, elaborating on Manne, and laying down a theme that Jensen would articulate for years: "The tender bidding process polices managers whether or not the tender offer occurs, and disciplines or replaces them if they stray too far from the service of shareholders. . . . The source of the premium is the reduction in agency costs, which makes the firm's assets worth more in the hands of the acquirer than they were worth in the hands of the firm's managers."[27] The logic of this would make every acquirer more discerning than every former-bidder-turned-manager. Incumbency was like a blinding disease. The insurgent was pure; the officeholder was corrupt.

Strangely enough, both Lipton and the Chicago pair viewed stockholders in a similarly harsh light. Lipton, of course, believed that shareholders were fixated on short-term considerations, coerced by interests inimical to long-term corporate health. Easterbrook and Fischel argued that shareholder limitations made outside raiders (who were also shareholders—just better) necessary. These true outsiders performed tasks that absentee, absentminded shareholders never would— or could. Outsiders are thus active, enterprising seekers for *control*. This desire for ownership seems to increase their acuity, based solely on the fact that they are putting their own money into the game (even if sometimes it's not really their money). Easterbrook and Fischel do not delve into the differences between the raider-as-shareholder versus the investor-as-shareholder. But as a general rule, both Lipton and the Chicago pair are empirically correct: throughout the modern era of M&A, most institutional shareholders—investors-as-shareholders— demonstrated little interest in monitoring. Passivity has been the rule. Governance may depend upon the shareholding institutions, but from the very beginning, both sides of the conflict were agreed upon one thing: they haven't been up to the task.

This created an unresolved tension. Easterbrook and Fischel demanded obedience to the general stockholders' will, while admitting that the bulk of shareholders didn't behave as good corporate citizens. In fact, they argued that shareholders should be restrained from any say in corporate actions, such as defense against takeover. There was a major exception: raiders-as-shareholders received enormous benefits— they did not need to struggle to triumph. They inherited the earth at a very low premium. To work at optimal efficiency, managers and boards (they saw boards as captive agents of managers) had to abandon competitive impulses—which, like Freudian analysis, always seemed to cover deeper self-interested drives—and blindly follow the dictates of the market. And yet the free market's defining virtue is competition. This odd form of competition, in which most players had their legs tied together, was best for everyone, now and in the future. "All parties," they promised, "benefit in this process," not just target shareholders, who get a premium, and bidding shareholders, who get an asset, but all shareholders, even society itself.[28]

Fischel and Easterbrook's passivity imperative applied even to what Lipton insisted was a key justification of an effective defense: to reward shareholders with larger premiums. The pair hammered away at this seemingly noncontroversial practice. High premiums made market performance difficult. "Any strategy," they wrote, "designed to prevent tender offers reduces welfare." They did not define how that welfare is spread around. "Even resistance that ultimately elicits a higher bid is socially wasteful." The reason: Target shareholders' gains are bidding shareholders' losses. "Shareholders *as a group* [my italics] gain nothing; the increase in the price is simply a transfer payment from the bidder's shareholders to the target's shareholders." Even worse, defense, or as they called it with a trace of moral opprobrium, *resistance,* consumed resources, which they also declared a waste. They recognized, they were lawyers after all, that this no-defense view conflicted with traditional fiduciary duties, in which boards and managers are expected to maximize shareholder returns, a concept familiar to Adam Smith. (Like market efficiency, the invisible hand is a canonic principle until it's inconvenient and abandoned for higher ends.) But in a daring, if possibly overreaching analogy, they compared "resistance" to an externality like pollution. Just as a company that treats pollution as a free good harms society at large, so too, they wrote, resistance to takeovers will boost costs and "generally discourage prospective bidders for other targets; when the price of anything goes up, the quantity demanded falls." This may not actually be the case. Some goods, from fine art to tulips to—as we're about to discover—companies, under certain conditions, become more valuable as prices rise.

This may not be "rational," but it is empirical—that is, observable or testable: It happens. (With its deep faith in efficient markets, Chicago has struggled over the years to explain sudden asset swings, like bubbles.) In addition, they clearly conflate "social good" with shareholder welfare.

The bottom line: Easterbrook and Fischel rejected any defensive strategies, mostly with the broad statement that defense attempted "to second-guess the market," which, they noted, "is unpersuasive." They cited Lipton arguing that widespread tenders "decrease social welfare" (again, promiscuous welfare) because they "adversely affect long-term planning and thereby jeopardize the economy."[29] (Their argument contra Lipton spills over into a long footnote that warred with his attack on arbs, who, they insisted, played a constructive role by buying shares from stockholders who wanted to sell and making markets more efficient.[30] In Chicago, arbitrage is *the* essential market process.) Again, the thrust of Easterbrook and Fischel's argument came down to markets. If markets recognized a long-term strategy, they rewarded the company with a higher stock price; if not, shares tumbled. Companies wracked by hostile bids, on the logic of smoke-and-fire, are managing for the short run and piling up agency costs. A takeover bid is, by its very nature, evidence of agency problems. The pair scoffed at Harold Williams's charge that tender offers gobbled up capital better used for investment into new equipment or R&D, or that raiders gained working majorities only to loot companies. They denied that such cases are possible in a rational, efficient, mechanical market system, even as the likes of Victor Posner rampaged through one company after another, leaving a smoldering trail of ruin behind. (Although Posner, no relation to the Chicago judge, fended off lawsuits and regulatory actions, he died in 2002 at eighty-three a very wealthy man: so much for Easterbrook and Fischel's reassurance that there were rules against looting.) Lastly, the two turned to bidders, dismissing widespread beliefs that "self-aggrandizing" buyers often overpaid for acquisitions that hurt shareholders. A bidder's share price would eventually fall if he overpaid, they noted; the company would become a takeover candidate and "managers would fare poorly in the employment market."[31] They offered no evidence or time frame for this process. They did not pause to consider that a wealthy manager might have little need for the job market, or that a rich if lousy manager could transform himself into a principal, a shareholder, or a raider-as-shareholder. They did not struggle with the possibility that a buyer might be someone else's agent, thus conspiring to advance his own self-interest. They did not worry over-much about the company as a living, organic operation run by people. Only the stock mattered.

For all of that, Easterbrook and Fischel's argument appealed to many. There was a gnawing sense that US companies had grown inefficient and uncompetitive, that managers and boards had entrenched themselves, that shareholders only cared about themselves. The system needed shaking up. There may have been some truth to that diagnosis, though it's difficult to truly know. A stakeholder model can entrench "empire-building" management and boards; companies may need restructuring after decades of prosperity and globally driven technological innovation; and shareholders, to this day and despite drumbeats of predictions to the contrary, have not shaken their passivity. The problem, however, was the foundational belief that markets are the wisest arbiter of all questions in all circumstances. Markets can be efficient and investors may be rational by their lights. And when companies act irrationally or incompetently, or stray from the "will" of shareholders, markets discipline them. This is not wrong, just simplistic. Easterbrook and Fischel, like their colleagues, ended up indulging in fantasies by demanding a single answer to complex socioeconomic and psychological matters. They expected too much of managers, shareholders, and, notably, markets. Their mechanical model ignored the ceaseless change that buffeted companies and the fact that they make choices in the face of Frank Knight's uncertain entrepreneurial future. Markets may be the best judge of current conditions—the one-eyed man in the land of the blind—but so are managers. And generally the light is dim, the shadows deceptive. Markets are efficient processors of available information; but information is rarely complete, available mostly about the past, not the future, and humanity is imperfect. The insight that agents and principals may differ in self-interest is indisputably true; but drawing an accurate bead on agency costs by insiders or outsiders is difficult, if not utopian. And simply saying that uninhibited takeovers will boost accountability and all good things ignores the reality of companies that have been bought and sold in a serial fashion, altering strategies, changing policies, eroding ties that bind workers to firms, disconcerting customers. Companies can be imagined as a nexus of contracts, but that's not how employees experienced the workplace. Motivating managers by constant threat of takeovers may produce unforeseen consequences, including a dispirited acceptance of fate or a short-term, self-interested culture of greed. Again, a self-fulfilling quality. Unleashed M&A is a blunt, risky, and, yes, sometimes necessary instrument.

True believers in Mr. Market envisioned a constructive and ceaseless process of arbitrage, a karma-like return to equilibrium and rationality. But there are reasons to be skeptical of that in its daily reality. Yes, arbitrage exists; but whether it is always wise is another matter. Whether it's asset prices, companies, or technologies, markets confronted by unknowable futures struggle to settle on a single price. What seems to make sense one day—say, the portfolio theory and diversification that drove conglomerates—may, a decade later, appear misguided. Markets enabled conglomerate buying in the '60s, then presided over their destruction in the '70s. Which was the efficient market? True, conditions change. But markets drew qualitatively different conclusions from the same companies and declared each gospel. Are these ideas purely relative? Are there no deeper truths beneath what Keynes called the market's penchant for beauty pageants? Even if markets can detect agency costs with precision, they're certainly not very good at sniffing out malfeasance—or predicting the future beyond tomorrow. Retroactively, M&A premiums may seem too low or too high; at the time they often seem just right. There are periods when markets cheer every deal by bidding up shares and others when they shun M&A like leprosy. (Studies demonstrate that the best results come in the most skeptical markets.) Some of this, again, involves a changing macroeconomy; but except for true believers, it's difficult to contemplate cycles of M&A and conclude that markets are omniscient. Markets, faced with the unknowable, may be of multiple minds and revolve around multiple equilibria, like souls fated to wander the earth. In reality, they are no different than the men and women who operate them.

Chapter Seven

THAT ELUSIVE BALANCE

THE SUBTLETIES OF Easterbrook and Fischel did not go unchallenged, even among the law and economics crowd. The movement was spreading beyond the South Side, beyond Evanston, from coast to coast. By the early '80s, the law and economics tent contained a group of bright, relatively young lawyers and law professors. They were argumentative. On the West Coast, Ronald Gilson, thirty-five years of age, from Stanford Law, wrote a sharp rejoinder to "The Proper Role," while on the East Coast, a research fellow at Harvard Law School, Lucian Bebchuk, born in Poland, educated in Israel, at twenty-six already the recipient of multiple degrees (math, economics, law) and soon-to-be law school faculty member, offered a few thoughts as well.[1] Neither of them defended Lipton, of course; he was banned from the tent. Both, however, rushed to remedy what was, from a practical standpoint, the weakest argument, if a central one, put forth by the pair from Chicago: the idea that companies should not struggle to resist even if they boosted the price and improved returns for target shareholders—the passivity notion that drove Lipton to write in the first place. The passivity argument threatened to render Manne's M&A-as-monitoring project vulnerable; counterintuition, paradox, nuance might be catnip in academia, but they threatened realism and common sense. By restraining shareholders, Easterbrook and Fischel threatened shareholder hegemony, not to say shareholder democracy. And so, wheeling out different arguments, Gilson and Bebchuk rushed to rescue the takeover as an ongoing auction whose goal was the highest price for shareholders.

Meanwhile, M&A was boiling over, making Easterbrook and Fischel's argument that resisting companies rendered takeovers uneconomic, and that defense was emasculating hostile offers, seem silly. It had been valid once: in the '60s, about two-thirds of contested takeovers had been defeated. (Even Lipton thought the Williams Act threatened tenders in 1973.) But that was then. As one journalist noted, "By 1979 or 1980, the shame of hostile takeovers had all but disappeared. Those who hesitated to make an unfriendly bid were now the exceptions. Just as important, nearly every major corporation found itself part of the process."[2]

Part of the violent expansion of M&A was the appearance of "The Proper Role's" theoretical raiders, agent-scourging principals wielding tender offers, seemingly conjured up from nowhere, at least in the newspapers, and suddenly able to borrow unprecedented amounts of money. But the likes of Carl Icahn, T. Boone Pickens, Saul Steinberg, Victor Posner, Irwin "Irv the Liquidator" Jacobs, Harry Gray, J. Ray McDermott, Michael Dingman, and later, Ted Turner, Sir James Goldsmith, and a host of others were not theoretical at all. In fact, they had always existed, but in the sideshow of the circus, not atop elephants in the center ring. They were very real, very individual, and very quickly larger-than-life figures. The press doted on them, academics hailed them as forces of accountability and efficiency, and anxious corporations demonized them. They were portrayed as iconoclasts, entrepreneurs, mavericks, or (depending on where you were sitting) thugs, blackmailers, pirates. An entire mythology grew up around them so that at least one academic pair compared them to the psychoanalytically oriented fairy tales of Bruno Bettelheim.[3] They hunted in packs, as corporate or as individual raiders. Icahn, raised in Far Rockaway, Queens, and educated at Princeton (BA in philosophy, a short stint in medical school), started off as an arb and options trader and slid into stock picking, then by 1978 began taking larger and larger stakes. He quickly and loudly popularized Jensen and Meckling's core agency conflict shorn of theory: he, as a proxy for shareholders, would battle executives, notably CEOs and their lackey boards, who were mostly corrupt, stupid, foolish, incompetent, or possibly nuts. (As late as 2014, in an interview, Icahn admitted with his usual off-kilter charm that he had a genius for reductionism.[4]) His core message would remain unchanged for nearly forty years. Others, oddly enough, wielded considerable corporate power. Gray (who picked up a nickname, the Gray Shark, but whose public profile was pretty tame compared to some of the lone raiders) was a throwback: a conglomerateur who ran United Technologies. McDermott, the scion of a New Orleans oil-rig outfit, who outbid Gray for Babcock & Wilcox in 1980, was diversifying through M&A. Dingman was actively growing and reshaping Wheelabrator-Frye with acquisitions. A rare few, like Pickens, who ran Mesa Petroleum, seemed to tap both wells of metaphorical energy.

Much of the high-profile action involved energy and natural resources companies, some of the largest in the world. With share prices low, the public cost of assets looked a lot cheaper than the private cost of replacing them; an arbitrage play suddenly yawned opened. By the late '70s, inflation had become as chronic as smoker's cough. Inflation reshaped economic relations: It depressed stock prices, making underlying assets, mostly energy reserves like oil and gas, even cheaper. As Peter Drucker wrote, trying to explain this hostile M&A eruption in American capitalism: "Inflation distorts. It distorts values. It distorts relationships. It creates glaring discrepancies between economic assumptions and economic realities. . . . And the most predictable, indeed the most typical distortion of inflation, is between the value of assets and their earning power."[5] Anticipating another oil crisis, a mad scramble to acquire natural resource assets began. This represented a sharp break from a period when energy companies recklessly grabbed anything that was *not* oil and gas and ran counter to what Columbia law professor Louis Lowenstein dubbed in a 1983 paper "the pruning deadwood model of M&A"—that is, roughly the Chicago worldview. "The cheapest oil is on Wall Street," Lowenstein wrote. "No one suggested that the natural resource companies, such as Conoco, Marathon, and St. Joe Minerals, were undermanaged. [Well, Icahn and

Pickens did.] Indeed, acquiring companies like U.S. Steel and DuPont went to great lengths, even after the transactions were consummated, to reassure their more experienced target managements."[6]

Once begun, the M&A frenzy fed upon itself, even after Paul Volcker's Federal Reserve hiked interest rates in 1980 and sent the economy crashing, inadvertently ensuring—it was always a possibility but, combined with Iranian hostages, Volcker sealed the deal—that Carter would lose to Reagan in the election of 1980. Volcker snuffed inflation, too. The subsequent recession, named for Reagan, lasted until 1982, at which time new forces emerged to feed the already blazing M&A phenomenon. And even as inflation ebbed, assets looked remarkably cheap from a market perspective.

The M&A boom evolved in other ways that threatened the clear dichotomies of Easterbrook and Fischel. Corporations battling other corporations for assets confused the principal-agent distinction. As CEO, J. Ray McDermott was both an agent for shareholders of his oil-rig company, when he won Babcock & Wilcox from Gray, and a principal, since he owned much of the stock. So were many other corporate buyers. These hostile raids also spawned more players than a Restoration drama; five or six corporate entities circling a target, like wolves about a lamb, was not unusual. And it took considerable theoretical dexterity to discern how raiders contributed to a "general" shareholder interest, except share prices popped when they wandered into the neighborhood. (If the stock elevated even for a few days, the Chicago folks viewed that as justification for nearly anything.) Pickens, for instance, was a shrewd, smoothly articulate oil wildcatter-turned-big company hunter, who used his corporation, Mesa Petroleum, to stalk larger and larger energy targets. Joe Nocera was one of the few reporters who saw through the image and noted Pickens's "impression of ordinariness." As Nocera observed in *Texas Monthly:* "He does not exude charisma. He favors unostentatious business suits and shuns accouterments like flashy rings and cowboy boots."[7] Generally, though, Pickens was happy to exploit the cowboy image, as filtered through Clint Eastwood movies and Marlboro ads. As one account said: "Larger than life, frightening and maddening to those who would feel the brunt of his power, he appeared to emerge from nowhere."[8] (Amarillo, home of Mesa, was obscure, but hardly "nowhere.") Pickens was persuasive in his attacks on the performance and failures of bloated, imperial, integrated oil companies. And eventually, nearly every major US oil and gas company found itself either seeking a merger partner or defending itself against Pickens, Icahn, or various Texas oil interests (like Sid Bass or the Cullen family) awash in the financial resources they stirred up. And why not? The pickings were so easy. Borrow, buy, dump the debt on the target balance sheet—or walk away with easy share gains. Pickens was not alone, but he was a particularly devoted practitioner of greenmail, the then–perfectly legal practice of shaking down a company until it either surrendered or paid you a premium on your shares to go away, a kind of insidious conspiracy of principal and agent. Icahn referred to greenmail as "a kind of arbitrage" and Chicago justified it, calling it "targeted repurchases," an element of a beneficial management-monitoring process. Still, it was difficult to wrap your head around how greenmail fit into the moral dichotomy of principals and agents.

Inflation was the economic trigger, but it wasn't the only factor. More technical matters were tripping switches deep in the regulatory circuitry. By 1980, the Williams Act was only twelve years old, but it was a worn-out, much-traveled, *old* twelve; it had led a hard life—and it was about to get harder. The Williams Act is a case study in unintended consequences, mistaken views of the future, and wishful thinking. Williams proposed the bill in the mid-'60s during the conglomerate craze initially provoked by a 1966 tender-offer statute in Virginia. He first said he wanted to protect small shareholders, but from a political standpoint he was clearly responding to complaints from "proud old companies" confronted by sudden, fast, take-it-or-leave-it, no-choice conglomerate bids: dawn raids or Saturday Night Specials. In fact, the initial version of the bill was so tilted toward stifling tenders that the Securities and Exchange Commission took the uncharacteristic step of asking Williams for a rewrite. His next proposal eased up a bit, the bill passed, and Williams publicly acknowledged the goal of using M&A as a monitoring mechanism, without, in the SEC's words, "tipping the balance of regulation either in favor of management or in favor of the person making the takeover bid."[9] Instead, surprising nearly everyone, the act opened floodgates of M&A, including hostile takeovers. (After he left office in 1968, Manuel Cohen, who headed the SEC when the act was passed, declared the legislation "obsolete" and its use of disclosure "inadequate" to safeguard investors caught up in "mid-20th-century economic warfare." The date: March 1969.[10]) This occurred in part because that sacrosanct constituency, small shareholders, who accounted for 80 percent of all stock holdings in the late '60s, began evaporating as institutions took over. By the early '80s, institutional ownership neared 50 percent, far higher for larger stocks. For all their buttoned-up passivity, performance-fixated institutions were apt to reflexively grab M&A premiums, as Lipton argued, and, aligned with that dawning consciousness of self-interest, to embrace M&A as a monitoring mechanism. Institutions had their own problems, particularly the pension funds. They were large, powerful—and insecure. Vanishingly few could beat the stock market. And the defined-benefit plans they provided funded fixed (and growing) obligations with performance from fluctuating markets, a big problem in the grim '70s. Declared Drucker: "In the long and checkered history of investment and finance, there is probably no more uniformly dismal record than that of the American pension fund management in the last twenty years."[11] Moreover, he argued, as "trustees" both for companies sponsoring the plans and for beneficiaries—a bit of an agency problem right there, not unlike CEOs acting as raiders—they *had* to take any premium offer, no matter the "deleterious" result on the company. Added Drucker, channeling Lipton: "But they [the institutions] cannot consider the welfare and interests of their 'property.' They are not 'owners.' They are of necessity 'speculators,' even though they are legally vested with the owner's power.'"[12]

As for those once impregnable corporations, the decline of small shareholders left management politically exposed and isolated, though the romance of the small shareholder, like that of the family farm, lingered in Washington and among the public for decades. Drucker made the point that large corporations defended themselves successfully only when they rallied "constituencies" to their cause, as Phillips

Petroleum mobilized employees and its home community of Bartles-
ville, Oklahoma, to drive off Pickens. But that was a rare application
of a rapidly fading stakeholder model.

THE WILLIAMS ACT was a fragile vessel that was not designed to channel the tsunami of M&A that slammed into it. Tender offers were
about as tender as a punch to the face. As Stanford's Gilson wrote,
"The tactical history of the tender-offer movement resembles an unrestrained arms race."[13] The act hinged on regulatory themes enshrined
in the New Deal reforms of 1933 and '34: transparency, disclosure,
neutrality. The SEC, typically, viewed the act as forming a kind of
neutral site, a demilitarized zone, where all parties could gather to
transact; the agency envisioned itself as a fair-minded cop or referee,
enforcing a balance among an array of interests, without intervening
overtly. This would prove to be very difficult. In tender offers, shareholders and managers required a modicum of information and, very
importantly, time, to decide whether to accept a bid. Investors were
protected with withdrawal rights—that is, the ability to change their
minds, particularly in the event of a better offer—and a complicated
method of pro-rating, or valuing, shares in the case of partial bids for
cash. This ensured a zero-sum game between those shareholders who
grabbed the high cash bid and those who were left with a weaker offer
of shares, or a falling market price. Guessing where that sweet spot was
located in any given offer would prove to be tortuous as M&A engaged in a frenzied evolution. As a result, the SEC altered elements of
the bill—the share threshold, the filing deadline—in 1970, 1973, and
1976—and boosted disclosures. In 1979, hardly a decade after passage,
the SEC again revisited the act, under the pressure of mounting numbers of M&A deals that were increasingly large and hostile.

This balancing act was no science, and neither the SEC nor Congress had much in the way of an underlying governance theory to support it. Much of this stemmed from what Joel Seligman, in his
authoritative history of the SEC, blamed on the "breadth of the SEC's
jurisdiction" and "the vagueness of pivotal provisions" of its enabling
statutes. "Congress," he wrote, "created an extraordinarily broad

mandate that all but ensured that significant portions of it would be ignored." He cited James Landis, one of the architects of the agency and an early chairman, in his cogent primer from 1938, *The Administrative Process:*[14] "Agencies will be led most efficiently by experts when their jurisdiction is narrow."[15] The SEC had long been slow to confront governance. It had never spent much time on proxy rules and viewed most problems, such as cases of corporate bribery, as remedied by disclosure. "At no time, however, did the Commission systematically study corporate governance, as it often earlier had the securities markets or investment companies," wrote Seligman. "No SEC special study of corporate governance investigated such fundamental questions of how it was possible for so much fraud and falsification of corporate records to have existed despite existing SEC and state laws. Or how, in fact, the giant corporation was governed. Or whether it would be appropriate to replace or augment the corporate board of directors with new mechanisms to ensure accountability." In short, he wrote, "[i]t never seriously considered the possibility of postwar changes in the structure of the giant corporation."[16]

This left both Congress and the SEC exposed, particularly at the end of the '70s as the political scene lurched to the right. By 1979, when the SEC felt pressure to reset the dials again on tender offers, there were new complexities. Federal courts were hit by tender-offer suits and, over time, developed a variety of views on the practice. Under pressure from mounting M&A, the states, thirty-six of them by 1981, had begun writing their own takeover regulations—more accurately *anti*-takeover rules—mostly to protect agitated local companies and unions from what they viewed as predation. This confused the scene considerably, gave the lawyers a lot of work, and raised constitutional issues. Initially in 1979, under political pressure, the SEC anticipated raising the offer period to thirty days. And the agency seriously pondered taking the startling step of actually *defining,* in a tentative way, what a tender offer was and when it applied. This was more significant than it seems. In 1968 Congress and the SEC had deliberately avoided defining the technique, leaving the shaping process to judges and circumstances, like wind and rain sculpting a lump of sandstone

over many eons; this was part of its New Deal heritage.[17] It was a con-
cession to the belief, stemming from the late 1930s, the "second" Great
Depression, that government intervention often spawned more problems than it solved. It was, paradoxically, a recipe for a large, active
administrative state. As historian Alan Brinkley wrote:

> Liberal prescriptions for federal economic policies were becoming
> more detached from the vision of a harmonious capitalist world [in
> the late '30s]. The state could not, liberals were coming to believe,
> in any fundamental way "solve" the problems of the economy. The
> industrial economy was too large, too complex, too diverse. . . .
> The new breed of administrators would operate from no "master
> plan." Nor would they ever reach a point where economic reforms
> obviated the need for their own services. Rather they would be
> constantly active, ever vigilant referees (or as [FDR's antitrust chief
> Thurman] Arnold liked to put it, "traffic managers"), always ready
> to step into the market to remove "bottlenecks," to protect effi-
> ciency and competition, and to defend the interests of consumers,
> who were replacing producers as the ultimate focus of liberal
> concern.[18]

It was an idea of governing by technocrats, with its roots in Veblen
and Walter Lippmann, which informed Harvard economist John
Kenneth Galbraith's belief in a balance of countervailing powers in
the late '50s. By then, Berle, too, had accepted the need for a kind of
"managed capitalism."

In a sense, regulation as a balance of forces was a variant of stakeholdership, an acknowledgment of diverse interests and points of view.
The problem was that by the late '70s many of those stakeholder constituencies were either losing power or being redefined as illegitimate
or irrelevant. In its place, a kind of *realpolitik* took over, embodied in
rising litigation that Flom's Skadden, in particular, came to symbolize.
Skadden was self-consciously aggressive; Lincoln Caplan in his history
of the firm called it "hardball" and viewed it as a decline in legal standards. He quoted a female Skadden partner: "Don't forget, I'm at

Skadden Arps now. We *pride* ourselves on being assholes. It's part of the firm culture."[19] (There was a lot of handwringing over this. Caplan recounts a panel of lawyers trying to define "hardball." One panel member described it as "'meanspiritedness,' 'son-of-a-bitchedness,' and different from being stern, firm, and seizing the strategic advantage." He finally came up with a name: Ramboism. Skadden, he said, practiced Ramboism.) And the lawyers, who served their clients, actually had restraints—a leash, Caplan calls it—that the bankers, the raiders, the managers generally lacked. In any event, the strongest, most active, most powerful, wealthiest constituencies that could hire the most aggressive lawyers, tended to win. And as the forces at play shrank in number, they grew more powerful and their collisions became more violent.

Neither Congress nor the SEC in 1968 saw M&A as part of a fundamental governance problem—"governance," at the time, had few contentious issues; rather, they viewed it as as a technical matter that provided balance and order to legitimate interests. Tender-offer reform arose after a series of abuses: secret tender offers (attacker unidentified), side-deal tenders (secret cash payments for stocks), and coercive midnight raids. The no-definition policy provided flexibility and allowed for natural change to occur. Besides the fact that the SEC didn't want to expend the time and labor involved in micromanaging every M&A deal (since its birth the SEC had favored self-regulating organizations, such as stock exchanges, whenever possible), why knowingly plunge into a political tar pit that might stir up Congress, draw unwanted attention, and trigger ever-more budget-busting rules to be administered? And there were further implications to this balancing policy. Where were the political inputs coming from? Clearly, the law firms, the institutions, and a rapidly reviving Wall Street, with fewer but far larger firms, all effectively argued their cases, which were allied to their self-interests. The academic voice of the law and economics movement was also growing louder, supporting shareholder hegemony, magnified by Reagan's ascent and by the quiet support of the institutions. On the declining side, individual shareholders were losing power—their lack of organization didn't help; Lipton believes the balance tipped from retail to institutional around 1980. Corporate managements certainly had their own case to make, but they increasingly accepted the corporation as a shareholder-owned entity, not as an institution defending the interests of workers, communities, customers, the nation; this became clearer as more corporations took to the offensive in hostile M&A. (Perhaps they never had protected their stakeholders very effectively, which may explain why so few tried to mobilize those constituencies in defensive battles. What if no one responded?) As to "consumers," they were far too amorphous and atomized to play any role beyond lip service, except when a major, politically explosive scandal erupted. Then they became that scariest of constituencies—angry voters.

M&A was one factor driving a powerful self-fulfilling process: loyalties, from both employer and employees, were fraying. In particular, and as with the small shareholder, the power of labor had peaked and was receding as American industrial preeminence and the collective power of organized labor slipped. The '70s saw a major migration of industrial jobs around the country, around the world; the '80s welcomed the Rust Belt to American iconography. Management was making more money, but living with greater uncertainty. The lifetime job was increasingly rare. Theory met practice: this was an agency world, a nexus of contracts society, and an arena of clashing self-interests. It's no surprise that public choice, the study of self-interested agents in politics, became a growth field in academia during this period.

By 1979, the SEC was losing the courage of its no-definition conviction. In June, John Evans, one of five SEC commissioners, tackled the subject before a meeting of the National Association of Corporate Directors in New York. Evans was a moderate Utah Republican who had been a minority staffer on the Senate committee that passed the Williams Act and had been appointed by Richard Nixon as an SEC commissioner, then reappointed (after a painful delay) by Jimmy Carter. He believed in regulation. The SEC, he admitted in a speech, faced a conflict that had to be resolved between the need for certainty by practitioners and the "need for flexibility to assure that the statutory purposes are fulfilled."[20] The SEC had feared, he said, that defining tender offers would "facilitate circumvention of the statutory goal," that is, skirt the rules, engage in loophole management and manipulation—he did not utter that later phrase, regulatory arbitrage, that borrowed from Chicago's favorite market practice. Clearly, some of that had already occurred. Evans, a longtime advocate for small investors—an increasingly anachronistic stance—told his audience he believed that with so many tender offers, practitioners and the SEC had developed adequate certainty in terms of action; he may have been optimistic, given the frenzy of change. But the objectives of the Williams Act, he admitted, were under fierce attack by both states and practitioners; he needn't mention clever tacticians like Lipton and Flom. And so Evans blandly announced that the SEC would offer for the first time a clearer definition of the tender offer. Those nodding off that day after lunch could easily have missed the powerful forces Evans was gingerly referring to:

> [T]he tender offer field is occupied by participants of perhaps unparalleled financial and legal sophistication. The constant evolution in tender offer practice is a tribute to their ingenuity and resourcefulness. What is now considered a tender offer was ill defined in the 1960s. Since the beginning of 1978, we have seen increasing attempts to acquire control through novel transactions. These transactions serve to illustrate the difficulties inherent in attempting to articulate a static definition of an activity that is dynamic in nature. This is presumably the basis for the view attributed to Congress by an often-cited treatise that the absence of a definition is due to the fact that Congress . . . believed that a tender offer might well encompass transactions yet unborn, which were not considered tender offers in general custom or usage.[21]

This was a significant admission, and one that, consciously or not, conceded that administrative techniques built on balancing forces were giving way under blows of very smart, inventive, highly paid practitioners. These blows put the SEC on the defensive. The cop, outgunned and outmanned, contemplated retreat into a bunker of

definitions and rules, mandating stability, leveling the playing field—
that is, enforcing a theoretical, and often elusive, equality. This was a
step regulators hesitated to take. Leveling the playing field demanded
an active effort not to balance forces but to reorder them: to make
choices, to pick winners and losers. In the Chicago worldview, this
amounted to usurping a market prerogative, provoking charges of politics, regulatory overreach, inefficiency, inequity, corruption. In the
new Reagan administration, any mention of leveling the playing field
was anathema—despite recommendations from Fischel and Easterbrook, such as the passivity mandate, which demanded just that. Increasingly, the free-market crowd energized by Reagan declared *any*
regulation to be a form of leveling the playing field, or social engineering. Regulation came to mean a binary option: standing pat or, when
things went wrong and stirred political pressures, furiously tossing up
vast structures of new rules, which were rationalized as simple right
and wrong answers but only produced greater complexity, greater ambiguities, and, paradoxically, greater leeway for regulatory action. The
latter was a few years off yet, but coming.

In November 1979, the SEC, retreating from its thirty-day plan,
issued a new, twenty-day deadline rule for tender offers. There was no
definition included in the package. The agency instead suggested eight
factors, which lawyers could use to determine whether or not a tender
offer had actually been made, as opposed to more conventional open-
ended or privately negotiated transactions that lacked the protections
of the Williams Act. (The federal court in the Becton Dickinson, Sun
Oil case used these factors to determine that Sun had violated the
Williams Act and was criticized for it.) This "test," as one law review
article said, "is to be applied flexibly—all indicia need not be present
in each transaction and the weight accorded each factor is determined
on a case-by-case basis, resulting in after-the-fact, *ad hoc* judgments
by the courts."[22] Someone had to make the judgment, and it wouldn't
be the regulators; they resisted exposing themselves to the crossfire.
The federal courts did try to use the multifactorial guidelines. But the
test, as the authors noted, had unintended consequences: the federal
guidelines, as one critic offered, "invites litigation, makes planning

difficult and implicitly acknowledges interstices in the structure of the Williams Act which bidders will continually exploit to escape pervasive regulation. In addition, it forces judges to unscramble completed transactions, which judges are reluctant to do unless the behavior is egregious."[23]

M&A was on a slippery slope, which it was rolling down with increasing speed.

Chapter Eight

JUICY BRUCEY

Most people don't think.

—BRUCE WASSERSTEIN to *Esquire*, 1984[1]

T HE WORD THAT came to mind when meeting Bruce Wasserstein was rarely *balance*. He was a figure of a bewildering number of parts, few of which seemed to fit together snugly. He was lumbering, overweight, and famously disheveled. His thinning hair was often awry; his shoelaces were often untied; he could make the most expensive suit appear ill-fitting; and he rarely convened a meeting without food, from cookies to egg cream, within easy reach. He was one of those people for whom appearances do not seem to matter. This went way back—his college friends endearingly recall him as a slob—and ran against the grain of your typical corporate attorney-turned-investment banker.

In some ways, Wasserstein resembled the character of Kenneth Widmerpool in Anthony Powell's *Dance to the Music of Time,* a figure of portly ridicule who inexplicably grows ever-more powerful in London's financial center, The City. But Wasserstein was far too complex for comic caricature to capture, though the *New York Post*, which for years ran a photo of him with two bosomy models, tried. Nicknames attached themselves to him; even as a child he was "Bruce the Moose." Wasserstein was notoriously brilliant, though many found him off-putting and baffling; interpreting him was a full-time job, and there was always the suspicion that perhaps he was just talking nonsense. Like Widmerpool, he was both sensitive to slights and *seemed* oblivious to insults. Brilliance was his calling card; he played neither golf nor tennis (he did captain the tennis team in high school) nor did he accomplish much physically short of walking on the beach. Everyone has a running conversation in their heads: Wasserstein's inner voice must have been very compelling. He did not so much converse as produce monologues, often looking up as if he were offering these ideas to a higher authority. He suffered deficits of small talk. This could create a strained social dynamic; his conversants, even CEOs and clients, felt he was either talking over them or looking past them, or engaged in endless games of negotiating. His humor could sting. Often, these monologues crested in his "Dare to be great" speech, which convinced one commentator, without evidence, to argue that he had a Nietzschean übermensch complex—in other words, that he was sort of a Nazi.[2] This was crazy. He developed a reputation for arrogance, self-absorption, and self-aggrandizement, but he was capable of great kindness and generosity and could engender considerable loyalty. Politically, he remained a fairly standard liberal Democrat, which fit uneasily with his merger magnate role. "He's exceedingly goal-oriented," a source close to him told *Institutional Investor* in 1984. "And he cares as much about how his goals are perceived as he does in attaining them. He's certainly insecure that way. He not only has got to do things, he's got to tell everyone about it."[3] In 1987, financial journalist Jeff Madrick cast him as the epitome of the Baby Boomer for his uneasy mix of liberal politics and lust for "worldly success": "If anyone fit into the simplified description of his generation found in the movie *The Big Chill*, it was Wasserstein." Madrick was correct about one thing: *The Big Chill* was, like the analogy, simplified, not to say clichéd. (He wasn't there first, either: *Esquire* applied that same movie reference to Wasserstein in 1984.)[4]

He was born into a family of five children, one of whom was the playwright Wendy Wasserstein, another of whom was a pioneering female executive at American Express and Citibank, Sandra Meyer; his father, Morris, had emigrated from Poland and developed a successful ribbon business: Bruce was another son of the garment trades. He was born in Brooklyn, made the then-epochal leap to tony

Manhattan where he attended the private McBurney School (as had Rohatyn), then enrolled at the University of Michigan at sixteen. For years he was drawn to journalism. Despite his tender age, he won the job of executive editor of the *Michigan Daily* in 1966 and 1967; one of his predecessors, Tom Hayden, used that same editorial soapbox to help found the Students for a Democratic Society in 1960. Wasserstein never lost his affection for the newsroom, for trying to net reality in catch phrases, though his long, fitful, and often too-clever-by-half interplay with the media in the end could not be described as successful. He committed some fatal errors: talking to everyone, then leaking to a few, then going mostly silent—proving to be fallibly human after epic success. Public humility did not come easily to him. Besides, he often made many reporters feel dumb or, worse, manipulated. After his death in 2009, the *Michigan Daily* published an obituary accompanied by a photograph of the newsroom, circa 1966. Wasserstein stands in the center, dressed in a dark suit and tie with a mop of dark hair and black glasses. Everyone around him is talking, but he is staring off into the middle distance, a pencil balanced upright in his left hand, lost in thought, ready, like a young Cicero, to declaim.[5]

For all his talk, few knew Wasserstein's mind. Perhaps he didn't either; there was a lot of stuff crammed in there. His later book on the merger business, *Big Deal,* was thick, heavy, but unrevealing of his personal feelings.[6] His Michigan friends discerned no special turn to high finance, despite his "amazing" intellect and nascent feel for "strategizing," the latter of which could have been a retrospective judgment. "The key thing about Bruce was he was incredibly smart [and] he was a total slob in college," said one of his classmates.[7] Another of his colleagues once noted, "People don't know how seriously to take him because he did, and does, like to present himself as a parody."[8] After graduating with a degree in political science, he continued to pursue politics and journalism. He spent the summer of 1969 as an intern at *Forbes Magazine,* after which he decided—or not—to become a practitioner, not a reporter. He married in 1968 and enrolled in a joint Harvard Law, Harvard Business School program. He excelled everywhere: a Baker Scholar at HBS, in the top 2 percent of his HLS class—though, unlike Flom, he did not make the *Harvard Law Review,* editing the civil rights law review instead—and graduated with a JD cum laude. One of his Harvard Law classmates was a young, politically engaged New Yorker, Mark J. Green, who brought Wasserstein into Nader's operation, Nader's Raiders. In 1970, Green and Wasserstein edited a book for Nader called *With Justice for Some: An Indictment of the Law by Young Advocates.* Wasserstein wrote about the law and campus affairs. Two years later, the pair helped edit a Nader study-group publication, *The Closed Enterprise System,* which condemned the federal government for failing to enforce antitrust laws. In 1972, he won a Knox Traveling Fellowship to study British merger law at Cambridge University. On his return, he published his findings in the *Yale Law Review.* He later reviewed a late book of John Kenneth Galbraith's for the *Harvard Law Review.*

In 1974, he became a first-year associate at, of all firms, the corporate firm *par excellence,* Cravath Swaine & Moore. Wasserstein was certifiably bright but he hardly resembled anything Paul Cravath imagined. He had divorced and remarried, and he tacked steadily toward M&A. He didn't need to read Brill to recognize what was happening. He had a habit of dominating his surroundings, even as an associate; some Cravath partners must have quickly grown tired of hearing him declaim on British merger law. In 1977 Joe Perella, a tall, bearded, balding, rail-thin accountant and Harvard Business School graduate at First Boston—another top-drawer Wasp haven, though Perella's background was Newark Italian and the drawer had gotten shabby—walked into a deal meeting with some Cravath attorneys and First Boston bankers. Perella had begun building that firm's first merger department in 1973. (Perella later told *Institutional Investor* he was struck by a cover story on Rohatyn in *Business Week:* "I remember reading about all the fees he had collected working on deals. I was so impressed. I said: 'God, this is really a great business to be in. You don't use any of the firm's capital—at least you didn't in those days—and you made these nice fees. You know, this is a *great* business.'")⁹ Twenty minutes into the meeting, Perella said, this Cravath associate had "virtually taken charge. He was telling everyone the way the deal should be done from a lawyer's perspective and I said, 'Holy cow, this guy is unreal.'"[10] In another interview, Perella described the moment as if it were an infatuation out of Tom Wolfe. "He talked once, made a couple of points and bingo, *boing!*—it happened like that. I don't know who that son of a bitch is, but I gotta get to know him—he is something else. What a piece of work!"[11]

Perella, who had been lunching with Flom regularly since 1973 after meeting him on a deal, was eager to build deeper ties to Cravath and called up Samuel Butler, the firm's M&A expert who would become managing partner of the firm in 1980. Butler was the very model of Paul Cravath's dream: a small-town Indiana kid who attends Harvard College (plays football) and Harvard Law School and is astoundingly successful at *everything.* Butler sent Perella a list of his partners, but Wasserstein's name wasn't on it. Perella inquired. Cravath, said Butler, rotated its associates through various departments and Wasserstein had just left for municipal finance. Perella pressed on, requesting Wasserstein for a deal in which Cities Service, represented by First Boston, was considering acting as a white knight for Otis Elevator, which was under attack from Gray's United Technologies. He got him. On the plane back from Tulsa, where Cities Service was headquartered, Perella impulsively offered to hire him. In at least one telling of this tale, Wasserstein uttered words rarely heard from him: "Gee, I never thought of that."

Wasserstein then went to Butler to seek advice—and to get a sense of his future at Cravath. In a 2006 interview, Butler said he told Wasserstein, "It is not that you're not going to be a partner here; you might very well, as you're a bright, imaginative guy. I think from your very own personal preferences, you would be better off on the business side of things."[12]

Butler may have been right, but there are unplumbed depths to his advice. Wasserstein was a naturally disruptive force. As Butler also said, "Bruce even then was brash, obviously intelligent, outspoken." Intelligence was necessary at any major law firm, but not enough. Cravath wasn't clientless Skadden Arps hiring Joe Flom. It was stuffed full of talent, ego, and veins of lock-jawed prejudice. Law firms are delicate social organisms, semi-democratic in nature at the partnership level and often full of divas (not to say dependent on serfs, that is, associates, like ancient Greek city-states), and the selection of new partners hinges on many factors, even in a firm transforming itself for new transactional times. Wasserstein undoubtedly had already annoyed partners; he rarely knew his place. But Perella, in actually requesting an associate for help rather than a partner, may have sealed his fate at Cravath. Wasserstein went off to "the business side of things"— Cravath, in Butler's view, was not a business but a calling—and took his eccentricities to First Boston. Butler's message had been smoothly conveyed, as one would expect. Butler knew Cravath might need First Boston just as much as Perella needed Wasserstein. Besides, Perella was willing to double Wasserstein's $50,000 associate's salary. Butler was an articulate advocate for Cravath's traditional lockstep compensation system in which partners move up the income scale by seniority. His "personal preferences" comment may simply have been a recognition of Wasserstein's impatience and appetite for money and power. Or it was a sign that he would never be offered a Cravath partnership, that he was not really a Cravath Man.

The history of First Boston's rise to M&A preeminence has been told many times. Wasserstein recalled just how slowly they had started in 1977. Note the royal "we."

> From the date of my arrival at First Boston in the summer of 1977 through the following Thanksgiving, we had no business, we didn't have one deal. But we did a lot of work on long-term strategies to differentiate First Boston in mergers from other firms. We realized we could not be competitive arranging deals on the golf course. Therefore we tried to figure out whether we could be effective through the elbow-grease route and what we saw as an opportunity to professionalize the M&A business. We said we will be more knowledgeable about the conceptualization of transactions, the analysis of transactions, and the implementation of transactions.[13]

What remains striking, and underplayed, is how skillfully Perella handled Wasserstein. There was his realization that this pudgy, wild-haired, tieless, jean-clad savant without socks was a talented M&A tactician; that, in a sense, was the easy part. But Wasserstein was only the second Jew in First Boston's corporate finance department; the firm, with its Waspy veneer and its ship pictures, was struggling, and made Cravath look diverse. Perella didn't care; he wasn't exactly bred for the firm, either. He referred to Wasserstein as "Juicy Brucey." But Perella also recognized that to keep Wasserstein, he would have to share power with him. *We.* Wasserstein characteristically had already made clear he wanted to run a firm. Wall Street firms are not sand-boxes; Wall Streeters play rough for both money and power, which are tightly bound together. But Perella, who had built First Boston's merger department, clearly saw how his own considerable talents, par-ticularly for handling clients and superiors, meshed with Wasserstein's knowledge of tax and M&A law, thereby reducing their flaws as indi-vidual bankers. And so in 1979, after J. Tomilson Hill, an impeccably coiffed and adept banker, left Perella for Smith Barney, Perella went to Jack Hennessy, then head of investment banking, and offered to share power with the thirty-two-year-old Wasserstein. As Perella, then thirty-eight, said in a quote that appears in a number of accounts: "Jack frowned and said, 'This doesn't usually work on Wall Street.' I said, 'It doesn't because it's usually imposed on people. I'm imposing it on myself. I can't come and bitch to you, ever.'"[14]

Their competitors were not gracious about this partnership, which built its business by taking clients away from other firms, often in mid-deal, or as Perella called them, "street brawls," a distant echo of Demas's "fights." Wasserstein was the lightning rod. As one banker "hissed" to *Institutional Investor,* "It's a real tribute to First Boston and Joe Perella that they can tolerate Bruce's motivated flamboyance."[15]

The rise of Wasserstein and Perella's First Boston represented the coming of age of the Wall Street firm as a power unto itself in M&A. First Boston's M&A business was a long way from Felix Rohatyn's conception of the client-centric banker. Rohatyn remained a true be-liever in the proper role of the intermediary, the middle man, in that violation of agency theory, the loyal advisor; Wasserstein, First Boston, and the major firms—even Goldman Sachs, which still refused to advise on hostile deals, but was softening—were well on the way toward conceiving of themselves less as agents than as principals, less as relationship bankers than as globe-girdling transactional financiers. Unlike André Meyer, they did not cloak their eagerness for success and wealth in elaborate manners and art collecting. They talked the language of sports, war, manhood; they were tough guys, workaholics, metaphorical killers. It was no longer Wasps and Jews, gentlemen and *arrivistes;* it was macho men and the rest of flawed humanity: hard and soft. Perella recalled working with Greenhill on a deal and feeling the power of his personality: "Greenhill was different from the people who worked around here [First Boston]. I didn't say better, just different: much more aggressive, much more persistent—dogged—in pursuit of the client's objective. And *very* tenacious. Investment bankers tended to have a softer touch."[16] At First Boston, they referred to their entrance into deals as "forced entries." Inside First Boston, the M&A unit was known as the "Manson gang"; outside, it was dubbed, sneeringly, "the genius franchise." Perella was ambitious and, despite a genial exterior, driven, ruthless, and hard; but Wasserstein added an element of tactical aggressiveness that had not existed before, even in the heyday of Lipton and Flom, who were, after all, legal counselors and careful to couch their own self-interest in more enlightened sentiments. The lawyers may occasionally have thought their clients to be fools, but they retained a basic respect for them as clients (with some notable exceptions) despite their willingness to engage in the knifework of litigation, to operate like the Skadden partner described by one of his colleagues: "He's warm and friendly, with that angelic Irish face, and he'll cut your balls off."[17] But there were legal ethics, albeit loosened, marking those borders of proper behavior. The bankers had little more than fuzzy and often derided tradition as restraint, which was easily eroded and evaded. Increasingly, bankers viewed themselves as prime movers, scornful of corporate hesitation, vacillation, or fears—led by Wasserstein and Perella, who felt they had to be more aggressive to climb into the top tier. When Wasserstein left Cravath, he seemed to shed some of the traditional sanctity of the client-advisor relationship like an overcoat—though, like everyone else on Wall Street, he ritually genuflected to that ideal. Changes in control, he huffed in 1984, are a way to increase economic efficiency and vigor. As a professional, his first allegiance is to his client's desire to sell or acquire. And, echoing Flom, he said that it's just so much fun. "These fights are a lot like chess, only the rules change after every move."[18]

Wall Street had a clear-eyed view of its developing self-interest. By the early '80s, the surviving Wall Street firms were growing rapidly again, and making fat returns, much of these driven by M&A. In 1981, First Boston advised on $32 billion in announced or completed M&A deals, picking up $75 million in fees—three times that of 1980. In 1982, that grew to $93 million. By then, Wasserstein and Perella's M&A unit dwarfed everything else First Boston did. This got everyone's attention, within First Boston, within Wall Street. Once begun, pressure mounted to keep the profits coming, as with any corporation, both at First Boston and everywhere else. And a quiet struggle broke out over who received the bounty: bankers like Wasserstein and Perella, others in the firm, or its owners. A few of the major firms, like Merrill Lynch & Co., already had public shareholders; others, such as First Boston, had big bank parents, like Credit Suisse, that were publicly listed; others, like Morgan Stanley, were contemplating selling shares. Partnerships were fading, with Goldman Sachs as an outlier. The stakes were rising—both for individuals and for firms. Strangely, Wall Street firms in M&A may have been the most blatant proof, if anyone needed it, that Jensen and Meckling were right and that agency costs did exist, though in a difficult tangle of roles and complexities.

Wasserstein brought to Wall Street a deep understanding of the legal aspects of takeovers; soon after joining First Boston, Perella introduced him to Lipton and the pair began a three-decade-long friendship. Lipton was one of the few figures in M&A whom Wasserstein consistently deferred to. In 1978, Wasserstein quietly published a book, *Corporate Financial Law: A Guide for the Executive,* that was a very Lipton-like play for authority and clients; it quietly came and went. Years later, when Perella and Wasserstein bolted from First

Boston to form their own firm, they camped out in Wachtell's conference room for weeks, crashing the phone system and eating all the food. More importantly, Wasserstein recognized the centrality of M&A tactics fueled by a deep understanding of the legal and regulatory thicket. "What set him apart was his legal training," Jim Maher, a First Boston banker, once said. "Young lawyers were taught to control things, and how you do that is to control the documents, then you're more in charge. When Bruce came, he had a good sense of how ultimately to control things. Make sure the lawyers working on the transaction were our lawyers. Make sure they're loyal to us because they are going to control some part of the transaction. That sort of thought process Bruce brought to the table early on."[19]

And there was an added, explosive element. Wasserstein saw the business as a deep, inherently fascinating game, one with flexible, ambiguous, fluctuating rules, and not just a game as a rhetorical device beloved by slick magazines. He was good at games (his sister Wendy famously wrote about his penchant for applying his own rules to Monopoly as a child), skillful at untangling their complexities: he was, in many ways, a practical game theorist. "Wasserstein thought through the technical aspects of the takeover law as it evolved," noted Robert Lovejoy, a Davis Polk attorney and later a Lazard partner. "His mind permitted him to game theory out. When you are trying to get an advantage over a target or another bidder, understanding how the rules worked was very important. You would have coercive tender offers. The front-end bid would be worth much more than the back end. It was important to put your money where it mattered in those days because the guy who bid the most didn't always win. The guy who got 51 percent first did."[20]

The characterization of Wasserstein as a high-level practitioner of game theory probably comes closer than anything else to pulling the unruly strands of his personality together: the constant negotiations, the stream of speculative possibilities, the tendency toward abstraction and generalization. In his head, he was constantly engaged in a manipulation of a model shaped by legislation, regulation, the law, and the fluid ways of the market. Like any model it was a simplification; it was

useful if, as Milton Friedman once famously wrote, the model generated the right number, the winning answer—that is, if it was predictive—as opposed to being an accurate reflection of economic reality.[21]
M&A was a game; money was the reward for winning. Wasserstein's
mastery of this game was more compelling than nearly anyone else's,
possibly short of Lipton and Flom's, for a stretch of five years or so.
This was truly what he loved to do: juggling the permutations, moving
pieces back and forth, searching for the winning play. True, he had to
get clients to play along, to keep the game going. And he had to use
their money. But that, in many ways, was Perella's *métier*, though in
his talkative years, Wasserstein boasted of his sales prowess. In a career
that saw many triumphs, he may never have excelled at the game as
completely as he did in the early '80s, when he singlehandedly changed
the face of M&A and almost destroyed it in the process.

Chapter Nine

TOOLS OF COERCION

IN 2009, AT Wasserstein's memorial service at Lincoln Center, Lipton speculated that the Legend of Bruce began in 1981, during the war over Conoco won by DuPont. It was, Lipton noted, the largest takeover in history at that time. And it was a classic case, he said, "of the complexity and tactical maneuvering that were features of the takeover battles that caught the attention of the nation for most of the decade of the '80s." But Lipton left quite a bit out; it was a memorial service, after all, with eulogies and the Preservation Hall jazz band. It was not the time for reservations. Conoco was the culmination of a style of tactical maneuvering in M&A that had begun at least a year earlier, 1980, driven by First Boston and Wasserstein. This period displayed Wasserstein at his most fertile, creative, and explosively innovative. That creativity not only drove M&A bids higher and higher but was the very embodiment of what Evans was suggesting in his 1979 speech: Wall Street, financed by banks now willing to fund hostile bids and by companies eager to engage in high-stakes bidding contests, skillfully exploited the complexities and nuances of tender-offer rules that all but destroyed any semblance of balance between offense and defense, raiders and managers, autonomy and coercion, friend and foe—between, ironically, notions of agent and principal. It was remarkably lucrative for a few, though *Esquire*'s notion that Wasserstein "and his team" was billing $125,000 an hour on the Getty takeover was not only exaggerated but absurd.[1] It was a game. At the very heart of the First Boston breakthrough was the manipulation, the herding, the coercion, of the two groups—arbs and institutions—that Lipton had pointed out in "Takeover Bids in the Target's Boardroom."

Wasserstein was, in many ways, inevitable—though it wasn't just because of his personality and skill at an increasingly abstract, tactical game. He reacted to the situation he found himself in, and, not surprisingly, took advantage of it. If Wasserstein, or Wasserstein and Perella (Wasserstein Perella, or "Wasserella," as the firm they later formed was known), had not come onto the scene, would M&A have evolved in roughly the same direction? Undoubtedly. It was a climate that rewarded aggressiveness, boldness, chutzpah of the highest order; you got no credit for thinking small, for not grabbing the maximum reward, for daring not to be great. Riches flowed to the bold. Wasserstein himself had a characteristically odd, ironic relationship with money. Some of his oldest friends denied he cared that much about his accumulating wealth. And yet he was often grasping, squeezing the last dime in fees, and paid himself very, very well. Even many on Wall Street, both early and late in his career, thought he was fixated by money. Defense was breaking down as the money to finance M&A swelled; the politics shifted; the tender-offer rules, riddled with complexities waiting to be exploited, buckled; and the internal dynamics of the trade, particularly the psychological effect on managers thrust into a corporate version of anarchy, unfolded. Self-interest was unleashed as Wasserstein arrived on the scene at a perfect moment for his set of skills. He saw how to exploit this developing, complex, seductive game. He mastered its psychology, with its decision trees, probabilities, and timing issues. And in doing so, he—not the law and economics folks, with their passivity argument, or Jensen with his agency costs—made Lipton's already public fears, of a total breakdown of defense, more than just talk.

This was ironic. For Wasserstein was also Lipton's progeny. He had absorbed the steady escalation and sophistication in tactics developed by Flom and Lipton through the '70s, then drove them forward with his clever manipulation of lock-ups, legs-up arrangements, Pac-Man defenses, and, most devastating, the front-end-loaded, two-tier bid. Wasserstein, in truth, invented few tactics, though he got credit for them; but, like a boxer or a jazz musician, he proved a master—at least for a few years—of their blurringly rapid combination. What he did was to *imagine*—and that word recurs in descriptions of Wasserstein's methods—them in bold, new ways on a huge scale. And he and Perella managed to prod major corporations to fund their tactical weaponry at higher and higher costs; to escalate. Like inflation, M&A escalation appeared inevitable. In the end, and for all the wizardry, the First Boston message came down to: If you want to win, you must escalate. Higher bids were part of the Wasserstein kitbag, partly because he talked so much about them—thus the later nickname "Bid 'em up Bruce." (No one called Perella, who was also voluble, "Bid-'em Up Joe.") But they also sprang from his methods, which were determined by what the tender rules provided. In short, tactics, not bankers, fueled higher bids, even if they did satisfy bankers' own interest in higher fees. And though it was often forgotten in the press's tendency to turn Wall Street bankers into heroes or villains, the final decision to escalate ultimately came from principals, managers, and boards, and the ultimate enablers, lenders, not agent-bankers. Wasserstein (or any banker) might have imagined himself a Faustian principal, but clients made the calls, if they could get the financing.

The Conoco struggle with DuPont, and later deals like the epic war over Getty Oil or Bendix and Martin Marietta, were M&A situations that, like a European war, started quietly, drew in more and more armies, exploded, then subsided away, leaving a blasted battlefield littered with both combatants and civilian casualties. The turn to hostile tactical complexity can be traced to the struggle over a railcar company, Pullman, a longtime First Boston client that had declined along with the railroads. Meanwhile, J. Ray McDermott's eponymous offshore oil-rig company wanted to diversify, believing the oil boomlet had ended. McDermott craved Pullman's petrochemical plant construction unit, Kellogg; he figured he could sell off the rest of Pullman and pay down the debt. In mid-1980—it was the day before the Independence Day weekend—McDermott announced a partial tender offer for Pullman, hoping he could grab it cheap. Wasserstein waved off McDermott's strategy: "I'm not sure they understood its full potential. We don't run a dream factory around here. We simply take the philosophical possibilities provided by the market and apply them. We didn't invent the partial offer. We invented the partial offer that works. We didn't invent pools. The SEC gave them to us. And we used that invention to our client's ends." He was in full sell-promotional bloom. "The point is, people create rules without understanding their full implications. We consider more thoroughly than anyone else the second- and third-order effects of things and we've also refined Wall Street's taste for our kinds of variations."[2]

First Boston had already drawn up a list of white knights for Pullman, which the firm contacted—"chumming" in the lingo. And Wasserstein prepared to exploit the new tender offer rules. Under the Williams Act, there were two key deadlines set by a tender offer: one to buy all the shares; the other for a partial offer (saving cash), in which tendering shareholders would have their shares accepted on a pro-rata basis. This latter involved the famous, and poorly understood, proration pools, which provide the underlying rationale for two-tier bids. While the SEC had extended the all-shares offer period to twenty days at the end of 1979, it left the partial-offer period at ten days: a tighter window. This set up an incentive to tender. If the total shares tendered for cash exceeded the percentage required by the pool, everyone's pro-rata percentage would fall, and they would be forced to sell their remaining shares into the less valuable "back-end." Better to tender quickly and decisively, before everyone realized what was happening. It was a variation on the proverbial rush for the doors in the event of a fire: you had to recognize the situation and move fast to get yourself out and not be crushed or left behind. But you also wanted the best deal, which required a sense of what everyone else was thinking—Keynes's beauty pageant again. What if there was only smoke, no fire? Sit tight. Madrick summed up the possibilities, and the expertise required, not just to engineer a rush to tender but to judge what offer to grab:

> The rules provided takeover players with many tactical alternatives. They could raise the minimum or maximum number of shares they would accept, and therefore cause greater or lesser value for their

bids. A higher maximum meant more shares would be paid for. A lower minimum meant that a tender offer would be affected even if fewer shareholders tendered. The rule complicated the subsequent raising of bids, because that changed the timing requirements. And proration pools, more than ever, turned takeovers into contests designed for savvy arbitrageurs who understood how to evaluate competing offers, prorations and alternatives. If the arb controlled enough of the outstanding shares, that would affect the way a takeover bid was played.[3]

Wasserstein and the arbs were made for each other. Pullman was small enough that the arbs, who were wielding larger and larger funds, could determine victory or defeat alone; Wasserstein didn't have to cater to slower-moving institutions. If you set up a cash pool for 51 percent of the shares, you might be able to induce arbs to tender with a cash bid—and win with them alone. That left nearly half of the shares still outstanding, which might get a lower price or less desirable currency, like shares, or worse. For the arbs, the game was to judge which offer would triumph, setting up the rush for the door. The resemblance to blackmail was not a coincidence. Powerful incentives, as a tool for shaping behavior, are first cousins to blackmail.

First Boston applied these insights when the firm found a white knight, Wheelabrator-Frye, a company that had been reshaped under Michael Dingman, an engineer by training, into an industrial firm selling cleaning equipment, carbon paper, and ink. Wheelabrator was not sexy—and smaller than Pullman. Dingman, however, wanted to grow, and was also drawn to Kellogg, the crown jewel. Wasserstein used lock-up and legs-up arrangements to help Wheelabrator's cause and to apply nut-cracking pressure on shareholders and rival bidders. The legs-up gave Wheelabrator the option to buy Kellogg if the deal didn't work out. Pullman then boosted the pressure by changing the legs-up to a lock-up, in which Wheelabrator signed a contract to acquire the crown jewel. A legs-up or a lock-up not only made shareholders pause, and recalculate their options, but were blows to other bidders, who were now trying to buy a diminished asset. Both techniques had been challenged in the courts and their legality was murky, which was risky, but then Wheelabrator was an underdog. Next, Wasserstein designed the front-end to be far more valuable than the back-end. More pressure. Dare to be great.

McDermott didn't just slink away. His company possessed a number of advantages, including size and money, and it also maneuvered to take advantage of the timing gap between various withdrawal and offering deadlines set up by the Williams Act. The complex dance resulted in a series of tense, topping bids by both parties. "It's like playing a football game in a bathtub," Wasserstein said.[4]

Bid-topping was one result of the aggressive tactics Wasserstein and First Boston employed. A bidding contest *was* like a football game: you pounded, you schemed, you faked, you punished, and you rode momentum. Wasserstein saw the rational necessity for bold action; his attitude was Don't play if you don't play to win. (And Perella was there to keep the client focused.) Wasserstein did not say: Carefully calculate agency costs available at each bid. In the real world of M&A, information was imperfect, emotion powerful, and rationality was, as the economists say, bounded—that is, limited by, at best, things that are knowable. You needed to reach a tipping point. Note the shift of allegiances that occurs. First Boston began as Pullman's banker for the defense. But everyone "knew" Pullman couldn't win against McDermott. Loyalties drifted. As soon as Wheelabrator showed interest, First Boston dedicated itself to its eventual triumph, no matter the cost. Pullman became a set of assets to be manipulated, and if its shareholders could extract a higher premium, all to the good. In fact, at least in this struggle, most of the gains went to the hottest of hot money: the arbs. Other shareholders will either have sold out earlier, accepted a lesser deal on the back-end, or played the high-risk proration-pool game. Everything, on both sides, is dedicated to convincing arbs to tender, driving premiums higher and higher. And one other thing became apparent: the higher the bidding went, the more the investment bank took home in fees. (Arbs and banks thus shared the same incentive to escalate.) First Boston got $6 million just for the Kellogg lock-up. That's a nifty incentive to transact.

Wheelabrator-Frye eventually outlasted McDermott, after Wasserstein lobbed in a final bid, raising even before Wheelabrator's previous bid deadline had expired. Dingman, for his part, kept finding more money from the banks. The arbs rushed to accept Wheelabrator's bid, sensing a winner (and creating the self-fulfilling result). Madrick, who dug deeply into the deal, called it "perhaps the most tactically complex of all time."[5] Despite the crushing premium, Dingman successfully sold off assets, raised capital, paid back the bank, and moved on. Dingman would use this capital to engineer other deals, finally merging Wheelabrator into The Signal Cos. and taking the president's job in 1983. Two years later, Signal was swallowed up by a conglomerate, Allied, which spun out a clutch of business that Dingman took over, and started all over again.

The battle over Pullman produced a headline or two, but it was never a kitchen-table story; Pullman sold for only $600 million. The struggle between Mobil, Seagram, Cities Service, and DuPont for Conoco a year later was different. Wasserstein thrived in this shifting, multifront, multidimensional field of play: it was like the Gettysburg of takeover struggles. Once again First Boston, representing DuPont, rolled out a two-pool bid structure—one that Flom apparently helped design.[6] The deal quickly spawned lawsuits: antitrust, Williams Act violations, even a restraining order Flom won against Seagram in Florida, where Conoco owned several gas stations that sold liquor, for a potential violation of a state prohibition against a liquor distributor owning a retailer. Seagram got the order reversed. Then Flom filed again in North Carolina. Again, a reversal. The bidding mounted throughout the summer. No one had seen anything like it. Wasserstein, aware that because of Conoco's size he needed arbs *and* institutions to tender for DuPont, pressed the company to make an aggressive two-tier bid, offering both ends at the same time, with the front-end in cash and the back-end in stock. DuPont and Seagram swapped topping bids. Cities Service, tapped out, dropped out. Mobil entered the fray. But as Wasserstein himself admitted, the deal was ultimately decided on a technicality: Mobil got hung up by antitrust authorities, delaying its bid, and DuPont won with a slightly lower offer. It was, as we've seen, a Pyrrhic victory for DuPont. Cities Service and Mobil later fell to mergers.

Arguably, First Boston proved to be the big winner. The firm had shown every major firm on The Street that it was now a top-tier M&A bank. The deal produced a huge payday for the firm. Better yet, First Boston had out-strategized Morgan Stanley, and won a continuing set of assignments from DuPont. This was true respectability, Wall Street style. Much of the credit accrued to Wasserstein, which he encouraged. Wasserstein and Perella had to be listened to now, inside and outside First Boston.

The DuPont acquisition of Conoco brought the sheer madcap excess of M&A fully to public notice; you could not avoid it. Then it got crazier. Other over-the-top extravaganzas like late 1982's Bendix, Martin-Marietta battle turned M&A into what one commentator called "a cannibalistic orgy."[7] The Bendix deal had everything: a panoply of white knights (Harry Gray's United Technologies, Ed Hennessy's Allied, with Combustion Engineering, LTV, and other big companies hovering nearby), flocks of advisors (First Boston and Salomon for Bendix, Kidder Peabody's Martin Siegel for Martin Marietta, Rohatyn and Lipton with United Technologies, Flom with Allied), mind-bending complexity, and headline-provoking tactics (the Pac-Man defense in which Martin-Marietta, under attack after a Bendix tender, spun around and made a tender offer for Bendix), all topped by gossip about a bored Bendix CEO, Bill Agee, and his younger lady friend-turned-second wife and advisor, the very Catholic Mary Cunningham, who at one point declared that she was providing her husband with decision trees. The pair appeared to treat Bendix like a toy. And Bendix and Agee turned out to be the big losers, gobbled up by Allied, which shared the proceeds with United Technologies. Wasserstein and Salomon's Tom Pownall blamed each other—and Agee and Cunningham—for the fateful decision to attack. And Goldman, turfed out of an advisory assignment, made a fortune on the arb play; that was Rubin's operation. *Forbes*'s Allan Sloan called it "the messiest tender offer ever."[8] Four books were published about the deal (one by

Sloan, another by Cunningham); M&A was now indisputably main-stream. Bendix had everything but polygamy.

And Bendix raised a deeper question: What was the point? Early '80s M&A stirred a sense of violation that was beginning to break the hard shell of public disinterest: an aversion to chaos and reckless change among the conservatively minded; a sensitivity to inequities and thoughtless greed among liberals. Ordinary Americans had no reason to master lock-ups, proration pools, or tender offers (individual investors were lambs to slaughter in these deals); they did know Pac-Man, but in a somewhat different context. What was apparent was the instability suddenly rattling corporate America's china closet. Familiar names—names that had sailed through depression and war—were engulfed or threatened. New names, new faces, strutted across the stage. Colossal resources were mobilized and deployed, without evidence that companies were better, more efficient, more competitive, except that some shareholders walked away with giant gains, even as the first stories of post-merger layoffs appeared; they were like movies with mind-blowing special effects and no discernible point. The public did dimly discern that technicalities and judges were deciding enormous and complex deals. Wall Street grew rich; some CEOs, too. Assets were shuffled like three-card monte, but how did anyone know that the corporation, the economy, the nation itself, had the winning card? All this, in a post-Vietnam, post-Watergate era, with insecurities high, with competitiveness anxieties building over Japan, was accentuated by Wall Street's fixation on war metaphors that suggested boys gone mad. Which was the optimal owner of, say, Conoco's reserves and know-how: a liquor company, a chemical company, or another energy company? And how would all the debt piled up after these fantastic bidding contests be paid? Debts, in the populist worldview, *always* had to be paid, usually by some poor slob who had nothing to do with them. And they called it a game.

Many of these questions hit home harder at the state level, where jobs and powerful corporate interests were tangible presences, than at the better-insulated, more distant, more constituency-diverse federal level. Nonetheless, by February 1983, the SEC was gearing up for another run at Williams Act reform, its fifth in fifteen years. This time, the agency assembled a seventeen-member expert panel. The committee was a who's who of M&A moxie, the embodiment of the SEC's increasingly quixotic effort to achieve balance: chaired by Dean LeBaron, chairman of institutional investor Batterymarch Financial, and graced by Easterbook (about to be named a federal judge), Dingman (now running Signal), Allied's Hennessy (soon to acquire Signal), SEC chief economist and Chicago product Gregg Jarrell, former Supreme Court Justice Arthur Goldberg, Lipton and Flom (of course), Greenhill and Rubin (an arb!—and soon to be co-CEO of Goldman with M&A chief Steve Friedman), and the *wunderkind* more responsible than anyone else for disrobing the Williams Act, thirty-six-year-old Wasserstein. The group basked in mutual celebrity: it was an elite club, albeit not as exclusive as Lipton and Flom. The group met, formed subcommittees, and by July, well ahead of its deadline, had cranked out fifty recommendations, which the SEC chewed over and filed. The panel produced a lot of noise, but little substance. There was no consensus on reform. Most of the committee members were profiting from the status quo, including CEOs like Dingman and Hennessy (who did occasionally express regret about what was going on) and the advisors, financial and legal. Goldberg, a cranky outsider, later decried the whole exercise in a blistering dissent.[9] No one, he complained, was thinking about the public. That was mostly true. The Reagan SEC had selected a group whose self-interest was firmly in the camp of keeping the game going.

The effort got a lot of attention, particularly in academia. Around that time, Lowenstein, a former merger attorney, general counsel, and president of Supermarkets General, turned Columbia University law professor, wrote a long and thoughtful piece on the current state of hostile M&A.[10] In an era where opposing views had dug deeply in, Lowenstein was a rare, unattached voice: neither a Berle apostle, nor in the Lipton camp, nor a member of the law and economics fraternity, and certainly no fan of Wall Street; he was, if anything, a devotee of Graham and Dodd's value-investing and Warren Buffett.[11] He recognized that "some of the assumptions of the congressional policy of neutrality [on tender offers] were faulty even then [in 1968, when the Williams Act passed]."[12] And he was skeptical of the fundamental role efficient markets played in M&A, or even that "takeover bids are 'good for the world.'" He believed that the theory and practice of governing public corporations would be violated if shareholders were given the unilateral right to liquidate the business. He had lost faith in the tender offer. "Early on, the tender offer was viewed as an alternative to the proxy contest and was used by individuals seeking, with minimal personal investment, to obtain consent," he wrote. "With few exceptions, however, the tender offer has become instead the means by which one large corporation attempts to purchase outright the business and assets of another."[13]

The center was giving way, with the problem located in the structural dynamics of M&A tactics as shaped by tender-offer rules and by the rapid adoption of tactical innovations. Market competition, in the form of undiluted arbitrage, was a problem, Lowenstein wrote. "Each successful new tactic by bidders or targets, even if they may have damaging consequences, is quickly imitated in succeeding bids, so that the intensity of the struggle inevitably escalates. If a lock-up of the target company's best business, its crown jewel, will help the management's chosen white knight win the auction, lock-ups there will be. If the nature of the market for stocks is such that, absent regulation, a two-tier bid proves effective in coercing acceptance of a partial offer, even if followed by a much lower price on the second-step 'cramdown,' two-tier offers will become commonplace."[14]

BY 1982, LIPTON was disturbed as well. Lipton continued to write—he offered an update of "Takeover Bids in the Target's Boardroom" in 1981 and argued that both judicial decisions and "several commentators" had backed his position, particularly on the importance of the business judgment rule.[15] But the reality of M&A was starkly different. "We were not doing so well defending these companies," he admitted decades later.[16] He was snappish even about Wasserstein. Lipton reacted with unusual acerbity to a question posed by an *Esquire* reporter writing a Wasserstein profile in 1984: "Bruce is an intermediary who is paid vast sums of money to arrange gigantic deals that affect a tiny universe of people," he snapped. "In the aggregate, the deals are part of the free play of the marketplace, and have no perceptible influence on American life."[17]

Lipton believed that companies could not escape the lethal weapon of the two-tiered, front-end-loaded bid. No one was safe. In the updated "Takeover Bids," Lipton boasted about his successful defense of McGraw-Hill against American Express. McGraw-Hill's board rejected the offer, and two years later the share price exceeded $40 a share. Lipton claimed that this validated the arguments he had made in "Takeover Bids."

In fact, McGraw-Hill was a lone, unique deal from an earlier, even a lost, time. M&A had moved on.

The new tactics shredded defenses. Defense came down to attracting a white knight. Defense was left to squeezing out a slightly better price. Defense was hoping bidders made a mistake, which with practice grew less common; everyone had the basic playbook, written by Flom and Lipton.

In early 1982 Lipton began to play with an idea for a gambit that could restore defense, albeit at great cost. Wasserstein later described it, aptly, as a spring trap;[18] it also resembled a kind of landmine or a lethal jack-in-the-box. It was a desperate ploy, a startling, almost diabolical tactic: an attacker would make a tender offer only to discover the cost exploding as shares wildly proliferated. In some ways, it was related to the Pac-man defense or counter-tender offer most spectacularly used by Martin Marietta against Bendix. Triggering Pac-man swung defense to offense. Lipton's defensive scheme transformed apparent bidding success into a fiscal armageddon. The scheme was designed to be coercive not to the shareholders of target companies but to the bidders. The target board controlled its use. In Lipton's later words, it "evened the playing field."[19] By September 1982, Lipton had written an internal Wachtell memo describing a version of what he benignly called A Warrant Dividend Plan. The scheme had been quietly discussed with the New York Stock Exchange and vetted by Lewis

Black, an attorney at the elite Wilmington, Delaware, law firm of Morris, Nichols, Arsht & Tunnell, who offered the opinion that "there would be no difficulty under Delaware law."[20] Today, Lipton laughs at that. "Ninety-eight percent of the lawyers we talked to said it would never fly. He was the one that didn't."[21]

The memo meant Lipton's scheme was ready for action. "Accordingly," said the memo, "the plan may be discussed with clients and implemented if the client so pleases. If any client goes forward, please let me know as soon as possible."[22] Yes, please. In fact, the Warrant Dividend Plan would sit on the shelf for nearly a year, a potent weapon waiting for its moment, while cruder variations were taken for spins.

The tactic was on Lipton's mind as 1982 ended. In December, with Bendix winding down, Lipton and Wachtell picked up two defensive assignments in Texas: Pickens was moving on General American Oil in Dallas, and Burlington Northern (timber, railroad) was threatening El Paso Natural Gas. Lipton recommended the Warrant Dividend Plan to General American. But the controlling family quickly decided to sell to Phillips Petroleum. Meanwhile, Lipton's partner, James Fogelson, flew to Houston to meet with El Paso, which had received a takeover offer just before Christmas. El Paso had no defenses and was in dire financial shape. What El Paso had, Lipton realized when he showed up, was "blank-check preferred" shares, a class of stock that had already been approved by the board but not yet issued. Preferred shares have more rights than common stock, usually in the form of a higher dividend—a payout to shareholders. Preferred could be configured to provide shareholders with a dividend consisting of more common shares, which could be triggered either by a bidder's acquisition of a given stake—say, 30 percent—or by change of control, thus launching that deadly proliferation of shares. The El Paso board passed a plan that would offer shareholders twenty shares of preferred for every share of common stock if control changed hands, thus vastly multiplying Burlington's expense. Burlington rushed to court for a restraining order, which was denied.

Beside the preferred, El Paso had no options. No white knights appeared and an attempt to kill the deal on antitrust grounds failed.

By January 10 Burlington had agreed to buy 42 percent of El Paso for the original bid, as well as to invest $100 million in more shares to resolve its financial woes. The board never activated the plan. The *New York Times* story about the episode never mentioned Lipton's first attempt to set into motion what Wachtell began to call "the shareholder rights plan," which, a few months hence, Kidder Peabody's star M&A banker Martin Siegel dubbed "the poison pill." Siegel had a talent for phrasemaking: he also coined the phrase "golden parachutes." Siegel, like Lipton and Goldman Sachs, specialized in defense: both the pill and the golden parachutes quickly became part of most defensive game plans.

Adoption was slow at first; the pill was new, untested, and legally suspect. The pill was like riding around with nitroglycerin in the trunk—it limited a company's options and could weigh down its credit ratings. Shareholders didn't like poison pills; neither did academics; neither did politicians. Early attempts with the preferred shares were not wildly successful. But improvements were made. A few months after El Paso, china manufacturer Lenox, advised by Siegel and Lipton, brandished a poison pill at liquor company Brown-Forman, which was threatening unwanted advances. This pill was a more sophisticated version, though it also used preferred stock. It could maim or kill in two ways. First, a "flip-in" gave Lenox shareholders one share of stock for every one they already owned, doubling the cost of Brown's bid. Second, the "flip-over," which was triggered by a change of control, provided each Lenox shareholder with forty shares of Brown-Forman. The flip-over, if triggered, would have massively diluted the stake of the family controlling Brown-Forman from 62 percent to 30 percent. Faced with those consequences, Brown raised its offer and Lenox agreed to a sale. As in El Paso, the courts denied a motion for a restraining order.

A handful of other companies adopted variations on the preferred pill. But most held back. In fact, the most effective poison pill was the original Warrant Dividend Plan, which dealt with many of the drawbacks of the preferred. Warrants, which give shareholders the right to buy common stock under certain conditions at a certain price, were more flexible than preferred. And as laid out in that 1982 memo, warrants could accommodate both a flip-in and a flip-over. There were legal questions. The flip-in "discriminated" against a bidder by restricting the warrants to pre-bid shareholders. Wasserstein argued that the flip-over was retained as an option because of fears that the flip-in would be disallowed.[23]

The early pill did not kill offense, but made it more difficult. It was a controversial, desperate step—the suicide bomb as the ultimate defense—splitting practitioners, stirring backlash. In 1984, Democratic congressman Timothy Wirth of Colorado wrote a tender-offer reform bill that reflected a laundry list of concerns. The bill wanted to tighten disclosure on bidders, shrink the time they had to communicate their intentions, and hike the duration of a bid to forty days. The bill forbade any change in compensation for an officer or director during a tender offer—an early sensitivity to golden parachutes. It banned greenmail. And it attempted to foil aspects of poison pills. Companies could use the pill if they got shareholder approval first. This was an attack on Lipton's board prerogative and an attempt to legislatively limit the business judgment rule.

From a political standpoint, the bill was incoherent, though reflective of liberal thinking on M&A in the last years of its long ascendancy in Congress. It was sensitive to practices that were beginning to be viewed as public abuses. The anti-greenmail provision hurt raiders; golden parachutes and pill provisions annoyed managers and boards; the forty-day notice made life difficult for bidders and Wall Street. In any event, it was, as legislation, a dead letter. The public was not fully energized. As with the earlier, tender-offer blue-chip panel, the balance of power leaned toward the status quo. Introduced in May 1984, the bill expired in the heat of early August.

Chapter Ten

EVIDENCE OF ORTHODOXY

I N 1983 Felix Rohatyn, not Wasserstein, not Greenhill, not dashing, young Marty Siegel, was the most famous merger banker in America, not quite at the level of, say, Elvis, but not bad for a slight, pale, fifty-six-year-old immigrant. Rohatyn was The Man Who Saved New York from collapsing into bankruptcy, not to say The Man Who Saved Wall Street, a subject of cover stories, a figure lionized, respected, in demand. He appeared to be omnivorously smart. He remained chairman of the Municipal Assistance Corp., which oversaw New York's finances as the city balanced its budget and crept back into the bond market. "This chairmanship had been the most rewarding experience of my professional life," he admitted later.[1] He swung from crisis manager to watchdog to earnest talking head. He remained at Lazard, now relocated to studiedly shabby quarters at Rockefeller Center; he liked to walk to work, down Fifth Avenue, past St. Patrick's, among the tourists. At last, the humiliation of the ITT scandal had faded, though the nickname, Felix the Fixer, persisted. (Felix the Cat also cropped up.) And he was still raking in fees for himself and for Lazard. As he noted in his memoir, "Despite the demanding hours I spent as chairman of the MAC board, I continued to bring a great deal of business into the firm."[2] He possessed an unsurpassed network. He transcended investment banker-dom; he was a legitimate statesmen. He hobnobbed with politicians and socialites; he hung out at Elaine's; his opinion mattered whether he knew what he was talking about or not. And yet—he was restless. He had done so much. What next? In 1984,

Institutional Investor caricatured him on its cover in a top hat and tails for a story headlined "The Making of a Celebrity."[3] He seemed poised to head off in different directions. But *which way?* He was writing. He was involved in the Democratic Party, though he was hardly your press-the-flesh retail pol. Talk began that he might be a future secretary of the Treasury in a Democratic administration. But he stayed at Lazard, still battled for deals, still took calls. He remained intensely competitive and prickly proud, and came across as thin-skinned; some of the financial crowd thought him vain, a conscience-wracked Cassandra. Wall Street lacks both a long memory and a generous soul.

He was a free man. Geneen gave up the ITT CEO's job in 1977 and retired as chairman in 1979; his successor, Rand Araskog, effectively sold off much of the by-then ramshackle conglomerate, aided by Rohatyn. Meyer had grown ill in 1977—cancer—and settled in a chalet in the Swiss Alps, while still running the firm by phone.[4] He summoned Rohatyn and asked him to take over the firm. Rohatyn says that Meyer had asked him many times before, but he had always refused. He rejected the idea again. But, always the banker, he offered a solution: Michel David-Weill, a direct relation of the firm's founders then working at Lazard Paris. As a bourgeois Jew, Meyer, says Rohatyn, "was both fascinated and resentful of the David-Weills' aristocratic pedigree."[5] (Rohatyn, of course, shared Meyer's bourgeois background.) His analysis of the firm shares the anachronistic quality that the firm embodied: "Authority at Lazard, I believed, could come from only two sources: either you were a member of the controlling family, or you generated significant and prestigious business. I fulfilled one of these criteria."[6] Of course, Michel David-Weill fulfilled only one, too—as did Meyer himself. It is odd that the man who ran MAC and who still did deals felt he could not run Lazard and advise on M&A at the same time. But he had broader interests. Rohatyn, unusual in such a shrewd advisor, also did not foresee problems with a firm that had two poles of power: the proprietor and the rainmaker. David-Weill took up residence in New York, operating out of Meyer's old office, with the great financier's desk sitting in the middle of the room. When Meyer died in May 1979, Rohatyn and David-Weill repaired to Rohatyn's "small summer cottage" on Long Island—it was a substantial home in Southampton—to plot the next decade at Lazard.

Rohatyn recalls that he had grown uneasy as firms consolidated on Wall Street and a "great deal of new money was in play." He had had a hand in that consolidation: as the NYSE's crisis manager during the near-collapse of Wall Street, he had orchestrated many firm mergers to take pressure off the exchange's rescue fund. Lazard itself suddenly appeared small and undercapitalized; it was certainly idiosyncratic. But beyond Lazard he grew disturbed by the mounting waves of mergers: "What distinguished these corporate deals from those of the previous decade, however, was the aggressive nature of many of these transactions, their previously unimaginable size, and the character of the new warrior bankers who with an armory of new financial weapons led the charge."[7] His deep-seated ambivalence reemerged. Deals, he recalls, had once been negotiated or friendly. Senior management of American companies, not to say their lawyers and bankers, went to the same schools, belonged to the same country clubs, came from the same class, "cut from similar wholesome, Waspy cloth." Was that "wholesome" sarcastic or admiring? Hostile deals had been frowned upon until Morgan Stanley "ripped up" this "unwritten social contract."[8] The rules had changed for everyone, including Lazard. Rohatyn yearned for a lost world. The new crowd—Flom and Lipton, Wasserstein and Greenhill, and this mysterious purveyor of junk bonds, Michael Milken—made him nervous. They were combative, high profile, and they were interested in money in ways he thought unseemly. "But I personally did not care for hostile takeovers, and would participate in such an activity solely on behalf of a large, well-financed, longtime client of the firm and only after exploring all other possible alternatives," he writes.[9] That was a loophole capacious enough to provide a nice living.

In 1983, Rohatyn published his first book, a compilation of his columns, commentaries, letters, and addresses, *The Twenty-Year Century: Essays on Economics and Public Finance.*[10] Once again, he was early: he was a fiscally conservative Democratic with liberal social instincts. But

Reagan, not Clinton, was president. Rohatyn was for fiscal prudence and an activist government. He urged the creation of a new Reconstruction Finance Corp. to tackle social problems. He favored a mixed economy, and "though I believe the marketplace knows best most of the time, I am skeptical that it should always be the ultimate arbiter of economic action, and I am more than willing to interfere with it when it becomes a disturbing, rather than benign influence."[11] Given his history, he was sensitive to alarm and disaster, but in none of the essays did he mention the threat of hostile takeovers. His public actions jostled uneasily with his private discontent. In July 1984, the *New York Times* rang up Rohatyn to ask him his views about "the surge in takeovers." Rohatyn offered a well-honed sound bite: "All this frenzy may be good for the investment bankers now, but it's not good for the country or investment bankers in the long run. We seem to be living in a 1920s jazz age atmosphere."[12]

Some folks liked the jazz age.

IN 1984, Michael Jensen cited Rohatyn's jazz-age quote as an example of the "enormous amount of criticism" generated "not only from politicians and media but also from high-level corporate executives" over hostile takeovers. He saw two other unsettling developments: the July 1983 SEC blue-chip tender-offer committee and a bill by Democratic congressman Peter Rodino that proposed making larger mergers meet a standard that they "serve the public interest." (Neither went anywhere.) Jensen characterized the debate over takeovers as a kind of *götterdämmerung* between forces of scientific light and ignorant darkness, with the edge going to the latter—the armies of Lipton and his defense-empowering poison pill. He dismissed Rohatyn as a folklorist. Of course, he and his financial confederates were scientists.

Jensen had been productive since 1975. He and Eugene Fama, with whom he had co-founded the *Journal of Financial Economics,* had collaborated on a series of papers extending various aspects of agency theory. Jensen was a powerful voice asserting the essential truth of Fama's market efficiency. In a 1978 paper he famously declared, "There is no other proposition in economics which has more solid empirical evidence supporting it than the Efficient Market Hypothesis." And he had published a book, with Clifford W. Smith Jr., *The Modern Theory of Corporate Finance,* in 1984, a compilation of key papers outlining the new thinking. (In the introduction, they summarized the building blocks: efficient markets, portfolio theory, capital asset pricing theory, option pricing theory, agency theory.[13]) In 1977 he had become the founding director of Rochester's Managerial Economics Research Center, and in 1984-'85 he served as a visiting professor at the Harvard Business School; he retained both institutional bases, Harvard and Rochester, until 1988, when he settled full-time in Cambridge—that is, when he wasn't consulting, speaking, or attending conferences. His collaborator Meckling had retired as dean of Rochester's Graduate School of Management in 1983 and moved to California.

Jensen moved from exploring agency theory to, by the early '80s, championing a Manne-like unrestrained takeover market. In 1983 he published a survey of the research on the takeover market, "The Market for Corporate Control: The Scientific Evidence," in the *Journal of Financial Economics,* with a young Harvard Business School professor, Richard Ruback, who had done research on share returns in M&A. The paper is noteworthy on several levels. Again, it argued the view that the Chicago perspective on hostile takeovers was "scientific"— that is, proven and objectively true; he often said he was part of a larger scientific revolution. He said again and again that agency theory lay at the heart of what he called a revolution in the science of organizations. Science implies the presence of its opposite: cant, dogma, fantasy, superstition, false idols, the stuff in the newspapers. Science implies evidence.

"The evidence indicates that corporate takeovers generate positive gains, that target firm shareholders benefit, and that bidding firm shareholders do not lose," they wrote.[14] In short, M&A is a non-zero-sum game: target shareholders win; bidders *do not lose.* Jensen and Ruback defined effectiveness precisely—as short-term stock gains by shareholders within a month of the announcement of a deal—and they were not concerned by the rapidity of change in an M&A phenomenon that was less than a decade old. For many years, their survey would be cited as proof of the proposition that takeovers were broadly beneficial. It was the orthodox interpretation.

The vast bulk of the evidence came from another Chicago big idea: the event study. Jensen had participated in some of the early work on event studies. But Chicago graduate student Gershon Mandelker gets credit for the first *merger* event study in 1974, part of his PhD dissertation.[15] Fama, Fischer Black, and Merton Miller made up his thesis committee, and he thanked Jensen and one of his Rochester grad students for "editorial and technical aid." The event study stemmed from the confluence of two Chicago innovations: the development of the capital asset pricing model, a technique for pricing investments based on risk and expected return over time, and machine-readable securities prices from the Center for Research on Securities Prices in Chicago, the CRSP data that Jensen had utilized. The result is what one commentator in 1987 called "the economics and corporate finance profession's closest analogue to the automated factory. Scores of papers have been written on how the announcement of a merger, takeover or related corporate control transaction affects the normalized price of a target and acquiring firm."[16] The math in an event study is relatively sophisticated, but increasingly automatable. The idea is straightforward: How does "an event," such as a merger announcement, affect the price of shares of buyer and seller within a window of time, and what are the "abnormal returns" beyond the overall rise or fall of the market? The trick is to separate out the "noise" of the market from the "signal" of the stocks in question. The assumption making this work is market efficiency: that investors are absorbing, and reflecting, all available information.

Nearly all of Jensen's estimates for takeover benefits came from event studies. In "The Scientific Evidence," Jensen and Ruback synthesized a mass of event studies on mergers and takeovers. Their conclusions were striking. Target firms in successful takeovers "experience statistically abnormal stock price changes of 20% in mergers and 30% in tender offers." Bidding firms realize "statistically significant abnormal gains of 4% in tender offers and zero in mergers." In deals that fail, both bidders and targets suffer small losses, statistically close to zero. The pair then concluded that the studies justified Fischel and Easterbrook's passivity argument—though they equivocated. If managers oppose a takeover or do anything to reduce the probability of a deal, well, that's bad. But if they squeeze out a higher bid, well, that's good. They described this situation as "an empirical matter"; that is, presumably, management would be judged by short-term share prices.[17]

They then introduced a subtle, if important, change in the standard rationale for takeovers. Chicago orthodoxy had begun with Manne's notion of takeovers as a force for managerial accountability. That had been refined to the notion that financiers and activist shareholders—investors—buy control of companies and "hire and fire management to achieve better resource utilization." Now they narrowed this further—and fundamentally changed its thrust. Takeovers were competition by *managerial teams* "for the rights" to run corporate assets. You could easily pass over this alteration in phraseology—it was just words—but something odd was afoot here. For one thing, they declared that takeovers were now the exclusive province of one group, managers—undoubtedly top managers, the kind of folks they taught at Harvard. "Managerial competition" has somehow replaced financiers and activists—that is, a variety of investors or shareholders. They downgraded the status of arbs and "takeover specialists" to intermediaries—agents. Other stockholders played a passive, and vague, "judicial role." And directors, in normal governance the decision-making representatives of shareholders, are (as usual) absent: tools of managers. Indeed, they argued, echoing Lipton, that shareholders are often disloyal—to *managers:* "Stockholders have no loyalty to incumbent managers; they simply choose the highest dollar value offer from those presented to them in a well-functioning market."[18] Well, yes.

Jensen and Ruback suggested that this new formulation was an advance on more conventional Chicago doctrine. But in fact it's almost reactionary: "Managerial competition" sounded a lot like Berle's managerial governance without stakeholders, but with M&A. How this fit into agency theory was a mystery. Agents somehow disciplined agents.

Moreover, this abstract discussion didn't really fit into Jensen and Ruback's basic survey of scholarly results. They bolted the managerial model, like helicopter rotors atop a car, to the empirical survey. And they engaged in a methodological sleight of hand. The managerial model first appeared as a hypothesis—we think this might be going on—and within a few paragraphs morphed into a definition, one they claimed was anchored in earlier work from Fama and Jensen: managerial competition was the "analytical framework" in which takeovers must be viewed. In short, they didn't set out to prove the validity of the model by looking at empirical realities but, rather, stated it as a possibility, then declared it to be the reality they were depicting. Then, by stowing the managerial model into the survey, they allowed the former to ride along with the latter. But the managerial model had little connection with the success or failure of takeovers, except to leave the impression that progress of the Darwinian kind was taking place: good managers were triumphing over bad through M&A. When shareholders see a higher share price, they vote for the managerial group that offers it, blindly accepting the wisdom of the market. Everything depends on that wisdom—that is, on market efficiency.

A year later, in 1984, Jensen returned with "Takeovers: Folklore and Science."[19] This was shorter than the paper co-written with Ruback and more polemical; it ran in the *Harvard Business Review.* He did not bring up the role of managers. He listed a number of popular beliefs about M&A—the "folklore"—and dismissed them, one by one. Jensen repeated the "facts" about target shareholder gains and insisted that M&A is a tool for the efficient deployment of assets. He denied that takeovers siphon off capital for new plants and equipment, generate shareholder gains by monopoly power, allow managers—so much for his own agency theory—to "feather the nests at shareholders' expense."[20] Maybe you could shirk, but that didn't mean you were feathering your nest. Prohibiting plant closings and layoffs following takeovers "would reduce market efficiency and lower living standards." Golden parachutes are actually good for shareholders—"the evidence indicates that shareholders gain when golden parachutes are adopted." His evidence is again hitching a free

ride on previously declared certainties: evidence, for instance, that target shareholders' profit means that takeovers are, *ipso facto,* efficient
and productive. There are a lot of *ipso factos* in "Takeovers: Folklore
and Science." This is a system built upon the foundational assumption
of efficient markets, which, as one critic observed, is accepted as an
axiom (a truth that does not need proof), not a hypothesis to be
tested.[21] "The vast scientific evidence on the theory of efficient markets
indicates that in the absence of inside information, a security's market
price represents the best available evidence of its true value," Jensen
wrote.[22] "Vast" is way more persuasive than "sizable" or even "considerable"; in fact, "true value" remained a thorny subject. And a lack of
evidence—"no evidence with which I am familiar indicates that takeovers produce more plant closings, layoffs and dismissals than would
otherwise occur,"[23] he noted dismissively—is not a problem for Jensen
but, rather, a back-door confirmation of his thesis: M&A is vastly
beneficial. If he didn't know the evidence, it obviously didn't exist.

JENSEN MIGHT HAVE been disturbed by criticism raining down upon
unrestrained hostile takeovers, but he had a powerful ally: the White
House. In February 1985, the White House Council of Economic
Advisors weighed in on M&A in its annual *Economic Report to the
President.*[24] This was not really for the eyes of Ronald Reagan; this was
for Congress, the media, and some wide-awake part of the public. This
was an official, policymaking pronouncement, far more powerful in
impact than the hairsplitting debates articulated by the law and economics group, Jensen, or even Lipton and his supporters. Most of the
time, advocates wrote either as academics, in the case Jensen or Fischel
and Easterbrook, or as practitioners, like Lipton. They were undoubtedly aware of larger politics. But they were also sensitive to their own
self-interest, either commercially, scholarly, or career-wise. The Council of Economic Advisors had a different, more overtly political mission: to shape public opinion. With Jensen or Lipton, politics was a
subtext. With the CEA, academic argument, the recitation of theory
and evidence, was a loud trumpet for larger political ends (which
ended, among other things, speculation about what the SEC was

really up to when it came to M&A: nothing much). What was once arcane and counterintuitive was now official White House policy. This report was thus one of the milestones for a former heterodoxy from Chicago on its road to orthodoxy.

The *Economic Report to the President* dealt with any number of important subjects. Chapter 6 tackled "The Market for Corporate Control" and immediately set the theme, competition, with a breathless, bracing sweep, presenting competition as a universal mechanism, a benign force for good. (Competition and arbitrage are roughly synonymous.) There was no ambiguity, no sense that too much competition might be a bad thing, or that competition could, in certain circumstances, lead to less-than-inspiring ends. Competition even has a goal: "to break down entrenched market positions" and unsettle "comfortable managerial lives."[25] There's a stack of novels in that last phrase.

Thus began a theoretical defense of unrestrained takeovers. This was not the veiled, constituency-balancing act of the SEC. This was the bracing essence, the orthodox recitation, of the Chicago law and economics view. It is actually one of the most accessible summaries of the Chicago view of M&A. The academese has been scrubbed away. The sentences are active, direct, and clear. There are no mathematical formulas. The authors assume a mildly instructional stance, speaking not from an economic Olympus but from an easy chair. Having established that competition is an unalloyed good, the anonymous authors then explain in broad generalities, channeling Manne, though not by name (there are no names, no footnotes, no instances of *ad hominem* intellectual sparring—the report is above polemics, where truth resides), how "competition plays a particularly important role in the market for control of publicly traded companies. This market determines who will operate the Nation's largest business enterprises and influences the business strategies that many of these organizations follow." The corporate control market provides, like Constitutional government, a set of "checks and balances."[26] The report does not mention other theories of the firm that were once so compelling, or states that took a different view of things; there is, beyond a brief outline of M&A waves, no history at all. The authors explain the essential governance structure as they saw it: stockholders, who generally own companies, hire managers to run them. Directors never appear. The term *stakeholder* also goes missing. This delegation of authority, they note, is very efficient. It promotes a class of talented managers (executives did tend to be Republican), reduces "the costs of diversifying investors' portfolios and facilitates mobility of financial resources among companies competing for capital." They then offer a mildly paradoxical admission: "Separation of ownership and control has been a major reason for the success of the modern corporate form as a business entity."[27]

Then comes the inevitable "but." The modern public company has merit, but separation of ownership and control is not without risk. Delegation of authority creates potentially divergent self-interest in managers, who may operate the firm in a way that's not in the best interest of stockholders. How do you define stockholder interest? A short jog ahead we find out: by the stock price and the stock price alone. At the very foundation of a swaying tower of benefits and interests is a flickering, often randomly dancing, if profoundly efficient, stock price. This situation gives rise to an agency problem. This is a serious issue. "The adverse consequences of this agency problem can be significant because, if unchecked, it can deter socially beneficial mergers, keep assets from being allocated to higher-value uses, impede adoption of more profitable capitalization plans, and otherwise prevent publicly traded corporations from making the largest possible contribution to aggregate performance."[28] So it's not just that wayward managerial self-interest undermines shareholder interest, which is somehow captured by the share price, but that self-interest can be ratcheted up to the level of a national problem. Quietly, the CEA anointed stockholders not just as true owners of public companies but as proxies for the public good—"socially beneficial."

This was the standard Chicago formulation, which tended to look past matters of shareholder passivity or neglect. The report did not touch on Jensen and Ruback's quietly heretical notion that managerial competition was at the heart of takeovers.

A little later, the authors do drop that other parties may have an interest in the fate of corporations, particularly in takeovers. "When takeovers succeed [no mention of when they fail], some individuals [not workers, not unions, not middle managers, just random individuals] and communities may be adversely affected if jobs are lost or plants and offices are shut down. The problems raised by such reallocations of assets are a proper subject of social concern, but they are not unique in takeover transactions."[29] Ponder how quickly disrupted individuals and communities become "a reallocation of assets" issue, or possibly "a social concern." Maybe the government should do something to "ease local adjustment problems." Or maybe not. This, however, leads to a generalization presented as irrefutably objective—but one, in fact, that tiptoes a subjective line. The CEA employed the classic Chicago move Jensen often used: limiting reality to a solvable problem, then defining reality that way. "Contests for corporate control are largely economic [phenomena], and they can and should be understood as such. The policy debate need not be guided by anecdotal evidence that emphasizes isolated incidents that some critics perceive as abusive."[30] Again, note the volley of loaded verbiage: anecdotal, *isolated* incidents, *some* critics, perceive, *abusive*. Economic fact—quantified, factual, objective, scientific—is all that matters, though that's stated, declared, not argued or proven. It's folklore versus science again.

And what of that evidence? The rest of the chapter tangles with those carping, self-involved, subjective, and anecdotally fixated critics. Again and again, the authors redefine the problem to matters of economic efficiency and national wealth, which they insist can be quantified and fixed, and dismiss objections as lacking in evidence, which they claim to possess but rarely reveal. Even Jensen, at his most casual, rattles off more facts than this CEA report does. But the CEA still gestures toward evidence that it declares to be self-evident. Evidence becomes something of a chanted theme, a subliminal message of rational belief. Even the lack of evidence speaks to proof. If there's no evidence, it's because it's so obvious. There is "no *evidence,*" said the authors, that M&A has, "on a systemic basis, caused anti-competitive price increases." (This is a sensitive point, because critics charged the administration with dismantling antitrust, which Chicago had long attacked. But the public grasped the concept of monopoly and accepted antitrust. Big was bad. The chapter reiterates three times, nearly word for word, that there's no *evidence* of anti-competitive effects from M&A, which, given the rapid evolution of the takeover boom and the long-term perspective required to judge these things, can't really be justified.) The *evidence,* however, is "overwhelming that successful takeovers substantially increase the wealth of stockholders in target companies. . . . Economic theory therefore suggests, and the available *evidence* confirms, that merger and acquisition transactions are, on average, beneficial for stockholders in both bidder and target firm." That shareholder benefit then becomes the claim that there is also *evidence* that M&A adds to "aggregate wealth." And there is "substantial *evidence* suggesting" that stock markets don't penalize long-term investment. But there is "no systemic *evidence*"—systemic as opposed to unique or circumstantial?—that two-tier offers have a coercive effect, and there is "substantial *evidence*" that the market actually prevents such abuses. (Wasserstein would be surprised: the entire purpose of his complex orchestration of bids and deadlines was to press, panic, bully, and coerce shareholders into tendering for his client.) The SEC, in fact, has found *evidence* that there's no difference in premiums between single-tier and two-tier bids. While the CEA believes the Williams Act was unnecessary, that's water under a long-washed-out bridge: the twenty-day offering period "appears to provide ample time for many targets to find alternate bidders." In any event, a longer minimum period, which some states were pressing for, would raise the cost of takeovers, reduce benefits, limit aggregate gain, and increase "the resources spent on non-productive bargaining over the allocation of those gains"—a recapitulation of Fischel and Easterbrook, just shorter. The CEA is really arguing for passivity in targets, which, for everyone's benefit, should agree to neuter their competitive urges and surrender.

And while the authors insist "there's no credible *evidence*" that any offensive tactics are abusive, that's not the case with defense. Defense is different. Offense is the prerogative of motivated principals; defense is a tangled web of agent self-interest. Again, this all turns on a definition. "The more fundamental debate," they write, "concerns when, *if ever,* a target management should be permitted to oppose a takeover that promises a significant premium to the corporation's stockholders. [There's no definition of *significant.*] The question arises primarily because of the possibility that management will maintain control over corporations despite the fact that stockholders could benefit by tendering their shares." Here, the report hesitates. That *if ever* is a sign. The risk, they decide, is not enough to ban defensive tactics. And they make a striking admission for the CEA in 1985: "There is no economically correct solution to the question of how the gains resulting from acquisitions should be distributed among bidders and targets." In other words, everyone benefits so why shouldn't targets get some of the gain? And so, like Jensen and Ruback, they grudgingly retreat a step from passivity.[31]

The authors wrap up by defending defensive tactics that are "not proper subjects for Federal regulation." (*Proper* again.) Once more, they're following Jensen on greenmail and golden parachutes. Greenmail is actually a benefit because it drives the stock of a target company up, always a good, and signals a potential takeover. But after the board pays greenmail, the stock often plummets like a rock. That's not so good. The evidence from share prices, the authors admit, is mixed, with insignificant gains. But everything works out because most companies that engage—or are victimized by—greenmail tend to either find themselves targets again or undergo a recapitalization or management change. The greenmail acts as "a signal of vulnerability" and "may therefore be a valuable stimulus for more fundamental and beneficial corporate change." Greenmail actually reduces takeover costs, and thus catalyzes bids. Legal and moral aspects of greenmail play no role in this economic calculus. As for golden parachutes, the authors assert that the phenomenon is too new for "the market" to judge.

Evidence against golden parachutes is inconclusive. Regulating the practice would be difficult and "constitute a major intrusion into an area that is traditionally subject primarily to State regulation."[32] In fact, nearly everything they discuss had traditionally been a matter of oversight by the states, not the federal government.

Still, for all its confident declaration of reality, the report, upon publication, was already slightly stale, out of date, 1983-ish. The CEA team did not wrestle with two innovations that by early 1985 were already, beneath the surface, struggling for control of a shape-shifting takeover phenomenon. The *Economic Report to the President* never mentioned Lipton's poison pill, the ultimate defensive tactic. And it never brought up the gathering storm of Michael Milken's offensive juggernaut of junk-bond-fueled takeovers.

Chapter Eleven

MICHAEL MILKEN, SURPRISED BY SIN

THE POLITICAL SIGNIFICANCE of Michael Milken's junk-bond insurrection was not obvious to the world outside Wilshire Boulevard, Beverly Hills, where his Drexel Burnham Lambert
high-yield—that is, junk-bond—department operated, until he decided to take over M&A. That was in the mid-'80s. Throughout the
'70s and into the '80s, Milken built his sales and trading operation
with intense, monomaniacal energy and, for the most part, did it outside the public eye. Like Jensen, he saw no need for the press. If
Rohatyn was a Name, Milken was still a Nobody. He was, to an extraordinary extent, a furtive creature of the markets, not a public figure. He was not a habitué at Elaine's or 21 or the Regency for breakfast.
He was a control freak, a workaholic, and still young, at thirty-nine, in
1985. He was a man who kept his information close, including a few
items that probably weren't secrets to his colleagues, like his toupee,
which he donned in his twenties. (A few observers insisted he avoided
publicity because he was sensitive about his hair, but he had far better
reasons to avoid attention.) All that ended with Drexel's decision to
join the takeover wars in 1985.

Milken had grown up, the son of an accountant, in Southern California, and like a character from *Ozzie and Harriet*—a common reference in Milken profiles—he was a high school cheerleader (Sally Field
was on the squad, too) and prom chairman and he worked in a diner.
He neither smoked nor drank nor indulged in recreational drugs nor

sipped caffeinated or carbonated beverages. He attended the University of California at Berkeley during the free-speech movement, joined a fraternity, was elected to Phi Beta Kappa, then went to the University of Pennsylvania's Wharton School, graduating in 1970. He appeared untouched by political events: he was a finance junkie, which in those days was a more unusual preoccupation than it is today. At Berkeley or Wharton—accounts vary—he stumbled across, like Joseph Smith in the New York woods, his golden plates: bond studies going back to 1900 by W. Braddock Hickman, an economist at Princeton and Rutgers universities who in 1963 had died while running the Federal Reserve Bank of Cleveland. Hickman's study (later updated by T. R. Atkinson to the year 1965) argued that over time those bonds, which carried higher interest rates than investment-grade corporate bonds, generated better risk-adjusted returns than more traditional fixed-income portfolios. In other words, the higher rate more than compensated for the greater risk. This was Milken's revelation: investment grade, he repeated endlessly, could only go down. Junk had upside. There was some salesmanship here: Milken saw his bonds as speculative tools; he was a trader. Investment grade rarely went bankrupt, which meant bondholders got paid; junk did, at varying levels, which meant investors maybe didn't. This is where the debate over junk really began.

"Adam Smith," the pseudonym of a latter-day financial writer named George Goodman, not the Scottish political economist, was pondering go-go financial truths around the time Milken was leafing through Hickman. (Goodman was particularly entertaining on the then-novel subject of the tendency of stocks to move randomly—random walks, in the jargon, a pillar of market efficiency—which he discussed with Chicago's famous "Professor Fama." At the time, Goodman had not heard of junk beyond the contents of his attic.) One of his themes in *The Money Game*,[1] an iconic text in modern financial journalism published in that lively year, 1967, was the increasing fixation on calculating value as Wall Street was emerging from what he called its long, post–Black Friday purgatory, "the Street of iniquity."[2] Goodman recognized that it was an age that increasingly saw salvation in quantification and rational models in the figure of *homo economicus,* and that attempted to eliminate those experiences that were not reducible to numbers:

> Hopes, fears, greed, ambition, acts of God—it would be hard to put it more succinctly. It is hard to program these into anything as unforgiving as an IBM 360. There is a school that says all these things are in the numbers already, but actually the study of numbers is rational, a search for some shining inner Truth called Value. Value is there, like Bishop Berkeley's tree that made a noise when it fell in the forest whether or not anybody heard . . . [but] value is only one part of the story.[3]

Milken believed he had discovered the entire story in patterns of junk-bond defaults and returns. Like Jensen, it all came down to definition. But his larger tale, his personal story, particularly when it came to M&A, shared many aspects with what Goodman claimed his 1976 book on the new finance was all about: "image and reality and identity and anxiety and money." In short, wrote Goodman, jauntily donning the Smith name, which to some was like borrowing the name of God. "The world is not the way they tell you it is."[4]

Milken went to work at a triple-barreled firm on a respirator, Drexel Harriman Ripley, in Philadelphia, a partnership launched in 1835 with a deep Wasp genealogy, which included, looming in its rhyming past, an ancestor he would later be compared to: J. P. Morgan Sr., who had worked there when it was his father's firm, Drexel Morgan. In 1971, the then–Drexel Firestone (the firm had been bailed out by Firestone family money a year earlier) underwent a shotgun merger with a second-tier, New York retail brokerage, Burnham & Co., run by "Tubby" Burnham, who we've earlier met. Connie Bruck, in her definitive Milken book, *The Predator's Ball,* has Burnham, who was Jewish, asking his Drexel counterpart if he employed any Jews.[5] He did: 3 or 4 out of 250, including a brilliant one, he said, who would probably leave—Milken. Burnham, who had borrowed $100,000 from his grandfather to start the firm in 1935 and was not really overweight (the nickname was a vestige of a childhood illness), talked to Milken and asked what he required to stay. More capital, he replied; Drexel had been starving his tiny trading operation for capital. Burnham gave him $2 million to play with. He also appended the ritzy Drexel name in front of the more plebian Burnham on the all-but-inarguable advice of Goldman Sachs's Gus Levy and Morgan Stanley's Robert Baldwin. Drexel Burnham. Burnham's mother complained about that decision, but the newly christened Drexel Burnham celebrated by ordering up Lucite "tombstones" containing two brass balls each.[6]

By then, Milken had already begun to build a desk that traded his low-rated bonds. Milken dealt with bonds from once-solid companies that had come down in the world—"fallen angels"—or (less often) "Chinese paper," issued by conglomerates in acquisitions. Years later, he opened up huge new markets in debt for emerging companies, for leveraged buyouts (LBOs), and for hostile takeovers—very different from the bonds Hickman studied. Early on, Milken traveled the country, like Johnny Appleseed, making a case for his low-grade bonds. Milken was a shining example of that emerging business species he did so much to ennoble, the entrepreneur, breathing as much life into that out-of-favor concept as he did into these zombified junk bonds. (Milken's rise roughly paralleled that prototypical New Age entrepreneur, Steve Jobs—another figure who made a vast amount of money by claiming he wasn't interested in money.) He started out trading but he had bigger plans. In 1972 he convinced his first major investor, a pension plan for an industrial company, to buy a 5 percent allocation of junk; conventional bond funds then gobbled up junk from Milken to make up for steep losses in the oil crisis and the subsequent slump in the economy in 1974; in 1977, he launched his first junk-bond fund, tapped insurers, money managers, and S&Ls desperate for yield, and began issuing new bonds, all the while building widening circles of unorthodox financiers—entrepreneurs—who were both buyers and sellers of his bonds: Meshulum Riklis, Saul Steinberg, Steve Wynn, Victor Posner, the Belzberg Brothers, Carl Lindner, William Farley, Fred Carr, and Tom Spiegel; later, John Malone, Craig McCaw, Steve

Wynn, Ted Turner, Nelson Peltz, Ronald Perelman, Icahn, Pickens, and the LBOers. It was quite a crowd.

In 1978, Milken, then thirty-two, took his entire operation and moved it to Los Angeles. Explanations have proliferated about that exodus. He and his wife had grown up in the San Fernando Valley; he wanted to spend more time with his three children; his father was sick. He could get a three-hour jump on New York by starting every day at 4 a.m. (He worked until 7:30 p.m., not leaving a lot of time for the kids.) Wasserstein says he left to avoid "the watchful eyes of competitors," which may tell more about Wasserstein than Milken.[7] Bruck talks about how he resisted prying questions from senior executives at Drexel; the move was clearly a declaration of independence.[8] One of those execs was Burnham, then closing in on seventy years of age. The much-younger man's aggressiveness and penchant for secrecy worried Burnham, who had grown up in an age when capital was dear, liquidity could disappear like water in a colander, and disaster was always in the forecast. Milken believed that the money world had changed; *he* had changed it. Junk released powerful energies. Money was flowing, liquidity abundant, risk at bay, despite the '70s gloom. (Goodman as Adam Smith: "The one thing we have, whether or not we will ever find true Value, is liquidity—the ability to buy and sell momentarily and relatively effortlessly. Liquidity is the cornerstone of Wall Street."[9] Liquidity, to say the least, was related to but not the same as jingling, crackling money-in-your-pocket. A liquid cornerstone may be a sly Smithian joke.) Six years later, in 1984, Drexel would run an ad campaign with the tag line "How to Invent Money." The two worldviews—scarcity and abundance, the dead past and the lively future, prudence and risk—clashed. So Milken put a continent between himself and New York.

IN THE EARLY years, Milken had commuted in the pitch-black of an early-morning bus from Cherry Hill, NJ, to Drexel Burnham on Wall Street, poring over bond data wearing a miner's cap with a light. (The detail comes from Bruck. Just before she published her book, a group of Drexel insiders gathered to read it. Richard Sandler, an old

Milken colleague, erupted over the miner's cap anecdote. "It was a gift. It was an eye doctor's thing. He never wore it; he only wore it once."[10] Bruck never revised.) The miner's cap packed a metaphorical punch: this intense guy with the burning eyes was peering into the dark—literally and figuratively. It wasn't just that Milken, like Flom in his proxy days, operated in an arena that was so marginal as to be almost invisible to much of American business, but that his bonds were considered lost, fallen, tainted, cast into stygian gloom. In retrospect, the fact that Milken could retrieve and resuscitate these bonds was one of many consequences of broadly rising American financial wealth, one that Harvard professor John Kenneth Galbraith, for instance, in *The Affluent Society,* never envisioned, though he did worry about the pernicious effect of installment credit. There was enough money—*liquidity*—around to jolt junk to life, and there was a feedback loop attached: once launched, Milken's junk network turned synergistic. Bonds, one form of debt, had once been the primary currency of a capital-poor, risk-averse financial world, the prudent man's investment (many a Wasp fortune sat upon a mound of corporate bonds); by the time Milken came along, in the '60s, the upside appeal of stocks had made bonds appear dull, dusty, antiquated, boring; institutions were buying stocks. In M&A, bonds generally had, at best, marginal standing. Or worse. Even loans, another form of debt, were senior to bonds in the capital structure: banks got paid before bondholders. And as deals grew more leveraged (that is, featured more debt) and complex, bondholders often found the value of their bonds beaten down as new loans and debt were piled atop them. In Jensen and Meckling's concept of the nexus-of-contract corporation, bondholders were creditors possessing an explicitly contractual relationship with the firm, which agreed to pay interest on a schedule; so-called bond covenants set other, more technical, conditions. Unlike shareholders, who were recipients of the residual income of corporations, and thus principals, bondholders existed in a netherworld, more agent than principal. Jensen considered them intermediaries, in the same class as workers, customers, and local residents eager for companies to fund museums and support local house prices.

Bondholders were not party to the elemental struggle between managers and shareholders. They were not within the ambit of fiduciary duties (except to their own investors). Beyond contractual details, bonds and bondholders, like loans and lenders, were not thought of as actors in the daily drama of corporate governance. They needed protection; they required lawyers.

Milken changed all that. Milken made the issuance and use of junk bonds (he invented the term until some genius realized it sounded bad, *high-yield* was rolled out, and critics were then ritually castigated for using the term *junk*) an essential step in financing a new company or engineering a hostile takeover. American companies, Milken believed, were underleveraged: too little debt. Debt got a nifty tax deduction, but it could make equity seem far more potent (earnings per share skyrocketed if there weren't many shares). And debt forced agents to serve principals, a concept Jensen would soon embrace. Debt was, in James Grant's phrase, "the new Archimedes lever."[11] (Grant, a former *Barron's* credit reporter and founder of a well-read bimonthly newsletter, *Grant's Interest Rate Reporter,* who started getting random phone calls from Milken trying to cure his skepticism over junk, was being ironic; he lacked faith in Milken's new age.) Milken's junk broke the stranglehold that equity financing had held over companies. The only "real" company had been assumed to be a *public* company. The conventional path toward growth and maturity was the initial public offering, in which a company listed on an exchange and sold shares to the public, a rite of passage attracting equity capital necessary for expansion and prosperity. The SEC oversaw public companies and mandated a regular cycle of disclosures; this system was the keystone of New Deal reforms, lifting transparency—in Louis Brandeis's oft-chanted phrase, "sunlight is said to be the best of disinfectants"—to the summit of regulatory virtues. Public companies were supposed to be transparent to investors, as opposed to the suspicious, if legal, opacity of private companies. A public listing brought with it the SEC's major constituency, shareholders, thousands of them, of all varieties, and thus produced the separation of ownership and control, not to say a milling, hard-to-shepherd mob of investors. Traditionally, financing of private companies was perilous and scarce—mostly bank loans and the odd angel investor. Junk provided fresh sources of capital. Bonds had their complexities and compliance issues, but they were, by definition, *private*, and ownership and control were direct, aligned, undivided, unambiguous: prelapsarian. The SEC was more remote from bonds, junk or investment-grade, than stocks. (The Federal Reserve, for obvious reasons, kept a keen eye on the Treasury market.) A company financed by bonds—which increasingly meant Milken's bonds— could retain its privacy, entrepreneurial freedom, and creativity, while avoiding the governance challenge of shareholders who owned but didn't monitor and a government that regulated, taxed, and harassed. And joining Milken's magic circle also provided protection from attack, better even than Flom's retainers.

In his first fifteen years at Drexel Burnham Lambert (the latter arrived with an infusion of capital from Belgian bank Groupe Bruxelles Lambert), Milken barely appeared in the press and rarely publicly articulated a case for junk bonds beyond the fact that they were a big opportunity. That began to change in 1984, when the sales job began to a larger public. *High-yield* was now part of the nomenclature. "Why buy 'high-yield' bonds? Because they offer an opportunity for better performance without undue risk; a chance to earn an incremental rate of return compared to risk-free Treasuries or investment grade bonds." That came from "The Case for High-Yield Bonds" produced for the 1984 Drexel Burnham Lambert High Yield Conference in Beverly Hills, a gathering of clients that had begun as a modest confab in the '70s. As Grant noted tartly, that very "bullish" case seemed to come from Milken himself.[12] True, the "case" was a marketing document. What few saw at the time was that the very fact that junk represented such an opportunity—that mispricing was so persistent—also meant it violated Chicago's efficient-market faith.[13] And this wasn't just a tiny inefficiency either; for Milken it lasted two decades. (What was the source of this inefficiency? Milken blamed credit-raters, and their fixation on past performance; but some of it clearly came from Drexel's stranglehold on a very private business and the fact that information did not flow very far from Milken himself. Milken's companies had promise and potential: they were about the future, not some failed past. This was a powerful message in the Reagan '80s, but it suggests a flaw in the arbitrage process that Chicago did not acknowledge.)

This violation captures a little-noted difference between Chicago and Wall Street: the latter, whether on Broad Street or Beverly Hills, reflexively resisted the strong form of Fama's efficiency argument, as did the investing public. If Wall Street had embraced it, it might as well have closed up shop—or attempted to replicate the fixed rules of the old Club, which, in a sense, was what Milken was quietly doing in Beverly Hills. A purely efficient market is one without profits for intermediaries. Without inefficiencies, without opportunistic mismatches, without smart guys versus chumps, Wall Street can't generate a decent return on its capital—certainly not the kind to send shares soaring. That tension between efficiency and inefficiency—the opportunities that eventually are eliminated by mounting and remorseless arbitrage in the form of competition—shapes much of the history of post-'70s Wall Street, from junk bonds to M&A to mortgages, and fed Milken's reticence bordering on paranoia. The easiest way to lose a windfall inefficiency in a remorselessly arbitraging Wall Street is to blab about it; and yet the only way to grow profits, to retain control, is to bring more people and money into the game, to expand the market, to feed the beast, to *grow*. That tension could be explosive. In hindsight, Milken controlled an inefficient market, but his grasp, in time, naturally eroded as its profit possibilities dawned upon, first, Wall Street, then the public. Milken probably realized this; the folks in New York might not have. Milken's increasingly Herculean efforts as the '80s unfolded to dominate and retain personal control over a market that was expanding, diversifying, drawing in more and more players, and more and more money, is one that some observers, like Bruck in *The Predator's Ball* and James Stewart in *Den of Thieves* (a title that telegraphs its punch), interpreted as a descent into a cult of personality. Whatever you think of Milken, the fact that he retained *personal* hegemony over junk for as long as he did is an amazing feat, like a man pulling a tractor-trailer, requiring an almost theological level of belief in himself and his product and a staggering will. But his loss of control was also inevitable, though the nature of his fall was not.

Milken ran a private firm within a private firm. He resisted Drexel going public for years, which resulted in the Groupe Bruxelles Lambert infusion. What good would that do *him?* He made the bulk of the firm's profits; he generated the capital. Public ownership would simply be another threat to his grip on the market. Milken's troops referred to the junk-bond unit as the Department; he was nominally a mere vice president. At his first address in Century City, Los Angeles, there was no name on the door; he claimed never to have had an office; his photo never appeared in the annual report. He had no need for acclaim as he built, layer upon layer, name upon name, his network of investors and clients. He felt no necessity to talk about what he was building, to justify it to a wider world—though he was, by all accounts (and there are many), a driven, evangelical salesman. He lived on the phone to *his* market; an endless queue of high-powered executives and financiers showed up at 5 a.m. to talk to *him.* Bruck quotes casino magnate Steve Wynn, an early Milken client: "Mike would always say, 'You can't make a dime off publicity.'"[14] Milken himself told Bruck that if his people started getting into print they'd think they were famous. "They won't work as well. I want them in at four or four-thirty, ready to work, until eight o'clock at night. That's what we do, that's our responsibility. I don't want them to think of what's outside." Outside did not mean on the sidewalk, but outside the market.[15]

He controlled compensation, which mushroomed into a tangled, luxuriant, and eventually toxic undergrowth of bonuses, bond and equity stakes, warrants attached to underwritings, private side deals, and reciprocal arrangements; it was every bit as complex as the off-balance-sheet bestiary that Enron later gestated, if marginally more legal. Money was fungible. Complexity provided options; options spawned temptations. Compensation was control—not just over his team but over his burgeoning network, which eventually included major corporations. Members of the Department talked about Milken's loyalty and charisma, but the constant circulation of money that only he fully comprehended (at least until the unraveling) fed the muscles and tendons of the operation, justifying the 4 a.m. start. He understood the network effect, the tendency of liquidity to be drawn to liquidity, of growth to fuel growth. He rewarded, he punished, he incentivized, he linked buyers and sellers. Mike gave; Mike taketh away. Your self-interest was his self-interest. And he didn't ignore the feast. He and his younger brother Lowell, a lawyer, got the first and best cuts, accumulating stupendous personal wealth; annual comp for Milken rose from over $100 million to, in 1987, over $500 million, an eventual net worth estimated at somewhere between a billion or two, which was a lot of money in the '80s, even as he went home for three hours of sleep to his everyman ranch house on the Encino *cul-de-sac*. (In later media treatments, this contradiction—egoless guy, ridiculous wealth—was never satisfactorily reconciled.) There was the most basic of hierarchies at Wilshire Boulevard; there was Mike, at the center of the X desk, and everyone else, many of whom would turn out to be very talented professionals. (Many thought that Leon Black, the son of conglomerateur Eli Black, who ran the LBO group in New York, was Milken's greatest talent—but there were others. Bruck notes that in the New York group Milken only really respected Fred Joseph, who ran it before becoming CEO, and Black.) The org chart was an office joke. No one outworked Milken or exceeded his fine-print knowledge of the product, down to individual bonds for long-forgotten companies. No one knew what Mike knew. Again, none of this was necessarily illegal. But it became more and more difficult to sustain the mounting contradictions, even as his very-real enemies, both on Wall Street and the government, multiplied.

Ironically, Milken embodied the best argument *against* the reductionism of agency theory. Milken was an intermediary, a trader, an analyst, an underwriter, an advisor, a market maker, a salesman, a financier. He was, Black said, "a man who sees the big picture all the time—and also the small picture, down to the details."[16] *Forbes*, in a 1986 story called "One-Man Revolution," acutely noted: "Stories that have appeared recently comparing him to J. P. Morgan or calling him the junk bond king miss the point: Essentially Milken has created his own universe. He isn't just a step ahead of his Wall Street peers—he's a quantum leap ahead, acting as a venture capitalist, investment banker, trader, investor."[17] As the grand orchestrator—"the grand sorcerer" or "the magnificent," as Cary Reich in *Institutional Investor* called him[18]—Milken determined which deals got done and which did not: he was the ultimate authority. Leon Black told Bruck in mid-1996: "We are increasingly on all sides of transactions."[19] The market existed in Milken's frontal lobe. Yea or nay? Ask Mike. He was the prime mover behind the curtain; he regularly set prices in thinly traded issues, a sin of sins in a market economy. Even though he was in California, he represented the apotheosis of Wall Street as a principal in takeovers. He served as both agent and principal: the very embodiment of conflict. He never managed any of these companies (like Rohatyn, he didn't even manage his own firm). The rest of Wall Street envied him, hated him, imitated him. You could—and many did—argue endlessly over what Milken did with those multiple roles, what his state of mind was; but less debatable is the fact that he fulfilled those roles. And given the typical diagnosis of agency theory—if a conflict exists it generates agency costs—Milken was a walking, talking, deal-making transgression. And yet, no one, certainly not Jensen nor Fischel, who later wrote a book trying to exonerate him.[20] In fact, because Milken restored offense to the takeover market, his supporters argued that the very forces that were trying to dethrone him, such as US attorney Rudolph Giuliani, were illegitimate and damaging, rather than just arbitrage by another name.

Only later, when Milken was on the defensive, did he and Drexel get around to overlaying a larger *public* rationale on his labors that didn't involve the accumulation of wealth and power; his ideological supporters preached those ideas, ranging from credit as the mother's milk of commercial democracy to M&A as a restructuring force for good to his views on family raising and global financial problems. Like Rohatyn, he became a celebrity, albeit one harassed by prosecutors. He became, by necessity, political. His life was probed, interpreted, explained in a dozen books and a hundred magazine articles. There's a tendency with Milken to ascribe later thoughts to earlier beginnings, as if he knew the pattern in history's financial throw rug: Milken, by this mindset, had always been Milken; history led to him, culminated in him. Wasserstein, without citation, mentions in *Big Deal* that Milken grew interested in low-grade bonds when he was helping his father with a client.[21] Milken once told Bruck that Hickman's junk study was "consistent with what I had been thinking for a long time." Perhaps that's true; much of his later thinking did align with his early salesmanship. In 1970 he said he submitted an op-ed to the *New York Times,* arguing his own brand of idealism: "Unlike other crusaders from Berkeley, I have chosen Wall Street as my battleground." (Hard to imagine what motivated that confession, and how the paper could reject it.) The world hadn't realized that Milken's higher intent began as a civil rights gesture after the 1965 Watts riots when he was nineteen; he didn't offer that up publicly until 2000, when he began to write about the democratization of finance.

Meanwhile, the size and scope of Milken's network, power, and wealth edged into sight only when he began to finance ever-larger, ever-more-public takeovers, fueling LBOs and providing jet packs of money for Icahn and Pickens and Perelman and Peltz. Even when Drexel controlled the fates of hostile takeovers, to a far greater extent than even a Wasserstein could imagine, Milken remained reticent; he appeared happiest as Mike, the one true God of his expanding universe, the evangelist of junk, comprehensible only to himself. He may, as some accounts suggest, have resisted the move into M&A, uncharacteristically allowing himself to be bullied by New York, Fred Joseph, and corporate finance, and he may have wanted to retreat from takeovers once the storm broke. But he didn't; he couldn't; he found himself driven forward by the dynamics of the network he had created and controlled. He was, in any event, more ambivalent about M&A than about the junk market itself.

But who truly knew? Grant argued that Milken fundamentally misunderstood Hickman and ignored his work on the deterioration of low-rated bond quality in bull markets. Grant called it the "Law of Decay," and laid out a cyclical scheme—theory was probably too highfalutin—of credit growth, euphoria, and decay, which in some ways resembled economist Hyman Minsky's notions about macroeconomic cycles and bubbles. Grant, an elegant writer, also provided a snapshot of late Milken, the increasingly besieged Milken, in a book, *Money of the Mind:*

> In person, Milken was soft-spoken and unassuming. His suits and hairpiece had an off-the-rack appearance, and his shoes were middle-class. If a phone rang, he would answer it directly: "Mike." His eyes darted. Not seeming to meet yours, they would suddenly engage them. . . . In conversation, there was no wit, no thrust and no parry. His style was literal, factual and persistent. On the telephone, he was garrulous and given to broker's slogans (such as in the heat of the 1987 boom): "What you have to understand is the world is awash in liquidity," or, "You've got to look at the United States as a takeover candidate," or "Often, what's old is weak and what's new is strong." He used your first name like an index finger with which to poke you in the chest, and keep your undivided attention. But in the middle of a monologue, he could also say something unexpected.[22]

Grant questioned Milken's assumptions. He did not pretend to read his mind.

IF MILKEN IN 1984 had decided that moving aggressively into financing takeovers was a bad idea, and better left to the banks, he might not have ended up in prison. He would have had no reason to deal with Ivan Boesky, the self-styled king of the arbs, who was drawn to Milken as Drexel edged into M&A and, after he was indicted for insider trading, implicated others, including Marty Siegel and Milken himself. If Milken had resisted that move into takeovers—and it was a step corporate finance in New York was eager to take—the volume of M&A might have been lower, but the M&A phenomenon would not have differed significantly. The size and number of takeovers had reached historic proportions—outstripping, as Jensen noted, even the conglomerate wave of the '60s, which made concerns from the White House that defense was making take-overs difficult, a reach—before Drexel took the fateful plunge. Junk accelerated existing trends; it did not create the movement. Pickens, Icahn, Steinberg, Riklis, and Posner were already notorious players. A decade had passed since the first blue-chip takeover, Inco-ESB. But politically, Milken shaped much of the second half of the '80s by agreeing to finance hostile takeovers. He dominated the scene—the public scene. You can, if you choose, see junk bonds as a democ-ratization of finance; and you can view the opening up of M&A to *all* comers—as long as these new financiers happened to gain admis-sion to Milken's club, which many often forget—as a beneficial re-structuring of an entrenched corporate sector (Black saw them, with admiration, as new robber barons); you can even, though this is a leap, accept Milken as the embodiment of the invisible hand. But there are also factual realities. The internal debate at Drexel turned on sheer self-interest: it was about making more money. The firm had grown so quickly and was minting money, nearly all of it from Wilshire Boulevard, and dominated the issuance, underwriting, and trading of junk bonds. Drexel needed new markets to feed an in-creasingly insatiable machine, to build a more diversified firm (Fred Joseph's dream), and, as Milken knew better than anyone, to retain an increasingly precarious control over a whirlwind.

For a number of years, Joseph had held brainstorming sessions with a hippy-dippy, up from the '60s, Bombay-born consultant named Cavas Gobhai. Joseph was trying to construct a diversified firm around Milken. He ran a corporate finance department that was as second rate as the old Burnham, though full of talent. A number of Gobhai sessions beginning in the late '70s focused on building an operation that could play with the big boys in takeovers. It was aspi-rational. Milken sent emissaries to the early meetings (he now rarely left the office), which tackled subjects like how corporate finance could more effectively use—leverage—Milken's operation, that is, in Gobhai's summation: "Merge with Mike."[23] In 1982 the group, meet-ing in New York, drew up a list of who they might recruit as a rain-making M&A banker: on the admittedly blue-sky list was Flom,

Lipton, Rohatyn, Wasserstein, Ira Harris, Lehman's Eric Gleacher, and Kidder's Siegel. (Joseph eventually bagged Siegel, only to discover he was caught in the Boesky insider-trading scandals.) Drexel did become one of Skadden's top five clients; the firm even used Lipton once to resolve a dispute over dividends (or the lack of dividends) with shareholder Groupe Bruxelles Lambert, before he turned decisively against the firm, Milken, and junk. The group also wrestled with another issue. The firm had few clients capable of large deals, but it had, through Milken, access to, as he said in 1985, a trillion dollars in wealth. Rather than depend on a client, why wouldn't Drexel itself, rather than a bank, put up the billion dollars or so necessary for a takeover? As Bruck asks, paraphrasing, "Or what if they said they did [have the money] (and got it later)? And what if, by staking the word of the firm on this claim, the world believed it and acted accordingly? In the new lexicon—and universe—that Drexel would soon create, this concept would become known as the 'highly confident' letter. But for now it was christened (for its emptiness) the Air Fund."[24]

The Air Fund was a remarkable leap. It was using Milken's network in a provocative and radical new way. It was capturing Milken's evangelical thrust: *believe me.* Over the next year—and the fact that it took a year is significant—Milken grew comfortable with it, saw how it fit into his machinery, and what a step he was taking. Like the two-tier, front-end-loaded bid or the poison pill, the Air Fund was a game changer, turbo-charging the network. There was risk, of course. Drexel posed a direct threat to the banks, which had powerful allies like the Federal Reserve. Milken expressed his trepidation of the banks at one point to Grant: "Recalling Saul Steinberg's failed attempt to take over Chemical Bank in the late 1960s, he advised never to get crosswise with it or others like it. They were powerful and unforgiving institutions, he said, and he seemed to fear what they might try to do to him for taking so much of their corporate-finance business."[25] In fact, the banks had a big problem, which Milken was about to exacerbate. M&A was a lucrative line of business for them. They were already feeling the pinch of what, in regulatory jargon, is known as disintermediation—a process in which nonbanks, such as Wall Street firms or mutual funds or even computer companies, peel away profitable parts of their franchise and take banks' customers. Banks were still snarled in regulatory red tape; unregulated rivals had a big advantage. But that regulation, such as that New Deal centerpiece, Glass-Steagall, which separated investment banking from commercial banking, was beginning to crumble in a larger, globalizing financial world that from a customer's perspective didn't care about regulatory niceties and organizational divisions.

Milken had already edged onto the midway of the takeover circus. In 1982, Drexel had offered mezzanine financing for two leveraged buyouts. Financing these deals required multiple layers of capital in different forms. Mezzanine was a form of mostly unsecured financing that sat just below, and supported, bank loans (and sat just above the equity) in increasingly intricate capital structures. Allan Sloan argued in the first of a series of revelatory articles about takeovers, junk, and Milken in *Forbes* from 1984 to 1986[26] that one of the keys to LBOs was the development of mezzanine debt, mostly junk sold to pension funds, which gave bank lenders cover to participate in highly leveraged deals.[27] LBOs had been a specialty transaction for years, mostly involving small, private, and mature industrial companies or corporate spin-offs. But by 1984 they were exploding—and they were targeting larger public companies. Engineered by firms such as Kohlberg Kravis Roberts, Forstmann, Little & Co., and Clayton Dubilier & Rice, they were a variant of M&A, though rarely hostile. The firm, usually with the cooperation and participation of management, would "buy out" the company (that is, put up a small amount of equity), then have the company take out a large amount of debt, which, given the leveraged nature of the post-buyout company, usually included junk. In short, they purchased a company, which then paid for the acquisition. The game, in theory, was to remove the agency costs, upgrade operations, and sell at a higher price, paying yourself and your investors.

Once they began to scale up, LBOs quickly became controversial. First, the technique seemed too good to be true: You used the company to finance its own acquisition? The process, in fact, was rife with potential conflicts, particularly with management participation. The management buyout also, as with Milken's role, mixed agent and principal roles: management was an agent absconding with company assets to become a principal. (The strange thing was, the buyout itself was a governance disaster but produced a more aligned governance structure, albeit a private one, in the new entity.) Second, the LBO left an initially low-debt company burdened by debt. You could take this two ways, depending on how you felt about agency theory. You could look at this as pillaging the company, or you could see it as providing incentives to work harder and more creatively. In fact, depending on circumstance and practitioner, there was a little of both. Moreover, as Sloan pointed out, all this debt was tax-deductible. "The key reason for the frenzied growth [in LBOs] is that Uncle Sam, in his wisdom, subsidized the LBO business. Not directly, of course, but through the tax code."[28] Many of these deals were unthinkable without the tax code. Third, some of these LBOs proved to be fantastically profitable for the buyout or LBO firms—like junk, *LBOs* as a term was sanitized in the '90s into *private equity*—mostly because of that leverage. If the debt-heavy company prospered and was sold off, the buyout firms made windfalls; if it failed, the firms lost a tiny amount of equity, while workers lost their jobs and creditors absorbed their losses. Some of these windfalls were off the charts.

Two stood out. In 1982, former Nixon treasury secretary William Simon and his partner at Wesray Capital, Raymond Chambers, bought a greeting-card company, Gibson Greetings, from conglomerate RCA in an LBO for $80 million. (This was a conglomerate breakup deal: Gibson had been gobbled up by CIT Group, a business lender, which in turn was consumed by RCA, a Rohatyn relationship.) Wesray put in equity of $1 million; the rest was borrowed for an 80–1 leverage ratio. In 1983 Wesray took Gibson public, and ended up holding about half the shares, now worth $290 million. Simon had personally put up $360,000 and made a quick $66 million. Gibson was a straight play on leverage and opportunistic timing. It was a mind-boggling windfall. At that point, Milken was an interested observer, not a participant.

He *was* involved in a second spectacular LBO, for Metromedia; in fact, he made it happen. In June 1984 John Kluge, the chairman and CEO of Metromedia, the old client of Seligson & Morris and the re-named successor of TV pioneer Du Mont Broadcasting, decided to LBO the company with three colleagues—technically, it was an MBO, a management buyout. Kluge, who started as a food broker, had a long and controversial career at Metromedia exploiting a variety of tax-avoidance and creative accounting schemes. By 1983 the stock was falling and he launched an LBO, the biggest up to that point: $1.3 billion in bank loans, the cost of which was crushing. As Grant pointed out, the interest on the loan came to 14.9 percent, while the junk—it was an early junk LBO deal—that Drexel raised to take out the loan was 15.4 percent, though payment was stretched out like a rubber band. This elongation of payments enabled enormous leverage: after the junk offering, Metromedia had a capital-to-equity ratio of 100 to 1. Kluge himself, who had owned 26 percent of the company, put up only shares, no cash, in the LBO (unlike his colleagues); after the junk offering, he ended up with 75.5 percent of Metromedia, *without spending a dime* of his own money. He then began selling off assets, including television stations, to Rupert Murdoch (these formed the basis for Fox) and Hearst for $2 billion, followed by the sale of a billboard subsidiary, nine radio stations, the Harlem Globetrotters, and the Ice Capades for a billion more. Kluge, for a time, reigned as the second-richest man in America.[29]

Metromedia made capitalists everywhere try to figure out the math, which shocked even sophisticated financial reporters like Sloan, who deconstructed the deal in *Forbes* in 1984 under the headline "The Magician," focusing on Kluge's "hocus-pocus."[30] The true magician in this case was not Kluge but the still-behind-the-curtain Milken, whose junk bonds made the deal possible. Sloan tracked the flow of junk over the next few months. He and his co-author Howard Rudnitsky accumulated piles of bond filings, arranged them in stacks, then began to painstakingly trace the money: who bought, who sold. What they discovered were the first lineaments of Milken's self-reinforcing, mutually beneficial network. The illustration on *Forbes*'s cover for "Mike

Milken's Marvelous Money Machine" was a merry-go-round populated by Milken and some of his crowd: Steinberg, Posner, the Belzberg brothers, Fred Carr, Thomas Spiegel, and Carl Lindner.[31] Sloan recalls *Forbes*'s legendary editor James Michaels looking at the art and saying, with chilly prescience: "Do you realize all of them are Jewish?" Sloan, who like Michaels was Jewish, replied that he thought Lindner was a Baptist. Michaels shot back, "That's the worst kind of Jew."[32]

In retrospect, Milken was perfect for the needs of the LBOers. Milken was willing to take risk, thus enabling the construction of fantastic towers of debt sitting atop a layer of mezzanine resting upon a few cinder blocks of equity contributed by the LBO sponsors—a kind of upside-down pyramid. He was not overly concerned about getting his junk bonds written down; through the deft manipulation of his network, he had made a practice of not allowing his clients to lose money, though that became increasingly difficult, then impossible. He quickly became a go-to stop for Kohlberg Kravis Roberts and a number of the bigger LBO shops. One exception was Forstmann Little, whose principal, Theodore "Teddy" Forstmann, used subordinated debt rather than junk and developed an animus toward Drexel and Milken. Despite its controversies, the LBO market suited Milken. The deals were private. They involved a fresh group of financial entrepreneurs, much like his raiders and empire builders. This was a relatively small group of firms but they were very active: they were *transactional.* And they were thrilled to find a supplier of financing that competed with the banks, which they viewed as stuffy, conservative, and capricious—and, most importantly, parsimonious and pricey.

LBOs led to takeovers. A Gobhai meeting in November 1984 aired out the Highly Confident letter scheme. There was consensus: Milken, Joseph, corporate finance, and key clients were ready to go. By April, at the 1985 High Yield Conference—the first true Predator's Ball—Drexel was prepared to announce that it would participate as both a backer and as an advisor to hostile deals. The conference, orchestrated by Donald "Donny" Engel, a Milken client finder (he reeled in Posner as a client and received the nickname "the Prince of Schlock"), had grown, year after year, since the late '70s. Engel ran the exclusive Bungalow 8 cocktail party for the most important clients at the Beverly Hills Hotel, filling the room with starlets (his other nickname was "the house pimp") and clients. During the day, some one hundred issuers of Drexel-backed junk lined up to speak at the Beverly Hilton. Joseph made the announcement in the afternoon. He explained the Highly Confident concept. As James Stewart wrote in *Den of Thieves,* touching on the underlying governance canker of the Drexel Way: "Joseph elaborated on his own philosophy: Companies should belong to those willing to take risks—in other words, to Drexel's clients rather than public shareholders. That's what capitalism was all about. Anyone with Drexel's backing could buy a company. 'For the first time in history, we've leveled the playing field. The small can go after the big,' Joseph concluded."[33] The American dream, at least since Andrew Jackson: level the playing field, at least for our crowd.

Stewart finished his set piece at Bungalow 8 that evening, carefully noting the bodies. "Boesky was in a corner talking quietly with Icahn; Sir James [Goldsmith] was in a group with Pickens and Flom. Murdoch and Lindner were chatting with [Drexel banker David] Kay and Engel, the affable host. Within only a week, Pickens would launch his bid for Unocal, Peltz would bid for National Can, Sir James would attack Crown Zellerbach, and Farley would go after Northwest Airlines—all with Drexel financing."[34]

As the latter-day Adam Smith wrote: image and reality and identity and anxiety and money. That was the money game. The revolt of the fallen angels had begun.

APOPLEXY REIGNED. JUNK was either the destruction of western civilization or its salvation. In late 1984, Lipton, who had begun to send out regular communications railing about abusive takeovers to clients, strung together epithets—"The combination of bust-up takeover threats with greenmail has become a national scandal. The junk-bond bust-up takeover is replacing the two-tier bootstrap bust-up takeover"—that drove the *New York Times*'s William Safire in his language column to translate. "'National scandal' is the only phrase I recognize in that burst of tycoonspeak," Safire wrote.[35] A few months later, in April 1985, Lipton elaborated to the *New York Times:* "Junk bond financing of takeovers is a further exacerbation of increased leverage in the economy."[36] The debt is "creating a system which historically goes back to the tulip bubble in the 17th century, the South Sea bubble in the 18th century, the money panics in the 19th century and in 1929, which have resulted in crashes, panics and great devastation." In that same story, First Boston's Mahar expressed an eagerness for the firm to get into the junk financing, which, he noted, "raises the horizons of what some clients can do and makes the probability of winning a takeover higher."

By the end of 1985, a new cop appeared. Paul Volcker's Federal Reserve, which oversaw national banks, proposed to apply margin rules to junk used in takeovers, effectively restricting the sale of high-yield bonds to 50 percent, thus fulfilling Milken's fear of payback. Volcker, the tall, cigar-smoking central banker who had killed inflation, had been, like Lipton, publicly worrying about high debt, particularly in takeovers. The administration reacted to the attempt with rare collective fury: Treasury, Justice, Labor, Commerce, the SEC, the CEA, and the OMB all lined up to deny the central bank's right to intervene. Assistant attorney general for antitrust Douglas Ginsburg, a Chicago Law School product—he had worked on the law review with Easterbrook—harrumphed, "The board's decision would destroy the market for corporate control, which disciplines inefficient managers and allows shareholders to maximize return on their investment."[37] Volcker ignored them and the measure survived two 3–2 party-line votes (Volcker and two Democrats against two Republicans) on the Fed Board of Governors—an unusual dissension at the Fed and widely seen as a sign of Volcker's weakening clout.[38] Immediately after passage, the stock market plunged, then recovered.[39] Lipton was pleased but wary. Rohatyn came across as more ambivalent. "I think it's a very significant thing for the Fed to take a position on the more extreme types of leverage involved in some of these junk-bond takeovers," he said. Not that he opposed all high-yield bonds, he added, just the extremes. Skadden Arps represented Drexel at the Fed, but lost. The apocalypse, M&A version, became fact. But in the end, as the *Times* noted, "A check of Wall Street lawyers, entrepreneurs and investment bankers yesterday indicated that many felt there would be ways around the rule." There were.

Chapter Twelve

THE FLAW IN THE PERFECT MACHINE

MILKEN'S SPECTACULAR EMERGENCE was the *deus ex machina* that Chicago needed to counter the poison pill. Milken swung the advantage back to offense. He defibrillated the Chicago dream of takeovers as a cleansing process of arbitrage back to life. The fact that Milken was a one-man market for junk bonds, which was hardly the way efficient *free* markets worked, was conveniently overlooked, at first through lack of knowledge of how Drexel operated, then, for true believers, more deliberately, and long after Allan Sloan in *Forbes,* Connie Bruck in *Predator's Ball,* James Stewart in *Den of Thieves,* and various federal investigations had produced detailed views of Milken's machinery. But in 1985 Milken not only provided a potent new fuel for the takeover market, he was, his advocates declared, democratizing takeovers, both by selling bonds of formerly downtrodden companies and by financing swarms of raiders, many of whom had been obscure or marginal in the past. (Some of them, to be fair, built considerable empires.) Milken was the deity the theory demanded. Again, the fact that he "democratized" takeovers only for those buyers who he personally allowed into his club was not apparent or part of his growing reputation. Eventually he would lose control of determining that membership—Wall Street was already scheming to break his stranglehold—and the jig would be up.

Milken was the triumph of ends over means—of reality bending toward desire. He kept the means under a large blanket as long as he could. But it wasn't just the mounting tension between his near-absolute control and an exploding market. Milken refused to allow his deals to be seen to fail. The ultimate source of his power was the belief that he knew more, that he was smarter, that he had many options to deal with distress, loss, or bankruptcy. Milken seemed infallible. So great was this power that Chicago viewed Drexel and Milken as models for effective private restructurings that avoided the bankruptcy courts. But the Chicago crowd did not spend a lot of time trying to figure out how those restructurings were actually accomplished. Milken made it seem as if he never lost, or that his deals never flopped. They did; he was just a master at burying failure and moving on. And as long as the market and the economy grew, he could continue to play that game.

Still, one potential problem always lurked at the edges of the take-over market. Shareholders might be strolling off with fat premiums, making event studies appear spectacular. But what was happening within those merged or acquired companies? What long-term effect—and event studies, measures of abnormal stock gains in takeovers, were, by definition, short-term—did M&A have on the resulting companies? Did the question of success and failure end at a deal's closing party, and involve only a new owner and a higher share price? Over the short term, Milken and his raiders appeared to be omnipotent forces. But some observers had their doubts. They knew that markets rose and fell, and that the turn often came with shocking, even destructive speed. They understood how fragile the inner workings of a corporation—systems, practices, technologies, products, cultures, *people*—actually were. They saw them as organic entities, with complex lives, psychological and material; individual, diverse, shaped by their pasts, not as abstract nexuses of contracts that could be engineered without cost, re-imagined without stress, dissembled, re-assembled with frictionless ease. They recognized them as empirical entities, not as theoretical constructs—and they saw difficulties.

But in the endless vistas of a bull market, few cared.

IN 2006, as M&A was beginning another surge in volume, economist Frederic "Mike" Scherer, who had just settled, after a long academic career, at Harvard's Kennedy School of Government as an emeritus professor, wrote a paper that looked back on a long career thinking about, among other things, mergers. "Thirty-six years after my first published struggle with the issue, I have three itches that still need scratching," he wrote. First, he felt the need to look again at the underlying trends of a merger boom. Second, he noted, "the debate over the success of mergers continues." And third, he was interested in a kind of meta-question: "How mergers and the consequences are being treated in business schools."[1]

Scherer had graduated from the University of Michigan, received an MBA at Harvard in 1958, and began a long exodus through academia—Princeton, Northwestern, Swarthmore, Haverford, with stints overseas at the University of Bayreuth and the Central European University. He spent two years as the chief economist at the Federal Trade Commission in 1974–1976. Scherer's perspective on economic matters was fundamentally different from that of the Chicago school—a group he referred to as "the finance specialists." Scherer was drawn to an economic specialty known as industrial organization that involved an attempt to understand the behavior and performance of industry—that is, companies that produce tangible, tradable commodities or products: grain, oil, cars, pharmaceuticals, beer, steel, semiconductors. Like any field with "industrial" as a prefix, industrial organization does not have the stature it had a half-century ago. Scherer studied industrial markets rather than financial markets, which Chicago often saw as the very ideal of markets; he undertook grinding empirical research, not mathematized theory and model-building. In his 1996 textbook on the subject, *Industry Structure, Strategy, and Public Policy,* Scherer noted the three strands he was weaving together: history, theory, and policy.[2] His methodology of choice was the case study, which was really to say he found value in economic history: "The case studies are organized historically in the belief that real-world industries are complex organisms whose evolution can be understood only through careful attention to historical dynamics. An historical approach is adopted also to help readers avoid the trap of which George Santayana warned: that those who fail to learn the lessons of the past condemn themselves to repeat its errors."[3] Scherer, in short, was an empiricist, trying to make sense of observable facts, data, evidence that emerges over time. Chicago, for the most part, favored a more theoretical, timeless, and perfect market present, a properly scientific, *normative* standard.

In the '70s, Scherer and one of his graduate students at Northwestern, David Ravenscraft, began working on a project analyzing mergers, originally under the aegis of the Federal Trade Commission's Bureau of Economics. The FTC pioneered antitrust in the United States (today it shares the franchise with the Department of Justice). Chicago had long been skeptical of the antitrust enterprise, from Friedman, Stigler, and Director to Richard Posner, who in a 1976 book described it as an "intellectual disgrace," to Robert Bork, who slammed it again in yet another book two years later.[4] The focus of Chicago's ire was the Harvard-centric school of industrial organization.[5] Chicago had a point: antitrust policy had not always been, in retrospect, sensible, discriminating, or wise. It was not a science, despite its attempts at quantification and rigid guidelines. It had often been a blunt instrument and prone to ossified convention, particularly on questions of size. And innovation and technological change have a way of undermining—arbitrage again—what seem to be anti-competitive corporate bastions. But antitrust also embodied a tension involving market performance and efficiency, and one that had intrigued earlier Chicago economists as well: Can size, concentration, and market power distort the efficient setting of prices? Or are market tendencies, like arbitrage, powerful enough to naturally counter what may appear to be monopolistic behavior? And—this is the difficult part—where is the line drawn? *Who* draws the line?

Scherer, in fact, was no true believer in the rigid break-'em-up school of antitrust, though he did not dismiss it quite as cavalierly as Posner and Bork. (He became a noted expert on Harvard economist Joseph Schumpeter, with his dynamic notion of "creative destruction.") In the '60s, Scherer had done graduate work with Jesse Markham, an early scholar of mergers, at the Harvard Business School. Markham argued the "rule of reason" in mergers—"reason, in this case, meant sensible pragmatism as opposed to rigid guidelines on concentration and market-share that the antitrust agencies adopted," he once said.[6] Markham had served as chief economist of the FTC in the mid-'50s, after Congress had passed legislation mandating a number of constraints on mergers. The 1930s wisdom that not just the Depression but the rise of Nazism and fascism were fueled by cartels and monopolies still held Congress captive, and academic structuralism had grown up to justify it. Big was bad, and the economy was dominated by a relatively small number of large industrial companies. Antitrust enforcement was tight. As Markham once said, "The Eisenhower administration saw me as a voice in favor of a standard of work, as opposed to perfect competition. I could advocate the benefits of letting certain firms work together to foster innovation, which buyers value just as much as temporary price advantages—the traditional yardstick of competitiveness."[7] Markham's book[8] argued that conglomerate diversification probably posed less of an antitrust threat than the authorities (particularly in the Nixon administration, which established a particularly tough anti-conglomerate stance) claimed.

When Scherer took the job of FTC chief economist himself, he had grown convinced that some mergers enhanced efficiencies, though they might trip antitrust triggers. "I struggled with that for years," he says.[9] As chief economist, he had to sign off on mergers based on the economics of the transaction. Near the end of his term, a merger deal landed on his desk, in which big agriculture commodities producer Archer-Daniels-Midland won control of Clinton Corn Processing. The FTC rejected a merger that appeared to Scherer to be highly efficient. "I was torn," he says today. "I dug in my heels and prepared an efficiency defense, which was unusual." He soon left the FTC, which did halt the merger, but he began thinking: "How can we test this?"[10]

Scherer and Ravenscraft recognized that takeovers were creating two perspectives on mergers.[11] One school of thought, the finance specialists, "sought to explain the causes and efficiency benefits of mergers through the study of stock-price performance." The second, "straddling academia, the consulting profession and the business press, focused with growing skepticism on the fruits of past mergers."[12] In this latter camp was Peter Drucker, who decried how many mergers were utter failures as businesses. Scherer and Ravenscraft wanted to analyze a wealth of data generated by the FTC on mergers over a cycle, specifically that of the conglomerate wave, and provide tangible evidence to guide policymaking. They tried to examine not stock prices but, rather, what they saw as the underlying phenomenon: actual profits generated by real companies. From 1974 to 1977 (much of Scherer's tenure there), the FTC gathered so-called line of business data from nearly 500 large US manufacturing companies, sorted into 261 manufacturing and 14 nonmanufacturing categories. Scherer and Ravenscraft used that information to analyze in detail what exactly happened in a merger wave that peaked in the late '60s, with effects that lasted into the '70s. The database contained some 6,000 mergers, which were linked and coded to individual lines of business. Accounting methods were identified. And the pair tracked "sell-offs"—that is divestitures and traced them to specific lines of business. They assembled some 15 cases studies of sell-offs.

This was a massive amount of laborious work—Scherer says it was the biggest project in his career—just as computing was arriving on the scene. The FTC had a mainframe with remote terminals, which Scherer used to write programs to analyze the data. Scherer bought himself his first desktop, a minicomputer. The problem with analyzing what occurs within a company after a merger is complexity. Even relatively simple companies have a remarkable number of moving, and interactive, parts. The need to ferret out what exactly is going on explains the extreme methods Harold Geneen of IT&T developed to extract information from herds of managers. Mergers may affect only one line of business in a company with five or fifty lines. A merger may have a big effect or a small effect, a positive effect then a negative effect, an accounting effect and an operating effect; as soon as the deal closes, the relevant line of business begins to change, evolve, buffeted in a dynamic environment. That the accounting often varied was the most common criticism against Scherer's kind of empirical research. How do you extract change attributable to a merger—the signal—from all that noise? The answer, Scherer and Ravenscraft believed, lurked within the lines of business data—"the best data," Scherer still says, "anyone ever had on mergers."

BY THE MID-'80s, the pair were writing papers on their analysis, the first stages for a book the Brookings Institution in Washington had agreed to publish. They were excited by the results—only to run into the takeover debate at its polemical height. They found themselves in the middle of an increasingly polarized ideological scrum, inflamed by junk, the poison pill, politics, and deeper theoretical, methodological, and institutional disputes.

These intellectual currents collided at New York's Morningside Heights in November 1985, just as Drexel-financed raids mounted. Academic conferences were ubiquitous. But this one was a little different: a matter of timing, luck, and ambition.[13] Columbia Law School, after decades dominated by giants like Adolf Berle and William Cary, was trying to regain relevance in corporate law; Columbia in the '70s had turned inward after the student strike of 1968. In 1980, the law school launched a law and economics center. Later, in 1985, Louis Lowenstein and John Coffee (the Adolf Berle professor of law) helped bring together many of the various combatants in the takeover debates, mostly academics, to break down some walls. The conference featured a bloc of Chicago-style economists and finance types (Jensen was there, but Henry Manne had refused the invitation and tried to talk Jensen out of it[14]) and a number of other voices, from empirical researchers like Scherer to Robert Shiller, a young Yale economist doing early research on what came to be called behavioral economics.

Ellen Magenheim was a graduate student in economics at the University of Maryland who had collaborated on a study of merger-related share prices with Dennis Mueller—like Scherer, a merger and industrial organization specialist. At thirty-one, Magenheim, today the economics department chair at Swarthmore, had worked for five years, then returned to grad school; Maryland was not, she recalls, MIT or Harvard and she was dazzled by these people she had heard about. "I think back now and I'm amazed I wasn't scared to death," she says. She recalls talking to Coffee and was struck by the focus on "real-world phenomena." She also remembers the Chicago contingent. "They were tough," she says. "They had the standard model." They viewed, she says, industrial organization types like Mueller and Scherer as old-fashioned, not theoretical, fixated on case studies and believing that structure determined behavior—the position Posner attacked in his antitrust book.[15]

Magenheim and Mueller presented a paper at a session with the unrevealing title "Evidence from the Gains of Mergers and Take-overs."[16] The session was, however, a session full of subversive ideas and challenging data. Richard Roll, an old Chicago hand most recently at UCLA, offered a paper on what he called the hubris hypothesis of M&A: the idea that bidders who often won in takeover contests were hubristic overbidders, who tended to overpay and underperform. He revisited some central issues: Why were some bidders paying large premiums if markets were strongly efficient? Were bidders aberrational, even irrational, or was the market not that efficient? And what if acquirer gains were roughly equal to acquirer losses and dealmaking costs? Lowenstein and Wharton's Edward Herman found underperformance in accounting data. Maryland's Mueller (who became a pioneer of public choice theory, the application of economics to politics), and Magenheim, argued that share prices after takeovers suffered, raising questions about the validity of efficient markets and event studies. "Long-term stockholders did not always fare well; the event studies focused on shorter-term, more speculative plays," Mueller and Magenheim concluded.

Scherer and Ravenscraft were focused not on share prices but on business operations and results—the engine, in the long run, they believed, not only of stock prices but of broader social ends such as employment, philanthropy, R&D, productivity, and growth. Their lines of business data suggested that corporate performance generally declined in years after an acquisition. But, as they noted, "This is too simple."[17] Companies that invested early in cycles—in this case the first conglomerates—often prospered, with better targets at generally lower prices. However, solid companies, they added, were bought and generally they retained their profitability and market share. Some experienced "traumatic difficulties" and had to be sold off. They then posed the spooky question that bedevils any kind of empirical historical analysis, as opposed to theoretical economics. This was the counterfactual one (meaning contrary to fact: an alternative reality), beloved of sports fans perched in bars: What if Mickey Mantle had good knees, or Ted Williams and Joe DiMaggio hadn't gone to war? What if Gore beat Bush? Some of this is the stuff of fantasy. Economic historians or econometricians, however, use counterfactuals in a more rigorous fashion. The counterfactual question shadows every attempt to judge an event—like a takeover—as better or worse. What was the alternative? Compared to *what*? What if the company hadn't been acquired? How would it have fared? Linking before to after is causality; comparing it to another, what-if alternative is counterfactual.[18]

These counterfactuals were particularly complex when they involved people, and M&A situations were people-intensive. As Scherer and Ravenscraft wrote, "Would acquired companies' profits have deteriorated even without a merger? Would the average acquired and then divested company have plunged into unprofitability had it retained its independence? Would companies that did well under conglomerate ownership have fared as well independently, among other things, receiving the capital required to sustain growth?"[19] Counterfactual questions are impossible to answer *definitively*, unless you're a complete determinist. Scherer and Ravenscraft were not. They observed one path from the past to the present, and could envision multiple paths into the future. They openly admitted how problematic studies of merger effectiveness were, even with good data. In a sense they were saying: You have to pick the counterfactual that makes sense to you. Does it involve immediate speculative profits for short-term investors or the longer-term operating performance of the resulting company?

Those distinctions were ignored in the ensuing debate. In a short comment on the session, two Chicago stalwarts—the SEC's chief economist (and member of the tender-offer advisory panel) Gregg Jarrell and the University of Michigan's Michael Bradley—lectured the empiricists to present their data clearly but not to try to interpret it, because they clearly did not know what they were doing.[20] (The sneering implication: Only Chicago neoclassical *economists* could handle theory.) Jarrell and Bradley were particularly dismissive of Scherer and Ravenscraft's work. In a few brutal paragraphs the pair scoffed at their data as inadequate and their conclusions about failed conglomerate mergers as obvious, suggesting that those failures were really caused by state and federal anti-takeover regulations, not by anything inherent in M&A. Jarrell and Bradley ignored the lines-of-business data and fixated instead on the case studies, suggesting that they represented a retreat from abstraction, econometrics, and a disciplined methodology into anecdote. They used those case studies to get off a good, if glibly duplicitous, line. "It is not clear what can be learned about the economic effects of hostile takeovers by studying 15 mergers that ultimately led to selloffs," they wrote. "This line of inquiry seems analogous to trying to understand the institution of marriage by talking only to divorced people, and to only a few of them at that."[21]

Jarrell and Bradley never mentioned the true targets of the empirical studies before them: the validity of efficient markets and event studies. Their view seemed to be that both were beyond dispute. Why defend them? Bradley had recently published an event study on takeovers. Jarrell had written a 1984 paper with Easterbrook that offered one of those sweeping statements that Chicago was famous for: "There is no debate about this subject [event studies] in the way monetarists, Keynesians and supply siders debate employment and inflation. The method of analyzing market returns is almost universally valid."[22] Universally valid—*almost*! In that paper, Easterbrook and Jarrell also clearly identified shareholders with the national good: "Because what is good for investors in this respect is good for the economy as a whole, the loss [if managers play defense] is felt widely."

Jensen presented his own paper, "The Takeover Controversy: Analysis and Evidence."[23] He made his usual points, about greenmail, junk bonds, and the evidence, from event studies, that takeovers benefit shareholders. He assumed a few provocative positions. His defense of golden parachutes, "a major component of the solution to the conflict of interest between shareholders and managers [that] has been vastly misunderstood," was particularly aggressive. Jensen noted that senior managers—those deeply self-interested, suspect, eager-to-keep-their-jobs agents, in his own characterization—have lots to lose in takeovers. Of all agents involved in operations, only senior managers seemed to Jensen deserving of protection against the disruption that takeovers wreak. (Previously, Jensen had rarely admitted there *was* disruption.) The logic is classic Jensen: bold, confident, employing a means-and-ends logic that makes sense only where a universal drive, self-interest, rules. "At times of takeover," he wrote, "shareholders are implicitly asking top-level managers of their firm to negotiate a deal for them that frequently involves the imposition of large personal costs on the managers and their families. These involve substantial moving costs, the loss of position, power and prestige, and even the loss of their jobs. Shareholders are asking the very people who are most likely to have invested considerable time and energy (in some cases, a life's work) to building a successful organization to negotiate its sale and the possible redirection of its resources."[24] Jensen was borrowing the Lipton view and using it for his own ends. Managers matter. Managers make deals. Managers engage in a life's work, which lesser souls do not—or if they do, it doesn't matter. He displayed little concern for workers, mid-level executives, researchers, technicians, salesmen, or any group below top executives; they are all, from a shareholder perspective, expendable; taking care of them isn't worth the effort. High position gets its just deserts; a sense of fairness is mere altruism.

Still, Jensen's "Takeover Controversy" is most interesting because he then galloped off in a new direction. He first provided covering fire to protect traditional Chicago verities (junk, greenmail, golden parachutes, the benefits of unrestrained takeovers), while he began to explore new ideas, which apply stress to those now-polished orthodoxies.

Jensen introduced a new theory of takeovers, free cash flow theory.[25] He admitted that free cash flow theory is just one of a "dozen theories that explain takeovers," suggesting, without perhaps realizing it, that none of them do so adequately. But he argued that the theory is consistent with a lot of the data, and it extends agency theory. Like

Roll's hypothesis that buyers with money often overpay from hubris, free cash flow theory adds a layer of predictive, psychological realism to the rudimentary dichotomies of conventional agency theory—dichotomies that dominate governance doctrine to this day.

Free cash flow is the money available to a company after operating expenses are paid. Managers who find themselves running companies producing generous amounts of free cash flow tend to produce agency issues, much as lottery winners have a tendency to go wild. In short, all that cash liberates them from any control, and they're able to spend it on mergers likely to destroy value. (Mark this moment: Though Jensen celebrated takeovers, he is admitting here that takeovers don't *always* work out well for shareholders.) Without constraints, managers waste money and erode shareholder value. There is a cyclicality buried within free cash flow theory that mirrors broader fluctuations in capitalism: managers run efficient operations until they have too much cash to play with, which they then squander. It's a psychological construct that's mostly anecdotal and empirical, not statistical: Jensen is constructing, on foundations of agency theory, a story, a narrative, then searching for data that fit. It's more complex and contingent than standard agency theory. Jensen always felt drawn to sweeping concepts—his models nearly always want to be theories—but in this case he clearly has a set of ideas that explain a particular kind of takeover. But the tug of the universal explanation is irresistible. Here Jensen used free cash flow theory to argue that it's to shareholders' benefit *generally* for firms to carry more debt (which will force managers to perform more efficiently) or to pay out that extra cash to shareholders; he called this "the control hypothesis of debt." Achieving this control over management would require shareholder intervention, which not long before he had earlier despaired of ever seeing. Or perhaps outside forces, like leveraged buyouts, might enforce that efficiency-enhancing debt.

This speculation on free cash flow captures Jensen's restless brilliance—a brilliance even critics admitted to. He did not invent free cash flow theory; but he seized upon it and applied it energetically, particularly to research about how managers at companies not under great competitive pressure and separated from ownership will prefer to enlarge staff and seek higher salaries and perquisites. Jensen effectively married that kind of insight to what was unfolding in takeovers. He was sensitive to trends, in this case the rise of LBOs, which were built on a free cash flow model with their overhang of debt, including junk bonds (a key aspect of his defense of junk): the often heavy debt load focused and disciplined managers. Governance in LBOs had fewer of the complexities of public companies: a small board of private owners intent on maximizing profits created a clear alignment of interests. Jensen, in hindsight, was slowly turning away from the tortuous complexities of public company takeovers as his economic panacea, toward private buyouts, LBOs, as the most straightforward and efficient utilization of capital. And he all but predicted that investors—activist investors—would one day demand that free cash flow be used not to make value-destroying deals but to reward shareholders, in the form of dividends and share buybacks. Much of that was far in the future; but he was on to something, and he was happy to elaborate on the relation between free cash flow and low-return mergers in various industries, mainly in oil and gas, where so many major deals had occurred.

Jensen also took a revealing swipe at Scherer and Ravenscraft.[26] Their study had no relevance, he began, including the lines-of-business data. The conglomerate transactions that provided their data, he said, were too small; the deals were done for stock and mostly involved private manufacturing firms, rendering their work "of limited usefulness in making inferences about recent takeovers of large public manufacturing and non-manufacturing companies (many acquired for cash)."[27] Jensen was torturing this point—arguing that conglomerate deals, which primarily used stock as a currency, were made for "growth" as opposed to big oil-type deals of the early '80s that spent their surplus free cash flow and were "non-growth," as if anyone went into an M&A deal hoping for non-growth. In fact, the stock that conglomerates used to buy companies was roughly equivalent to the free cash flow of the manufacturers: conglomerate shares were so inflated by a giddy market in the '60s that they appeared to be free money. Alas, when stocks crashed, as they did in the '70s, the growth play in conglomerates evaporated.

The elephantine issue Jensen ignored was the role of the market. How could a strongly efficient, omniscient market get things so wrong? If markets were not efficient, then shares were not accurate reflections of the mismanagement—the agency costs—that slack managers had allowed to build up. And the higher rationale for takeovers crumbled.

In fact, the Chicago takeover rationale was beginning to fissure— not just from the studies suggesting that M&A may not be as successful over the long run, but from within, by theories like Roll's notion of overpaying buyers and even Jensen's on the temptations of free cash flow. The transcripts of the conference hint of a struggle not just between Chicago theorists and empirical economists like Scherer and Mueller but also between the hard core of Chicago economists, like Jarrell and Bradley, against wavering financial economists beginning to question the market and the model that drove it. The Chicago school would continue to be the standard, as Ellen Magenheim said, and Jensen would continue to preach the Chicago gospel into the '90s. But the ideological movement, in terms of takeovers, had crested.

WHILE THE CONFERENCE at Columbia, not unsurprisingly, had no immediate effect on public consciousness, it was nonetheless an important milepost. Seeds had been planted, not just for the academics but, in the long run, for the practice of M&A. Scherer and Ravenscraft's work was really the first major empirical assault on concerns that Chicago had waved aside: culture, fit, price, post-merger integration, hidden liabilities, the difficulty of weaving together large and complicated organizations. Agency costs aside, it wasn't easy to run a large company in turbulent times; and it was even harder to buy and integrate large entities. The accumulated empirical research suggesting this—research that first appears en masse in Scherer and Ravenscraft's 1987 *Mergers, Sell-Offs, and Economic Efficiency*—would eventually lead to a belief that most M&A, or *all* M&A, or 42.5 percent of M&A, failed to perform over the long term.[28] In several decades, this, too, became a kind of reflexive conventional wisdom of the markets. If Chicago believed that a world without M&A would produce ruin and failing competitiveness, the all-deals-are-bad outlook was that companies were better off if M&A had never been unleashed. Both were caricatures; both were universal prescriptions for a profoundly diverse phenomenon. Like nearly everything else in finance, attitudes toward M&A would settle into tide-like cycles, a set of beliefs, often unmoored from data, that were deeply tied to the influence of waxing and waning markets. Deals are necessary; deals are junk. Perhaps Chicago was right that there are deterministic market elements at play. Bull markets spawned a sense of market efficiency; bear markets stirred skepticism.

But the all-M&A-is-bad school is also, like the all-takeovers-are-good claque, a raid upon reality. The counterfactual always looms, certainly for managers and for shareholders: What is the alternative? What if you do nothing? How do you measure success? How do you know what would have happened if you had *not* taken that fork in the road? Both universal prescriptions require a short-term horizon. Counterfactuals not only lurk in historical economic analysis; they also complicate the perspective of agents, who must act, make decisions, choose options, never knowing what the alternatives truly are—unclear, despite access to vast amounts of data, about the future. Still, Scherer remained the inveterate empiricist. He was skeptical of the belief that *all* M&A was good, that markets were strongly efficient, and that share prices were an accurate measure of long-term value. But as with antitrust, he also recognized that *some* M&A was effective as a strategy. The data spoke a complex language. Acquisitions accomplished while animal spirits were quiescent and prices were reasonable, or that involved smaller units that did not claim transformative effects, had a better chance of success than giant, highly priced mergers. One size did not fit all. He recognized that some companies practiced the craft more effectively than others, and that different industries—lines of business—varied in their suitability to M&A.

Scherer seemed most disturbed when enthusiasm for M&A outraced the data, ignoring the risk. In 2006, he offered a personal and historical perspective involving one of the institutional bulwarks of finance: the business schools. He noted that he had graduated from Harvard Business School in 1958, but he could recall in that two-year program only one case study that involved a merger. Scherer had researched the HBS list of case studies in 2005 and found thirty-one with a title containing the word *merger;* eleven with *takeover;* thirty-seven with *acquisitions;* and seven with *M&A.*[29] Three courses focused directly on M&A. In a study of finance textbooks he argued that merger content rose from 3.7 percent in 1955 editions to 22.6 percent in those published in 2005. Business school used to be about management; Drucker was their God, William Whyte their chronicler. MBA students wanted management jobs. Finance in the intervening years had mushroomed into the most popular of specialties. "Attitudes have changed in part because opportunities and market demands have changed," he wrote. "But in addition, it must be admitted that M&A is one of the most interesting, intellectually challenging topics taught in business schools. . . . How much more excitement there is in 'doing the numbers' to estimate the internal rate of return from a big proposed merger, devising takeover strategies and financial incentives to force mergers despite the reluctance of well-known corporate leaders, and structuring merger partners' payments to minimize taxes!"[30]

Generally, he said, there was less interest in management and leadership than in economics and theory. "It is easy to impress one's students with quantitative analyses that have crisp, definitive right and wrong answers," he wrote. MBAs had once been a tiny elite, destined to run large companies or teach. That changed in the '80s. In 1958, he said, 4,041 master's degrees in business subjects were conferred; in 2000 that number was 112,258—an annual growth rate of 7.92 percent. "Receiving an MBA is far from an elite distinction, and although there is a sorting based upon the much-publicized quality of the program from which the young person graduates, there are many more people one must overtake to move up the corporate hierarchy. Working on an important acquisition helps one to stand out."[31] He then concluded:

Thus, we in the United States have created a sizeable professional establishment that sees as a significant justification for its existence the making of mergers. Business school curricula emphasizing mergers are a reaction to corporate sector demand, but the supply in turn reinforces the demand. That would be troubling enough, if business program training provided the members of the establishment deep insight into what they are doing. But there are grounds for skepticism.[32]

He then pondered his earlier work on mergers. "Our finding that mergers during the 1960s and 1970s were on-average efficiency-reducing and similar conclusions from other more recent studies challenge one of their [the business schools'] most popular educational offerings," he wrote. "It is like telling Ford Motor Company that its SUVs have a high propensity to roll over, or like telling Coca-Cola that its Coke Classic contributes to obesity and eventual diabetes. It can hardly expect to receive an enthusiastic reception."[33]

Chapter Thirteen

THE OMNIPRESENT SPECTER
OF THE PYGMY STATE

T HE ACADEMIC ARGUMENTS about takeovers sorted themselves out only over the long run—over a span of years, even decades. In that long run, they had, in hindsight, a major effect on the way takeovers were perceived, albeit one that was shaped by other factors as well. Meanwhile, in the real world of this rapidly evolving deal culture, events were unfolding like a house falling down, creating their own winners and losers. The noise was deafening, the dust thick, the consequences very far from theoretical. Michael Milken was raising junk financing and backing a swarm of hostile takeovers. No corporation was safe. And in response, companies were reaching for the most practical defensive tactic on the books, Marty Lipton's devilishly clever snap-trap of a poison pill. The latter half of the '80s thus saw the collision of seemingly unlimited financing for takeovers and a defensive tool that appeared immovable. Something had to give.

Washington appeared paralyzed. The bias of the Reagan administration was by this time explicit: takeovers, the more the better, were socially and economically beneficial. Defense represented the protection of entrenched interests, which was bad. Offense involved, as Jensen and the Chicagoans regularly noted, the optimal rechanneling of cash flows from inefficient to efficient managers. But the White House was also tangled up in its own political contradictions. Ideology was one thing; interest groups dominated by corporations like the Business Roundtable and the Chamber of Commerce had great influence within regulatory agencies and in Congress; corporate interests were particularly powerful in the states. As the administration aged, politics began to trump ideology. This begins to explain why neither Congress nor the SEC ever moved to implement the dream of dismantling all defenses that Chicago law professors Frank Easterbrook and Daniel Fischel had articulated—most importantly, the bane of the takeovers-are-good school, the poison pill.

In fact, for much of the early '80s no one was willing to step in and bring order—balance—to a battleground that was spreading and growing more lethal. Takeovers accentuated deeper conflicts between states and the federal government, between administrative agencies and courts, between Wall Street, executives, shareholders, and employees. Finally, the escalation did induce one legal venue to intervene and try, in its distinctive way, to bring some order to the scene: the courts of the nation's smallest state, Delaware, which required from them the kind of judicial activism they had spent eighty years or so avoiding.

THE PILL AND junk bonds had exploded on the M&A scene at a particularly fraught moment in corporate law and financial regulation. Traditionally, if not constitutionally, regulation of corporations was a prerogative of the states. This went back to the post–Revolutionary War period when state legislatures took over a task of chartering corporations formerly controlled by Parliament and, before that, the king. Corporations were rare and often monopolies, like canal and road-building companies. They were often unpopular, and viewed as corrupt. But by the Jacksonian era the frontier was furiously expanding, the fever for commerce was surging, and the chartering of corporations shifted from a unique legislative act to something more routinized, like filling out a form and paying a fee. The monopoly aspect faded, and legally chartered companies proliferated.[1]

The tradition that the states, as opposed to the federal government, determined corporate law made sense when corporations were small and local. But the rise of industrial, multidivisional, multistate, economies-of-scale-driven corporations in the half-century after the

Civil War—the railroads, DuPont, AT&T, U.S. Steel, General Electric, Standard Oil—created new stresses. Corporations like the railroads had a significant effect on people's lives at great distances; they had immense power to shape economic development, create (or stifle) markets, determine winners and losers. And their source of power increasingly outstripped municipalities, counties, even states.

The authors of the Constitution, even Hamilton, envisioned a nation full of self-reliant Jeffersonian yeoman farmers, supplemented by, at best, a scattering of small manufacturers. There was a populist streak in American democracy that resisted centralized power—an instinct toward federalism, or state's rights. But there was ambivalence toward federalism as well. Tocqueville touched on the contradictory nuances of this American populism: "Our contemporaries are ever prey to two conflicting passions: they feel the need for guidance, and they long to stay free. Unable to wipe out these contradictory instincts, they try to satisfy them together."[2] This was the source of Tocqueville's so-called soft despotism of the majority. Often, when a corporation became powerful enough, as in the case of the First and Second Bank of the United States, their charters were allowed to lapse, and they were shuttered, broken up, and their assets scattered across the states: privatized. Nonetheless, the drive of industrial technology and economics, not to say the lure of sea-to-shining-sea markets to expand into, was such that by the early twentieth century, some corporations had grown sufficiently mighty to challenge a still-compact federal government, though still governed by laws and judges from individual states—that is, those states where they were legally incorporated, or domiciled.

It was an American innovation that companies didn't have to be legally domiciled in states in which they were founded, and where their employees, facilities, or headquarters were located; this was known as the internal-affairs doctrine. Companies in one state could operate in all others. They could restlessly move like settlers, seeking the best climate for their businesses. They were free to choose. (By the late nineteenth century, the courts had decided that corporations were also, in fact, legally persons, if fictional—a fascinating blend of the immortal and the mortal that has spawned, among many other consequences, unrestrained campaign spending by corporations.) But once they selected a domicile, companies had to submit to that state's corporate laws, which were often draconian by later standards. In fact, the states reined in the early trusts, disbanding some of them. As corporations grew, they exerted greater influence over state officials; the railroads famously bought and re-bought entire legislatures. Corporations were rich—and New Jersey recognized the possibilities first. By 1891, New Jersey had gone into "the charter-mongering business," one commentator noted, seeking big companies to set up shop there.[3] In 1896, New Jersey became the first state to adopt a modern "liberal" corporation statute, dismantling restrictions on the size and power of business units, welcoming holding companies, and, not by chance, rescuing the Standard Oil Trust, which the Ohio courts had tried to break up. Between 1897 and 1904, "New Jersey's statute facilitated the greatest merger movement in American history."[4] (That is, until the 1980s.) Other states followed, and battled to attract the largest companies. New Jersey, with its first mover advantage, gathered the largest numbers and became known, not happily, as "the Mother of Trusts" or, more pungently, "the traitor state."[5] Why did states care about accumulating corporate domiciles? Money. New Jersey generated such a robust revenue stream in corporate charters and incorporation fees that New Jerseyans paid no property tax. In 1911, corporation franchise fees amounted to a third of New Jersey's annual income. The business also enriched and deepened the local bar, provided cases and jobs for judges, and brought status and other rewards to state politicians.

Then came Woodrow Wilson, Princeton president-turned-governor and Progressive Democrat who attacked economic abuses with a Presbyterian personal moralism. Wilson felt that individuals, not companies, should be punished for transgressions—that is, until he met with Louis Brandeis, the Boston attorney and big-business scourge, who argued that monopolies were not immoral but "symptoms of a faulty system."[6] Wilson, not coincidentally, was running for president; he won that November against Republican William Howard Taft and Teddy Roosevelt, who campaigned under the Bull Moose banner. Roosevelt harassed Wilson for hypocrisy over New Jersey's coziness with the trusts. So in his final address to the state legislature, Wilson introduced seven bills that slammed the shackles on corporations in New Jersey. The legislation, quickly dubbed the Seven Sisters (not to be confused with multinational oil companies), passed and many of the largest corporations in New Jersey promptly fled to Delaware, which had slyly copied the Garden State's corporate law in 1899—eliciting an entertaining diatribe from muckraker Lincoln Steffens: "Little Delaware, gangrened with envy at the spectacle of the truck-patchers, sand-duners, clam-diggers and mosquito-wafters of New Jersey getting all the money into her coffers."[7] Wilson moved into the White House, leaving a budgetary hole for the clam diggers to fill; New Jersey repealed the Seven Sisters in 1917 but by then it was too late. Delaware had grabbed the lead and has held it, with an ever-tightening grip, ever since. In fact, the First State didn't see any reason to fundamentally alter the corporate statutes for another sixty-eight years. Corporate law became a major Delaware industry, like tourism and chickens. Today, corporation fees provide about a quarter of the state budget. Over 60 percent of the Fortune 500 companies call Delaware home, at least legally.

New Jersey was the first state to be excoriated for engaging in regulatory competition, or arbitrage; Delaware has been such a long-lived successor that the phenomenon is now known as "The Delaware Syndrome." In many spheres of life, competition is unthinkingly embraced as a virtue; that was certainly the critique of both the anti-monopoly, trust-busting crowd and the pro-takeover rump: competition enforced accountability. But competition in a crowded regulatory market can produce paradoxical outcomes. In a world replete with regulatory arbitrage, states compete for corporations, usually by rewarding management, engaging their self-interest. A law review note called this process "the survival of the unfit."[8] In 1933, by-then Supreme Court Justice Brandeis famously complained that "the [state legal] race was not one of diligence but of laxity." In a Berle and Means world dominated by professional managers, corporations are assumed to seek venues that give them an edge over their natural antagonists, shareholders; in fact, Steffens put his finger on that tendency in New Jersey long before Berle did, in 1905. Competition thus led to a steady deterioration of corporate standards. As one legal observer wrote: "They have watered the rights of shareholders vis-à-vis management down to a thin gruel."[9] *They* meant Delaware.

The race for the bottom assumed the air of historic inevitability. However, like describing managers and shareholders as eternal combatants, this devolutionary race did not tell the whole story, or at the least it was a tale whose meaning shifted based on where you stood: thus, it was profoundly political. As decades passed, as corporations evolved and the corporate system mutated and matured, the decision over where to domicile turned on more than just rudimentary dichotomies—lax versus diligent, manager over shareholder, pro-takeover versus anti-takeover, top versus bottom—particularly among the largest public corporations. The choice was rarely as simple as moving to the most permissive state. Companies needed many things, particularly as they grew more complex and litigation mounted. Many companies required access to a sophisticated judiciary and corporation rules that provided predictability, speed, flexibility, certainty, which in turn required stability and a legal system based on precedent—that is, a comprehensible logic. Longevity and consistency were advantages that accumulated over time; and they grew most successfully when there was at least some restraint on political interference. The needs and interests of shareholders changed as well: first, the tightly knit finance capitalists of the Morgan era; then atomized small investors; then powerful, passive institutions.

Besides, there were forces at work that had little to do with competition. As with Milken's junk-bond market, a network effect existed for corporate law: the state with the largest number of companies tended to attract more, because it both simplified matters and made outlier companies appear suspect. (The soft despotism of the majority is a kind of network effect.) The sheer amount of precedent mattered. Besides, it's not easy switching domiciles; once in, you tended to remain. Delaware was always just good enough, like IBM for decades in the computer business, to retain most of its incorporations. Delaware was the safe choice, the prestige choice, *the* brand.

Still, grumbling over Delaware's hammerlock on corporate law continued. Delaware's hegemony waxed and waned, though, again, large firms rarely left the state for good. Delaware would act, thus feeding its critics, when it felt it might be losing control over its corporate franchise. In short, it competed. In the mid-'50s, corporate contributions to total revenues began to slip, from 16 percent in 1955 to 7 percent in 1962.[10] The next year, Delaware commissioned a committee consisting of lawyers from Wilmington's three dominant firms to study its corporate laws. As one admitted: "The excellent and able committee consisted chiefly of pro-management attorneys. . . . [T]he only interest represented in the committee was management."[11]

Generally, this group of elders cleaned up, reorganized, and clarified the statute, though they also had as a goal "to ascertain what other states have to attract corporations that we do not have."[12] They operated pretty much free of the legislature, which one committee member referred to, not inaccurately, "as a bunch of farmers."[13] But they made some key additions to what had traditionally been an "enabling" set of laws—that is, as Lewis Black, the Wilmington attorney Lipton used to vet the pill, wrote in a piece of Delaware boosterism, a "statute intended to permit corporations and their shareholders the maximum flexibility in which to order their affairs,"[14] and which a critic once dubbed "enablingism—the state enables management to fill out the corporation law in the way it feels best."[15] They specifically tackled the subject of insider liability, particularly for officers and directors. Lawsuits were rising (you could debate why, but they were), and directors, in particular, felt exposed to litigation. So the new Delaware corporate code established "a mandatory right for reimbursement of expenses for a director successful in defense of any action or proceeding." Note the *mandatory*. That was unusual for Delaware. But it hit the sweet spot with corporations and their boards.

In 1967, the legislature approved the new Delaware corporate statutes. The next year, the state experienced a sharp upswing in new incorporations and re-incorporations. Franchise fees quadrupled between 1966 and 1971, and the percentage of franchise fees to revenue doubled to 24.9 percent. This success set off consequences. Other states scrambled to copy or modify Delaware's liability statutes to keep companies from leaving their state for Delaware. Few states, however, seriously thought Delaware could be supplanted.[16]

The muttering over Delaware rose to a full-fledged howl in 1974—the year of Inco's hostile attack on ESB Storage, three years before Jensen and Meckling's agency theory, and at the height of the liberal rediscovery of corporate governance—when Columbia University's William Lucius Cary, a former World War II OSS man-turned-law professor who had run a reformist SEC for John Kennedy from 1961 to 1964, launched his ferocious attack on the state. The *New Yorker*'s financial writer John Brooks described Cary as a man with "a gentlemanly manner and the pixyish countenance of a New England professor. . . . His reputation among his colleagues was, as one of them put it, for 'sweetness of temperament combined with a fundamental toughness of fiber.'"[17] Some pixie. Even today, Cary's polemic against Delaware and in favor of federal standards for corporations has a vehemence that strains uncomfortably against the grey, dense, proper pages of the *Yale Law Review* and the article's deceptively benign title: "Federalism and Corporate Law: Reflections Upon Delaware."[18] Cary had indeed reflected and concluded that Delaware was a bane, a pox, a plague upon the corporate law, a disgrace to all jurists, beginning with this initial sentence: "Delaware is both the sponsor and the victim of a system contributing to the deterioration of corporation standards."[19] And then Cary got angry: "The view is widely held that Delaware corporate decisions lean toward the status quo and adhere to minimal standards of director responsibility both to corporations and shareholders."[20] And: "Delaware decisions indicate a clearer penchant in favor of management."[21] And: "[Delaware's] consistent philosophy favors controlling shareholders and leaves fiduciary questions to the business judgment of an indentured board."[22] Delaware decisions are "labyrinthine" and feature a "tortured rationale" and meet a "low standard." Then Cary inserted the knife in what should have been a corpse: "Perhaps there is no public policy left in Delaware law except the objective of raising revenue."[23] He twisted the blade: "The first step is to escape from the present predicament in which a pygmy among the 50 states prescribes, interprets and indeed denigrates national corporate policy as an incentive to encourage incorporation within its borders, thereby increasing its revenues."[24] A denigrating pygmy! Low blow. Then came Cary's conclusion, featuring the fate of civilization, not to say the state of the soul:

> A civilizing jurisprudence should import lifting standards; certainly there is no justification for permitting them to deteriorate. The absurdity of this race for the bottom, with Delaware in the lead—tolerated and indeed fostered by corporate counsel—should arrest the conscience of the American bar when its current reputation is in low estate.[25]

Cary's purpose here—sometimes it seemed as if his higher goal was an afterthought to denigrating Delaware—was to argue for a larger federal role in corporate law. Cary didn't want to burden the SEC with the need to enforce a governance mandate it had received in the '30s; he undoubtedly knew its mission was too broad already. He also knew—he admitted—that wresting control directly from the states, meaning Delaware, was unlikely politically. Instead, he urged a workaround, which in hindsight is a sign of weakness: the creation of minimum federal fiduciary standards that would give the federal courts—which he had great confidence in, mostly because they weren't tainted by the self-interest of venal, revenue-hungry states—the opportunity to truly protect investors and "prescribe fairness as a prerequisite to any transaction." Cary's move was aggressive, but he wasn't alone. The New Deal had been a lunge toward federalizing corporate law. And there had been many calls in the '50s and '60s to shore up federal regulation and judicial reach when it came to corporations. The threat hung over Delaware. But federalization had only crept forward a few steps after the initial '30s legislation.

The fact that Cary wrote in the waning years of the New Deal consensus may have accentuated the harshness of his attack. He had assumed an orthodoxy of views both politically and academically on the reality of the race for the bottom and the necessity for a larger federal role. Part of his vituperation may have been that federalization seemed so obvious. That notion was shattered in 1979 by another product of Chicago's law and economics program then teaching at Yale Law School, Ralph K. Winter, who launched a frontal assault on the race-for-the-bottom mindset.[26] Winter was a federalist, favoring a multiplicity of states over the power of the federal government. He resisted the idea of federal intervention; he viewed regulation as a cost. What Cary saw as deterioration was perceived by Winter as rich in experimentation, a competitive market process. "No one denies that Delaware's open bidding for corporate charters has led to a steady lessening of the restrictiveness of state corporation law," Winter admitted.[27] But that was good, not bad; the top, not the bottom. What Cary attacked as disenfranchisement of shareholders, Winter saw as investor approval. The core of his case involved verities of the Chicago view: rational self-interest working its wisdom through the markets. If Delaware was so shareholder unfriendly, then earnings of Delaware companies should run below that of companies chartered elsewhere, and their share prices should be lower. These companies would be at a disadvantage when it came to raising capital, and as a result would face takeover threats. This was common sense. Why would shareholders and markets reward companies for choosing Delaware as their domicile if that was not in their self-interest? Private interests should be able to arrange private matters—"to make their own deal," said Winter.[28] That would reduce transaction costs and shift these issues to matters of contract law rather than regulatory fiat.

All the phraseology in the Chicago view makes its appearance here. Freedom. Private transactions. The reduction of transaction costs. The law of contracts as opposed to regulatory fiat. Of course, the notion that private transactions impose "no substantial cost" was at the crux of the disagreement, and was belied by unfolding events in an unrestrained takeover market.

Any perspective on whether state corporate law is, at any moment, evolving or devolving is murky because markets, and their participants, are shifting, changeable, and relativistic, and notions of the "best" depend upon the observer's view of the nature and purpose of the corporation and of deeper, often-antithetical virtues like efficiency or competitiveness versus job creation or fair play. There is no objective—quantifiable—way to measure this, Chicago notwithstanding. Share prices are reflections of value produced by complex inputs. They depend on market climate. They turn on politics of managers and shareholders. They swing on macroeconomic or *zeitgeistian* factors— optimism and pessimism, fear and greed.

In theory, a multiplicity of states, like a group of investors in a market, creates a laboratory for experimentation in the law,[29] though in practice many states simply copied Delaware doctrine or grabbed off-the-shelf Model Acts like one developed by the American Bar Association. They wanted not to supplant Delaware but to retain its crop of locally domiciled companies. This served to reduce incorporation choices (and competition) to softer matters, such as expertise and predictability, which favored Delaware and its near-monopoly. At the very least, Cary and Winter kicked off an academic debate that went on for years. Everyone seemed to take a shot at explaining, denouncing, rationalizing, deconstructing Delaware as either a saint or a sinner. Columbia University Law School professor John Coffee once bemoaned the fact that the subject "constitutes the most overwritten theme in the academic literature about corporate law," while, of course, writing about it himself.[30] The longer the debate continued, the more complex and nuanced it became.[31] The result: State competition as a moral drama faded, except in public political debate, where the race to the top or the bottom persists as provocative metaphors.

Meanwhile, by the early '80s, with Reagan in the White House, Delaware quietly edged back to its more traditional stance, which was to allow managers great latitude in making decisions for their shareholders.

THE POLITICS OF federalism collided with the politics of M&A and produced a terrific tangle. The free-market crowd favored federalism—that is, states' prerogative in corporate law, which traditionally played to the self-interest of managers, who resisted takeovers. This was, of course, a contradiction. Winter spoke for Chicago by supporting Delaware as a worthy example of the survival of the fittest, legally speaking. And yet, the most effective strategy to stifle hostile M&A emerged from the states that erected bristling anti-takeover provisions—approximately forty by the mid-'80s—some of which conflicted with federal law, the Williams Act. In 1982, the US Supreme Court, that bastion of federal sovereignty, knocked down an Illinois anti-takeover rule in a case called *Edgar v. MITE*. But lobbyists and legislators rewrote the rules and the anti-state movement in the states continued.

This led to some ideological confusion. Lipton may have discovered that he was at war with Chicago over a corporation's right to defend itself, but on the practical question of states versus the federal government, with its implications for managers and shareholders, he found himself aligned with Winter, Frank Easterbrook, and Daniel Fischel. Lipton's approach—the centrality of the board, the foundational nature of the business judgment rule—came from Delaware's playbook. Lipton articles like "Takeover Bids" anticipated many of the ways Delaware reacted to hostile M&A. Not that Lipton agreed with every Delaware opinion. He did not—and when he objected, he let the world know. But he recognized Delaware's preeminence. Likewise, Chicago and the Reagan administration defended state prerogatives, but also criticized Delaware opinions, often different ones from Lipton's. This split, between an embrace of state's rights and a belief in takeovers also played into the administration's passivity. It struggled to satisfy both ideological impulses.

Delaware's near-silence on the role of the board in the face of a hostile takeover was until 1985 deafening. Precedent was thin and aging and a small, if intense, struggle over the business judgment rule— Bayless Manning, the former Yale law professor who was at Paul Weiss in 1984, called it "a febrile theological controversy . . . resolved only by banishment, as heretics, of all who hold views at variance with accepted doctrine."[32] The first case, *Cheff v. Mathes,* was hardly controversial by Delaware lights. *Cheff* was decided in 1964 and involved a company, Holland Furnace, that sold home boilers door to door.[33] Holland's business was failing—and sketchy. (Holland salesmen were accused of dismantling boilers, then refusing to reassemble them unless homeowners bought new ones.) Family members of P. T. Cheff, the CEO, controlled the board. At one point, the CEO of an unrelated company began buying shares. To get rid of him, Cheff's wife offered to buy back his shares at a premium; eventually the board itself put up the money—an early example of greenmail. The board justified the action by insisting the investor was a shady character. The Delaware Supreme Court finally decided that Holland, despite the obvious self-interest of a number of board members, still received the right to the business judgment rule because the directors sincerely believed the company was at risk.

Cheff v. Mathes was a traditional application of the business judgment rule—that is, managers know best—albeit in circumstances that were novel. The case articulated a so-called standard of behavior: that directors in the face of a takeover threat show "good faith and a reasonable investigation." This is known in corporate law as a board fulfilling its duties of loyalty and care.

The second case, *Smith v. Van Gorkom,* occurred in the late '70s. This involved a deal—an early leveraged buyout—involving two major business figures in Chicago: Jerome Van Gorkom, the CEO of a railcar-leasing company called Trans Union, and Jay Pritzker, a powerful local financier and conglomerateur. The men served on the Chicago School Authority together and skied together at Vail. Van Gorkom was nearing retirement age and was looking for a buyer. Trans Union was a successful company that generated lots of cash flow and, because of the railcars, so much depreciation that it accumulated valuable tax-loss carry-forwards that were not necessarily reflected in the share price. Pritzker wanted both the company and the tax losses. Trans Union had an experienced and independent board that included deans of the University of Chicago and Rochester business schools, and four CEOs.

Pritzker made what to Van Gorkom seemed a generous offer and presented it to the board, which accepted it in two hours without discussing the valuation or consulting an investment banker, or even the CFO, who thought the price was low and that shareholders would have to absorb heavy taxes if they sold. Van Gorkom then signed the merger document without reading it a few nights later at a gala he threw every year for the Chicago Lyric Opera. He trusted Pritzker. None of the other directors read it, either. They trusted Van Gorkom.

A shareholder sued in Delaware. The case ended up in Delaware's "lower" court of Chancery, which saw it as a standard business judgment case: an experienced board and CEO knew what they were doing in accepting a premium offer.

The case was then appealed to the Delaware Supreme Court.[34] Shockingly, the Supreme Court overturned Chancery and argued that Trans Union's board did *not* deserve the protection of the business judgment rule. The majority on the Supreme Court thought the directors had violated their duties of care by embracing Pritzker's bid so quickly and casually. By *care,* the court meant the failure to consult outside experts and carefully read the merger documents. Accordingly, the court suggested the directors had failed to extract the best price for shareholders. Van Gorkom wanted to sell to Pritzker and did not really try to get the best price or find another bidder, although Kohlberg Kravis Roberts, the pioneering LBO firm, was briefly interested but backed off. The court dismissed the premium, along with the complexities of the tax-loss carry-forwards, and kicked the case back to Chancery to figure out what Trans Union *should* have gotten. The court didn't unwind the deal, which had long closed, but ordered the directors to pay damages based on the abstract "fair value" price that Chancery concocted. (The board's directors and officers insurance paid $10 million in damages, and the Pritzker family paid the remaining $13 million.[35])

This outcome was a long way from *Cheff* and stirred up a firestorm in Delaware.[36] The corporate lawyers were aghast—they were, after all, Delaware's prized customers. Director insurance premiums spiked as soon as it was apparent that the Trans Union board had been personally hit with damages. Delaware had committed a cardinal sin: surprise and a break with precedent, meaning *Cheff.* The case was quickly dubbed the "full employment for advisors" decision. Paul Weiss's Manning called the decision "atrocious" and scoffed at the Supreme Court's use of "fair value."[37] Chicago's Daniel Fischel argued that the Supreme Court had been influenced by Cary, had no coherent theory of the business judgment rule, and produced "one of the worst decisions in the history of corporate law."[38]

All this spooked the Delaware legislature, which quickly rushed through a bill that eliminated monetary penalties for directors in the event of a breach of the duty of care.[39]

Did Delaware know where it was going on takeovers? Undoubtedly not. As Manning wrote, apparently tapping personal experience, "It is not unusual for the common law to develop in a manner reminiscent of a shipboard passenger making his way from the bar to his stateroom, careening first against one bulkhead and then thrown against the other. Usually the passageway is quite narrow, and usually the law, like the passenger, arrives at its destination intact. But the life of a lower court judge in Delaware these days is not an easy one. In *Van Gorkom* the lower court zigged toward the directors . . . when, it now appears, he should have zagged."[40] Delaware was being forced to explore issues generated by takeovers, including the business judgment rule and beneath it, the nature of fiduciary duties. Delaware was still guided by managerial deference—enablingism. But it was reacting, albeit grudgingly. The Delaware courts were sensitive barometers, as self-interested as any agent, struggling for what Manning called "a jurisprudential diplomatic-political balance." But the courts also displayed the deep inner loyalty—both for itself and its cases—that agency theory routinely glossed over and ignored in managers, as judges proceeded on their wandering, often seemingly random, legalistic way, one opinion at a time.

And *Van Gorkom* did have an effect—like a punch in the face. As Weil Gotshal's Ira Millstein said: "I have never been in a board room where I couldn't get directors' attention by saying: 'Remember *Van Gorkom.*'"[41] It was one thing to lose a cozy directorship; it was another to get sued because you failed to take adequate care.

MAJOR CASES BEGAN to appear in greater numbers, and the Delaware courts struggled to define the responsibilities—the duties—of directors in the face of hostile bids. *Van Gorkom* opened up new threats to Delaware's seemingly ancient business judgment rule. Could a board simply reject a takeover offer without consulting shareholders? How did the role of directors change as a takeover bid progressed? Where did the power lie in deciding these elemental matters—with directors or shareholders? Could Delaware create a standard that was sensible and fair to all the parties? And what about the poison pill?

The Supreme Court began its long consideration of these issues with a 1985 case involving Boone Pickens and an old Standard Oil unit, Unocal.

In 1984 Unocal, fearing a takeover attempt, began erecting defenses, including signing up as a Delaware corporation. Late in the year, Boone Pickens started buying shares, through an investment group called Mesa Partners II. Pickens began a proxy contest, then a hostile tender offer for Unocal, scooping up 13 percent of the shares, then launched a two-tier front-end-loaded cash tender offer that gained 37 percent more. A regular at Milken's Predator's Ball, Pickens loaded up on junk. This was one of the first uses of high-yield in a hostile takeover attempt; Unocal shareholders on the back-end would receive junk bonds in exchange for their Unocal stock. (Mesa claimed it had raised $3 billion in junk from Drexel, buttressed by $1 billion in bank loans.) Unocal, led by combative CEO Fred Hartley who despised Pickens, resisted; and unlike Trans Union, Unocal, aware of *Van Gorkom,* stepped carefully through the procedural minefield, hiring a Los Angeles–based law firm, and consulting Goldman Sachs and Dillon Read, which told the eight independent directors that the Mesa proposal was too low and presented defensive strategies. One scheme was for Unocal to self-tender—that is, buy back a portion of its own shares at a cost of nearly $4 billion. Unocal, however, specifically excluded Mesa from the buyback. Why enrich Pickens?

To no one's surprise, Pickens sued, and Chancery rejected the self-tender (that is, buying back one's own shares) as discriminatory and restrained Unocal from making the offer unless it included Mesa—basing this decision on what's known as an entire-fairness standard.[42] Pickens's investors, however, were getting nervous. Mesa could walk away with $180 million if it could just sell into Unocal's self-tender. Pickens appealed to the Delaware Supreme Court.

The Supreme Court acted with unusual speed. As Andrew G. T. Moore II, one of three justices on the case and the author of the opinion, later said, "expedition was required by the sheer force of marketplace demands."[43] Three justices had disqualified themselves, and a superior court judge, Clarence Taylor, was recruited to fill out the three-man panel.

After a packed hearing, Moore ordered the doors locked and forbade anyone to leave, torture for arbs who desperately needed to get the word—and their trades—out.[44] In the oral decision, Moore, speaking for the justices, argued that the case was a straightforward *Cheff*-like business judgment case, seeming to lean toward great managerial deference after *Van Gorkom.* He cited an earlier case he had decided, *Pogostin v. Rice,* that declared the business judgment rule applicable in takeovers, which some see as a move that led to years of wrangling and needless litigation.[45] In any event, the Supreme Court reversed Chancery and allowed Unocal's discriminatory self-tender. Pickens, in short, had lost. But more importantly, in the written opinion a few months later, Moore elaborated a new standard for director behavior. Moore, a Lipton admirer, had clearly read "Takeover Bids," and the court embraced a board's right to oppose a takeover bid and "protect the corporate enterprise, which included shareholders."[46] Moore seemed to include within the corporation a responsibility to stakeholders and rejected Chicago's passivity in the face of a takeover stance. The board's role "is not a passive one," he wrote, "and even the authors [Fischel and Easterbrook] conceded that no court or legislature had adopted it."[47]

Moore also recognized the role self-interest played among directors and managers, and how that might distort their reactions to takeover bids. In one of the more famous lines in Delaware jurisprudence,

Moore noted that there exists "the omnipresent specter that [the board] may be acting in its own interests, rather than those of the corporation and its shareholders."[48] The board had to show that "it has reasonable grounds for believing" that a dire threat exists and its responses "must be reasonable in relation to the threat posed."[49] Directors, in short, had to earn the right to the business judgment rule by passing a two-pronged test. The first prong extended *Cheff*'s call for "good faith and reasonable investigation" into the facts of the threat. Moore noted that a proper process often hinged on the presence of directors independent of management. A board with a majority of independent directors received "bonus points." The second represented something novel: it slapped limits on a board's response and opened the door to an "enhanced duty," which really meant enhanced scrutiny. "A corporation does not have unbridled discretion to defeat any perceived threat by any Draconian means possible," wrote Moore.[50] There must be "an element of balance," a proportionality, effectively thrusting Delaware into the M&A arena as an arbiter—a role that called for what one paper later called a "regulatory test"[51]—in a manner the federal government continued to avoid and that was novel for Delaware. There were threats that directors could erect defenses against (the court lifted wholesale Lipton's enumeration of reasons for rejecting offers from "Takeover Bids"), including an inadequate price or questions of illegality.[52] And Chancery had already recognized that Mesa's bid could be seen as low, that the junk bonds at the back-end could be judged inadequate, and, here was an eye opener, that Pickens' reputation as a greenmailer posed a viable threat. The court viewed Mesa's bid as coercive.[53]

Unocal had passed Moore's new intermediate test and could take refuge in the business judgment rule. Years later, Moore noted the inadequacy of "the Chicago School's notion of passivity by the board in a takeover contest," which "in the jargon of the financial community . . . left companies and shareholders naked in the street ready to be flattened by a steamroller." He also argued that efficient markets involved "a simplistic math calculation," and that Delaware had rejected it in *Van Gorkom,* as if that would make it disappear.[54]

Mesa settled with Unocal, which agreed to allow it to participate in the self-tender if it promised to go away for five years. Pickens agreed and walked.

JENSEN REACTED WITH fury at *Unocal.* He dashed off a denunciation, "When Unocal Won Over Pickens, Shareholders and Society Lost," arguing that the Supreme Court had "shocked the legal, financial and corporate communities" with the decision, calling it a "stunning loss for Unocal shareholders and society," and declaring it was now "suicidal to launch a takeover against a Board willing to use its new powers to discriminate against shareholders. A determined Board could, in the extreme, pay out all the corporation's assets and leave the acquirer a worthless empty shell."[55] This was wildly overstated, though Jensen, as usual, backed it up with math. He calculated that Unocal's "victory" cost its shareholders $1.1 billion, or 26 percent of its pre-takeover value, a $2.1 billion increase in value during the struggle. And he defended Pickens. "For his services in generating this $2.1 billion gain for Unocal shareholders [albeit temporarily], Boone Pickens has been vilified in the press, and Mesa Partners II has incurred net losses, before taxes." He didn't provide an after-tax calculation.

Everyone lost, declared Jensen: shareholders of Unocal, of Mesa, of all Delaware companies, society in general, "because the evidence indicates that takeovers are beneficial." As for the greenmail charge, the practice of "targeted repurchases" causes no damage to shareholders and can easily be prohibited by management. Therefore, the fact that it exists is the fault not of raiders but of management, who use it to protect themselves. This was a stretch, particularly if you accepted the popular identification of greenmail with blackmail. Still, Jensen did note—accurately—that Delaware had permitted a discriminatory offer to repel a discriminatory bid.

For Jensen and the Chicago crowd, the news was about to get worse.

JOE FLOM DID not like the way things were going in Delaware. Flom and Lipton often disagreed, though amicably. But this poison pill was a problem. Flom recognized that far more than anything from the SEC or Congress, Lipton's pill could change the nature of the increasingly junk-bond-fueled M&A market and slow it to a dog trot; the pill threatened to make the triumph of defense plausible. Flom was not overly concerned about the fate of executives or shareholders or the nation; they could take care of themselves. He was concerned about his firm, Skadden Arps, which was growing like topsy, mostly on high-octane M&A, and his clients, including Drexel, which paid the bills. Flom personally believed the pill would never pass muster legally. If he had doubts, he did not express them, though what he said to Lipton over bagels might have been entirely different. Then the *Harvard Law Review* got into Flom's face.[56]

In June 1984, the *Law Review* had published a Note that focused on the new development: "Protecting Shareholders Against Partial and Two-Tiered Takeovers: The 'Poison Pill' Preferred."[57] This was not aimed at the crowd that eagerly consumed Brill's "Two Tough Lawyers" article (see Chapter 4). But that didn't make it better from Flom's perspective; it might have made it worse. Flom knew who was reading this stuff. Corporate lawyers, of course. Academics. And Delaware judges. Flom was enough of a master of opinion shaping to be worried, especially by the conclusion: "This Note has argued that the issuance of poison-pill preferred stock provides legitimate protection against partial and two-tiered tender offers, and should therefore be deemed legitimate under both state fiduciary law and the Delaware corporate statute."[58]

Lipton had immediately sent copies of the Note to clients. Flom went ballistic. Lipton and Flom were involved in a bruising battle between New York investment company Dyson-Kissner-Moran, which had hired Flom, and Household International, Lipton's client. DKM had invested in Household, and its CEO, John Moran, joined the board. But Household, like so many other companies, had grown insecure, hiring Lipton (who warned against the possibility of a "bust-up" takeover) and Goldman Sachs, and decided to put a pill in place. Moran objected, voted against it, then offered for DKM to acquire Household in an LBO—confirming the board's paranoia.

Moran hired Skadden and Flom. Moran's approach was not overtly hostile. But DKM did sue in Chancery to kill the pill.

Both Flom and Lipton knew that this might be The Big One: finally, a test in Delaware of the legality of the pill.

Given that, Flom did not need the *Harvard Law Review* offering its damn opinion, particularly one at variance with Skadden's interests. He complained to the dean of the law school. Flom had heard that a Harvard student, who had been an associate at Wachtell the previous summer, wrote the Note. "This article may have a taint on it," he told the *New York Times* in late September. "I'm not accusing anybody of anything, but the appearance of impropriety ought to be dealt with. The issue is merely one of making sure all the cards are on the table."[59]

Flom managed to appear uncharacteristically exasperated. Harvard Law rebuffed him, arguing that Notes are collaborative processes, and that another student who worked on the piece had a wife who had recently accepted an offer from—Skadden Arps. How had Flom found out about the Note in the first place? Lipton had told him. "It boggled my mind," muttered Flom.[60]

FOUR DAYS AFTER deciding *Unocal,* the Delaware Supreme Court heard arguments on the poison pill case, *Moran v. Household.* On the panel sat Moore, John McNeilly, and Chief Justice Andrew Christie. They convened in the old supreme-court courtroom off The Green in snug Dover, the state capital. Moore associated the day with repulsive invasion. "Normally," he wrote, "one can stand on the Dover Green and almost feel transported back to those historic [colonial] days—but not on that particular Tuesday. The streets surrounding The Green were clogged with stretch limousines, giving it the appearance of some out-of-place, unsavory gathering."[61] But he wasn't alone. Moira Johnston noted that the highway leading to Dover "looked like a mafia convention. 'Every limousine in Delaware had been rented,'" said Stuart Shapiro, Irving Shapiro's son and a Skadden M&A attorney, who drove in from New York.[62]

The case had been highly anticipated since Chancery approved the pill under the business judgment rule and DKM appealed. (Jensen and Michael Bradley had appeared as expert witnesses, arguing that the Pill would reduce the value of Household shares. DKM found support from investors, the law and economics crowd, and the federal government. The five SEC commissioners debated whether to intervene, a direct federal threat to Delaware, but at the last moment voted 3 to 2 to hold off. Instead the agency wrote a brief supporting DKM and sent attorneys to the trial, joining representatives from various industry and union groups. "We sort of sat back, we looked at it, and we said, 'Well, let's monitor what's going on here,'" recalled Grundfest, who had been appointed as a Democratic SEC commissioner in October 1985, after serving on Reagan's Council of Economic Advisors. "Instead of saying, 'Gee, we need immediately to respond'—because at the time I viewed this as inconsistent with a more free-market approach to takeover activity—I said, 'Let's not do anything rash. Let's not do something from the regulatory perspective at the SEC. Let's not try to get any federal legislation through Congress. There were people who wanted to do that.' I said, 'All right, let's run the experiment.'"[63]

There were tensions within Delaware as well. Would the Supreme Court again overturn Chancery on such a public case?

The arguments before the court drew an all-star gathering of legal talent. It was Skadden Arps against Wachtell Lipton. Skadden's lead attorney was none other than Irving Shapiro, the compact retired DuPont CEO, who hadn't argued a case since the '40s. Flom had raised a fuss over what he had called a "tainted" Harvard Law Note on the poison pill issue but he was perfectly happy to go to battle in Dover with that preeminent insider, Irving Shapiro; Stuart Shapiro, who had led the case for Skadden, sat at the counsel's table with him. Shapiro, still a formidable courtroom performer, insisted that Delaware law gave boards no power to authorize a pill and that the technique usurps the rights of stockholders to receive hostile tender offers.[64] Wachtell countered, with six-foot-ten Charles "Charlie" Richards of Wilmington's Richards Layton & Finger making the pro-pill argument. Moore was particularly aggressive in questioning.[65] In its opinion, the court immediately raised the question of the business judgment rule and cited *Unocal* on the board's responsibility to judge "whether an offer is in the best interests of the corporation."[66] Household, the court noted, was unusual because it adopted a pill preemptively, without a specific threat in mind. The court worked through arguments that the pill was illegal under Delaware law, deciding, finally, that it was not. Then it turned to the business judgment rule—and the *Unocal* test. Did directors have "reasonable grounds for believing that a danger to corporate policy and effectiveness existed?"[67] Was the mechanism a reasonable response to the threat? Was the board negligent or entrenching itself?

The court announced its decision orally on November 19. McNeilly, the senior justice, assigned it to himself, but it took him six months to write, causing "great anxiety among the parties and their counsel," Moore wrote.[68] (McNeilly retired in October 1986 after twenty-five years on the bench.) The Household board could receive the benefit of the business judgment rule. The pill—at least that variation of what Moore called "Martin Lipton's ingenious conception"[69]—was legal under Delaware law, at least if the *Unocal* test was met. The anonymous author of the *Harvard Law Review* Note had been correct, though, at the time, he had had no idea about the role that yet-undecided cases like *Unocal* would play and the tortuous complexities that would ensue. Flom was angry. And, of course, Lipton had emerged triumphant and appeared prescient, though it had been a close call and the relationship with Flom never quite recovered. Delaware had spoken; the federal threat was (for the moment) in retreat. And defense did appear to be firmly on the ascendant, even with the junk-bond insurrection.

A year later, the SEC adopted "the all-holder's rule" that banned discriminatory self-tenders, like Unocal's—a shot at the *Moran* decision. By then, takeovers had moved on.

Chapter Fourteen

THE PURSUIT OF SELF-INTEREST

M EDIA-WISE, MICHAEL JENSEN was ahead of his time. At the
height of his public activities in the mid-'80s he filled all available channels with his views—though he rarely hit the popular press.
And without an Internet, he was mostly stuck talking to other academics and to a growing group of practitioners who agreed with him.
Like a proto-blogger, he engaged in quick hits: cross-fertilizing one
paper with another, as new events, issues, and decisions provoked responses. He revised regularly. This explains footnotes that refer to papers written after the document in question. Some he published;
others stayed in the dark of the drawer, waiting. His arguments often
remained the same, but they were tailored for the occasion. Some were
argumentative, short, dashed-off; he rarely wrote at the length the lawyers did, and his prose, which had a tendency to bolt like an excited
horse, was not nearly as precise or polished.

Not long after the Delaware court's *Moran* decision approving the
use of the poison pill, he revised a paper first written for a 1983 corporate governance conference on the business judgment rule; parts of it
appeared in his presentation at the Columbia conference (see Chapter
12). The paper itself is an obscure work in Jensen's oeuvre, but it reflects his views in a particularly unvarnished way. Jensen was wrestling
with where Delaware fit into the larger struggle. On one hand, Delaware was the apotheosis of a *laissez-faire* impulse, embodied in the
business judgment rule. On the other hand, that produced unhealthy
managerial entrenchment. Delaware, in some of its decisions, looked

suspiciously soft on takeovers, which Jensen insisted "have generated enormous efficiency gains by forcing the restructuring of many firms in mature and declining industries."[1]

Jensen found himself caught in crosscurrents of federalism and takeovers. Delaware courts, he admitted, had "created a highly productive fabric of corporate law, which has generated large benefits for the nation." He was, in short, a race-to-the-top adherent—though he did not explain how the glory era of Delaware law coincided with the golden age of managerial prerogative and stakeholder governance. In more recent times, Delaware's struggle to sort out takeover issues resulted in "a confusing set of decisions, which in contrast to much of the courts' previous history made little economic sense." Jensen had a theory of how Delaware had gone awry: its model of the corporation, which had once worked so well, had a fundamental weakness. That "model" rested on the business judgment rule, which, in turn, was based on the notion that directors would act "altruistically"—that is, shorn of self-interest. This "altruistic model," Jensen wrote, "is incorrect as a description of human behavior." All individuals are "presumed" to suffer from self-interest. He did not elaborate on how such a fallacious model could work for so long, then suddenly fail. The altruistic model, he declared, did not provide "proper answers to the conflicts surrounding corporate control disputes."[2] Once again, the matter came down to providing "proper answers," that strangely prim locution redolent of the classroom.

He did offer a prediction. Eventually, the Delaware courts would have to adopt "the now well-developed agency model of the corporation," which envisioned all conflicts as contract matters—that is, the Jensen-Meckling agency model.

Jensen was particularly irate about the poison pill. He offered his own legal theory about where *Moran* had gone awry. The pill "unilaterally changed the nature of the contractual relationship with Household's shareholders in a fundamental way."[3] He raced on, as if Delaware *had* embraced the nexus of contracts model. The contractual violation packaged in the pill was implemented "without vote of approval by the shareholders"; that is, it represented a failure of shareholder democracy.[4] Shareholders could force a change to restrict a board's power, but that wouldn't be easy, since pension funds tended—this wasn't his exact phrase—to fold like cheap suits for management. Unlike Lipton, he did not delve into the nature of that submission except to accept it as a fact, like gravity. So once again, shareholders had to be saved from themselves. What does it mean for agency theory as a key to governance when principals—shareholders—seemingly can't act on, or fully comprehend, their own self-interest?

Jensen accepted another contradiction: the desire to leave companies alone while mandating passivity for boards. He blamed Delaware for continuing to embrace the business judgment rule, which would result, he predicted, in the erosion of, well, the business judgment rule. He admitted that he favored a business judgment rule (which, remember, he believes is based on a fallacy)—just not in takeovers. Takeovers were special. By empowering management, Delaware allowed managers to elude the corrective hand of the market—to become *permissive*. "We can expect to see managers who are protected from disciplinary forces of the control market begin to abuse their obligations to shareholders in more serious ways outside the control area. The court will likely be drawn into these conflicts and in so doing the business judgment rule will be eroded even more seriously."[5] It's a slippery slope, which, he added, will "seriously handicap the corporation as an organizational form." Seriously, this sounds a lot like a race to the bottom. Jensen did not seem to realize that decisions like *Unocal* and *Moran* had already drawn Delaware deeply into what he called, a little chillingly, "the control area."[6]

Jensen's view of Delaware has a cartoon quality. Historically, Delaware enabled a wide latitude of management behavior—too broad, of course, for many—through the business judgment rule, but it was never based on "altruism" or "the altruistic model." The foundation of the rule, for good or ill, was the belief that boards and managers possessed the best information and, as Lipton suggested, were most resistant to coercion: they were best positioned to act *rationally*. As chancellor of the Court of Chancery William Allen wrote in a long sentence a few years later: "Because businessmen and women are correctly perceived as possessing skills, information and judgment not possessed by reviewing courts and because there is a great social utility in encouraging the allocation of assets and the evaluation and assumption of economic risk by those with such skill and information, courts have long been reluctant to second-guess such decisions when they appear to have been made in good faith."[7] That is, Delaware expected managers and directors to rise above their natural self-interests: they had a duty of loyalty. As the opinion in a 1939 business judgment case known as *Guth v. Loft* declared: "An undivided and unselfish loyalty to the corporation demands that there shall be no conflict between duty and self interest."[8] Jensen assumed such a transcendence of self-interest was a fantasy, a daydream. Agency costs persist, even if hidden, like herpes. He does not have to see into hearts and minds; he *knows*. He has a theory and models. Meanwhile, cases that ended up in Delaware often involved investigations into unique, individual, endlessly diverse varieties of self-interest. It was as if Jensen was happier assuming that the sin of self-interest existed while at the same time not delving too deeply into the Pandora-like black box. Delaware shouldn't look, either.

How to understand, and judge, this large, growing, and elusive M&A phenomenon? Was it good or bad? Fact or fiction? Constructive or destructive? Following the debates of the mid-'80s produces a sense of overload, fed by academics, the media, and lobbyists, and by the cross-fertilization of professions like law and economics swollen like tadpoles with metaphors: shareholder democracy, stakeholder governance, agency theory, neoclassical economics, the property, entity, contract, trustee, managerial, free-market, and altruistic models. Metaphors, like corporations themselves, are packages of fact and fiction. At their persuasive best, they have a beguiling, self-fulfilling quality, and they engage in spontaneous generation. The idea begets the reality, slowly, then quickly, like osmosis. Once begun, the breakdown of the corporation ten years after the first, big, public hostile takeover, Inco-ESB, took on this self-fulfilling quality, both intellectually and in fact. Few viewed major corporations any longer as impregnable, permanent, or—as Bayless Manning once said—"a little bit sacred." Famous, even venerable corporate names, came and went as deals tripped over deals. This flux bolstered the seeming validity of the corporation as a nexus of contracts, with its atomized workers and self-interested managers whose behavior was determined by economic and legal factors. Loyalty to the corporation by workers, managers, and directors appeared to be anachronistic, even naive. Compensation was beginning to radically diverge from bottom to top. The prevailing free-market metaphor with its cash flows that "want" to be liberated and seized by more efficient users, a kind of Aristotelian desire to fulfill a corporation's inner nature, seemed a more accurate reflection of competitive reality than the belief in the corporation as a Platonic, organic, social satrapy run by wise, technocratic managers. Corporations, with ties to sovereign power, whether chartered by a king or approved by a legislature, had been depicted as immortal essences, while shareholders were transient, quick to take "the Wall Street walk"—that is, to exit by selling. Now, increasingly, shareholders had become the permanent interest, whereas corporations, despite their tangible, countable assets, were transient, flimsy abstractions, barely real.

BILL ALLEN, WITH his bald head, thin black mustache, and spectacles, was no bomb thrower. If he had been he would never have gotten within spitting distance of the old Chancery building, with its brick and columns, on Rodney Square, near the Hotel DuPont.

Allen grew up in Philadelphia, attended New York University, and got his law degree from the University of Texas. He clerked for Walter King Stapleton, a major figure in the Delaware bar who, as a young associate, assisted on the rewriting of the new Delaware corporate statutes, and went on to become a federal judge in Wilmington, then Philadelphia. Stapleton, by Allen's own testimony, was a powerful influence—and a powerfully influential figure in Delaware.[9] Politically, Stapleton was a Republican, mildly conservative but reform-minded, a strand of the GOP that has faded. But he was (and is—he's still working) above all else a model judge: hardworking, serious, self-effacing, nonideological, a legal craftsman. After the clerkship, Allen went to work as a litigator at Stapleton's old Wilmington firm and clearly impressed the local power brokers as capable, reliable, and smart.

Delaware was discretely awash in crisis in 1985. The M&A boom was mounting and other states were getting attention for corporate-friendly, anti-takeover rules. There was an extremity of views, a chill of ideological reductionism that was profoundly unsettling to the Delaware mindset. The business judgment rule was a formidable dike; but it was giving way under the pounding of interests intent on corporate control. Delaware officialdom began quietly making changes: like the papacy, Delaware acts as if change occurs by divine fiat. The chancellor in 1985 was Grover Brown, a big, bluff, former family court judge who Allen once delicately praised "for his legal sophistication and simplicity of expression."[10] Governor Pete du Pont had named Brown the first Republican chancellor in sixty years in 1982; Brown described himself as a "country lawyer," who wrote his opinions out in longhand.[11] Delaware judges occasionally resort to the affectation that they're just a bunch of rubes pitted against big-city sophisticates. It's often a conceit, sometimes a joke, though in Brown's case it may have had some validity. Brown finished only three years of his Chancery term; in 1985, at forty-five, he abruptly retired. Allen, who in a variation of the rube routine, once insisted he was someone who does his work "not on the hilltop but on the shop floor of the corporate law foundry, amid the bang, gurgle and whirl of temporary restraining orders, expedited trials, and all the commotion of a busy trial court,"[12] was hustled into Brown's still-warm seat in late June 1985. His confirmation hearing before the legislature lasted twenty minutes. The Supreme Court had just wrapped up *Unocal;* the *Moran* arguments had just been heard; the junk-catalyzed frenzy had begun. A lot of work lay ahead. *Unocal*'s intermediate standard, which fit somewhere—but where?—between the business judgment rule and the harder-to-meet entire-fairness doctrine, as Ronald Gilson, a law and economics scholar who had recently left Stanford for Columbia, later pointed out, shifted the argument from whether managers or shareholders got to make the decision on takeovers, to whether the board's process of decision-making is good or bad. That "meant," he wrote, "that the court would decide the outcome of control contests."[13]

Chancery is an unusual judicial institution in the United States. Chancery courts developed in thirteenth-century England to decide matters of equity or fairness that were beyond the reach of the common law, with a lone judge settling disputes without a jury: over time, precedents and procedures grew up next to the great mass of common law. In nearly all the former American colonies, Chancery courts were abandoned after the Revolution, tainted by monarchical ties. But colonial Delaware had never had a Chancery court and had nothing to reject. Its creation, moreover, was shaped by personal politics. Under the state constitution of 1792, there seemed to be no position for William Killen, the chief justice under the 1776 constitution, who, as one history notes,[14] was Irish, Presbyterian, a Whig, and a Democrat in a state that was "rock-ribbed Federalist." Killen had important legal friends who felt he was owed a position for putting his life at risk during the rebellion, despite his politics. Killen got this odd little court of Chancery and presided over it for nine years until he died.

In fact, this odd little court proved particularly well suited to resolving internal disputes produced by that most aggressively modern of organizations, corporations (external illegalities were the province of more conventional courts). With the rise of industrial corporations, and through several Delaware constitutions, Chancery became *the* commercial court, with a chancellor as sole judge. As Delaware tightened its grip on corporate domiciles, Chancery slowly expanded, though it remains remarkably small for the quantity of major cases that land there, the power it quietly exerts, and the controversy it sometimes provokes. In the mid-'80s, Chancery still had a chancellor and three vice chancellors; it now has five judges, as does the Delaware Supreme Court.

This structure has its complexities and idiosyncrasies. In the background looms the state's crown-jewel corporate franchise. The governor appoints judges, whom the legislature confirms. The legislature, advised by the bar association, also regularly reviews corporate statutes and makes (nearly always small) changes. Everyone in this legal-political complex knows full well that their mutual, and ultimate, customers are corporations, which vote with their well-shod feet, advised by their bespoke attorneys.

In the foreground unfolds the complex relationship between Chancery and the Delaware Supreme Court. Chancery handles the vast bulk of daily cases, mostly corporate. Chancery cases are often fact-finding exercises. It is a trial court. The equity philosophy allows latitude and rewards imagination in judges, particularly in offering remedies.[15] The Supreme Court, on the other hand, is an appeals court; it takes a longer view and decides matters of precedent and principle as a group; consensus matters. The Supreme Court can take Chancery cases and, using the same facts patiently accumulated by a Chancery judge, draw very different conclusions.

By the time Allen arrived, Chancery had turned over almost entirely. The first female Chancery judge, Carolyn Berger, thirty-five, a rising star at Skadden Arps's Wilmington office, had been named early in 1985 (just in time to be overturned on *Unocal*). And Harvard-trained Jack Jacobs, forty-three, came in right behind her. The result of all this shuffling was a Chancery that was generally younger and less experienced judicially but perhaps more worldly wise than the Delaware Supreme Court. The Supreme Court, particularly Andrew Moore who made M&A his specialty, was aware of the rising debate over takeovers, but as a group the justices did not confront it daily like Chancery judges.

There was a discernible tension between the two courts. Chancery dashed off opinions as complex takeover cases came faster and faster— outpacing the more leisurely, more deliberate Delaware Supreme Court. As Gilson later wrote, "[Because of the sheer volume] the Court of Chancery was the first and last resort for many takeover contests and was restructuring corporate law on the fly. At the same time, the Court of Chancery had to remain sensitive to the views of the Supreme Court that was less experienced with the dynamics of control transactions, especially in this hectic period."[16]

What was not immediately apparent was how a court of equity like Chancery would react in a period of upheaval. In case after case,

Chancery confronted empirical facts: who did what, when, and, importantly, why. The judges needed to be efficient, flexible, and *useful*, not just right. The law, Allen argued, was not just a series of bulkhead-like rules; it changed, but hopefully at a controlled pace. "People who think of law as a system of legal rules alone fail to understand that law is a social product, inevitably complex, at points inescapably ambiguous, and always dynamic—always becoming something new." Allen understood the logic of those who resisted defining the tender offer: rules could be dangerously inflexible. "But if we were to learn the content of legal rules alone we would achieve only a dry and brittle power that would quickly snap under the dynamic cross-pressures of complex and contradictory real life."[17]

None of these were necessarily sentiments shared by the Delaware Supreme Court. The higher court piled new definitions and distinctions upon new takeover standards after seeming to break with the past in *Van Gorkom,* where the Supreme Court, seemingly out of the blue, punished a board for lack of care, and Chancery had to cope with the result. The Supreme Court was focused on establishing doctrine, not articulating viable practice. The Supreme Court overturned Chancery an unusual number of times, often in attempts to clarify its own earlier formulations; Allen, in turn, sometimes seemed to toy with the higher court, with his academic notions, and did not display the same concern for Delaware's continuing preeminence as Moore. The Supreme Court often appeared out of sync, at odds, with decisions pouring from Allen's Chancery, unusual in a court system and legal culture that made a fetish of consistency, consensus, and balance. But in the end, under these unusual conditions, Chancery drove the conversation, with Allen in the lead. As one legal commentator noted, during the oral arguments in the *RJR Nabisco* case an attorney confessed while standing before Allen: "It is difficult for me to stand here and talk to you about the law of the State of Delaware, and cite all the decisions—*and the only decisions see[m] to be your decisions*—but you will accept my apologies for constantly referring to those cases."[18] An exaggeration certainly; perhaps an attempt at flattery. But, as Gilson wrote, Chancery often seemed to be "restructuring corporate law on the fly."

What were *not* discernible in this long, complex, if occasionally barbed, conversation were partisan differences. Delaware resisted partisanship. The corporate law was too important and, as with white-shoe law firms, Delaware insisted it had a higher calling. Delaware lawyers of both parties tended to migrate to the middle. Managerialism was the consensus. Moderation meant reliability. Precedent produced an anchoring tradition that you dislodged at your risk. Much of the crackling tension in Delaware in the late '80s arose over how judges defined that tradition. In an essay, written after he left Chancery, Allen complained about the Supreme Court's "moralistic" opinions in cases like *Van Gorkom*. Allen blamed it on differences of taste: "I am frank to say that my opinion-writing tastes typically were not satisfied with this approach as a technique for resolving questions of power in the corporate form."[19] This verged on the gnomic, as if to say he was affronted by sloppy dress and a bad haircut. Taste, in his hands, was a loaded concept. He may have been criticizing a lurch toward shareholder protection that Moore took, or how the justice sometimes seemed to write from emotion, not dispassionate logic. He may have been referring to the Supreme Court's reaction to events by creating new standards and duties, muddying traditional practice.

In 1999, after Allen had left the bench, he poked at the Delaware Supreme Court at a 100th anniversary celebration of Delaware's corporate statute. "It is, I think, no disrespect to the extraordinary work of the Delaware Supreme Court to suggest that over the last fifteen years the style of opinion writing that has dominated Delaware corporation law has far too often not helped conscientious corporate lawyers who sought understanding that they could apply in their work."[20] Again, note the almost Mandarin-like focus on style, taste, and craftsmanship, which results in a critique of *usefulness*. Surprise, innovation, instability were not useful. In the *Moran* poison-pill decision he noted: "Approval of board adoption of poison pills meant that as a default national policy would be made in Delaware on a case by case basis." That put Delaware at risk. He called *Van Gorkom* a "shocking opinion to corporate law specialists and to businessmen and women alike . . . and was positively disorienting to the [Delaware bar]." The opinion, he said, was radical, but pretended it was not. He even suggested that Chicago law professor Daniel Fischel's characterization of *Van Gorkom* as "the worst in corporate law history" might be right.

But Allen also had his own taste for ambiguity and paradox. *Van Gorkom,* for all its flaws, he added, like a comedian delivering a punch line, was an "important political and social success." The opinion, he said, "exploded on the world of corporate directors," which took notice of its stern message and had "a positive effect on corporate governance." And he noted: "In this light, *Van Gorkom,* which, from a professional view, I think, is one of the worst cases in corporation law history, can be seen as one of the greatest opinions of modern corporation law. Thus, we're reminded that life is not always simple, and that, in the end, we're condemned to be philosophers."

Of course, what unfolded in Delaware was more than just about Chancery and the Supreme Court, or about Allen and Moore. The tendency to distill hundreds of cases in two courts over a number of years to two judges is tempting. In 1989 *Institutional Investor,* in a rare long-form look inside Delaware jurisprudence, pitted the young "liberal experimentalist" (Allen), backing shareholders, against the "crusty 53-year-old conservative" (Moore), defending management, both widely trafficked distortions.[21] Allen and Moore exploded those neat divisions: Allen was both "conservative" (returning again and again to the business judgment rule, resisting innovation and fragmentation, as one law review piece argues, for unity[22]) and "liberal" (accepting the primacy of shareholders, within limits, and working, case by case, to define board responsibilities to a range of corporate players). Moore could be combative, even arrogant, "an enforcer,"[23] but he was "conservative" in the sense that he adhered to a traditional sense of judicial prerogatives and had a visceral dislike of bomb throwers, agitators, and what he viewed as show-offs or incompetents. But his positions, particularly on fiduciary duties, initially worked to restrain the power of directors and limit the reach of the business judgment rule, and, despite his problem with Boone Pickens, he was not always "a staunch ally of corporate managements."[24] He broke with Delaware tradition by protecting shareholders driven by his sense of Delaware's self-interest. He had both "liberal" and "conservative" moments.

To this day, Moore may not get the credit he deserves for nudging Delaware into takeovers. Moore was not a Delaware native, and he defended the system with the zeal of a convert. Born and raised in New Orleans, he attended Tulane and Tulane Law School and clerked for Charles Terry, a chief justice who presided a year before resigning to run successfully for governor. In 1964, Moore went to work at a local firm and for eighteen years practiced corporate litigation. He had no mentor like Stapleton, but he paid his dues, serving on boards and committees, working Republican circles. In 1982, du Pont appointed him to the Supreme Court. He quickly gravitated to takeover cases no one else seemed interested in handling.

He had his ticks. He could be prickly and bullying. He disliked Pickens, and famously once refused to attend an event where he was speaking, which created the appearance that the Mesa CEO couldn't get a fair shot in Delaware. He regularly snapped at lawyers, some of whom had considerable reputations and clout in the Delaware bar. "Justice Moore is strong-willed and has very definite ideas about the way the takeover game works," *Institutional Investor* quoted Wilmington attorney Charles Richards of Richards Layton & Finger in 1989. "But there is a pronounced morality streak running through him. If he thinks you're taking advantage of the court's deference, you're finished."[25] Richards here is using the word *morality* differently than Allen: a defensiveness, a tendency to lash out at what he sees as error or impudence. Moore once described the court's anger in *Van Gorkom* over the fact that Trans Union's directors remained "stalwart in their unified defense of what occurred . . . even though it was obvious that certain directors were more culpable than others," and even though some might have been exonerated. "In a way, they were 'daring' us to find them all liable in a strategic maneuver to save certain insiders."[26] So they did—but he made *Van Gorkom* sound like a playground squabble.

Somehow, despite all these pressures, tensions, and imperfections, Delaware courts shaped rules and principles of behavior—of duties— in hostile takeovers, and provided a point of stability. Allen was philosophical about the effort. No judges were going to solve every problem. Delaware existed to provide stability in an unstable world, but it was a tent in a typhoon. Delaware could not fully stanch the venom or calm the deal whirlwind, which was, if anything, peaking in the late '80s, fueled by an over-ripe economy and a junk-fueled liquidity boom. It took a market break, recession, scandal, and public backlash to drain some of the poisons. But in time Delaware made the M&A process more transparent, predictable, fair (or at least acceptable): *legitimate,* in Allen's phrase. Despite the Chicago belief that M&A was about efficiency and profits, Delaware focused on rights, accountability, and responsibility. Despite missteps, Delaware inserted itself between skilled, ruthless, hell-bent-for-wealth operators contending for control. Not everyone was happy with this, or understood it. The literature that grew up around these decisions is a mass of interpretation, argument, criticism. As Manning once wrote of the Delaware Supreme Court, "As the nation's high court of corporate jurisprudence, it works daily under the klieg lights. No matter what it decides, or how it articulates its decision, the court will be roasted by reviews and, by some, or all, of the constituencies that populate the corporate world."[27] NYU Law's Marcel Kahan was more pungent in his description: "They have referred to the Supreme Court's takeover jurisprudence as mush and mud; disparaged the court for waffling and wavering; criticized its opinions for drawing distinctions 'without foundation,' being 'equivocal,' and lacking clarity; asserted that its rulings generate 'shock waves,' keep changing the framework 'dramatically,' and 'break with precedent;' and remarked that it first 'boosts powers of takeover target boards' and then 'boosts right of shareholders.'"[28]

But Delaware acted as few in authority did. As former Delaware Supreme Court chief justice Daniel Hermann liked to declaim: "It is almost as important that the law be settled as it is that the law be right."[29]

ALLEN APPEARED TO know where he was going, whether he did or not. He negotiated various concepts, theories, models, and metaphors tossed up by academics, by Lipton, by bankers, by politicians, by the Supreme Court, and by the media. He was a connoisseur of theories of the corporation. He had a sense of the moment and generally was favored by legal academics.[30] Between 1985 and the early '90s, he pressed Chancery to encompass a far more diverse group of participants than in the past, balancing shareholder rights with director prerogatives and bringing other intermediaries—lawyers, bankers, independent directors, bondholders—into the mix. This was not always obvious; the pattern emerged only in hindsight—and to the larger, democratic public it remains obscure and arcane.

Allen and his Chancery colleagues clung to fact and precedent, some useful, some not. Allen had a busy court and three other judges to manage. (He and his colleagues also made less than $100,000 a year.[31]) As chancellor he had the power (and the chore) of assigning cases—he increasingly took cases he wanted to try, that he thought fit into larger themes—but the business of the court was conducted, at its best, as a consensual enterprise. In yet another essay, Allen argued that good judges needed technical knowledge of finance and the law, but they also required what he called "artistry."[32] He noted the coiled spring embedded within that quintessential American project of getting as rich as humanly possible—accumulating what, as one of his successors, Leo Strine, once described in an opinion as the goal of shareholders: "Moolah, cash, ching, green, scratch, cabbage, benjamins—to obtain that which Americans have more words for than Eskimos have for snow—money."[33] Allen saw the need to provide wealth-maximizing managers broad discretion to create profits and the complementary need to limit managerial power: an uneasy synthesis of Jensen and Lipton. "The judge confronted with a problem involving fiduciary duty . . . knows he has no science to alert him to the fact that he has entered the dangerland where he threatens to interject excessive uncertainty into the process," he wrote.[34]

Allen abhorred uncertainty. It threatened the predictability and reliability that drew companies to Delaware and allowed managers and shareholders to make sensible decisions. Lawyers needed the court's guidance. A typical reaction to that uncertainty, he argued, was for judges to retreat into a bunker of high moral dudgeon, as he implied Moore had. For his part, Allen said that he reacted to unavoidable uncertainty, a manifestation of ambiguity, with a combination of the pragmatic and the pedantic. Pragmatically, he wrote opinions that were highly specific and fact-based. Pedantically, when he and his colleagues felt on solid ground, they turned to instruction, guidelines to "right action." Corporate lawyers read these carefully, intent on grasping the most recent twist on allowable behavior out of Chancery. Allen was making a subtle point here, because many of these dicta took on a preacherly quality, admonishing certain behavior, acknowledging moral transgressions. Allen himself said that "directors are members of moral communities with allegiances to moral codes."[35] How did these moral dicta differ from "moralistic" Supreme Court decisions? Many of these "shaming" dicta had no legal consequence, except that Chancery exposed the shamed party to damage suits. They were outside the law, providing a guide to Chancery thinking.

Allen was no bearded law-giver, Moses with a mustache. Like Stapleton, he was self-effacing and discrete. A year into his tenure, Allen said about his lack of judicial experience: "It's not sub-atomic physics. Reasonably intelligent people can decide these cases."[36] He was a judge sorting out close calls for parties hell-bent on getting rich. He was a slave not to principle or consistency but to circumstance. He clung to precedent. He was a judge operating in a commercial democracy, which raised questions, as he often noted, of legitimacy. Why Chancery? Why Delaware? Why *him*? A little honesty about the task at hand couldn't hurt. But honesty—candor—had its ambiguities, too.

> Candor is the first among a list of essential virtues of judicial opinions in a democracy. Candor is not, however, without social risks and costs. It can expose uncertainty in choice and thus it may be thought a risk to judicial legitimacy in a democracy. . . . It is more important, in my opinion, that the citizens who willingly subject themselves to the rule of law understand what the process really is; understand when and why choice is unavoidable; understand that the choices made have been made openly in an intellectually honest way and that the judicial process, as a whole, is subject to democratic control.[37]

Allen was an optimist; he was making a leap of faith in the democratic public's interest and expertise. He saw the possibility of a transcendence of self-interest. But he was no fool. He also recognized the impossibility of establishing a single fair and equitable order in a world of relentless change without a broadly accepted concept of the corporation—that is, in the jargon of the economists, an equilibrium, a "right" answer. Unlike Jensen, he did not claim to *know*.

There was only the act of judging that, while hardly perfect, struggled toward equity, fairness, and legitimacy. He didn't have an answer; he had a process.

IN 1997 GILSON of Columbia Law offered his own generous, if grudging, judgment of Allen's tenure: "By sheer force of his intellect, Bill Allen has given substance to what Manning described as 'our great empty corporate statutes.' . . . Allen has sought to rebuild corporate law on a more realistic and intellectually challenging foundation that recognizes the compelling decision makers who contend for influence behind the corporate veil."[38]

So, what did Allen believe the corporation was for? What was *his* theory of the corporation? In fact, he didn't have one; instead, he offered a kind of pluralistic liberalism of many equally valid beliefs and practices that have to be ordered and tolerated: so-called negative liberty.[39] The corporation had no essential nature. There were only conceptions—simplifications—that flipped in and out of fashion, a formulation that echoes Madison's ambiguities of federal and state sovereignty contained in the Constitution, which made it a "living" document able to change with the times.[40] In a series of essays, Allen argued the case: the nineteenth century had come to believe in the "property" model, in which directors worked as trustees for shareholders, who were true owners. The property model rose with the industrial corporation, prevailed, then fell with the Great Depression and the separation of ownership and control. This conception is the one that returned in the '70s, with Manne, Jensen, and the takeover crowd. "This model," Allen wrote, "might almost as easily be called a contract model, because in its most radical form, the corporation tends to disappear, transformed from a substantial institution into just a relatively stable corner of the market in which autonomous property owners freely contract."[41] Sweeping it aside was the "social entity" model, long associated with Berle. Social entity corporations have multiple stakeholders, none of which is preeminent. The company has greater goals than maximizing short-term wealth. It has a responsibility to workers, communities, customers, society. The corporation is less an economic entity than a social one: "The corporation itself is, in this view, capable of bearing legal *and* moral obligations."[42]

We have seen this dichotomy before. What makes Allen fascinating, if little known outside corporate law, is his observations of how Americans, and the law, have allowed the two concepts to coexist for long periods, papering over inconsistencies and conflicts. The emergence of the cash tender offer ended, at least for corporation law, the avoidance of "choosing between the alpha of property and the omega of relationships."[43] Takeovers drove up stakes, not just for shareholders but for stakeholders as well. Hostile takeovers undermined the prevailing belief that corporations could generate both long-term and short-term capital creation—satisfying both social entity and property believers, shareholders and stakeholders—and pitted interests against each other in a struggle of all against all: Hobbes again. This was a zero-sum game, putting intense pressure on directors who had the traditional power to choose. Allen recognized the depths of the clash. Courts and legislatures generally endorsed the entity view. (He was thinking of the anti-takeover movements in the states, the defense of the business judgment rule, and public reaction to excesses of the deal culture in the late '80s.) But "as the world becomes a fiercer place for American business, corporate management is forced to consider financial performance at every stage." That favors the property model. "Courts," he dryly noted, "were not anxious to grapple with this question."[44] Neither were regulators.

So Allen offers no answer to the larger question: What is the purpose of the corporation? At the end of the day he's a judge, not a philosopher. And as a judge he must accept the realities of the democratic *zeitgeist.* "I suppose there will be no final move in defining the nature or purpose of the business corporation. It is perhaps asking too much to expect us, as a people—or our law—to have a single view of the purpose of an institution so large, pervasive and important as our public corporations. These entities are too important to generate that sort of agreement. Within them exists the tension that a dynamic market system creates between the desire to achieve increases in total wealth and the desire to avoid losses and injuries—the redistribution—that a dynamic system inevitably engenders."[45]

Where does that leave us? These aren't legal, financial, or economic questions, says Allen. "Rather, in defining what we suppose a public corporation to be, we implicitly express our view of the nature and purpose of our social life." Since we can't agree on that, corporate law is fated to be "contentious and controversial . . . worked out, not deduced. In this process, efficiency concerns, ideology and interest-group politics will commingle with history . . . to produce an answer that will hold for here and now, only to be torn by some future stress and to be reformulated once more." And he ends, a classic compression of one of his most profound insights, with a touch of Poe's raven: "And so on, and so on, evermore."[46]

Chapter Fifteen

CALL OF DUTIES

"So you fear you're having a post-midlife crisis?"

I want to talk about the bottom line.

I want leverage.

I want to say things like, "The bottom line is that I've got plenty of leverage."

I want to put together equity pools and engage in leveraged buyouts.

"Why do you want leverage?"

How do I know? I don't even know what leverage is. If I was engaged in a leveraged buyout, I wouldn't even know what I was engaged in. I don't know what an equity pool is, either, or how to put one together.

"You have a romantic yearning for a world in which you are pathetically ignorant?"

—RUSSELL BAKER, "Creature of *Fortune,*" *New York Times*[1]

CORPORATE LAW, MEANING mostly Delaware law, has, like the military, sports teams, the Boy Scouts, and religion, a thing about duty. The heart of corporate law is fiduciary duty. That breaks down into the duty of care, the duty of loyalty, and into various minor, and much debated, satellite duties like candor. Duty often seems to harken back to an age when life was hard and rheumy-eyed folks read the Bible to each other by candlelight. They may then have gone out and done wrong—broken a trust relationship, particularly one involving money or property—but they felt the scourge of their violation and a sense of accountability. They had failed their duty; they had betrayed a trust, a promise, an oath, a commandment, a covenant; they had failed to transcend their self-interest. Defining that duty, like defining a tender offer, could be tricky. But a duty suggested that somewhere out there was a higher standard of behavior that you, in all your fallibility and self-interest, had failed to meet. Duty was less a psychological model—original sin was a theory that fed off more primitive emotions of guilt, imperfection, mortality, crime, and punishment—than an aspiration; not a right but an obligation. Once you start dwelling on such subjective, human tendencies, you can easily toss up more rules than Puritans deciding who can join the local church. Immanuel Kant, the child of duty-wracked German Pietists, divested himself of all the religious trappings in his attempt to put morals on a rational philosophical basis. Essentially, what he came up with as a foundation for morals was a sense of duty.

The Chicago academics were ambivalent about the traditional adherence of corporate law to fiduciary duties. Chicago generally viewed duties as outmoded, arguing that most relationships that matter in public companies could be defined by carefully written and enforced contracts—a lawyers' solution. Eventually, fiduciary duties might wither away, as companies learned to use contracts to cover the extraordinary range of corporate activities. Michael Jensen reflected that belief when he confidently predicted that Delaware would embrace agency theory, with the corporation as a nexus of contracts. In a modern market-fueled world shot through with models and theories, money and power, Delaware's focus on duties seemed anachronistic, a throwback, like wigs and penmanship and sin.

But the triumph of the contract had yet to come. Contracts were rigid, inflexible, rules-based in a fluid, increasingly dynamic world—seemingly more suited for a bureaucracy than for a new-age, nimble, networked company. (And "implied" contracts really meant no contracts.) Contracts required lawyers, negotiation, monitoring: that is, frictions, costs, delays. Even Chicago's leading theoreticians, Daniel Fischel and new federal judge Frank Easterbrook, acknowledged limits in a book they wrote in 1991 that outlined the contractual approach to corporate law: "For contracting to work optimally, the markets must be completely free. That is, all possible contracts must be completely free. That is, all possible contracts must be lawful. They must be stable and enforceable at low cost; breach must be detectable and remediable. Finally, the contracts concerning one firm's operations must have no effect on other firms. Each of these steps is problematic."[2] In short, contracts, at least in tender offers, work wonderfully well in a world that doesn't yet exist.

By then, the Delaware courts had already examined, outlined, debated, enumerated, and argued over a class of fiduciary duties that applied to directors who found themselves in hostile takeover struggles. This was not the Ten Commandments. This was a handful of imperfect and fallible judges struggling to balance key principles, from the age-old business judgment rule, giving great leeway to decision-making managers, to expectations of shareholders that they could have a say in the fate of *their* corporation. Takeover jurisprudence may have begun in the 1980s with *Unocal,* where Moore laid out a new test to determine directorial duties of care and loyalty, but it took off with a new duty named for a company that peddled what its founder called "hope in a jar."

RONALD O. (FOR OWEN) PERELMAN was, in a term Martin Lipton began using in the mid-'80s, a classic *takeover entrepreneur.* Five foot five inches tall, cigar-puffing (five a day), energetic, talkative, occasionally vulgar, and exceedingly litigious, not to say intently focused on his own self-interest, Perelman grew up in Philadelphia and, like Milken, graduated with an MBA from Wharton. He married a wealthy woman, had four children, managed her money, and worked for his father, Raymond Perelman, the son of Lithuanian émigrés, and a man who apparently defined the term *hardball.* Raymond ran a metals-fabricating company, Belmont Industries, which he built into a mini-conglomerate; his son tagged along on deals.

In 1978, at the age of thirty-five, Ron bolted for New York after his father refused to make him president. The two didn't speak for six years. Perelman was driven, detail-oriented, and shrewd, as evidenced by his advisors at MacAndrews & Forbes, his takeover vehicle:

Howard Gittis, a longtime Philadelphia attorney and Perelman's closest associate; Bruce Slovin, a Harvard lawyer; Fred Tepperman, a Warner veteran. Soon a Skadden Arps partner and Flom protégé, Donald Drapkin, would join the club. The boys spent the days talking, smoking, scheming together in a townhouse stuffed with modern art on the Upper East Side of Manhattan. Perelman was relatively unknown, and at the time press-shy, but they were all experienced professionals, adept at buying and selling, at financing, tax, and particularly law. "God knows, Ronald has an ego," a Perelman banker once told *Business Week*. "But this is not a reverent crowd. It's like being around the dinner table at someone's home. They don't kiss the ring. I've heard them tell him he's a putz."[3] In fact, that's exactly what Drapkin liked to call him, when he wasn't referring to him as the Dwarf. Perelman in turn referred to Drapkin in more scatological terms. For a while, this tomfoolery was masked by a take-no-prisoners attitude toward the outside world. Unfortunately, Perelman had a way of falling out with colleagues, eventually battling both Tepperman and Drapkin in court.

Perelman, free of Philly, was a cat on the prowl. He and Gittis—the full team didn't assemble until later—searched for undervalued assets, used debt, and sold off assets: he was a bust-up guy and he wasn't averse to greenmail. Right off, he borrowed $1.9 million and bought a jewelry business, Cohen-Hatfield Industries. He then sold off everything but a wholesale watch distributor and pocketed $15 million. In 1980 Cohen-Hatfield merged into MacAndrews & Forbes, a maker of licorice extract for cigarette flavoring, and a chocolate wholesaler, for $45.7 million. The company borrowed $35 million from a group of banks and repaid them by selling junk bonds, underwritten by Drexel Burnham Lambert and Bear Stearns, his entree into Milken's network. In 1983 he nabbed Technicolor, which owned the movie color process. He sold off five divisions but the core Technicolor business took off with the advent of multiplex theaters. The deal, alas, left a trail of ugly charges that included paying off board members and cheating a Technicolor shareholder, Cinerama. Despite the lawsuits, Perelman sold a controlling stake in Technicolor to Carlton Communications. Faced with divorce from his first wife—Perelman seemed to specialize in personal ruptures that required a judge to sort out—he took MacAndrews & Forbes private in 1983 to shield his assets. Milken provided the junk to take out the debt. When bondholders refused to buy the bonds, Milken sold them to the Drexel network and Perelman paid them off in cash. He immediately stalked Consolidated Cigar, a part of conglomerate Gulf + Western that was trying to restructure itself into an entertainment company. Why not? Perelman had a personal interest in the product. In 1984 he bought Consolidated, maker of Phillies cigars. Soon after, he grabbed Video Corp. of America.

Although he was new to the big time, Perelman was Milken's kind of guy. He targeted beaten-down Pantry Pride, a Philadelphia-based owner of three supermarket chains that, like Trans Union, had tax-loss carry-forwards that could be used to shelter profits. In June 1985, he won control by buying preferred stock; Drexel represented both buyer and seller—which was both unusual and a sizable conflict. Quickly, he sold off all three chains, leaving Pantry Pride a corporate shell—his acquisition vehicle. He didn't bother to change the name.

In July 1985, Perelman raised $761 million in Drexel junk. Part of it—$200 million—went right back to Drexel "to pay down inventory" and the rest became Perelman's war chest. He insisted he wasn't sure what company he'd be targeting until he found Revlon, which was widely viewed as ludicrous. Revlon was a famous, global cosmetics company run by a tall, my-way-or-the-highway French-born executive, Michel Bergerac, who had no intention of selling out to a tawdry former supermarket chain run by an obscure bust-up acquirer: Peril-man, they called him at Revlon. Panty Pride.[4] Bergerac, who had run ITT's European operations under Harold Geneen (see Chapter 3), succeeded Revlon's legendary mercurial founder, Charles Revson, and had begun to build his own healthcare (of sorts) conglomerate: contact lenses, lab testing, prescription drugs, acne cream, antacids. Perelman believed that Bergerac had allowed the cosmetics operation to slide.

Perelman approached Revlon to make what he called a friendly bid. Bergerac—tall, bald, with a handsome mustache and beautiful suits—dismissed it as much too low, though even the Delaware

Supreme Court's Andrew Moore took note of "Mr. Bergerac's strong personal antipathy to Mr. Perelman." The two sides manned up. Bergerac hired Paul Weiss's powerfully connected litigator Arthur Liman and, not surprisingly, given his ITT pedigree, Geneen's old banker, Felix Rohatyn, who returned from a vacation in Austria. This was a tight knot of relationships and interests. The rumpled, absent-minded Liman, famously described once as "Walter Matthau doing a Perry Mason impersonation,"[5] was a top-tier courtroom cross-examiner, a power at Paul Weiss, and the protégé of Simon Rifkind, who had built the firm. Rifkind—a New Dealer, former federal judge, and Rohatyn's attorney in his nightmarish ITT hearings—sat on both Revlon and MacAndrews's boards; he had been the executor of Revson's estate. Perelman had asked Rifkind to arrange a friendly meeting with Bergerac, which the lawyer did, then regretted after realizing what Perelman was after. Rifkind felt he had vouched for Perelman with Bergerac, and quit MacAndrews's board to join the Revlon defense. Paul Weiss in the past had represented both companies, so Liman felt he could only advise Revlon, not engage in litigation; he hired Wachtell for that, and got Lipton and his founding partner, a litigator in Liman's class, Herbert Wachtell.

The Liman, Rifkind duo seemed beyond reproach. But under the intense white-knuckle pressure of the struggle for Revlon, reputations broke down. The Revlon board had a leaking problem—Perelman's team always seemed to know exactly what was going on at Revlon—and paranoia took hold, which eventually fixed upon the Paul Weiss pair. Ezra Zilkha, a legendary investor, longtime Revlon board member, and Bergerac confidante, years later in a self-published memoir[6] speculated in a particularly damning, if indirect way: "Neither [Rifkind nor Liman] is still alive, and the dead cannot defend themselves, but some people suspect there was a mole on Revlon's board who leaked our deliberations to Perelman." *Some people suspect.* If there was evidence beyond the circumstantial, Zilkha failed to offer it up. Suspicion was enough.

Perelman gathered his own advisors, led by Drexel's Dennis Levine—who later played a key role in Milken's demise. Morgan

Stanley got the assignment of selling off Revlon assets if Perelman won, a key part of his plan; still, some bankers at Morgan Stanley groused at playing second fiddle to the parvenus of Drexel. Bergerac, who had once gone big-game hunting with Greenhill, called to pro-test—"They hang horse thieves," the CEO snapped at him, suggesting the takeover attempt was akin to theft—but that failed to move him. Perelman's big catch was Flom, who brought in Donald Drapkin, who was a Skadden partner but who had grown close to Perelman.[7] Drapkin had been a Cravath associate with Wasserstein, and his office was right next to Flom's at Skadden. Even the banks chased their interests, which trumped some vague establishment loyalty. Chemical Bank, which had once defended itself against Steinberg, agreed to lend to Perelman, setting off more howls from the Revlon camp. To no avail. Chemical was about to launch its own merger campaign that involved gobbling up most of the New York elite banks, including Manufacturers Hanover, Chase Manhattan, and J. P. Morgan & Co.

Bergerac was so self-regarding he seemed like a parody, but principles did seem to emerge from his sniffy Gallic self-regard: the Perelman forces were baffled by how resistant he was to carefully dangled sums of money—especially golden parachutes. He was, in that regard, a faithful agent, bolstered by his considerable net worth. Perelman had never operated a company the size of Revlon. But it didn't matter. He had Milken's seemingly limitless financing. This was thus a clash of Perelman's will and Milken's resources and Bergerac's will and Revlon's size and prestige. As Connie Bruck points out in *Predators' Ball*, the initial takeover deals Drexel had backed had fizzled, notably Icahn's attack on Phillips and Pickens's move on Unocal. This deal was crucial for both Perelman *and* Milken.

The battle shifted back and forth, with each side believing it had won at different times. (The *New York Times* all-but-declared Revlon the winner at one point.[8]) Perelman's initial meeting with Bergerac occurred in mid-August. By mid-September, Wachtell attempted to show in federal court that Perelman had had designs on Revlon when he raised the junk (a disclosure violation) but failed. So, too, did Revlon's attempt to prove that arbs had been tipped off early to swing the shareholder base in a speculative direction, which was probably true since trading volume spiked; but the firm couldn't nail it. Revlon, on Lipton's urging, installed a poison pill. And the board authorized the purchase of a quarter of its shares in exchange for bond-like notes—again at Lipton's recommendation. Perelman waited several weeks—then upped his bid, contingent upon getting 90 percent of the shares. Revlon began to suspect, in typical takeover fashion, that it had two crappy choices: liquidate and pay investors, or find a white knight. It was September 24, 1985. A smaller buyout shop offered to buy the cosmetics business. One of the biggest of the leveraged buyout firms, Forstmann Little & Co., said it would acquire the rest with Bergerac and his senior management team. Perelman raised his bid again, then again. More ominously for Revlon, Milken sold more Pantry Pride junk. In a meeting arranged by Liman, in which Bergerac, Forstmann's founder Theodore "Teddy" Forstmann, and Perelman tried to settle matters, Perelman blurted out that every time Forstmann raised his bid, he would top it by a quarter a share, which amounted to between $30 million and $35 million with each raise. The idea apparently came from Drapkin. Perelman felt he *had* to win no matter the price; and he had Milken. Bruck quotes one of Perelman's bankers on his "incredible tenacity. He was like a dog with a bone. He would not stop. I think if he'd had to bid ninety dollars he would have done it."[9] Only Forstmann had no personal stake, beyond the urge to win. Still, while Perelman had advantages—Milken, the tax-loss carry-forwards, the divestitures, even the fact that he didn't have to pay excessive carrying costs on the junk—he was in uncharted territory. This wasn't the kind of rational bidding Chicago imagined. And he was being backed by Milken, who was also not operating in an efficient market—who *was,* within limits, the market.

To clear the way for a Forstmann buyout, the Revlon board took steps that triggered a cascade of unfortunate consequences. They had to dismantle the poison pill so it would not wreak its retribution on Forstmann, and to abandon limits on the amount of debt Revlon could shoulder. But when the board waived those limits, bondholders rushed to sell, fearing the damaging effect that a large new load of buyout debt would have on existing bonds. This produced a kind of cardiac shock: the value of the bonds collapsed. Forstmann hurriedly agreed to raise his bid and support the notes, but in return he demanded a lock-up to buy two key units of Revlon and a $25 million fee. Notes from that board meeting, which ended up in court, underlined Forstmann's disdain for junk bonds and Perelman. *He* used respectable financing. *He* had been invited into the deal by Lazard. On Saturday, October 12, the board voted to sell Revlon to Forstmann. Pantry Pride rushed to sue in Chancery.

Delaware Chancery judge Joseph Walsh played up the drama. He ended his recitation of the facts of the case with a novelistic touch: "At 5 p.m. on October 18, within three hours of the conclusion of oral argument on the present motion, Pantry Pride announced that it had increased its offer to $58 cash for any and all shares of Revlon and that it would match Forstmann Little's support of the Notes."[10] Perelman would not be denied. Bergerac was toast.

THE REVLON ACQUISITION was a tactically sophisticated deal that offered a graphic demonstration of Milken's growing power and Perelman's guts. But Revlon, for all of Bergerac's pretensions and all the attempts by Lipton and Rohatyn to present it as a profound moral clash, was hardly some rare corporate treasure in the IBM, AT&T, DuPont, General Motors, or General Electric class. Perelman was right: Revlon had begun to fade like an aging model, particularly on the cosmetics side, well before Charles Revson died. Bergerac had acquired assets, but it was a jumble, which made it easy to disassemble. The sagging stock was evidence of trouble, and of a negative view by the market of conglomerates. And at the end of the day, the company's much-vaunted brand was built on selling over-the-counter beauty aids to masses of women—a legitimate, if ephemeral, business. It was a smoke-and-mirrors company, dependent on advertising, packaging, brand, and manufactured allure. Celebrity—the fact that millions of ordinary people knew Revlon, bought Revlon, even loved Revlon, and "knew" the famous women who pitched Revlon—made it catnip for the press. The fact that hard-bitten Perelman, son of a metal-bender, shelled out a huge premium, suggested that he too believed in peddling dreams (much of his later career, marital and business, confirmed that tendency, though he and his team did fix Revlon up before the heavy debt required to acquire it extracted its toll, demanding reorganization and refinancing. But that was years later.) Still, Perelman undoubtedly recognized what winning Revlon would do for him. Revlon turned him into a winner, a big-time player, a *macher,* eventually a billionaire. Success brought success. It made him in 1986 one of *Fortune* magazine's "50 Most Fascinating Business People: Revlon's Striving Makeover Man," a headline that channeled all kinds of class judgments.[11]

Whether he meant it or not, Rifkind, by then eighty-three years old, neatly deflated Perelman's triumph: "Here, then, is a transaction which has absorbed countless hours of labor and many millions of dollars to accomplish something which is devoid of any redeeming virtue."[12]

Connie Bruck captures what Adam Smith in *The Money Game* called status anxieties rippling through this deal in a single anecdote. Liman has tried to broker a peace, and Perelman and his entourage have headed up to Revlon's "gilded, rococo foyer" on the thirty-ninth floor of the General Motors Building, across from the Plaza Hotel in New York. She quotes Bergerac: "I'll never forget those twenty or thirty guys coming off the elevators. All short, bald, with big cigars! It was incredible! If central casting had to produce thirty guys like that, they couldn't do it. They looked like they were in a grade-D movie that took place in Mississippi or Louisiana about guys fixing elections in a back room." Her perspective then shifts like a camera on a boom: "For their part, Perelman's group thought little of Bergerac's décor: the animal heads from safaris mounted on the walls, the elephant-leg stools, the Abercrombie and Fitch–type murals of lions and tigers, the antique commode, throne-like, in Bergerac's private bathroom. As Drapkin commented, 'It was the tackiest.'"[13]

The anecdote undercuts Bruck's conclusion: "The conquest of Revlon signaled the end of an era. Those who defended it were struggling to perpetuate a way of corporate life—plush, congenial and secure, un-menaced by anyone but perhaps another corporate giant—that had lost its ability to prevail in the economic world. The junk-bond marauders had won here, and if they had won here, they could win anywhere."[14]

And yet, if there was an end of an era, it had ended years earlier. Somehow, managerial excess survived, un-menaced. The defenders had been defending for years, and would continue. What was the source of their privilege? The balance had shifted slightly, tipped by Milken's resources, which were deep, but as evanescent as liquidity— or a Revlon fragrance or lip-gloss. But companies also had weapons: the pill, staggered boards, recapitalizations, buyouts. If there was less difference between Perelman and Bergerac than the spin suggested, then there was also less difference between takeover bids fueled by bank loans and those powered by junk. Milken did activate a new group of "marauders," but many of them had been marauding for years; even Perelman had been operating since the late '70s. Was there a substantive difference between Victor Posner, Carl Icahn, and new-comers like Perelman or Nelson Peltz? Was there a difference between old Perelman and new Perelman, or Perelman the father and Perel-man the son? Only that as recipients of Milken's favors, and con-trolling pools of capital that Milken could tap, they could set sights on larger targets and dream bigger dreams. But the notion that some de-cline and fall were at hand because of junk bonds tested credulity. The marauders were not taking over. They had been inside for years, with their silk-stockinged feet propped up on the elephant-leg stools.

How had Perelman won? Because Revlon lost, betrayed by its own self-interest. Walsh, who had also been the Chancery judge in *Moran* and who would soon move to the Delaware Supreme Court, was not concerned with matters of taste; his job was to explore the working— or not—of fiduciary duty. On October 24, 1985, he had enjoined— blocked with an injunction—the Forstmann buyout, effectively handing the company to Perelman. He stepped gingerly through prec-edents on board behavior. He cited *Van Gorkom* on the duty of care and *Unocal* on the duty of loyalty. Even informed boards operate un-der limits, he noted. The response had to be proportional to the threat.

Walsh pointed to a turning point: in late September it became clear that Revlon had lost; the board realized it was going to be broken up, and it was just a question of who would get the spoils. (Walsh offered the nugget that Bergerac had discussed a buyout with Forstmann *before* Perelman made his offer. Bergerac resisted Perelman's money but was happy to take Forstmann's.) At this point, Walsh said, the board's role changed. Its fiduciary duty now was not to defend Revlon but to extract the highest price possible for shareholders—that is, to act as an auctioneer.

Once you became an auctioneer you had to treat bidders roughly the same. Revlon had not, despite getting a rich price for shareholders. The company favored Forstmann with concessions like the lock-up and the waiver of the pill and a sharing of information. Revlon never invited Pantry Pride to make its case to the board. Walsh rejected Revlon's claim that it favored Forstmann because it seemed better able to finance the acquisition. Neither Pantry Pride nor Forstmann could buy all of Revlon without selling assets. And Walsh noted damning evidence of director self-interest: Forstmann provided the board a solution to the notes problem. Because the notes were imploding, directors faced bondholder lawsuits. The notes problem, in turn, originated with the initial decision to buy back the shares to keep them from Perelman. The board, Walsh concluded, saw Forstmann as a way to elude those suits. It had acted in its own self-interest. It had failed to fulfill its responsibility to shareholders and violated its duty of loyalty.

Walsh's remedy: He took away the board's right to the pill, the exchange offer, the lock-up, and a no-shop clause banning Revlon from soliciting outside buyers. He dismantled Revlon's defenses. He encouraged Revlon to renew bidding on other terms. In short, more bidding activity, not less, should define what had become an asset sale. The winner would be the higher bidder.

Revlon appealed to the Supreme Court. Andrew Moore offered an oral opinion a day later affirming the Chancery decision. Moore's written opinion agreed with Walsh on major points (and why not: Walsh was citing opinions Moore had a hand in developing), including the transition of the board from defending itself (which received the protections of the business judgment rule) to the point when the board clearly saw that the company was breaking up.[15] Moore zeroed in on that transition, and his language reverberated: he spoke of a moment when a sale was *inevitable,* when the board's duty changed from preservation to the maximization of the company's value.

Moore was articulating a new standard, seemingly born from *Unocal*'s proportionality standard, which in its emphasis on a balanced response to a threat was also subjective.[16] The responsibilities that descend upon the board when this inevitable turn from preservation to sale occurs became known as *Revlon* duties. It was like an end-of-life process. Technically, *Unocal* involved matters of general defense, while *Revlon* governed a final auction or sale. Under *Revlon,* directorial options narrowed to the role Ronald Gilson and Lucian Bebchuk had sketched out to Easterbrook and Fischel's mandatory passivity imperative: sell the company at the highest price in an auction (see Chapter 7). In Moore's notion of *Revlon* duties, only shareholders mattered; stakeholders, which boards could normally consider under the business judgment rule, fell away. It was as if a company was retracing the Chicago-driven shift from stakeholder to shareholder-centric governance, from Berle to Manne, in the space of a single takeover episode.

But what was this new test—and how did it differ from *Unocal*? What exactly triggered it—a sale of a company, a change of control, a change in ownership, a breakup, or something else? Was this state of inevitability always so obvious—or was it clear only in hindsight, like a burst financial bubble? Was it something new—another standard of review—or was it related to the traditional business judgment rule? In his *Revlon* opinion, Moore seemed to confuse whether Revlon was violating the duty of care or the duty of loyalty. This was important because the duty of loyalty is a far greater transgression, triggering the withdrawal of the business judgment rule, which a failure of the duty of care may not. "The Delaware Supreme Court's failure to decide whether *Revlon* claims implicated the duty of care or the duty of loyalty was a failure to decide the proper role of the courts," slashingly opined Northwestern law professor Gordon Smith in 1998, concluding: "The [Moore] opinion in *Revlon* is impenetrable."[17]

Revlon, in fact, was a sketch, an outline. While Moore had written about recognizing and reacting to defensive situations—the omnipresent specter of self-interest, enhanced scrutiny, proportionality, inevitability, coercive threat, reasonable price—the words were mostly empty vessels yet to be filled. But with what? And so the process began: not just in case after case, mostly in Chancery, which began to try to apply these precedents, but in law reviews and client notes, where these opinions and their rhetoric were unpacked in a running, bubbling stream of commentary. This was a rich, perhaps over-rich, brew— mixing fine points of fiduciary duties with debates about managers and shareholders, theories of the firm, federalism, and economics. It was a bewildering exercise for outsiders—like foreigners trying to figure out the fine points of professional football. But upon this play of definitions and legal concepts hung the fate of companies, careers, lives. This was, given the volume of cases, a legal arbitrage process. Any loopholes, any weaknesses or flaws, were likely to be ruthlessly exploited by legal practitioners and their clients. But the sheer volume of cases, each unique, also allowed errors to be corrected, planed away, hammered down, dropped, redefined, or amended in subsequent cases by Chancery and the Supreme Court. There were no guarantees of beneficial results. Still, in a nation that no longer spent much time rigorously parsing, or even necessarily believing, fine-grained moral strictures, this was an unusual exercise: the attempt to shape, tame, and channel brutally self-interested corporate behavior. At the end of the day, these strictures had little to do with claims of economic efficiency. They had everything to do, as Walsh said, with conduct and duties.

In *Unocal* and *Revlon*, the Supreme Court placed Delaware into complex, ambiguous, and perilous situations. Both potentially limited a board's power, albeit balanced by *Moran*'s approval of the pill. Trying to pin down that moment when a board had to sell in a mind-numbing variety of different takeover situations proved a challenge, both for Allen's Chancery and for the Supreme Court. Was it really necessary? Why couldn't the basic *Unocal* test, which determined whether the business judgment rule applied, be used? Or why not just update that old case *Cheff*, with its easy tolerance of board prerogatives? Conversely, why shouldn't the board simply default to shareholders on a decision as fundamental as a takeover? *It was their money.* Case by case, judge by judge, the debate rumbled on. In particular, Allen, who arrived at Chancery just after *Moran,* struggled to sort this out, to distinguish *Revlon* from *Unocal,* to carve away exceptions to both, to break down and define the elements and language, to come to some sort of legal consensus on how to define proper behavior over a vastly diverse set of issues stirred up by gargantuan takeovers—"to," as one law review article said, "dismantle [*Unocal*'s] impact."[18]

For all the technical distinctions and standards and duties, Allen and his colleagues' steady focus was on the presence, or absence, of self-interest. There were certain foundations of governance Delaware did not question. The board had the power to make fundamental decisions about the fate of corporations. Boards had this power because shareholders had voted them into office. Just as Chicago subsumed directors into the ranks of managers, so the Delaware courts ignored managers unless they were directors. The business judgment rule—the assumption that directors had the best information and the greatest autonomy—was the default option. But directors could find that freedom withdrawn if they strayed and sought their own self-interest rather than that of the corporation. This was a *judgment.* Contrary to Jensen, the Delaware courts understood agency costs, but as an aspect of self-interest, governed by a sense of duty. In fact, for all the talk going back to Berle about the separation of ownership and control, self-interest was a broader, more fundamental transgression. Delaware's business judgment rule always assumed—perhaps over-optimistically—that boards could transcend self-interest. True, Delaware courts rarely felt the need to probe board self-interest deeply—perhaps from their *own* niggling self-interest as Delaware judges. But hostile takeovers changed that. The takeover was self-interest in action. The takeover embodied a radical self-interest in individuals—Pickens, Perelman, Bergerac, Icahn—who often wrapped themselves in the abstract and unitary collective self-interest of shareholders. The ethos of takeovers said: Self-interest cannot be cured so we might as well seize it, embrace it, celebrate it. Anything that interfered with the expression of self-interest in takeovers should be dismantled as unnatural and inefficient.

That was not Delaware's view. By the mid-'80s, more and more takeover situations like Revlon included an innovative, potent expression of self-interest: the leveraged or management buyout (most LBOs had an element of management participation). From the manager's perspective, buyouts loomed as ideal white knights. Buyouts were seemingly wins for everyone: they rewarded both shareholders and participating managers—though, as with Milken's network, participation was sharply limited. Shareholders got premiums; key managers kept their jobs (and, with a change of ultimate ownership, got a new board), shared in as an often-rewarding upside; and, as a private company, faced no threats of further takeover or public disdain. (Buyouts often turned out to be tougher than they seemed: LBO firms frequently demanded more accountability of managers than ordinary shareholders.) Delaware, however, saw them as nests of potential conflict and self-interest. Delaware's solution: special board committees consisting of independent directors shorn of managerial representatives, formed when an LBO involving management surfaced. In a 1990 article focused on those committees, Allen placed buyouts in the same class as poison pills—mechanisms that had to be carefully scrutinized for self-interest. "I remain open to the possibility that such committees can be employed effectively to protect corporate and shareholder interests," he wrote. "But I must confess a painful awareness of the ways in which the device may be subverted and rendered less than useful."[19]

ALL OF WHICH brings us to *Macmillan,* a case that lasted for two years and involved two visits to Chancery and one to the Supreme Court, and that was a virtual anatomical dissection of self-interest. *Macmillan* was a saga that featured two executives, Edward "Ned" Evans and

William Reilly, who ran the New York publishing house, Macmillan;
a Texas up-from-oil investment operation, the Robert M. Bass Group;
a swashbuckling and egomaniacal Czech-born British tabloid entrepreneur and war hero, Robert Maxwell; and LBO shop Kohlberg Kravis Roberts. Wasserstein—initially at First Boston, then at Wasserstein
Perella—represented Macmillan; Lazard advised the Macmillan's special committee; and Wachtell Lipton served as the committee's special
counsel.

Evans was the middle son of Thomas Mellon Evans, one of the pro-
genitors of financial takeovers in the pre–Williams Act 1950s and '60s
(and a "poor" cousin of Paul Mellon), a figure most famously characterized by a New Jersey congressman as "the corporate embodiment of
Jaws, the great white shark."[20] Thomas Evans was a notoriously difficult man, one of *Fortune*'s Ten-Worst Bosses in business in 1981, and
not exactly a lovable father. Ned worked for him. In the late '70s, Ned
engineered a boardroom coup at stumbling Macmillan, became chairman of the board, then took the top operational role: he seemed to
have escaped his father—until Tom Evans capriciously unloaded his
stake in the publisher, threatening Ned's control. Ned survived, restructured, and rebuilt Macmillan through some sixty acquisitions,
rebuffing several takeover attempts, and he was generally viewed as a
success, driving the consolidation of publishing. He held only 2 percent of the shares after his father sold, technically providing neither
ownership nor control, but he was in charge. Reilly, a veteran of conglomerate W. R. Grace & Co., served as his right-hand man.

In May 1987 Evans and Reilly persuaded Macmillan's board to
adopt defensive measures, including a pill, and to pursue a leveraged
recapitalization, borrowing money to buy back stock to keep it out of
a raider's hands. They got the idea after Maxwell attacked but failed to
nab Harcourt Brace Jovanovich, which defended itself by taking on
debt to buy its own shares; the "restructuring" had been engineered by
Wasserstein and Perella at First Boston. Macmillan opted for a copy-
cat restructuring, with Evans and Reilly gaining control without putting up any of their own capital (the company borrowed to buy $120
million in shares through an employee-stock ownership plan).

Macmillan adopted, on Wachtell Lipton's urging, a flip-in pill, golden parachutes, and a hike in director compensation. In August, the board voted to break Macmillan in two, separating the publishing and information businesses, as another defensive move.[21]

Just as Macmillan was launching the plan, and two days after the stock market took one of its biggest one-day dives in history on October 19, 1987 (a challenge to market efficiency, particularly after the stock market bounced back without a recession), the Bass Group made a friendly offer for Macmillan. Evans and Reilly told the board that Bass was a gang of greenmailers, and the board rejected the offer. The pair decided a special committee was necessary and hired Lazard to advise it. Lazard then recommended that management's stake be whittled down from 55 percent to 39 percent of the information business, enough to ensure control while avoiding charges of handing over ownership. Bass raised its offer on June 4. The special committee and full board rejected the new bid as "inadequate."

Bass then filed suit in Chancery, asking the court to enjoin the restructuring on grounds of *Unocal, Revlon,* and a violation of the duty of candor (arguing that the board never disclosed that a new stock option plan would be essential for the later restructuring). Chancery's Jack Jacobs focused on the *Unocal* claim, finding both the board and the special committee to be self-interested and the restructuring "an unreasonable and disproportionate response" to the overture from Bass. He blocked the restructuring.

Rebuffed in Delaware, Macmillan's board adopted the pill, and handed out stock options and golden parachutes. Macmillan now explored a buyout with Kohlberg Kravis Roberts, which promised management a 20 percent stake. Maxwell Communications, however, made an all-cash tender offer and a bidding contest began, in which Evans and Reilly and their banker Wasserstein served as auctioneers. After several rounds, Macmillan declared KKR the winner but had to give the firm a no-shop (promising not to seek a buyer), a lock-up, breakup fees (payments if the deal came apart), and reimbursement of expenses, plus a deadline. Maxwell sued Macmillan in Chancery. Jacobs agreed that the auction hasn't been "evenhanded"—he was quite clear that management violated its fiduciary duties—but refused to reset the auction by enjoining the lock-up, arguing that Maxwell had not been misled and could have submitted a higher bid. He did, however, order the pill withdrawn, opening the door to another Maxwell bid. Maxwell appealed to the Supreme Court.

The Supreme Court, Moore writing the opinion, reversed Jacobs, invalidated the lock-up, and, as one commentary noted, was "even more contemptuous of Evans and Reilly, their investment bankers and the board than was the Chancery Court." Moore accepted Chancery's factual narrative and was "clearly conscious of the extent that this was a morality play." Moore underlined an auction process that was "systematically corrupted by management and their investment bankers and, in which, the special committee utterly failed in its task."[22]

This *was* a remarkably sleazy sequence of transactions, even for a period that was unusually tolerant of transactional ethics. Evans and Reilly treated Macmillan's board, and its special committee (one member of which never attended a single meeting), as if they were mere tools. The board, Moore wrote, was "torpid, if not supine, in its efforts to establish a truly independent auction, free of Evans' interference and access to confidential data."[23] He elaborated: "By placing the entire process in the hands of Evans, through his own chosen financial advisors, with little or no board oversight, the board materially contributed to the unprincipled conduct of those upon whom it looked with a blind eye."[24] Nearly every action Evans and Reilly took reeked of self-interest. They handpicked members of the special committee but didn't form it for weeks, instead consulting themselves with Lazard; they met with KKR without telling the board; their advisors, not the special committee's, ran the auction. They favored KKR in ways that made Revlon's relations with Forstmann seem demure. They wouldn't negotiate with Bass or Maxwell; they gave information to KKR but not to Maxwell; Wasserstein, in presenting guidelines for the final bids, urged KKR to go higher, in what became known as the "long script," while Maxwell merely received a deadline; they then offered KKR a lock-up after the board had ended its restructuring efforts and decided to sell, thus entering the *Revlon* zone, where a sale was inevitable.

And it got worse. During the final bidding round, unnamed "financial advisors" told Evans, Reilly, and an outside attorney where the two bids stood. Evans then tipped off a KKR representative, who hung up when he realized what was happening; if KKR hadn't reported the call (the firm disclosed it in an SEC filing), Moore says, it might never have come to light. Evans and Reilly failed to tell the board about the episode in the meeting that followed, allowing Wasserstein to present a false sequence of events. Moore was outraged. The directors had surrendered their "primacy" to management. They had violated their duties of care, loyalty, and candor. There was an omnipresent specter of board self-interest—it was a toxic cloud. Once it was obvious the company was breaking up, the board had conducted an auction lacking in fair dealing and fair price. Moore applied *Revlon* duties. "The voluminous record of the case discloses conduct that fails all basic standards of fairness," fumed Moore. "While any of the identifiable breaches of fiduciary duty, standing alone, should easily foretell the outcome, what occurred here, including the lack of oversight by directors, irremediably taints the design and execution of the transaction." At every step Evans tilted the auction to management or KKR. Wasserstein, as Evans' banker, should not have served as auctioneer; that role belonged to Lazard, as advisor to the special committee. Moore argued, in fact, that Wasserstein's long script to KKR on the final bids constituted a second tip—and violated every principle of fair dealing. Evans' silence on the tip was "a fraud upon the board."[25]

Moore's opinion was excoriating. As that same legal commentator wrote, "Consider what it must be like to live with such a public shaming, to see in acquaintances' eyes the unasked question, 'How could you have stood by and allowed this to happen?' Imagine how other managers and directors, when they read or heard about these opinions, felt about the prospect of being similarly pilloried. Anecdotal evidence confirms what we all would expect: No one, including directors and officers of Delaware corporations, Wall Street investment bankers, and Wall Street lawyers, enjoys being held up to this sort of public condemnation."[26]

Legally, Moore's decision significantly broadened the tasks of a board when *Revlon* duties applied—and it also drew Delaware even more deeply into a board's deliberations. Director duties of care and of loyalty required them to delve into relationships of management and directors and their chosen agents—to sniff out self-interest, particularly when management was a bidder. Advisers, particularly bankers, were also now targets of judicial scrutiny. "The courts are suspicious and will no longer accept blindly the advice of bankers," Allen told the *New York Times*.[27] Still, *Macmillan* was another Moore novelty, and some lawyers grumbled, privately and publicly. As one law review noted, "The key practical consequence of the Macmillan decision is that a board of directors must get actively involved in evaluations of financial data, communications with bidders, and decision-making with regard to specific merger provisions such as poison pills, no-shop provisions and lock-ups in order to protect against liability for a breach of fiduciary duties."[28]

The Supreme Court blocked Macmillan's deal with KKR. Six months later, after a shareholder vote, Maxwell acquired the publisher. Maxwell himself died in 1991, when he suspiciously tumbled off his yacht into the Atlantic and drowned; investigators were closing in on him on charges of a massive misappropriation of pension funds from his Mirror Group newspaper company. Evans retired to his Virginia farm. He died in 2011. The obituaries focused on his role as a thoroughbred owner, notably for a stakes winner named Quality Road.[29] His Macmillan tenure was an afterthought. Reilly went on to run Macmillan for a year under Maxwell, then took over a KKR property called KIII that was rolling up publications, including *New York Magazine*.

WASSERSTEIN'S ROLE IN Macmillan was particularly humiliating, though he shook it off. He told the *New York Times* that Delaware's conclusions were based on "verifiably erroneous facts," because bankers could not present their positions in court. "Bankers are extraordinarily frustrated. We're not parties, so we're not able to file briefs."[30] It was a feeble defense. In *Big Deal,* he mentions Macmillan once in 791 pages, introducing it with a bland, if tortured prelude: "The perceived conflict of interest inherent in management's dual role as a custodian for shareholders and as a self-interested acquirer had real vitality in the mid-1980s."[31] Perceived? *Vitality?* Macmillan, he noted, tipped off KKR, though he failed to mention his own role. On yet another occasion, he formulated a means-and-ends defense straight out of Chicago: everything was fine in *Macmillan* because shareholders saw their stock rise from $64 to $90 a share. "We're supposed to be jerking bidders around to enhance shareholder value," he said.[32]

He may not have realized it, but the *wunderkind* days were over. Deeper changes in takeover dynamics were reshaping the game, creating a climate in which Wasserstein's innate aggressiveness increasingly worked against him. Investment bankers often blurred the line between principal and agent; in one opinion, Allen had pointed out that Wasserstein and Perella's role as advisor, as an "expert" on the future price of the shares, and as a paid orchestrator of a share-repurchase program, was "a rather straightforward and conventional conflict of interest."[33] Milken had shown the way. The power had shifted from offering Rohatyn-like, objective, disinterested advice toward providing financing for M&A, for taking on risk.

In a discussion of *Unocal* in 1992, Moore made several fascinating points. The business judgment rule, he said, had been "inadequate" to contain conflicts generated by coercive, two-tier bids—the set of tactics that vaunted Wasserstein to the top—thus providing the rationale for *Unocal.* But *Unocal,* he said, "signaled the end of the coercive two-tier, junk-bond-fueled tender offer. The Court's opinion made it clear that such offers, usually couched in terms of 'benefitting' stockholders, were *per se* coercive and subject to strong defensive measures. The court's message was not lost on bidders."[34]

This was overstated. *Unocal* did signal that Delaware would be more actively involved in monitoring fiduciary duties; and less-coercive bids did subtly change the allowable limits on board defenses. (It's a historical irony that *Unocal* was formulated based on one of the last of the big two-tier coercive bids.) That, combined with the fact that financing suddenly seemed unlimited, hastened the end of the rococo era of takeover tactics: the Wasserstein era of high strategic gamesmanship. So it wasn't just that competition had caught up with his genius for the tactical game—though there was some truth in that—but that the complex tactics of DuPont and Conoco had ceased to be as necessary as they had once been. It was as if Napoleon found himself in a muddy trench on the Western Front. As Perelman recognized, with Milken behind you, you could make noncoercive all-cash bids that escalated until the other party was overwhelmed—or made a mistake. Meanwhile, M&A as a business was bigger than ever, with the real profits coming from betting your own capital. But that required larger, more complex organizations: traders, underwriters, analysts, salesmen—and capital. Firms bulked up, in part through M&A: Jimmy Robinson's American Express acquired Shearson in 1981, Lehman Brothers in 1984, EF Hutton in 1988. Wall Streeters hated Milken because he was beating them. But the firms imitated him, setting up a pattern of accordion-like fluctuations over the next three decades— yanking capital from yesterday's boom business and feeding today's. Across Wall Street, firms began building junk-bond operations and investing, like Drexel, in the same deals they advised on. Wasserstein and Perella's decision to bolt First Boston and set up a boutique was driven by these forces: the urge to become principals. Investment banking, however, was becoming a scale business, which they lacked, requiring a greater propensity on their part for risk. Meanwhile, firms like Morgan Stanley set up LBO units, not just to advise or finance but to participate as principals, spawning more layers of conflicts. The attitude of doing whatever it takes bogged down in a mire of conflicts, litigation, and disaster.

Chapter Sixteen

TIME AFTER TIME AFTER TIME

U NDER SCRUTINY, PRESSURE, and temptations like leveraged buy-outs, the clear division of agent and principal that characterized Jensen and Meckling's agency theory broke down. Few accepted that they were purely agents; in their hearts, they were also principals. Many did not see themselves as conflicted, either. As principals, real or imaginary, their self-interest merged, as it did for Evans at Macmillan or Perelman and Bergerac over Revlon, with that of corporations they felt heaven-sent to own, control, or run. As Bill Allen of Delaware's Chancery Court once noted in an opinion, "*Unocal* recognizes that human nature may incline even one acting in subjective good faith to rationalize as right that which is merely personally beneficial."[1]

Some of these complexities were deepened by the *zeitgeist*. The aspirations of principals were rewarded and lionized in the '80s: everyone was encouraged to be a free thinker, a doer, aspirationally at least, a principal. Who wanted to be a mere agent? Even as agency costs—the price of employing agents seeking their own self-interest—became conventional wisdom, the corporate world came to think of itself less as a hierarchy of masters and servants, or a maze of white-collar bureaucrats, and more as denizens of networks and matrices, free agents plying their trades: entrepreneurs. Like Milken, entrepreneurs looked resolutely forward, never back. The notion of a rigid hierarchy ruled by fiat seemed, like stakeholdership and unions, an industrial relic. Chicago wanted to dissolve the corporation into the market, like a bouillon cube in hot water. The corporation was a process, not a thing—always evolving, characterized by mobility, portability, fungibility, change: hope in a jar. Accountability, however, as Delaware envisioned it, was difficult to target, define, and pin down. The world of networks—each a nexus-of-contracts—consisted of middlemen, intermediaries, mediators, dealers, brokers, advisors, consultants. These were increasingly both agents *and* principals, like car salesmen, real-estate brokers, investment bankers, journalists, politicians, doctors, lawyers, salesmen, judges, and spies— maybe even as investor Ezra Zilkha insinuated about star attorneys Liman and Rifkind, double agents. This spawned suspicions of disloyalty, certainly on Wall Street, where conflicts proliferated. Who do you trust? Who is truly on your team? Executives imagined themselves as owners. To resolve that conflict, boards began to shower them with shares, a cause Jensen championed. This alignment of interests quickly became viewed as a panacea for the separation of ownership and management, as if governance was a matter of carpentry. Even Delaware saw the logic of directors who owned large stakes, who were aligned like straight edges with stockholders. But in the long run, in a world where takeovers and LBOs brutally separated winners from losers, this only deepened their status as go-betweens, men (or women) in the middle, unsure in their faith, divided in their loyalties, conflicted, cross-grained, bewildered, and profoundly self-interested.

These conflicts particularly bedeviled those deeply divided corporations whose head accepted shareholder governance but whose heart remained a stakeholder company. And as the '80s began to climax, the struggle to control and channel rampant self-interest was brought back to where it had begun, with the Williams Act, which legitimized the tender offer, over the chronic question of coercion. These complexities were on display when Time, Warner, and Paramount and their various agents, principals, and minions trooped into Chancellor Allen's Chancery courtroom in Wilmington on a warm July day in 1989. They had a problem. Allen's answer put a seal on Delaware's view of corporate governance.

IN SPRING 1987, senior management of Time Inc., the media empire built by Henry Luce and arguably America's preeminent publisher, quietly entered talks with Warner Communications, an entertainment conglomerate Steve Ross had built over the last decade or so. This was a complex collision of personalities and history. Luce, the Great Man of Time and flag-carrier of The American Century, had died in 1967. Time had prospered, and even made forays into related entertainment areas—Home Box Office, after almost failing, had become profitable—but on Wall Street, with its own share-price-driven lens for viewing the world, Time was increasingly viewed as self-regarding, poorly managed, with a Brooks Brothers culture fixated more on a glorious past than on a rapidly changing media landscape. Even Carol Loomis, a longtime writer at *Fortune* (a magazine dreamed up by Luce), in a piece on the deal in November 1989, "The Inside Story of Time Warner," quoted an investment banker who called Time "[t]he preppiest company I have ever seen in my life."[2] Time's ability to launch new mass products had faded (so had the mass market, but who knew); its rank-and-file perquisites were legendary (and envied); and it continued to follow a Luce-inspired division between church and state, which the business side of the company ritually celebrated while quietly planning to dismantle. Although the Internet was still more than a decade ahead, Time, high above Rockefeller Center, felt besieged by Wall Street, share performance demands, and ever-rising takeovers. As Allen later wrote, "Management and the outside board of Time have been concerned for some while that the company has in place certain of the protections against uninvited acquisition attempts."[3] Time, in fact, had reinforced its defenses: a staggered board, restrictions on shareholder action or meetings, and a poison pill, which would be triggered by someone buying a 15 percent stake in the company. Time was nervous.

Gentlemanly, if somewhat remote and passive, Time CEO Richard Munro had tapped Nicholas Nicholas, a younger (at forty-eight) hard-charger as president and successor. But Munro also kept Nicholas's longtime rival Gerald Levin—cerebral, verbal, casual, a boundless enthusiast for his own ideas—around as chief strategist. Levin was certainly different from the usual buttoned-up Time exec, and he had on his résumé both disastrous ventures and triumphs, including the use of satellites in cable transmission. Nicholas and Levin had an on-again, off-again relationship—Nicholas had once been assigned to clean up Levin's HBO, which he did successfully, embarrassing Levin—but they seemed to be working together effectively. Both believed Time had to change dramatically and they saw M&A as the best way to do it. But conversations with potential merger partners like Gannett, CBS, Paramount, and Capital Cities foundered on Munro's requirement that Nicholas run the resulting entity and that Time remain the preeminent partner. Levin, in particular, dreamed of transformative transactions, and he wrote a memo, cobbled from Nicholas's notes and his own fertile ideas, to that effect, which became a key document when affairs landed in Delaware. His dream: to combine Time, Warner, and Turner Broadcasting into an entertainment colossus.

Across Rockefeller Center, Steve Ross presided over Warner Communications. The silver-haired, silver-tongued Ross, a junior college grad who had moved from family funeral homes to parking lots to entertainment, had assembled a powerful bundle of media companies—television, movies, music, cable—which he ran with a genial, if ruthless, hand. Ross was not a micromanager; but he was an absolutist: Warner was his company. At sixty, he had no successor, and he craved one more big deal. He was a master of the artful exercise of power, a natural salesman; and he paid himself at a scale that shocked Time executives. Nicholas first approached him, after a day on jury duty, to talk about a joint video venture. Ross was intrigued. However, operating problems soon scuttled the venture. Nonetheless, at a Time planning session with outside directors, Munro and Nicholas brought Warner up as a possible merger partner. Warner had everything Time thought it needed. Internal Time analysis of entertainment-oriented targets concluded that Warner was the best fit. The outside directors pressed Munro and Nicholas to engage Ross—but raised control issues. Time had to be in charge; and that meant Nicholas ultimately had to be CEO. Nicholas told Loomis that he popped the question to Ross: merger? Ross thought about it and agreed to talk more. Ross easily accepted Time's demands about succession, with one caveat. He wasn't quite ready to retire and he would serve as co-CEO, first with Munro, then with Nicholas. He insisted he could share power. He was the nicest guy around and his own people loved working for him. He had a genius for handling the entertainment crowd, which was not a Time skill-set. As Arthur Liman, his friend and lawyer, told the *Los Angeles Times,* "Steve genuinely likes the talent who works for the company."[4] Connie Bruck, who wrote a Ross biography, *Master of the Game,* quotes one division head of Warner: "Steve said it [a Time deal] would be good for me, so I trusted him. I was a loyal servant." No apparent agency problems at Warner.[5]

Ross did have one internal problem: Herbert Siegel of boatmaker Chris-Craft, who Ross had sold a sizable stake to several years earlier—17 percent—to help him repel Rupert Murdoch, when he had displayed an interest in Warner. Siegel, a Warner director, had proven to be a thorn in Ross's side. He disliked Ross's extravagance and operating style. Ross, in turn, worked to isolate Siegel on the board.

Time had deeper dysfunctions. Both Ross and Munro wanted a merger. But Munro had board problems, not to say a building full of thin-skinned journalists. Much of the old guard at Time distrusted Ross, viewed him with distaste, associated him with the Mob (he had been implicated, but never charged, in a scandal at the Mafia-controlled Westchester Premier Theater in the 1970s, which also involved Frank Sinatra), and feared that Time's journalistic patrimony would be drowned in a company dominated by crass Hollywood values. (In fact, that was exactly what Levin and Nicholas envisioned.) Ross had allies at Time, however. Time director Michael Dingman admired Ross, and favored the deal. Felix Rohatyn, who had advised Warner and Time, and particularly Liman vouched for Ross with the Time board. Rohatyn, however, was skeptical that the board would ever accept Ross. Rohatyn told Bruck that Warner was "a company made up of executives with very strong ties to each other, mainly Jewish, who would appear to be parvenus, in a glitzy business. . . . And Time is the most establishment, white-shoe company."[6] Liman, for his part, was devoted to Ross. Time, he said, was Ross's transactional masterpiece, "the greatest deal in history."[7]

Negotiations dragged on, led by Levin and Ross's right-hand finance whiz, Jerusalem-born accountant Edward Aboodi. A new board
structure—twelve directors from Time, twelve from Warner—was set,
and a committee for editors to report to consisting of two Time directors and one Warner director was hammered out. In August, however,
the deal almost collapsed when Time tried to get Ross to sign a contract spelling out succession, with a hard five-year deadline. Instead,
Ross walked. When he returned in January—the catalyst was a dinner
between Ross and Dingman[8]—the Time board was more compliant,
if grudgingly so. (The Time board vote on the merger came in 12–0,
but four directors immediately resigned. Bruck quotes one Time director saying to another: "Mafia 12; Whiffenpoofs 0."[9]) The Time
board believed it was taking over Warner. In the share-for-share transaction, every Warner share got .465 Time shares, a 12 percent premium, and 62 percent voting power for Warner stockholders. Ross
disliked debt and much was made of the contention, notably in congressional testimony by Munro and Ross, that this transaction *wasn't* a
hostile, leveraged, bust-up deal. Still, price was a relative afterthought
to succession. The succession contract disappeared, replaced with a
brief memo written by Levin and Liman that said Ross didn't have to
retire after five years, but if he did, Nicholas would become the sole
CEO. Ross, in fact, based on comments to the press, seemed to be
thinking ten years, five as CEO, five more as chairman. On March 3,
1989, the two boards authorized a merger agreement. Warner would
be a subsidiary of a company called Time Warner. The two boards
agreed to a defensive share swap, taking sizable positions in each other—a mechanism to deter an outside bid. As Allen wrote, "Everyone
involved in this negotiation realized that the transaction contemplated
might be perceived as putting Time and Warner 'in play.'"[10]

Bruce Wasserstein, who advised Time, thought the timing favored
Time. The RJR Nabisco leveraged buyout (see Chapter 17), the largest
takeover to date, had recently closed and was gobbling up huge
amounts of junk bonds and the political climate, in part because of
the furor over RJR, had turned anti-buyout. Joe Flom was Time's outside lawyer. He had a lunch scheduled with Paramount CEO Martin

Davis. Munro didn't like his lawyer having lunch with a potential enemy—he obviously didn't know Flom—but asked him to find out whether Davis was planning a raid on Time. Flom inquired whether he knew anything about a raid on Time. "Time?" Flom testified later that Davis blankly replied. "It's 12:30. I'll have the soup."[11]

On June 7, Davis struck. Just two weeks before the shareholder vote, Paramount Communications made a cash tender offer for Time. The price was high: $10.7 billion or $175 a share—though a Wasserstein Perella analysis guessed Time was worth quite a bit more, a figure some board members thought low. Time stock immediately leapt by $44 a share. Time and Warner scrambled to redo its deal, with Time offering Warner $14 billion in a two-tier cash and securities deal—the front-end 51 percent for $70 in cash, the back-end $70 in stock. The deal now had total debt that would amount to $16 billion, and a change in accounting meant large amounts of goodwill would be dumped on Time Warner's books, eroding earnings for decades. Time really *was* buying Warner—at a higher price. But while the nature of the transaction changed, Warner made sure the governance provisions did not. Ross would still be co-CEO, the board was still evenly divided, and Warner's premium was even larger.

Time was caught in a trap of its own construction. Time needed Warner to rebuff Paramount. Davis was, in temperament, the opposite of the smooth, affable, silken Ross: short, volatile, with a legendary temper. (In other ways—tough beginnings, need to control, shrewd—they were a lot alike.) In a flash, Time's directors and executives found their jobs at risk and Time's "culture" threatened; a more cynical view, taken by Paramount, was that Time managers now found it expedient to wrap themselves in the Lucean culture. On June 16, the Time board voted to replace the share-for-share exchange with a tender offer, which did not require a shareholder vote. Paramount's offer was generous, the arbs were scooping up shares, and Time shareholders, heavily institutional, had long been restive, particularly unhappy with the rich deal Warner shareholders were getting.

There was part panic, part daydreaming about cashing in the Paramount offer throughout the Time-Life building. Many Time employees had shares accrued during long careers, none more so than Munro, Nicholas, and Levin, who received large awards of stock in long-term contracts to ensure the "continuity of the culture." "The contracts put Munro in the position of explaining to employees, including hundreds of journalists, that he and Nicholas accepted the extraordinarily handsome agreements to protect them," muttered Loomis.[12] Journalists can sense panic, particularly when it's happening down the hall. Munro, shades of Bergerac and Revlon, sent Davis one of those how-can-you-do-this-you-scoundrel letters, which only communicated the existence of a thin skin: "You've changed the name of your corporation but not its character: It's still 'engulf and devour,'" he wrote, referring to Paramount's predecessor, the old conglomerate Gulf + Western. The *New York Times* responded to the letter with a fulsome portrait of Davis as a post-conglomerate corporate builder.[13] Robert Hughes, *Time* magazine's art critic, knocked out a better line, being a professional: "It's another disaster of late capitalism with all these plastic dinosaurs bashing against each other in the primeval swamp."[14] It's always "late" capitalism—though Hughes had no idea how long that late phase might last.

Warner and Time agreed to the tender offer and triggered the defensive share exchange. Paramount then raised its offer to $200 a share and filed suit (with two Time shareholder groups) in Delaware's Chancery Court, making a *Revlon* argument that a sale was inevitable, topped off with a *Macmillan* argument that the Time board was protecting its control. Time had put itself up for sale with the original Warner deal—a change of control loomed—and thus the board had the responsibility to conduct an auction that maximized the price for shareholders. Allen took the case.

The Chancery hearing was scheduled for Monday, July 10, on Rodney Square. Delaware Chancery trials had become big news. The *Los Angeles Times* led with the fact that a record number of arbs were planning to show up, and quoted a clerk in Allen's office reporting that it was possible that they would collect more than the thirty or forty cellphones—the early "bricks," portable phones the size of walkie-talkies—that a normal big hearing attracted. "We've had nonstop calls for a month."[15] The paper described the case as a shareholder-manager dispute, and called an often-quoted Southern Methodist University securities law expert, Alan Bromberg, who offered the well-honed sound bite: "You can put the question as, 'Who owns the company—the shareholders or the management?'" Bromberg didn't define "ownership." The *New York Times* thought Paramount would win, reporting that "traders" were betting that since *Macmillan* was the precedent, which turned out to be wrong, shareholders would come out on top.[16] But Allen was a puzzle. As the Los Angeles paper noted, "While Allen has shown himself to be an advocate of shareholder rights in some decisions, in others he has shown a reluctance to order companies to auction themselves."[17] Even Bruck, writing a number of years later, tried to squeeze Allen into that shareholder-management straitjacket: "Chancellor Allen, who had earlier written decisions that expanded shareholder rights—particularly shareholders' rights to a choice between alternatives—had been feared by the Time and Warner lawyers."[18] And if Allen approved, what about Moore, who had, the lawyers said, a tendency to react against taking "personal advantage"?

Allen, in fact, was immersed in arguments, only the most obvious aspects of which poked above the surface, not to say resembled anything as rudimentary as a straight manager-shareholder conflict. In Time, Allen would decide specifics of a case involving three large companies, plus the fate of Time shareholders. The issues were technical, arcane; the translation to noncorporate lawyers, even those in M&A, was a ripple across a deep, dark pool.

A year earlier, Allen had wrestled with a case that turned on whether a board could block a shareholder vote in a takeover situation—as Time was attempting to do. He argued that if the bid was not coercive—that is, did not involve the kind of two-tier bidding based on bullying shareholders to tender—the board could not deny shareholders the vote. If the board did block a vote, it would not receive the protection of the business judgment rule. He summed this up in a classic line that explicitly referred to boards as *agents* of shareholders: "The theory of our corporate law confers power upon our directors as agents of shareholders, not their Platonic masters."[19] Four months later, Allen heard a case that turned on whether the board for a company called Interco could, as defensive measures, retain its pill and sell its prized asset—in its case, the Ethan Allen Furniture chain—without a shareholder vote. The all-cash bid was usually assumed to be *not* coercive. Allen argued that the board could use the pill—but not indefinitely. He cited a subtle form of coercion—substantive coercion—that applied when the board believes the price is too low, though shareholders might not realize it. This was a temporary condition, which should have been alleviated by an effective defense producing a higher price. Allen ordered the Interco board to pull its pill and hold a shareholder vote, but added that it could still sell Ethan Allen. Why? Because boards had the right to manage business affairs.

Interco, which *Institutional Investor* called "the most controversial decision framing shareholder choice,"[20] kicked up a *Van Gorkom*-like reaction from companies. Wasserstein, who had advised Interco, questioned whether "a judge like Allen" could analyze a complex restructuring as well as an investment banker.[21] Around that time, the New York Supreme Court had invalidated a poison pill that Irving Trust was using to defend itself against Bank of New York's hostile bid. The next day Irving surrendered. Some eleven New York corporations threatened to leave the state. Wachtell Lipton had represented Interco. Lipton, angry at this threat to the pill, was fully aware of Delaware's vulnerability to its corporate clientele. He penned a client note suggesting that companies leave Delaware for friendlier states.[22] He accused Delaware of encouraging takeovers, threatening the future, and depressing the standard of living—mentioning Allen specifically.[23] And he also urged a strategy borrowed from Nancy Reagan—"Just say no"—that advocated a kind of passive resistance by boards with pills to takeover threats. He probably knew that companies wouldn't flee the state. But he wanted to rattle Delaware's cage. "Nobody around here is afraid of Marty Lipton," shot back an anonymous source at Chancery. "*Nobody.*"[24] However, Lipton's missive clearly upset the Delaware Supreme Court, which was already touchy about Allen's jurisprudence.

THE TRIAL IN Chancery unfolded on July 11 and 12. Time and Warner had the legal stars: Robert Joffe from Cravath (with Charles Richards of Richards, Layton) represented Time and Herbert Wachtell from Wachtell Lipton (with a team from another Delaware firm, Morris, Nichols) led the Warner team. Allen produced his written opinion on July 14. In his closely argued—if, as some critics charged, "discursive"—decision, Allen, after a detailed recitation of the facts, put the issues in broad context. He batted away the notion that he was dealing with a straightforward manager versus shareholder dispute over "ownership" that turned on maximizing short-term shareholder returns. In short, he refused to be drawn into the issue of what outcome was best. As he had done in a number of recent cases, Allen parceled out responsibility and accountability for boards, shareholders, and, perhaps especially, the courts:

> Before turning to an analysis of the merits of the plaintiff's complaints, I pause to make one observation that should be apparent. It is not part of the function of the court to evaluate whether the Time-Warner deal is a good deal for Time shareholders or a poor one. The Time shareholders complain, feeling that under the revised merger Warner shareholders get all the premium and they get very little—except a promise that Mr. Nicholas will someday guide their company, and knowledge that they may be foreclosed from a comparable premium from Paramount. Plaintiffs find this to be cold comfort. Determination of the legal issues, however, does not require this court to try to evaluate, in light of the evidence, whether Mr. Ross and his negotiator, Mr. Aboodi, out-negotiated Mr. Levin and Mr. Nicholas in this transaction.[25]

Time's board, wrote Allen, believed that the future value of a Time and Warner merger would be worth more than the offer made by Paramount. This belief, he wrote, raised two questions. "First, does it make any sense, given what we understand or think we understand about markets, to posit the existence of a distinction between managing for current value maximization and managing for long-term value creation—a distinction which implies, unless I am wrong, that current stock-market values fail to reflect 'accurately' achievable future value?" Second, who gets to decide?

The first question dealt with the validity of efficient markets. Allen acknowledged that "for some"—and by *some* he seemed to mean Chicago and the academics—the distinction between short-term and long-term is a false one, and "there cannot be a premium for control," particularly in large, active, informed markets. He was skeptical of this belief. Perhaps, he wrote, "wise social policy and sound business decisions" ought to be based on these assumptions. "But, just as the Constitution does not enshrine Mr. Herbert Spencer's social statics, neither does the common law of director's duties elevate the theory of a single, efficient capital market to the dignity of a sacred text." In other words, economics and business are not the law; in fact, they're roughly analogous to nineteenth-century Social Darwinist ideas, like those of Spencer, that are more ideological than scientific. Directors can operate as if the market is wrong without breaching fiduciary duties. Directors, in fact, don't have to maximize "immediate value" except when they find themselves in *"Revlon* mode," with a sale of the company inevitable. Except under certain "radically altered states," boards can oversee their companies for the long run.

Had Time's board entered such a state? Allen argued that *Revlon* mode requires an imminent and inevitable threat of a change in control—a viable takeover threat, buyout, or share restructuring. Was Time handing control over to Warner in its original transaction? Paramount insisted it was, since Warner shareholders would have had a 62 percent control stake after the deal closed. Time insisted that the initial merger was designed to "preserve and improve the company's long-term performance" and that a stock-for-stock merger does not involve a change of control because Warner shareholders did not constitute a single control block. Allen agreed. Here he uses Chicago's fluid, atomized market to *defend* management against shareholder plaintiffs. At the same time, he is effectively limiting *Revlon* only to threats from large blocks of stock controlled by someone, which

Warner would have had only if it was a private company, thus narrowing its scope.

Allen then turned to *Unocal.* Did Time's board have the right to restructure the deal to block a shareholder vote it believed it would lose? Paramount made two arguments. First, in resorting to the tender offer, Time had violated its duty of loyalty and manipulated "the corporate machinery for the accomplishment of inequitable purposes." Delaware had come down hard in cases where boards had no justifications to override a vote that shareholders possess by statute, particularly in all-cash, noncoercive bids like Paramount's. But this was not the case with Time, Allen concluded. First, a shareholder vote on a share exchange was part of New York Stock Exchange rules, not Delaware law. Second, boards have a responsibility to manage their business affairs. That's their job. The Time board had developed a strategic plan out of real business considerations, not as a means of entrenching itself. Time was in a strategic mode, not a defensive one, when it signed the initial Warner deal. The shift to a tender offer occurred only when the board felt its strategic intent was threatened. It responded reasonably and in a not "overly broad" way. There was no "persuasive evidence," said Allen, that the board "has a corrupt or venal motivation."

And so Allen bestowed the business judgment rule on the Time board. Allen was providing a way for boards to ensure protection of the rule: engage in serious strategic considerations. He then offered a warning on the risks of undermining that central, key legal concept: he urged judicial restraint. Strategic thinking is an essential aspect of what boards are meant to do. If they fail at that task, if they prove self-interested, or find themselves with no other option but to sell the company, shareholders should get to decide that step through the vote. But short of that, boards should have latitude to call the shots.

Did Time's board make the correct choice? That wasn't Delaware's business. "The Time board may be proven in time to have been brilliantly prescient or dismayingly wrong," he wrote, circling back to where he had started, and unable to resist that wordplay on *time.* This might well be the mantra of the business judgment rule: no one knows, so you might as well allow those with the most expertise and knowledge to decide, and at least for a while. Time could merge with Warner. The arbs, betting on a Paramount premium, once again howled.

PARAMOUNT WASN'T HAPPY either and immediately appealed to the Delaware Supreme Court, which quickly affirmed Allen's decision; however, the final written opinion took seven months to appear, suggesting a degree of contention or uncertainty in Dover.

It is an odd decision.[26] It's an opinion that was not, in the usual Delaware fashion, restrained and careful; rather, it was personal, snappish, and confusing. It had an incoherence that suggested the presence of too many hands. You can sense the mounting pressure. Moore sat on the panel, but Justice Henry Horsey wrote the opinion. While affirming Allen's decision allowing Time to merge with Warner, much of the opinion was spent quibbling—or worse—over Allen's past handling of *Unocal* and *Revlon.* And as any number of legal commentators noted, the opinion managed to distort many of Allen's points. Moreover, the opinion did not tighten the rules or make the allocation of responsibilities clearer; it offered an easy path for boards to wrap themselves in the business judgment rule and thus fully embrace Lipton's "Just say no." Strangely, Horsey said little about Allen's argument that Time should be permitted to pursue larger strategic objectives. He did seem to respond to Lipton's protest of *Interco*—and aligned Delaware more closely with a number of virulently pro-management, anti-takeover states. The Supreme Court appeared to be trying to end this takeover foolishness, but doing so as if no one would notice that it was muddying Delaware's garden of precedent.

Interco and its predecessor cases seemed to loom large. In the opinion, Horsey snorted that Chancery (meaning mostly Allen) had "extrapolated a rule of law" that found its way "in the plaintiffs' [Paramount's] argument . . . that a hostile tender offer can pose only two types of threats: the threat of coercion that results from a two-tier offer promising unequal treatment for non-tendering shareholders;

and the threat of inadequate value. . . . We disapprove of such a narrow and rigid construction of *Unocal.*"

We disapprove. Not disagree: disapprove. The Supreme Court seemed to blame Allen for providing Paramount with arguments it felt compelled to reject. But those arguments were hardly radical, or unknown. Specifically, Horsey was reacting against Allen's discussion of coercion in *Interco,* which suggested that the Delaware courts should distinguish when defense was used to extract a better price and when it constituted an abuse. This involved the court using *its* judgment against that of the board, as if the directors were completely disinterested players. Horsey rejected that intervention as unjustified. Judges don't do math. And so, with tortured logic, the Supreme Court handed boards a huge victory: enablingism was back. The Supreme Court decision seemed to reject much of the jurisprudence in Delaware, with its exploration of self-interest, since Moore first suggested that the business judgment rule was not inviolable in *Unocal*—and it did so by claiming *Unocal* as a precedent.

Horsey's opinion also skipped past a theme Allen *had* identified, highlighted, and applied in a number of cases: coercion, the use of force or intimidation to obtain compliance. Coercion wasn't new: it ran through the long-running attempt to establish equitable governance in an era of takeovers. The Williams Act was designed to combat coercion of shareholders. Lipton, in 1981, made coercion a key element in his article "Takeover Bids in the Target's Boardroom." Lipton's governance depended upon boards, elected by shareholders, that were, in theory, the only bodies that had the potential for disinterest, autonomy, and freedom from coercion. Moore in *Unocal* drew from "Takeover Bids" and argued that the two-tier bid was "a classic coercive measure designed to stampede shareholders into tendering at the first tier, even if the price is inadequate, out of fear of what they will receive at the back end of the transaction." Coercion was a key element of the threat that determined a proportional response. Moore enumerated reasonable threats—coercive threats—that came directly from Lipton.

As cases piled up, Chancery wrestled with coercive bids, a task that grew increasingly challenging as the implicit blackmail of two-tier bids receded, replaced by the straightforward bribery of all-cash bids. Fueled by junk bonds, all-cash bids threatened managers but, in theory, left shareholders free to make up their minds. Nonetheless, all-cash bids did not mean coercion did not exist, only that it had grown more insidiously subtle. The courts labored to define what constituted a "reasonable" defensive response by a board under *Unocal*. They came up with three situations. First, when there's explicit "structural" coercion, as in a two-tier bid. Second, when a hostile offer would rob shareholders of a potentially better future bid. And third, when there's risk that shareholders will mistakenly accept an underpriced offer because they don't believe the board's promise of better value if the company remains independent—a situation called substantive coercion. If those three threats don't appear, then shareholders should decide with a vote. Substantive coercion, as the most subjective of the three, was also the closest call.

Boards, in theory, have better information than shareholders, and thus a better sense of when an outside offer is inadequate. Shareholders, on the other hand, may not believe boards, which they assume are self-interested, entrenched, greedy, dumb, or lazy. Judges can easily detect when a board is ignoring a higher bid or shareholders are being panicked by a two-tier bid. But substantive coercion is more difficult to discern. Judges, in fact, are just as limited to what management knows as shareholders. The burden falls on judges to give boards leeway, but to also understand that there are limits to that power. At some point, judges needed to step in, gather facts, and make a call. This seemed to be what the Supreme Court was resisting when it rejected substituting the court's opinion for that of boards.

The Supreme Court made a hash of the coercion issue. Time argued that the Paramount offer consisted of a threat of substantive coercion—that shareholders might make a mistake by reaching for that $200-a-share offer and thus miss out on the wondrous long-term benefits of a Time and Warner merger. Horsey described substantive coercion accurately, then plunged in the opposite direction: courts were not equipped to intervene when substantive coercion might exist. Anything that smacked of analysis was something directors could handle better than judges or shareholders. "Thus the court adopted a type of threat that requires the most judicial intervention, but took a very passive position under the guise of increasing the effectiveness of proportionality review," as one law review article said. "Such an analysis makes a mockery of proportionality review. The court used the business judgment rule in determining whether the directors' actions should be protected by the business judgment rule. The court could have been more deferential only if it had let Time's directors write the opinions themselves."[27] In fact, the Supreme Court looked particularly foolish in the footnotes, to the glee of the scholars in the peanut gallery, by getting tangled in various coercive threats and, as it had in the now-distant *Van Gorkom,* which Horsey also wrote, the complexities of market valuation. Since stock prices are ephemeral, judges can't calculate intrinsic values better than boards. They shouldn't even try.[28]

CAROL LOOMIS OF *Fortune* set up her self-examination of the Time, Warner deal with what's known in the magazine business as a nut graf, a neat package of prose tucked at the top of a story that tells readers why they should bother reading the many words that follow. It was a classic Time nut graf that characterized the relevant decades thematically, like rooms in a museum, with the Warner deal as a kind of culmination of the takeover '80s.

> The battle [between Paramount and Time] provoked tremendous controversy and touched every bare-wire business issue of the age: long-term vs. short-term value, shareholder rights, the significance of corporate culture, executive compensation, business ethics, management practice and merger and acquisition tactics. . . . It may prove a fitting sign-off to a decade in which both the Dow Jones average and corporate hostility reached new heights—for while it typified the '80s by being huge and vicious, it also suggested a new battle plan for the '90s by refuting the accepted wisdom that a cash offer is curtains for a target company.[29]

The deal, and the jurisprudence, was less epochal than it seemed at the time. Allen's warning of an unrestrained judiciary and its effect on the business judgment rule, slipped in at the end of his *Paramount* opinion, quickly took life in the Supreme Court's opinion. In fact, one legal commentator went so far as to speculate that Allen might have swung to an extreme position on *Unocal* as a ploy to get the Supreme Court to back off, but failed.[30] The case stirred great criticism and chatter. Still, you couldn't go back. Horsey's opinion represented a dead end that did not produce much in the way of precedent in years ahead. The issues inherent in *Unocal* and *Revlon* continued to be argued, and Delaware still toggled between boards and shareholders, building on Allen's narrow and carefully delineated analysis of interaction of the various parties of the corporate governance system.

As for the players in the Time, Warner, Paramount circus, their fates, once so entangled, now diverged. Davis and Paramount lost Time, but survived, only to succumb in a later takeover struggle—albeit to a buyer Davis wanted, Viacom's Sumner Redstone. Time Warner itself dragged around a crushing debt burden, shareholders were unhappy, and the stock price was a dog. Paramount's $200 a share seemed like an impossible dream with shares going for $95 each. Munro retired; Ross and Nicholas served as co-CEOs, before Ross booted Nicholas. Ross had developed prostate cancer and elevated Levin, who, after Ross died in December 1992, became CEO. Levin then engineered the merger with AOL at the height of the dot-com craze in 2000, a "transformative" deal that is today widely viewed as the single worst M&A deal in history—and the most egregious illustration of Scherer's suspicions (see Chapter 12) about market efficiency and the difficulties of post-merger integration. AOL brought Time Warner another decade of misery. Last heard from, Levin was teaching spiritualism in California.

In 1994, Moore came up for renewal of his twelve-year Supreme Court term; he was fifty-six years old. This was viewed as pro forma; a sitting justice had never failed to be reappointed if requested. Democrats, led by Governor Thomas Carper, now held the statehouse. Carper did not offer Moore a second term, selecting instead Carolyn

Berger as the first female Supreme Court justice in Delaware. This stoked long-suppressed speculation and an unusual rash of partisan sniping. Whispers about Moore's temperament and sharp tongue circulated, with the nominating commission leaking that he lacked "judicial temperament" and "civility." Moore was visibly angry, and declared the ouster "politically inspired." Various theories circulated. One even implicated Skadden in some mysterious role in Moore's demise—a murky plot that harkens back to Perelman's acquisition of Technicolor.[31] Flom responded by defending Moore and told the *New York Times:* "The suggestion [that Skadden was involved] boggles my mind. These conspiracy theories just don't stand the light of day."[32] Even Sarah Teslik, the executive director of the Council of Institutional Investors, defended Moore as a friend of investors.

Teslik was clearly recalling an earlier Moore. In 1992, before the rejection, Moore spoke to a corporate law symposium. The speech, "The 1980s—Did We Save the Stockholders While the Corporation Burned?," reflected not just the times but his own changing views. Much of it involved a review of the major takeover cases, in each of which he played a role: *Van Gorkom, Unocal, Revlon,* and *Paramount.* But the lasting sense that Moore communicated is that somehow it had gone wrong. True, Delaware did establish guidelines by which takeovers were fought. But he was still uncertain whether the courts provided balance "to an otherwise runaway situation" or simply interfered in free markets and meddled in corporate management. "Did the decisions of the Court feed the takeover frenzy or serve to limit it?"[33] This was candid, if hardly a confidence booster in Delaware.

And so Moore was gone. In restrained Delaware, this was an unprecedented episode. Was Moore dropped for his temperament, for his jurisprudence, or was he a victim of the era in which he worked? Or was it, as he said, politics? Moore remained in Delaware. He taught, spoke, and went on to join the man he had shamed in *Macmillan,* Wasserstein, whose personal private equity operation acquired the *New York Law Journal* and Steve Brill's *The American Lawyer* in 1996. Wasserstein, who suffered fierce criticism for his '80s deals and business reversals in the '90s, recruited Moore to the board of American

Lawyer Media (he was joined there by Donald Drapkin, Perelman's colleague and Flom's former partner at Skadden). Then, after Wasserstein sold Wasserstein Perella to Dresdner Bank for $1.4 billion in 2000 (Perella had left in 1993 for Morgan Stanley), he made Moore a senior advisor to the new firm, Dresdner Kleinwort Wasserstein. In 2002, Wasserstein left Dresdner to replace Michel David-Weill at Lazard. By then, the tide of takeovers was rising again.

Chapter Seventeen

ILL FARES THE LAND

Ill fares the land, to hastening ills a prey/
When wealth accumulates, and men decay.

—OLIVER GOLDSMITH, quoted by John Brooks
in *The Takeover Game,* 1987[1]

By 1985, Marty Lipton had grown concerned about the Jews—or rather, a backlash against the Jews. Takeovers had grown increasingly unpopular, which normally Lipton favored. But there was no controlling where the fire would move once a spark fell. Lipton's client letters had grown more vociferous as M&A mounted. Milken's entrance, sweeping out two-tier bids and bringing in all-cash, junk-bond-funded takeovers, were both effective and not quite-as-coercive, made it trickier to justify "Just say no" in Delaware. Debt-ridden LBOs were getting ever larger. Many of the raiders who gathered around Milken's Drexel Burnham Lambert, including the maestro of junk himself, were Jewish.

Connie Bruck pinpoints the Revlon deal, with the clash between Perelman and Bergerac, as the period in which Lipton's public declarations grew more extreme, and his private conversations dwelled on the possibility that takeovers would "unleash a backlash of virulent anti-Semitism."[2] As she points out, he wasn't alone. Many others in the Jewish establishment felt that way as well, and it was murmured, though rarely written about, in the financial press. Then came the insider-trading scandals: Milken, Boesky, Siegel, Levine (not to mention one of Lipton's favorites at Wachtell, Ilan Reich) and episodes like

Macmillan that revealed double-dealing and self-interest among bankers *and* management. Wall Street was now viewed as Jewish, as it had once been seen as Wasp. This was a tightrope of a problem. To speak publicly on *this* topic might inflame reservoirs of anti-Semitism that undoubtedly existed, and that had been agitated already by, among other things, the rise to preeminence of Jewish lawyers and investment bankers—the rise of a deal culture itself. In the long and sordid history of anti-Semitism, Gentiles have characterized Jews as untrustworthy go-betweens, agents of uncertain loyalties, rootless cosmopolites. Lipton would, in many cases, be defending forces he otherwise thought destructive. The problem was one that had often in the past accompanied Jewish secular success—one made worse by the fact that the triumph came on Wall Street, with its overtones of money and greed. And Lipton faced a more personal complication: to raise the question would only empower those who already thought that Lipton's ideas and commercial self-interest were too conveniently aligned; that he was using one issue, anti-Semitism, to burnish another—defense of management and boards. This was, in fact, a classic trap. Offering a defense would be construed as the very proof of the charge.

Anti-Semitism was only the most shocking manifestation of late-stage takeover fever. Blame was apportioned for a phenomenon that had once been viewed as cleansing and regenerative, but with the emergence of scandals, darkening economic and market conditions, and, not to be discounted, a political failure to respond, now appeared a matter of uncontrolled self-interest and greed. Companies were carrying more debt, an issue that grew more worrisome as the savings-and-loan industry began its wrenching, terminal collapse—never having recovered from '70s inflation, and trying to save itself by shouldering more risk (abetted, in this case, *by* congressional legislation), including loading up on junk bonds. And debt, that panacea, was proving treacherous. It was the Revlon problem: old debt found itself sinking in value as new debt was piled atop it.

IN M&A, THE debt issue came to a head when a Wasserstein client, a Canadian real-estate developer named Robert Campeau, raised billions in financing, including junk; went on a buying spree; then saw his vast, ramshackle, overburdened retail empire implode. It took two years, from start to disastrous finish. Wasserstein was blamed for talking Campeau into it, a version of the belief that clients were mere pawns; Wasserstein himself had seen Campeau as the key to First Boston's entrance into deal financing—that is, providing bridge loans and junk. (Campeau began as a First Boston client, then went with Wasserstein to Wasserella.) In *Fortune,* Carol Loomis called Campeau a "symbol of excess carried to its dumbest, most egregious limits."[3] A *New York Times* editorial noted, "Any corporate executive can figure out how to file for bankruptcy when the bottom drops out of the business. It took the special genius of Robert Campeau . . . to figure out how to bankrupt more than 250 profitable department stores."[4] Bust-ups and layoffs were now post-merger norms—that euphemistic term, *synergies,* made the turn from 2 plus 2 equals 5 to "necessary" merger-related cost reductions. Tales of affluence and misery proliferated. The press feasted on the return of Thorstein Veblen's conspicuous consumption—Hamptons mansions, Metropolitan Museum galas, elephant-stool excess. The argument over takeovers steadily morphed into an easily digestible cultural, rather than economic or legal, critique.[5]

The media broadly translated all this for the public. The takeover critique assumed increasingly Manichean tendencies—the kind of distinctions that traditionally fed anti-Semitism. Us versus Them. Anti-Semitism always taps the theoretical—the abstract "problem." Meanwhile, the fine distinctions of the Delaware courts only slowly, through practice, produced their effect. The culmination of this phenomenon, which put its stamp on the *zeitgeist,* was the notion that the barbarians had arrived. A lot of them seemed to be Jews.

ON FEBRUARY 1, 1989, Jensen testified before the House Ways and Means Committee.[6] He continued to promote the benefits of takeovers, never mentioning the evidence building about post-merger operating declines. He did not touch on challenges to efficient markets that his own free cash flow theory raised, or that of agency costs, except to say they exist as a result of the separation of ownership and control in public companies. He was, however, beginning to qualify his praise of takeovers. M&A, he now admitted, was not well understood. But while not all takeovers are productive, they are manifestations of "powerful underlying economic forces" that are. He dismissed charges of greed, even for Wall Street.

He promoted a new panacea: the leveraged buyout. He had developed a new historical interpretation, with a single transformative figure: the active investor. "By the active investor I don't mean one who indulges in portfolio churning," he wrote. "I mean an investor who actually monitors management, sits on boards, is sometimes involved in dismissing management, is often intimately involved in the strategic direction of the company, and on occasion even manages. That description fits Carl Icahn, Irwin Jacobs and Kohlberg Kravis Roberts."[7] (He also drafted Warren Buffett into a club the Sage of Omaha probably wasn't eager to join.) J. P. Morgan Sr. and his partners had been active investors, as the "investment banking and financial community" were, but they had been banished from participating in corporate matters by "the restrictive laws of the 1930s . . . after an outpouring of populist attacks."[8] Those attacks "led to the crippling of the American corporation in the 1960s and 1970s."[9] (He did not dwell on the self-inflicted crippling of corporations in the '30s or the corporatist triumph of the '50s and '60s.) He analogized that backlash to current criticism of Wall Street, which was attempting to return to active investing.

What's striking is how far Jensen had drifted from his mid-'70s agency theory that saw managerial-agents generating wasteful costs at the expense of shareholder-principals. He still acknowledged agency costs, but only in public companies, which he suggested couldn't be saved. Active investors, he argued, had no separation of ownership and control issues. He saw no creation of agency costs in the ambiguous agent-as-principal, the banker wearing many hats, the investor representing multiple constituencies, the share-rich CEO whose interests were aligned with shareholders, the LBOer.

The LBO was "a new organizational form"—which was true in public perception, if not historically. (Like junk bonds, it had older antecedents.) Jensen had once viewed debt as a way to control agency costs of excessive free cash flow, thus rationalizing junk bonds; now he applied it to LBOs. He analogized LBOs to conglomerates—odd, given his admission that the '60s and '70s were "crippling"—and to Japanese corporate groups, dominated by their active-investor banks. He predicted that "many CEOs of large diversified companies" had no future because of the success of "highly efficient" LBOs. "These partnerships perform the monitoring and peak coordination function with a staff numbering in the tens of people, and replace the typical corporate headquarters staff of thousands," he said, which was not wrong, just an exaggeration.[10]

As he had done with takeovers, Jensen offered research "proving" the benefits of LBOs. He described what he called "pay-for-performance sensitivity"—pay in relation to performance—that he insisted ran twenty times higher among LBO CEOs than in average corporate leadership, though the math was a little sketchy.[11] He cited studies that found hefty increases in operating earnings from the year prior to the buyout to the third year after, and even larger increases in cash flow. This was impressive—though Jensen didn't explain why flush LBO funds aren't afflicted by free cash flow problems. And there were other complications. The sample was relatively small and short in duration. More importantly, LBOs had flourished in a rising market, which was about to end. Since then, research *has* shown persistent above-market returns, particularly for top-quartile buyout firms. But that long stretch of market history is also punctuated by wrenching volatility and cyclicality.

LBOs shared and amplified the bandwagon effect of markets—a phenomenon similar to the cyclicality of free cash flow, and a kind of agency cost. As returns rose, more money poured into funds from eager investors. That money had to be put to work, often in less-than-sterling targets at higher prices. As a result, periods that produced stellar returns for LBO shops—investments could easily be sold in hot markets at high prices—tended to generate the poorest long-term future returns. Investments made in bear markets, where capital was dear and prices were low, produced the best long-term returns.

Like the poison pill, the LBO was a mechanism designed to buffer depredations of the market. One key was the prosaic fee. LBO firms picked this up from their former employers on Wall Street who, like car salesmen, could find a fee in a vacuum. Deals for investment bankers were increasingly festooned with fees—not just for proffering successful M&A advice but for providing fairness opinions, restructuring advice, and, of course, financing. Lawyers charged fees as well, mostly on an hourly basis, but that was, relatively speaking, small potatoes, except for Wachtell and Skadden, for which it was big potatoes. LBO firms even charged fees for arranging their own transactions; KKR got $75 million for pulling off the RJR Nabisco LBO. Fees are characteristic of the agent—that is, the provider of a service. Agents don't share in the economic gains of principals (they don't take the risk, either), but they score fees, which pile up.

The LBOers realized early on the advantage of acting both as agent and as principal—namely, providing a service *and* reaping the economic gains or losses: the real money was in principal investing—that is, putting your own money to work—magnified by investors' capital and by leverage, which, happily for LBO shops, is tax deductible. But investment gains might take years to harvest; fees are collected with clockwork regularity no matter the market. Like their brethren in venture capital, LBO shops adopted the 2 and 20 scheme: 2 percent in fees on the fund capital ($10 million on a $500 million fund) and 20 percent of the gain on the buyout. Fees paid the bills. Fees got you through dry periods and, for failing firms, provided income even if you just played golf, particularly if investors were locked in for, say, seven years. These fees didn't seem very large when funds were tiny, or onerous when investors were drawn by great waves of aspirational optimism. But as they grew, that 2 percent amounted to a tidy sum, an annuity.

So, from the start, the LBO shops were hybrids of agent and principal, embodied in the 2 and 20. Their success sparked imitation—on Wall Street—that deepened the layer-cake of conflicts and suspicions.

Jensen wrapped up his congressional presentation by praising debt as a control mechanism—"a monitoring and incentive device," the same rationale for takeovers—for wayward management. That high debt would lead to bankruptcies in bad times, he admitted. "LBOs," he said, "frequently get into trouble." But he insisted that this very fragility, caused by high debt, had produced a more efficient bankruptcy process outside the court—a "privatized" bankruptcy. Drexel Burnham Lambert, he noted, has been most active in facilitating the intensive use of debt, and had anticipated these problems, developing innovative workouts when the debt proved too heavy.[12]

Just about two months after Jensen's testimony, and in the midst of the RJR Nabisco buyout, Milken was indicted by a New York grand jury on ninety-eight counts of financial fraud. Two years later, Drexel collapsed into bankruptcy. The firm never got a chance to use its innovative, private workout medicine on itself.

FELIX ROHATYN ALSO trooped to Washington to testify at those Ways and Means Committee hearings. He had been an advisor to the RJR Nabisco board and he offered a different message. "Management can be highly motivated without mountains of debt to make them more efficient," he declared. Less than a month after his testimony, in the *New York Review of Books,* he offered his view in an essay titled "The Debt Addiction" aimed not just at LBOs like RJR Nabisco but "leverage—borrowing in general—takeovers, taxes, junk bonds, regulation and financial institutions."[13]

Rohatyn had abandoned his ambivalence. Remarkably, the popular anti-takeover critique, which he played a major role in articulating, shared an underlying sentiment with Chicago: the sense that American business was in decline, that it required a transformation, a revolution. Both the pro- and anti-takeover camps believed the time had come to return to first principles, to a golden age, which is where their critiques diverged.

Rohatyn offered both denunciation and affirmation: a kind of jeremiad, not far from guiding duty-wracked Puritans back to repentance, grace, and election. It was thus, despite its ostensibly financial subject, a cultural and moral critique—unlike Lipton in "Takeover Bids," who, for all his foreboding, focused mostly on corporate law and ended with a joke; even Lipton's client letters, for all their fury, did not go quite that far. Rohatyn had fully found his voice in a 1987 essay for the *New York Review of Books*, with its small, liberal, high-toned, influential, and mostly nonfinancial readership, which laid down many of his themes. He (or an editor) set the tone with the title "The Blight on Wall Street." His opening turned blight into a dread disease, with a passing allusion to Watergate: "As the revelations of illegality and excesses in the financial community begin to be exposed, those of us who are part of the community have to face a hard truth: a cancer is spreading in our industry, and how far it will go will only become clear as the Securities and Exchange Commission and the Federal prosecutors pursue the various investigations underway." Rohatyn fingered the source. "The cancer," he declared, "is called greed."[14]

Now, calling Wall Street greedy is a little like calling a shark a natural swimmer with a snappish appetite. The purpose of the place, like the corporation itself, is to make, accumulate, invest, and produce wealth, to maximize returns. One problem with Rohatyn waving the bloody shirt of greed is that he ran the risk of sounding hypocritical. He continued to be a preeminent M&A rainmaker, and he didn't live like a serf. This was *his* world. The other was one that Delaware courts were familiar with: defining exactly where the pursuit of profit bled into the excessiveness of greed. Greed is an aspect of self-interest, one of the motivating humors of the agent, like bile or blood. Like so many of the theoretical constructs of the agent, greed is a judgment, an opinion, by others; in a democracy, its determination requires a vote of the crowd—perhaps an angry crowd. Greed is relative, like market prices. The view from the inside may differ sharply from the outside; today's greed may differ from tomorrow's. Greed may submerge into socially worthy entrepreneurism, even philanthropy. Greed usually involves money, but it can also indulge in fame or power or sex, or any other pleasure. Greed is a voracious appetite.

Rohatyn wasn't just talking about a few cases of insider trading. Wherever Rohatyn looked, he saw evidence of greed: the budget deficit, the trade deficit, "the vulnerability" of the banks," by which he didn't mean the S&Ls but the failure (and bailout by the government) of Continental Illinois, one of the largest banks in the United States, which collapsed under bad oil-and-gas loans in 1984. The world was fallen. Somehow insider trading charges—that's what they still were in 1987 as Ivan Boesky quietly spilled the beans to federal prosecutors on his ties to Milken—were equivalent to budget deficits. Efficient markets? Rohatyn was skeptical; he was still the same fiscally conservative tyro at his first NYSE board meeting. He was always sensitive to race-to-the-bottom possibilities inherent in the wrong kind of competition. "The financial markets now have a life of their own, seemingly unrelated to any underlying economic realities." He saw old ways threatened; it was as if he could retain the ideals of the old Wall Street Club and abandon the price-fixing, backscratching, ethnic exclusion, locked-up liquidity. He saw too much trading, too much speculation, too much short-termism, too much Hollywood publicity: "Long-term relationships are no longer valued; this is the age of the freewheeling financial samurai."[15]

Debt and leverage were contagious. Junk bonds were high-cost securities that were eroding the solidity and stability of corporations. They were "unsound." Debt forces companies to sell assets (the bust-up strategy that "fails to take into account that a large corporation has responsibilities to employees, customers, and communities, and that it cannot always be torn apart like an erector set"[16]), reduce R&D, or slash capital expenditures. Debt is the sacrifice of the future to the present. Junk bonds are peddled privately, meaning to Drexel or private holders like S&Ls, and pose *liquidity* risk—that is, you run the risk of not finding buyers when you need to sell. Rohatyn feared illiquidity. These capital pools, engorged by debt, spawn collusion and conspiracy between arbs and raiders. Rohatyn tapped both the language of antitrust and the '30s critique of the House of Morgan, the latter of which Jensen dismissed as ignorant populism.

Junk bonds are time bombs. Rohatyn foresaw falling dominos: a stock-market crash and, as foreign capital fled America, interest rates spiking to Volcker-like levels. Rohatyn was pointing out what had long been ignored in the application of agency theory to takeovers: the ultimate principals, institutional shareholders, were agents in drag.[17]

As investors, they played the principal role, if passively. But they were also agents for union pension funds, mutual insurance policyholders, bank depositors, or trust accounts. Their responses to takeover bids were not pure, in a market sense. Their loyalties were compromised. Their investing strategies could be shaped by state and local government officials, by union sponsors, by social activists. Some loaded up on junk (certainly the S&Ls), others piled into LBOs, because they were desperately trying to catch up after the disaster of the '70s. Institutions thus suffered from the ambiguity not only between agent and principal but between market performance and political ideals.

Rohatyn proposed a blizzard of reforms.[18] He wanted to "level the playing field" by eliminating both defense *and* offense: universal disarmament. He wanted to limit junk bonds by federal- and state-insured institutions, eliminate the tax deductibility of highly leveraged companies, expand disclosure. He urged 100 percent financing commitments before a tender offer could begin and extension of the tender-offer period to sixty days. He called for a tax on securities transactions by tax-free institutions like pension funds. He wanted to limit votes on corporate matters to shareholders who held shares for at least a year— squeezing out arbs. And he proposed to outlaw greenmail, poison pills, shark repellents, lock-ups, and any state takeover statutes that "provide management and directors with an almost unlimited license to turn away *bona fide* bidders and entrench themselves."[19] The latter smacked of William Cary's sweeping federalism (see Chapter 13) and would have been a legal nightmare to define.

The reforms seemed designed to inflame opposition from nearly every interested group. "I am obviously not suggesting that all of these measures should be adopted," Rohatyn wrote, almost plaintively. (Nonetheless, two years later, he proposed a new raft of regulation to control debt—through taxation and re-regulation of takeovers, LBOs, and junk bonds, which would have required an even greater political upheaval.[20]) The objective was "to return as many major corporate decisions as possible to the hands of shareholders whose *central interest is in the soundness of their investment*."[21] Given systemic greed, and considering Delaware's struggle to identify self-interested directors,

Rohatyn failed to say how such sound, even proper, shareholders could ever be identified, probably because it couldn't be done. Rohatyn and Jensen stood on opposite sides of the debate, yelling past each other, but they shared a deeper tendency: they both divided the corporate and financial worlds up into moral categories: agents and principals, stakeholders and shareholders, greed and altruism, science and folklore, state and federal, good and bad. But these were categories that grew subjectively treacherous as you drew closer to their shifting, empirical realities. And their solutions—the free market or a kind of throwback regulation that dictated results—were impossible politically and practically. Both lacked Allen's larger view of American ambiguities and change. Neither could really answer the questions: Who were the sheep? Who were the wolves? And who gets to decide?

JOURNALISM, LIKE POLITICS, is most accessible to the public as stories—case histories. Journalists are natural empiricists. They are fundamentally anti-theoretical. Journalists tend to believe in facts, free will, a balance sheet of good and evil, patterns that produce conclusions, but, as Keynes once said of practical men, they are often "slaves to defunct economists" and, as H. L. Mencken so entertainingly argued, to moral nostrums from Sunday School.[22] Journalists must speak to audiences who do not know, and need to be convinced that they should. They are, like everyone, divided, and their moral instincts are basic. The temptation to simplify is strong.

Deals were complex. "Experts" were constantly consulted as if *they* knew. Even Rohatyn, who did not suffer from a lack of confidence and expertise, admitted in 1989: "The issues are at best very complicated and not easy to subject to quantitative analysis."[23] It isn't just that the future was unknown, or counterfactual—pasts are murky, too. Micro didn't easily link to macro, short-term to long, which was the task assigned to efficient markets, or cause to effect. The evidence tended to be circumstantial. M&A was regularly credited with spawning the Reagan bull market, with bringing America back, despite the fact that manufacturing was struggling—creative destruction!—and Japan was ascending. But that raised new problems when, in the late

'80s, stocks collapsed, recession loomed, and Japan fell apart. Financial innovations were often initially touted as transformative: conglomerates, tender offers, junk bonds, LBOs. But, in a lesson learned repeatedly, knowing required more data, over more cycles—and when that occurred, the pattern nearly always grew more, not less, nuanced, contingent, complex. Perhaps a managerially dominated, stakeholder-based corporate system might have done better, on balance, despite evidence of the '70s. This was a view that would have been greeted by derision from an '80s Wall Street crowd but seemed less strange in the mid-'90s. Often, it depended on where you stood—the corner of Broad and Wall or in a rusted-out car-parts plant in Michigan—and how your self-interest shaped your imperfect perceptions.

Journalists resembled Delaware judges, though there were more of them, and they lacked the compass of fiduciary duties. Hollywood also lived off stories, though without the redeeming faith in facts. In 1987 Oliver Stone, gripping the *zeitgeist,* made *Wall Street.* The movie's intellectual foil is the commencement address Ivan Boesky gave in the mid-'80s extolling the benefits of greed; in the film it's intoned by merchant-banker-arb-insider-trader-and-all-purpose-svengali Michael Douglas as Gordon Gekko, with his gelled hair and suspendered, white-collared getup. (The movie's haziness regarding Gekko's role and his nefarious scheme is a commentary on agent-principal confusion, though it undoubtedly wasn't meant that way.) But "greed is good" was hardly new. It was a simplification of Milton Friedman's *New York Times Magazine* reduction from two decades earlier—the social responsibility of companies is to make profits—and a compression of the market's invisible hand, a cliché of genius from Adam Smith in *Wealth of Nations* over two centuries ago. Boesky, of course, lacked Smith and Friedman's sophisticated bodies of work. *Wall Street* marked the full-blown revival of an age-old image of Wall Street sin that was actually deeply ambiguous—Gekko was not shallow, just greedy. The place came across as sexy, amoral, decadent, cool, rich: the last man's world outside the locker room. (Rohatyn once observed that no women had been charged with financial crimes despite their "significant growth in the industry."[24] In fact, women professionals were nearly invisible on Wall Street, including at Lazard, which he failed to note.) By the '80s M&A had become the hot career choice in those cash cows of academe, the business schools.

Journalistically, LBOs posed a particular challenge. Were they rational and beneficial? Were they coercive? Were their incentives good or bad? The distinction between the operation of self-interest in the buyout *process,* which often tortured the exercise of fiduciary duties, and the alignment of self-interest in post-buyout *operations,* were often conflated. Chicago blessed the underlying logic of LBOs, willing to sacrifice means for ends, and put its faith in diversity, market experimentation, and contracts; but as the Reagan administration aged, so too did the Chicago view of takeovers. Delaware viewed them more skeptically—and the unions and the left generally saw them as further opportunities to legally ransack and pillage. In any event, LBOs were peaking as the market shuddered, as if they were the ultimate expression of conflict, self-interest, greed, and cultural decline.

LBOs seemed like a Wall Street shell game—a trick, a scam, a con. LBO firms resembled conglomerates: five people overseeing an empire of assets. Conglomerates had blown up. When would the LBOs? The LBOer put up a toothpick of equity that ensured ownership; it didn't seem fair, possible, or sensible. Leverage assumed sinister powers. Junk bonds were fuel for bust-up transactions, asset-stripping, layoffs, and, as Milken and Drexel crumbled, iniquity. Debt carried ancient, even biblical overtones, which in turn could develop anti-Semitic overtones: Jesus in the Temple; the worship of golden calves. *Junk.* Debt was the road to doom or depression. The same soul that decried the debasing of the currency by the federal deficit saw no reason *not* to leverage up. And LBOs ran up against the acceptance of public ownership as the model of the modern corporation. LBOs spirited away public assets for private gain. They traded transparency for opacity, regulation for *laissez-faire.* They eluded democratic control. They rejected collective, public ownership, what the NYSE once ballyhooed as People's Capitalism, and denied the powerful parallelism of shareholder and democratic governance that Lipton had tapped in "Takeover Bids." They were either un-American or quintessentially American.

RJR NABISCO WAS the nineteenth-largest industrial company in
America with forty thousand employees. Its chief executive—
silvery-haired (fashionably long), slender, gold-braceleted, back-
slapping Ross Johnson, who liked a cocktail, a round of golf, and the
jolly company of his jock-squad buddies—had risen to run Nabisco,
with its legacy in baked goods and cookies, and agreed to its merger
with RJ Reynolds Tobacco. That was in 1985. Johnson had moved the
company outside Atlanta a few years later. Now business conditions
had deteriorated. In 1988, with the stock price down, federal pressure
mounting on tobacco products, and an experiment with an electronic
cigarette flaming out, Johnson proposed a management buyout to the
board. Johnson had shaped this board; but while he had great sway, it
members were hardly patsies. They agreed, but warned of the consequences. In fact, the proposal triggered a tempest; Johnson was suggesting the largest LBO in history—at $75 a share, a 36 percent
premium.

On Wall Street, the investment banks lined up potential buyers. In
particular, Shearson Lehman Hutton, American Express's unit, led by
a former Sandy Weill protégé, Peter Cohen, moved to work with
Johnson, desperate to join other Wall Street firms in merchant banking and takeover financing. Cohen was under pressure to prove himself—and there was his omnipresent boss at American Express, Jimmy
Robinson, a former investment banker and loser in the McGraw-Hill
battle, and his second wife, Linda Robinson, who ran a strategic PR
firm. The Robinsons were friends of the Johnsons; Jimmy was an Atlanta native and his father had been a big banker in town. Johnson
quickly hired Linda for the deal. The Robinsons were also socially
friendly with the Henry Kravises—Henry, a founding partner of LBO
firm KKR, and his second wife, fashion designer Carolyne Roehm.
Like Joe Flom and Artie Long, the two couples even owned a thoroughbred together.

Once Kravis decided to make an offer five days after Johnson's plan
was announced, he assembled a massive team of advisors: Drexel
Burnham, Morgan Stanley, Merrill Lynch, and Wasserstein Perella,
the latter mostly to keep Wasserstein from advising someone else.

Eventually others rushed to make bids: Salomon Brothers represented KKR's major rival Forstmann Little & Co.; First Boston, which proposed to sell RJR assets; and Goldman Sachs, which lined up companies eager to take choice bits. Around all this swirled the banks, eager to finance a winner. The money was oceanic, the fees astounding.

This was a deal for a new generation. One of Flom's stars at Skadden, Peter Atkins, advised the RJR Nabisco board's special committee, with Rohatyn as financial advisor. Like Rohatyn, Lipton had been warning about the unhappy end that all this LBO debt would eventually produce, so it wasn't a shock, though it was unusual, that he and the firm were absent. But when Kravis got blindsided by a savagely negative reaction to the deal in the press, topped by a *Business Week* cover screaming "King Henry: Why KKR's Kravis May Be Headed for a Fall—Even If He Wins the Battle for RJR Nabisco,"[25] he sought PR advice from Lipton and Gershon Kekst, his longtime outside PR advisor. They told him to ignore the fuss. But Kravis was, for all his discipline, volatile. After seeking advice from his wife, he fought back and regretted it. He was portrayed as a rich, short, thin-skinned bully.[26]

The mix was explosive. Kravis felt he needed RJR to ensure KKR's preeminence. Teddy Forstmann was drawn by the same hypercompetitive instincts—plus an aversion to junk bonds. Salomon and Shearson both needed a score, though Cohen and Robinson needed it more than John Gutfreund, the head of Salomon. The price escalated, tipping quickly from numbers that made economic sense—even accounting for harsher times—and the demands of a feverish auction. But that tells us nothing really. For the details, you need to read the authoritative book written about the deal, *Barbarians at the Gate*. Everyone did, which is how it became authoritative.

THE RJR NABISCO LBO crystallized views of takeovers and LBOs for a broad swath of the public—not just for investors, businesspeople, and Wall Street. This LBO was a big story, but it did not start or stop anything; it provoked no federal regulation, though it justified state anti-takeover statutes. It was, as an LBO, a dud, which haunted KKR for years. But RJR became a marker, a defining mood, which like *Wall*

Street gradually shed its overt meaning for a compact, if fading image, like a painted word on a worn barn door: *barbarians.* The word choice was brilliant. It captured the essence of the *zeitgeist.* These people were all barbarians; in fact, in retrospect, it was difficult to understand who wasn't a pillager of a corporation that once again was envisioned as a Platonic entity, with an ageless, all-American product lineup: Oreo cookies, Ritz crackers, Life Savers, Milk-Bone dog biscuits, Planters peanuts, Winston, Salem, and Camel cigarettes. These were icons. These were consumer brands: commercial ideals. The notion of barbarians returns us to Periclean Athens: a world divided between Greeks and barbarians, civilized and foreign speakers, with their ringlets and opaque ways. The struggle over RJR was a daily story. Then, in April 1990, the book arrived. *Barbarians at the Gate* by two *Wall Street Journal* beat writers, Bryan Burrough and John Helyar, was perfectly timed to put its seal on a dying era. (At least one other book with an in-your-face title, *True Greed: What Really Happened in the Battle for RJR Nabisco,* by Hope Lampert, appeared at the same time, followed closely by a number of books about KKR.[27]) And stories about other LBOs, many suffering in the downturn, followed—notably that of another *Wall Street Journal* reporter, Susan Faludi, on the human cost of KKR's LBO of supermarket chain Safeway, which won a Pulitzer, the sign that the journalistic establishment had achieved consensus on buyouts. Barbarians.

Barbarians at the Gate was such a raging success when it was published (Harper pushed it out fast, Helyar once said, because it was fearful that people would move on) that it came to define the reality of the LBO itself; its version of the deal—and for some, the caricature—became the accepted version. This involved a complex media transaction. The media, like share prices, reflect preoccupations of the larger public, or a marketplace of opinion, but never perfectly—or for long. (This is accepted by all but the most rabid of journalists: there's no efficient market theory of journalism.) It's often difficult to know what the public understands, and recalls—particularly when it comes to remote, complex issues like foreign policy or finance. Journalism brings scraps of news—right, wrong, in-between—to folks, who absorb some of it. *Barbarians* did far better than most: The book had a profound effect on perceptions of the deal itself. Memories fade; this scarlet-jacketed book remains. Even many involved in the transaction had their views shaped by *Barbarians*. It was more vivid than the reality.

Barbarians is a product of daily reportage. Daily coverage of takeovers had mounted through the '80s. The reporting tended to be episodic, built around discrete struggles. Takeovers were news, though rarely national news. Takeovers had the innate drama of sports writing, with *mano o mano* contests, winners and losers, an underlying mythology. Business journalism rarely got dramas, which is why the evening news sticks mostly to reporting on share prices, which in turn always seem to be heading to heaven or hell. Then came the insider trading scandals, bringing a broader, more inflammatory significance, not to say good and evil layered atop winners and losers.

Some of the best takeover coverage appeared in Brill's *The American Lawyer*. Brill had discovered a fascination with the legal business that had not to that point been obvious. He pursued a long-form style, heavy on personalities, intensely reported, sophisticated. He attracted an unusual number of talented reporters—some were lawyers by training, others not—including James Stewart and Connie Bruck. Stewart, a Harvard Law graduate and former Cravath associate, left *The American Lawyer* for the *Wall Street Journal,* where he reported on the insider cases (he shared a Pulitzer for that coverage in 1988) and published *Den of Thieves* about Milken in 1991. He also became editor of the *Journal*'s Page One, with its long, fact-filled leaders; after the magazines led the way, particularly with the rise of Milken and junk, the *Journal* dominated coverage of M&A in the late '80s and for years to come. The *Journal* had deep reporting resources. Its reporters and editors knew the business, which the business appreciated. It also had the nation's largest investor audience, which everyone wanted to reach. The paper's practice was to couple an M&A reporter, who presumably had sources on Wall Street, with a company specialist from the bureaus. This was often a potent combination. Burrough, son of a small-town Texas banker, was a few years out of the University of Missouri in 1988 and relatively new to M&A, while Helyar, a Boston University grad, was a staffer in the Atlanta bureau.

Barbarians was perhaps the finest marriage of the *Journal's* feature style to book length. The prose is crisp, the sentences punchy, the tone confident without being showy. It is, to this day, remarkably readable and accessible. This is not a book overladen with financial analysis or argument. It is hefty, at 515 pages, but moves fast, like a novel, in dramatic scenes; its roots were not just in *Journal* leader style but the New Journalism of Wolfe and Capote. That dramatic style required huge amounts of reporting, which is its greatest virtue. The drama is powerfully persuasive because it says: This is what it was like. It made claims to be a mirror to reality. Those claims included not just dialogue, which felt true because it was skillfully done, but also interior monologue. Burrough and Helyar descend like spelunkers into the psyche of their "characters." They reveal this overtly—in long passages of omniscience into mental states—and more subtly in the well-placed adverb, or qualifier, or description: "It was enough to make Cohen's head swim" or "Kravis' bid was Cohen's worst nightmare." The book is rarely abstract. The scenes unfold like a movie for a deal rich to the point of intoxication with crosscurrents of self-interest.

And yet, beneath this surface lurked the kind of tensions brought out by trying to make sense of such a complex, high-pressure deal. In a panel at 21 Club on the twentieth anniversary of publication—the authors chuckled that the *Financial Times* had declared *Barbarians* the second-best business book of all time, behind *Wealth of Nations*—Burrough noted that the two had never actually met until they signed the deal with Harper & Row.[28] At the Atlanta airport Helyar held up a copy of *Time*'s "Game of Greed" cover, which featured a smiling Ross Johnson, so Burrough knew who he was. The project was a flyer. Burrough recalled that "uniformly, everyone said, 'You guys have lost your minds.' The deal had been covered at such length and in such massive detail that everyone looked at us as if to say, 'What on earth is there to say?'" He then offered context. The '80s were a unique time for business and business journalism, he said. "We forget now [it was 2010], but the '70s were an awful time for business-as-celebrity, and mostly business. It was only with the discovery of a bunch of oil men led by T. Boone Pickens that the whole modern era of takeovers began. Once Pickens went on the cover of *Time Magazine* and *Forbes* discovered Milken about a year later, we suddenly had all these celebrities to write about and normal people, like my Mom and Dad, or people in Des Moines, started knowing who a lot of Wall Streeters were."

Helyar then formulated what he thought the book was about, which sprang from his early reporting on the unhappiness simmering among residents of Winston-Salem, North Carolina—Reynolds's company town for a century and full of RJR shareholders—with the flashy, nouveau-riche Johnson. Helyar attached a kind of after-the-fact nut graf to the book: "The kind of winds of change they [the main characters] represented, in terms of an old-line industrial giant put into play as an object for Wall Street to fight over."

Burrough wondered aloud why the book made such a splash. He denied that the pair were "editorialists" who thought LBOs or Wall Street were bad. They were just "trying to tell a good story." Helyar agreed, and ascribed the impact of the book to its novelistic treatment—it was entertaining, he said. "We were not going to get into the intricacies of resets and bond arcana. We were blessed with a twisted plot and twisted characters that gave us a lot to work with." And yet Helyar then promptly drew implications from the LBO. He argued, a little confusingly, that the period represented an end to corporate stewardship—and more:

> Even though the deal didn't have a legacy, I think the events we described [were] a watershed moment in American business. It was not just the high-water mark of the LBO era, which fairly soon imploded afterwards; it was a time that American business would never retreat from. . . . You were never going to see a corporate America as it existed before the 1980s, or particularly the late 1980s. You had a lot more CEOs that didn't have Ross Johnson's flamboyance, but they had some of his value set, in which there weren't any more corporate stewards, or hardly any; it was much more of a

mentality of what's in it for me. A spirit of corporate adventurism I think really took hold and we never went back to a stability that existed before. And I think Wall Street got into a situation where it constantly needed a new fix, a new growth engine, as LBOs had been, and as merger mania has been in the late '80s. And I think this helps explain how we get this succession of bubbles since then, whether it's the Internet or more recently, the unfortunate derivatives, the subprime mess, credit-default swaps. It's kind of like LBOs, a searching for the next big thing on Wall Street, so that what starts out as a good idea becomes a very bad idea and everybody is doing it and all the idiots are getting into the game.

Helyar nicely describes arbitrage at work on Wall Street, capturing a race-to-the-bottom ("all the idiots") driven by competition. This was, if not a legacy, a declaration of significance. To Helyar, *Barbarians* was not just a mirror to reality, as Burrough had said, an expression of journalistic objectivity without moral intent, a mere entertainment; it contained greater meaning: "It was a time American business would never retreat from." It represented corporate adventurism, instability, an end to stewardship, a *watershed.* It foreshadowed evils to come. Helyar wasn't alone. In his memoirs, Rohatyn views RJR as his personal watershed. "As for me, the RJR deal was a defining moment in my evolving thoughts about American business. In the aftermath, it became clear to me that despite the famous assertion that 'greed is good' in the movie *Wall Street,* the raging avarice of the 1980s was a pernicious force that would undermine the marketplace." Rohatyn argued that "the bottom line was no longer the simple bottom line" and that his "traditional banker's calculus drove him to see the wisdom of stakeholdership: the need to address laid-off employees, damaged communities, and cutbacks in employee benefits necessitated by higher corporate debt."[29] All this was a legacy, Rohatyn agreed, of RJR. "If market capitalism was going to continue to be an effective and revitalizing force in American business, it would need to focus not simply on executive paydays but on the widespread consequence of its actions."[30]

That's a heavy burden for any deal to carry. For all the self-interest and hubris at play, the RJR LBO featured neither illegalities nor the manic accumulation of a Campeau or the self-dealing of a Macmillan. The system actually worked: the incumbent CEO *lost*. Like Revlon, RJR Nabisco wasn't exactly a corporate paragon; its merit stemmed mostly from its age and size. Reynolds had undoubtedly done a lot for Winston-Salem, in the stakeholder sense—fueled by profits from toxic tobacco products. The company had employed many—fourteen thousand while the LBO was unfolding—and made many locals wealthy. But to celebrate it was a little like nostalgia for the plantation and the cotton fields. The company had been bolted together, and the rivets popped under pressure. The Nabisco part was on better footing, but it was experiencing the same challenges afflicting Time: it produced vast volumes of packaged-food products for a mass market that was both saturated and commoditized, and beginning to fracture. Growth was tough to come by. In some respects, it made financial sense to take at least Nabisco private. LBOs had been most effective in mature companies, particularly mid-sized industrial firms, with little growth but robust cash flow—out-of-favor companies that could handle debt. But RJR Nabisco was not a mid-sized industrial company. Johnson's initial bid, for $17 billion, was three times the next-largest private equity transaction at the time. The final price was $25 billion.

Did Johnson's drive to take RJR private represent legitimate economic interests? Yes—on that, *Barbarians at the Gate* is convincing. Johnson was nervous: he had requested a poison pill. He told the board he believed shares were undervalued, and that even if he didn't win control, shareholders would profit, which turned out to be the case. Johnson, in fact, does not come across as delusional. (He had discussed an LBO at least twice before: with KKR itself thirteen months earlier, and with an RJR shareholder Clemmy Dickie Spangler, the president of the University of North Carolina, who had gone so far as to talk to Citibank about financing the deal, shocking Johnson.) He saw problems clearly; and as the book makes clear, his staff understood LBOs quite well. The board, advised by Rohatyn and Atkins, met their fiduciary duties. Johnson lost, it's true; but he did so gracefully. The problem with Johnson was, as it had been with Bergerac and Evans, that he was an enthusiastic spender of corporate money—shareholder money. He was of the Steve Ross school: smooth, affable, a salesman and lavishly compensated. He delighted in the CEO life. As Helyar says, any book that has a story about a CEO who flies his dog out on the corporate jet after it bites someone is hard to beat.[31] Johnson enjoyed the perquisites of running a corporation too much. He was a philistine, a parvenu, a restless man with an entourage of highly paid jocks, a young, blonde wife the nice folks in Winston-Salem called Cupcake and viciously gossiped about (in the index, under Laurie Johnson, are references to "golf playing of," "gossip about," and "shopping of"). Johnson called the former Reynolds CEO, J. Tylee Wilson, "jiggerballs" behind his back.[32] The "RJR Air Force" had thirty-six planes, a bigger hanger than Coca-Cola's in Atlanta, and a landscaped three-story waiting area.[33] The details are devastating. Still, Johnson may have been, as *Time* suggested, greedy—but he was certainly shrewd. The book implicitly asks: Should a man of these tastes and free-spending ways be allowed to control a major corporation? Why should this man gain control of this venerable corporation? And if not Johnson, why should Kravis deserve such a treasure?

The deal made a stop at Chancery, which *Barbarians* never mentions. Allen took the case. The auction had turned on a close call by the RJR special committee, based on calculations of the two final bids, KKR and Johnson and Shearson, both of which consisted of complex mixtures of securities and cash. Rohatyn led the valuation effort for the committee. In *Barbarians,* Rohatyn tells the board: "Both bids are between one-oh-eight and one-oh-nine. [KKR was slightly behind.] When you get that close, and when you're dealing with securities in amounts that have never been dealt with before, in my business judgment these offers are essentially equivalent."[34] John Medlin, the CEO of Winston-Salem's major bank—Wachovia Bank—and one of the most respected bankers in America, urges the KKR bid. Others fall in line. Kravis wins; the board rejects its own CEO, a shocking outcome. Was this because of animosity from Reynolds partisans? Was it because directors were repelled by his lavish spending? Or did they actually believe KKR's bid was better? *Barbarians* seems to suggest a Winston-Salem backlash, while also portraying Johnson as felled by greed and a fatal lack of gravitas.

Allen saw it as a straightforward business judgment question.[35] Had the special committee fulfilled its duty of care in overseeing the auction? He thought it had. Were outside directors swayed by self-interest —would they profit from one side or the other winning? He could find no improper motivation: they fulfilled their duty of good faith. He rejected the motion for a preliminary injunction. But here Allen offered a striking comment. If such untoward motivations that were not necessarily financial *could* be proved, that *would* disqualify directors from protection of the business judgment rule. In short, directors can act against the best interests of a company even if they do not benefit financially. And he offered a truth far from a world of clashing ideologies: "Greed is not the only emotion that can pull one from the path of propriety; so might hatred, lust, envy, revenge or, as it is here alleged, shame or pride."

Allen recognized depths that lurked beyond the edge of *Barbarians'* magic mirror. There were others. Early on, *Barbarians* dwells on a leak indicating that KKR would jump into the bidding. Kravis initially suspected one of his bankers, Drexel's Jeff Beck, and banished him. But Kravis's partner and cousin George Roberts distrusted Wasserstein, and suspicion swung his way. Wasserstein supposedly leaked the story to prod Kravis to tender, thus preventing him from bidding for Kraft, which was under attack by another Wasserstein client, Philip Morris. Wasserstein then allegedly planted references to Drexel to implicate Beck. Later, after checking phone records, says the book, Kravis aides blamed Wasserstein *and* Beck. Both denied it. Was any of this true, or was it a conclusion, like Zilkha casting aspersions on Liman and Rifkind in *Revlon?* *Barbarians* never offers an answer; it's part of the entertainment. Today, the suspects are dead. Wasserstein spent the rest of his life trying to convince Kravis of his innocence. Beck, known as "Mad Dog" for his propensity to howl like a dog after a big deal, died in 1995 at forty-eight of a heart attack. He had been a technical advisor to Stone on *Wall Street*. Before he died, he was unmasked in the *Journal* by Burrough as an inveterate liar who made up stories about his nonexistent service in Vietnam.[36] Later, a *Business Week* reporter and self-described good friend wrote an entire book about Beck and Wall Street and his lies.[37]

BARBARIANS AT THE GATE symbolically marked the end of the takeover decade. There were other episodes, notably the epic collapse of Drexel Burnham in 1990, or First Boston's failed bridge loan for the LBO of a mattress company (as banks knew, financing had an upside and a downside)—an incident that became notorious as "the burning bed" and almost wiped the high-flying firm out.

By the early '90s, with LBOs and hostile takeovers receding, much had seemingly been forgotten. It was a new age. A more collegial, re-strained and prudent Wall Street had emerged, fixing its tie, polishing its shoes; the era of banking stars was reportedly over; LBOs became private equity, and junk—now the decorous high-yield—had been tamed. Anti-Semitism withdrew back down the sewer. Institutions were empowered; and CEOs supposedly put in their place. Takeovers were associated with the fizzy good times of those '80s. *Barbarians,* for all its success, could not close the gap between a democratic public and the complexities of finance and its intensely human motivations. Neither could Rohatyn, who eventually went to Paris as Clinton's am-bassador to France—not the Treasury secretaryship, but not bad—finally leaving Lazard. As a result, the takeover game, which, like the Kabuki maneuverings of the Federal Reserve on monetary policy that was transforming Alan Greenspan into a magus, and that affected mil-lions of Americans, was left once more to Thorstein Veblen's techno-crats: the lawyers, judges, regulators, bankers, money managers, and scholars, with their technical arcana and compelling theories. And the play of agent self-interest continued, everywhere and nowhere.

Chapter Eighteen

THE END OF HISTORY (IN THE BEST OF ALL POSSIBLE WORLDS)

A ND SO AN uneasy peace fell over the land, courtesy of recession and scandal. Takeovers and LBOs crashed in 1990, though they never approached the low norms of the now-remote 1970s. And by 1992, as the economy revived, M&A deals began to pile up again, setting new records. The politics of takeovers remained polarized. Hostile deals, layoffs, restructurings still occurred. But the aggression and outrage had ebbed away. Despite widespread pronouncements that junk was dead, it quickly bounced back, as bankruptcies eased and Wall Street firms grabbed Drexel's high-yield talent. Nearly all of Milken's raiders still operated, though without the self-righteous zeal and the nearly unlimited checkbook of the '80s. Even the American Law Institute managed to finally complete its work codifying the orthodox interpretation of corporate governance, though there remained dissenters and the effort seemed to end as much from exhaustion as from any sense of triumphant consensus.[1]

Throughout the Clinton '90s, calm prevailed. Partly, it was the influence of Delaware takeover jurisprudence, which did establish, in time, a sense of order, logic, and predictability—albeit one, in a world of change, that was always provisional. (And Delaware's continuing dominance marked the retreat of the anti-takeover movement in the states, as companies and their shareholders mutually embraced M&A,

albeit for different reasons.) But if Delaware was a brake on the machine, the powerful drives of self-interest still operated. Both schools of thought on corporations and takeovers—the manager or board advocates harkening back to Berle, with Lipton at its head, and the shareholder-centric school associated with Chicago and the law and economics movement—could tell themselves that they had won, that they had been proven (mostly) right. Managers embraced takeovers as a tool, not as a weapon of retribution or vengeance, and shareholders could take comfort in their continuing hegemony. But boards got to keep their poison pills and the business judgment rule, while institutional shareholders remained passive, particularly as more and more shares were taken up by index funds (a Chicago financial innovation), which bought and sold mechanically to rebalance portfolios against benchmarks, stripping active intelligence from the market. By the end of the late '90s, some observers declared that a post-ideological age had dawned for corporations as managers and shareholders pursued policies of peaceful coexistence. It appeared, as the title of one of their papers declared, to be the best of all possible worlds—the end of history, as another paper noted, at least in terms of the corporation.

But this reconciliation, which flourished in bullish Clinton years, stumbled in the more bearish markets of the George W. Bush era. And an upsurge in corporate scandals once again raised questions about a governance scheme that seemed to encourage cheating, illegalities, and failure. Lastly, and widely ignored, the practice of corporate governance, as opposed to the theory, dramatically narrowed to large shareholders and elite managers: from a theoretical democracy to a practical oligarchy. Jensen had aired this possibility when he talked about the need to reward top managers, and the rise of LBOs embodied it. This was, in fact, a development quietly celebrated as the answer to Berle's riddle of the separation of ownership and control: the alignment of interests between shareholders and management. And even today, when that alignment remains the shimmering ideal of orthodox governance, few recognize the consequences of attaining it: the effective disenfranchisement of the vast bulk of corporate workforces, the blind consensus of a short-term monoculture of top managers and shareholders, and deepening inequality.

IN 2002, OVER a decade had passed since the RJR Nabisco LBO; Milken had been in and out of jail, was recovering from prostate cancer and rehabilitating his reputation, though he could no longer directly work in finance. Bill Allen had retired from Chancery in 1996, and settled at NYU Law School. At seventy-one, Marty Lipton remained at the center of the deal culture and much else; he had been chairman of the law school board when Allen had been recruited. He continued to spar with academics, his client notes still bristled, and he still aggressively defended the pill; he was a powerful and controversial figure. Joe Flom, now seventy-nine, claimed to have semi-retired, but he still came to the office at Skadden. The two firms presided over legal M&A together. Wachtell, centered on New York, was relatively small but fantastically profitable; Skadden, global, diversified, and enormous, was neck and neck, the two most successful law firms on the globe, if as strategically different as Lipton and Flom themselves. The *doppelganger* of Lipton and Flom had been institutionalized.

The M&A machine rolled along, producing great wealth for Wall Street, shareholders, and top corporate executives. Economically, the more extreme predictions from the pro- and anti-takeover camps failed to materialize. The apocalypse had not occurred, nor had the Promised Land been reached—neither the destruction of American corporate competitiveness nor a return to the '50s miracle of growth and global dominance. While much of the '90s saw a rising stock market, the real economy still struggled with growth, productivity, and—in hindsight—mounting inequality. Global competition was intensifying. Top corporate executives were making more money than ever, particularly from stock-option-linked pay, but their tenures had grown shorter and increasingly volatile. Uncertainty, in fact, helped drive rising pay packages. Contrary to Jensen's prediction, the public company survived and LBOs, now known as private equity, slowly recovered after staggering through the recession; public and private grew symbiotically together—and a good portion of M&A involved flipping back and forth between the two. The public had generally lost its fascination with the takeover game and was now focused on the Internet, hot initial public offerings, and the waves of dot-com stocks that purported to make everything new: another manifestation of deal culture.

In some quarters, a sense of satisfaction bordering on the smug took hold. In 2000, Harvard Law's Reinier Kraakman and Yale Law School's Henry Hansmann produced perhaps the purest expression of that sentiment in a paper that borrowed from the popular essay and book written by political theorist Francis Fukuyama at the end of the Cold War: *The End of History and the Last Man.*[2] Fukuyama employed a Hegelian analysis to argue that with communism gone, de-legitimized, there were no other forms of governance that could compete with liberal democracy—and thus, in a Hegelian sense, "history," defined as the evolution of political systems, had reached a final synthesis. Hansmann and Kraakman borrowed Fukuyama's scheme for corporate law.[3] This was the polar opposite of Bayless Manning's 1962 footnoted declaration (see Chapter 2) that corporate law was an empty edifice. Corporate law had now been perfected, or close to it. Now, the "consensus that corporate managers should act exclusively in the economic interests of shareholders" not only had triumphed over a failed managerial, stakeholder model in the United States but would sweep aside "the labor-oriented model that reached its apogee in German co-determination [stakeholders such as workers represented on boards]" and the state-oriented model of France and, significantly, the top-down capitalism of much of Asia.[4]

Convergence had arrived—convergence to what became known as the market-driven Anglo-Saxon system. Convergence was consensus with evolution tossed into the mix. Other models would go to the wall, unable to compete. Even those of the Asians.

This represented perhaps the fullest reiteration of the Chicago view, a late blossoming of a now-mature set of ideas. These ideas took the shareholder model *global* and made its victory *inevitable.* And it was an American triumph, of a piece with the American Consensus that prevailed in global economic policy. Economics was the primary underlying determinant of corporate law. The managerial model had been preeminent but the collapse of the conglomerate movement "largely destroyed its appeal." Kraakman and Hansmann actually declared it "the conventional wisdom," apparently without irony (and avoiding the need for real evidence), that when managers gain control over investment policies, "they mostly end up serving themselves, however well-intentioned they may be"—in short, agency theory. While managerial firms may "be more efficiently responsive to non-shareholder interests" than those more focused on serving shareholders, the price paid in efficiency and excessive investment in low-value projects—Jensen's free cash flow theory—"is now considered too dear," that is, too costly.[5] Considered by whom, one might ask. Managerialism, corporatism, and stakeholdership were the communism of corporate law: relics of history.

There was an element of triumphalism here that may have represented a market top. These claims had little backing; in fact, comparing the two models, shareholder and stakeholder, in any scientific way couldn't be done. And yet Kraakman and Hansmann's "End of History" became one of the most-cited law reviews in 2001.[6]

In 2002 came a second paper out of the law schools that promised to reconcile the once-warring views on takeovers. Edward Rock from Penn and Marcel Kahan of NYU set out to explain why takeovers were no longer quite so hostile in the entertainingly titled "How I Learned to Stop Worrying and Love the Pill: Adaptive Responses to Takeover Law."[7] The pair noted subtle changes that had taken place within many corporations in the years since the '80s. Boards had far more outside directors. (They credited Delaware.) CEOs were increasingly paid in stock and their tenures had grown shorter. CEOs were more willing to sell their companies. Outside directors provided more monitoring, while payment in stock theoretically aligned the interests of managers and shareholders. As a result, shareholders were happy to pay top managers more, and had no reason to try to kill the pill, which could be a tool for increasing the premium in the event of a takeover bid. In fact, shareholders tolerated the creation of defensive moves like staggered boards for the same reason.

This happy alignment of interests, which the pair dubbed an "adaptive-response" (the terminology from evolution is deliberate) to the bruising conflicts of the '80s, appeared to satisfy everyone's interests. Corporate acquirers budgeted a payoff to top management into the price, much as they would an investment-banking fee (or, in days of yore, greenmail for raiders); target shareholders got their premium; and CEOs and senior executives grew very wealthy. The kind of "bilateral" decision-making between, say, managers (or boards) and shareholders that had been shaped by the Delaware takeover cases, Rock and Kahan argued, worked far more effectively than "unilateral" solutions—that is, giving either shareholders or managers total say: *both* board and shareholders had to agree on fundamental corporate decisions. Less contention, less ideology, was good. The system had, in a sense, healed itself. Balance and equilibrium had been naturally restored. The lambs bedded down with the lions. Even Wachtell Lipton, they noted, had begun to represent hostile bidders again. (Goldman Sachs had long since abandoned solely practicing defense as well.) After all, in this increasingly routinized takeover game, with institutions now contributing more than 80 percent of the shares, who could tell hostile from friendly? It was a distinction without a difference.

Balance and equilibrium, economically speaking, are ideals, goals, abstractions that markets drift toward, like the pull of gravity on planets and tides. They may never be attained, or a market may whiz pass them like a distracted driver missing his driveway. Some believe that in a world of constant change they do not truly exist. It's also a fallacy to posit an evolutionarily "perfect" organism: change is a constant, if variable in speed, and evolution is a random process that ends only in extinction. Generally, the academics wrote as if they had achieved a kind of evolutionary stasis, a resolution—a classic example of the present as the happy (and inevitable) culmination of the past, the best of all possible worlds, as Kraakman titled another 2002 paper.[8]

In any event, the best of all possible worlds theory was about to be tested.

No one in 2002 could have known that they were looking back at a beneficent period that had already ended—possibly in July 2000 when the stock market, fueled by the frenzy over dot-coms, topped out and began to slide; certainly after the planes hit the World Trade Center and Pentagon just over a year later. Recession, terrorism, and war proved to be deeply disruptive of the conventional wisdom.

The times challenged the fundamentalist faith in takeovers. The rise and fall of the dot coms offered another empirical argument against the strong form of efficient markets. It wasn't just that the market bid up fledgling Internet companies to dizzying heights (the tech-heavy Nasdaq didn't hit its 2000 high again until early 2015), only to smash them like light bulbs. Wall Street also had a chronic agency problem. One of the key components of efficiency is the analytical professionalism that exists throughout the markets, and the ability of performance-driven investors to arbitrage away excesses, like hyped stock, to equilibrium—that is, to bring it back to earth. Now, with dot coms and telecom stocks crashing, it was clear how fallible—or worse—Wall Street research had been, particularly when it came to hot, new, insubstantial companies that blew about like leaves on a gusty day. The popular story was, as always, a fall from grace, brought on by corrupt self-interest, self-regard, conflict, greed. The reality may also have involved a failure of market judgment, encouraged by an over-enthusiasm for an emerging and hyped set of technologies. A less obvious flaw came from the possibility that market arbitrage grew ineffective in extreme market circumstances like a bubble.[9]

It didn't matter all that much whether research was corrupt—shaped to meet the needs of M&A units and bankers and individual self-interest, as New York attorney general Eliot Spitzer insisted—or honestly misguided: the market turned out to be *wrong* for a significant period of time, and stocks, in retrospect, looked wildly overvalued. Spitzer was arguing that chronic agency costs were *part of the market itself.* If a conflicted market struggles to price a Web-based retailer accurately, would it be able to calculate, say, agency costs with any accuracy, or the true value of a large, complex company beset by raiders? And if a deep, highly professionalized market can appear to act in less-than-rational ways, why would a bidder, even a disciplined Henry Kravis, *not* get carried away by euphoria or competitiveness? Perhaps Kravis, Perelman, Dingman, Pickens, and other go-for-broke active investors were entirely rational—rationally irrational—recognizing that winners often accrued benefits as winners. (This may be what Wasserstein's "Dare to be great" speech really meant, though it didn't work for Canadian real estate developer Robert Campeau [see Chapter 17].) Perhaps there was something to Delaware's belief that boards and managers had information investors did not. All that wasn't to say that markets aren't often, or weakly or semi-weakly, efficient. They were and they are. They simply are not omniscient. And the line between strong and weak shifts like blowing sand.

That was certainly the case on January 10, 2000, six months before the dot-com market top, when Time Warner announced it was merging with AOL, formerly America Online (technically, AOL was buying Time Warner, like Time buying Warner). Gerald Levin, who had succeeded Steve Ross as CEO of Time Warner, beamed, tieless, at the news conference with Steve Case, the founder and CEO of America Online. Levin had fulfilled his dream, and topped Ross to boot. Total pro forma value of the resulting company that day: $350 billion. Both media and markets lustily cheered. The deal, another treasure chest of fees, included some of the sharpest advisors on Wall Street. Alas, a deal of this size took months to close, by which time the dot coms had crashed. The merger turned into an *auto-da-fé* of value—$200 billion went up in smoke. It was not just bad timing. AOL was already fading against waves of technological competition, and the economic downturn didn't help. Nearly everything went wrong: culture, timing, technology, pricing.[10] It was a disaster of wishful thinking over reality—though AOL shareholders did nicely, from an event-study perspective, it was a value-creating deal, and no one on Wall Street volunteered to return their titanic fees. Alas, anyone holding AOL Time-Warner stock had a ticket, like Japan in the '90s, for a lost decade or more; convulsive restructurings followed, including casting off AOL itself.

Evidence was now accumulating as to just how poorly many M&A deals, measured not by share price but by operating metrics, fared. Overpaying, particularly in stock, especially as the market crested, had been epidemic. The operational and integration risk of M&A—the knitting together of complex organizations—became more pressingly evident. Performance often suffered. Murmurs rose: Were *any* deals beneficial to anyone besides insiders? Were takeovers just a scam—an opportunity for managers to manipulate markets to drive their pay even higher? It became a kind of meme—that is, the conventional wisdom of the new age of the Internet: most deals failed. Most deals were orchestrated by CEOs trying to pump up their share price and get their stock options, or by fee-hungry Wall Streeters. Most deals were infected by insider trading. The statisticians, pro and con, went to war trying to quantify all this.

Distress brought more scandal. A cascade of corporate misdeeds and bankruptcies headlined by Enron, Tyco, WorldCom, and Adelphia—all built on M&A, complex mixtures of leverage, and piles of stock options—crashed. Shareholders were generally viewed as innocent victims, which was wrong: at least in terms of governance, they were, if not complicit, enabling. Executives went to jail. And boards were excoriated, despite those independent directors, sweeping the governance debate back to where it had begun in the '70s—What's wrong with boards?—and provoking the same reaction: the need for federal action. Congress held hearings, then produced Sarbanes-Oxley, a massive, unruly omnibus of governance-by-rules, provoking the revival of the federal-versus-federalism debate and fresh anxieties in Delaware[11] and years of protests from corporate lobbyists. So much for bilateral bargaining. Or perhaps this was just another shock to drive further evolutionary progress.

The reconciliation between managers and shareholders took on a different, more sinister light. Executives viewed themselves as principals—perhaps they always had—but now they literally *were.* Many now owned buckets of shares. Aligning interests with stock options had grown into the conventional wisdom of governance: we're all on the same team now. Few saw, however, the dysfunction of mixing agent and principal roles. Agency costs seemed relevant for a thin layer of options-compensated senior managers, which produced a queasy kind of ethics to buttress a governance system resting upon legitimacy. "The amounts you need to pay managers to do the right thing are generally small compared to the benefits that doing the right thing creates for shareholders," Marcel Kahan and Edward Rock noted.[12] This was an overly optimistic view of the power, and complex incentivizing and liberating effects, of money. This consensus view contained an ends-justify-means morality that was inherently unstable. The rising pay of senior managers resembled a new form of entrenchment. They were rich. What did *they* care? They had to be *paid off* to do their duty? The diagnosis of greed slid from Wall Street to CEOs—and required only scandal and failure to inflame it. Over the next decade, executive pay would become the default explanation for every financial and business failure—an exaggeration, but a telling one. Much of this could be traced to Chicago's conception of the corporation as a nexus of contracts—an appealing academic theory, but not one that created much sense of loyalty in employees. The tendency to view the corporation as something less than eternal, something fungible and disposable, was inherent in the nexus of contracts, and justified the pursuit of self-interest; the nexus of contracts arguably exacerbated omnipresent agency costs. But the free-agent nation had its deficiencies, too. One consequence was increasing inequality, which was initially most visible in corporate pay disparities, as wages and benefits stagnated in the middle and bottom and exploded at the options-enriched top. And symbolically it was enshrined in the notion that you had to be paid off to fulfill your fiduciary duty.

By the '90s, newly minted MBAs saw themselves as free agents, entrepreneurs, or dealmakers, not as lifetime employees, stewards, or trustees. As principals they were free to maximize their self-interests, and they didn't have to be lawyers to view the corporation as a tissue of breakable contracts. What was left, and forgotten, was everyone else, namely stakeholders, banished from the table: employees, communities, customers, the society, even the nation, which was not synonymous with shareholders. (True, employees who were beneficiaries of pension plans *were* principals—but at some remove. Technically and legally they were deterred from acting as true principals. They were not expected to meddle.) One big, if generally ignored, weakness with executives as principals—aligned with shareholders—is that they were increasingly incentivized to give shareholders exactly what they desired. Shareholders and the media applauded what Kenneth Lay and Jeff Skilling were building at Enron—until the day the company collapsed. This merger of manager and shareholder created consensus, but not diversity; independent voices needed to shout very loudly to be heard. The two sets of principals resembled twin mirrors reflecting light upon each other. Where is the space for longer-term judgment to gestate? Where are the views of skeptics, cranks, contrarians, short sellers, enemies of the conventional wisdom? Here again, in a corporate context, is another whiff of Tocqueville's soft despotism. What the gospel of the alignment of interests also ignores is not just this drive for short-term consensus but a gap in the interests of institutional investors overseeing massive and diverse portfolios of stock and the fate of corporations making their lonely way in a hard world. Institutions, like pensions, had their own needs and risk tolerances, which did not necessarily align with that of any single company. Institutions absorbed a blow; companies failed. This would become evident on Wall Street, as Judge Richard Posner, a seminal figure in the Chicago school, pointed out in 2010, after shareholders and financial executives, Wall Street *and* Main Street, marched hand in hand into the abyss of the financial crisis. He aptly called it, in the book of that name, *The Crisis of Capitalist Democracy.*[13]

To advocates of the conventional wisdom of shareholder governance, the alignment of interests produced a satisfying mutuality of interests. A win-win. But from the outside—where those contractual workers, among many others, stood—it only deepened the quality of takeovers that too often resembled a zero-sum game. There was even in a friendlier and more routinized takeover game the suggestion of a moral hazard—that is, the sense that you, Mr. CEO, Mr. Shareholder, and Mr. Wall Streeter, are insured against failure, which is a psychological relation to Jensen's free cash flow theory, and another concept that would become uncomfortably familiar in 2008's meltdown. The moment of gravest danger, and greatest risk, is when everyone who matters is fat, happy, self-satisfied, and secure.

FOR MICHAEL JENSEN, the decades after the '80s were a succession of revisions and recantations.

He remained an arresting figure. He was a big, commanding man with an air of ringing certitude. Jensen had never been a profound scholar. Rather, he was, at times, a skillful interpreter of the financial *zeitgeist,* a kind of prophetic critic of finance. The trouble with playing critic is that you drag your past like a lengthening chain behind you—consisting of triumphs, dead ends, and failed judgments. Jensen tended to ignore that past as if it had ceased to be relevant, except as evidence for this or that, and he assembled a remarkable number of contradictory positions. Agency theory would *save* public corporations; it was the key to understanding the corporation. Efficient markets were strong, scientifically inarguable, and essential for agency theory. Free cash flow explained takeovers, then merged with overvalued equity, but made sense only if markets *weren't* strongly efficient. Markets or Wall Street, not wayward managers, spawned agency costs, which undermined shareholder-centric governance. Public companies *couldn't* be saved.[14] As Jensen declared in 1989, "The publicly held corporation, the main engine of economic progress in the United States for a century, has outlived its usefulness and is being eclipsed."[15] In time, private companies developed flaws as well.

Once the '80s ran their course, Jensen drifted from the austere truths of the Chicago view. His position on these issues, which had once been so certain, grew hazier and less coherent, increasingly focused on individual behavior, and not on organizations, or governance.

In 1995, he looked back at corporate governance in the '80s.[16] Familiar themes appeared, from active investors to the disciplinary mechanism of debt and takeovers. He blamed the press for reviving populist hostility to Wall Street and providing the public with "villains by furnishing unflattering detailed accounts of the private doings of those branded 'corporate raiders.'" He had read *Barbarians,* which, he noted, "could best be described as an attempt to expose the greed and chicanery that went into the making of some Wall Street deals." Then he pointed out the existence of "corporate-wide inefficiencies at RJR Nabisco, including the massive waste of corporate free cash flow that allowed KKR to pay existing stockholders $12 billion over the previous market value for the right to bring change." The authors, he said, "seem to have failed to grasp that import."[17] Many readers would agree. After arguing that *Barbarians* unfairly portrayed deals and financiers, and missed Ross Johnson's real sin, he scorned *Fortune* for naming Johnson a model corporate leader just a few months before the buyout. The press, he argued, kept the story of how LBOs and takeovers were cleaning up inefficiencies from the public. "I know of no area in economics today where the divergence between popular belief and the evidence from scholarly research is so great," he said.[18]

He then, however, confronted an uncomfortable truth: LBOs had nearly expired from 1989 to 1992. Why? He did not take refuge in inherent market cyclicality. He blamed the press again, along with political overreaction and bad court decisions. Backlash fears cowed heroic active investors into submission. But almost in passing, he also suggested a more fatal flaw: markets overshot. All that excess free cash flow and inefficiency produced agency-cost issues, which markets were not fully picking up on; an over-shooting market is one with an efficiency problem. "Promoters," or the Wall Street crowd, were overcharging on fees and conflicted on financing, posing agency issues that LBO firms seemed unwilling to resolve. And LBO shops were putting up too little equity and buying assets with too little downside risk. And, because many LBOs were overpriced, they carried too much debt. All this seemed like a devastating critique of the foundations of the Chicago view: inefficient markets, conflicted intermediaries, private investors without adequate skin in the game, systemic mispricing, inadequate accountability. All engineered by *active* investors. But Jensen waved his own critique off, blaming the breakdown on "internal corporate control systems" and "intense political pressures to curb the corporate control market."[19]

In 2001, however, he rediscovered stakeholders.[20] The stakeholder model was "anachronistic," he declared, and "serves to reinforce a model of corporate behavior that draws on concepts of 'family' and 'tribe.'"[21] Family again! Jensen's solution was a concept he called value maximization—that is, maximizing the *long-term* value of the firm. A younger Jensen had been derisive on the subject of chasing long-term value; but he had changed his mind. He could save stakeholder theory by merging it with value maximization, forming what he called "enlightened stakeholdership." A year later he turned on Wall Street. The implication in "Just Say No to Wall Street"[22] is that The Street was forcing CEOs to overpromise to meet its unreasonable expectations. He denounced the "earnings expectations" game that had become a key aspect of the quest for shareholder value. He insisted Enron had been victimized by its own success, which may be true, but glossed over the criminality that resulted. The theorist of agency costs now demanded that managers tell markets to shove off. Two years later, in a keynote to the European Financial Management Association, he said, "Management should not let their stock price to get too high. By too high I mean a level at which management will be unable to deliver performance required to support the market's valuation."[23] Society was at fault for the dot-com crash, plus "misleading data from managers, large numbers of naïve investors and the breakdown of agency relationships within companies and within gatekeepers including investment and commercial banks, and audit and law firms."[24] In 2007, just before the financial crisis, Jensen and a co-author opined on the hot debate on compensation in a book, *CEO Pay and What to Do About It,* in which they demanded that *boards* negotiate tougher contracts with CEOs.[25]

Everyone seemed to be at fault. The rot was psychologically deeper than mere shirking. In 1995, Jensen had published a paper he had written with Bill Meckling that they had presented each year to a class they had once taught together at both Rochester and Harvard. (Meckling, by then, had died.)[26] The paper was their attempt to define the nature of man, which was its title. They dismissed other "nature of man" approaches, including Chicago's economically determined man, as inadequate and promoted their own model they called the Resources,

Evaluative, Maximizing Model, or REMM. This was a strange, if revealing, detour into philosophy for two finance guys. Then, around 2000, Jensen met controversial personal-growth guru Warner Erhard in California. Soon the two were partnering on a project they called the Ontological/Phenomenological Model, which argued that a failure of integrity lurked behind many of the woes of a troubled corporate world. Integrity began to crop up in Jensen's more mainstream efforts, like his paper on overvalued equity and a leadership class he had begun teaching. Together, they wrote articles, gave workshops, recruited instructors. Shoring up integrity and breaking down "ontological" barriers to financing soon loomed as the salvation of American business.[27] By then, Jensen was an emeritus professor, and he and Erhard worked the business school circuit in a kind of traveling Chautauqua show spotlighting integrity. This was a long way from Chicago-style finance.

In 2010, Jensen, now seventy-one, received the Morgan Stanley–American Finance Association Award for Excellence in Finance. The citation listed achievements like agency theory, compensation, and corporate control, noting that while his "classic research on agency" highlighted the importance of conflicts of interest between individual agents with differing economic incentives, his ongoing recent work [with Erhard and others] "seeks to address the interpersonal conflicts that play off within agents struggling to balance economic and ethical considerations."[28] (Actually, Jensen and Erhard technically deny that "integrity" is an ethical matter.) The citation noted Jensen's remark in 1978 that "no other proposition in economics . . . has more solid empirical evidence supporting it than the Efficient Market Hypothesis." But then, aware of his change of heart, it quoted a few later lines from that paper, as an illustration of what it described as Jensen's scientific philosophy: "Yet viewed as a whole, those pieces of evidence begin to stack up in a manner which makes a much stronger case for the necessity to carefully research both our acceptance of the efficient market theory and our methodological acceptance." But isn't "careful research" more a precondition for science than a scientific philosophy? It had been many years since Jensen, in fact, had generated the empirical research he suggested might be necessary. His papers and declarations were sometimes prescient, often insightful. But increasingly he had resorted to spinning theories that fit changing times, much like the journalists he loathed.

In lauding Jensen's career, the American Finance Association was also quietly admitting something quite extraordinary: the doubts about strong market efficiency were now official. The AFA did not elaborate on what that meant for governance, corporate law, and M&A. Neither did it note just how much instability and change had been perpetrated, how many lives had been disrupted, on the belief that markets were never wrong. It was enough that many, like Jensen, had once viewed it as inarguable truth and should be lauded.

Chapter Nineteen

THE DEATH AND LIFE OF M&A

Today, the M&A cycle is revving like a Harley doing wheelies across an asphalt parking lot: noise, smoke, leathery spectacle. We've seen the show before. Many declared in 2008 that the modern era of M&A, which had lasted far longer than previous takeover waves, had definitively ended with the financial crisis and what appeared to be the self-immolation of Wall Street. The banks were not lending, the markets were stunned, and the corporate triad of managers, boards, and shareholders—hit by credit crises, illiquidity, recession, and panic's hangover of uncertainty—rejected M&A as a strategy. Risk rose to the top of the agenda, despite the opportunity to buy at bargain-basement prices. M&A volumes fell dramatically.

Instead, in yet another adaptive response, boards, often urged on by that updated version of '80s raiders, shareholder activists (score one for Jensen), took their free cash flow, which they maximized by slashing costs, and bought back their own shares, thus rewarding shareholders by, at worst, supporting the share price and by, at best, lifting it. This was not new. The '80s also saw an upsurge in share repurchases, some related to takeover defense, so much so that Columbia's Louis Lowenstein, in a 1991 book, decried buybacks as "a lizard lunching on its own tail. It seems unnatural."[1] After the shock of 2008, companies again borrowed to repurchase their own shares in large numbers, taking advantage of historically low post–financial crisis interest rates. This was widely viewed as another win-win in a post-consensus age. Companies insisted there was no better, safer, and more rewarding use of corporate cash—not acquiring another company nor investing in expansion, modernization, or R&D—than buying back their own stock. After all, channeling the business judgment rule, who knew their prospects better than they did? True, the rank and file had to sacrifice. Wages were frozen; budgets were cut; layoffs were necessary. And buybacks contributed nothing to future growth; some buybacks, in fact, were followed by falling share prices, which meant that often-hefty expenditures went down the rat-hole exactly like failed acquisitions. As Lowenstein had warned in 1991, a buyback is an "ambiguous transaction"—an admission that managers can't find any better use for their capital. "Buybacks," he wrote, "are also suspect thanks to CEOs who want to manipulate the market."[2] Buying back shares produced the sight of options-compensated managers helping to inflate their own shares, using insider information. That said, the attitude toward buybacks remained remarkably benign. Buybacks *are* a logical extension of the shareholder model: a way for management and boards to preserve their relationship with shareholders—to protect themselves (and reward themselves, since, of course, they are shareholders, too). And once begun, and given continuing uncertainties (the world being a very dicey place to do business in), accentuated by aftershocks like the euro-zone crisis and a China slowdown, buybacks remained the default option for up-to-date boards and CEOs and growing numbers of activist investors.

Buybacks continued at extraordinarily high volumes through 2015, seven years after the crash. The death of M&A lasted until early 2014, when, like Lazarus, it staggered to life once again, shrugging off its time in the tomb. That turn occurred quickly. By then, the conventional wisdom about M&A had become dogmatically mummified. *Most deals fail,* the pundits chanted. *Why bother?* M&A would *never* recover its former role; it was a crude tool from a barbarous age. Depending on your point of view, the experts blithely tossed out their favorite percentages of failed deals, rarely offering context, source, or duration: 40 percent, 60 percent, 100 percent. Studies proliferated, disagreed, accumulated—cited if unread. This again, however, was a counterfactual problem; you knew AOL Time Warner was a disaster, but in most cases, you could never know the cost of *not* doing a deal, of strategic passivity. This complication was generally ignored. So, too, was that eventually companies had to grow. Meanwhile, Wall Street, enmeshed in its own woes and shattered credibility, tried to counter the *most deals fail* chorus. Year after year, surveys of gloomy, if self-interested, industry insiders and Wall Streeters predicted an M&A revival, fueled by low rates, rising share prices, reviving economic growth, and the necessity, at some point, to re-ignite corporate growth, above and beyond cost-cutting, dividend payouts, and buybacks. And year after year, M&A numbers would pop for a quarter or so, generating headlines (excited, if nervous) about how deals were back, then fall to the levels of a decade or more in the past—1992, say, or 2003.[3]

And then, just as many on Wall Street capitulated to the conventional wisdom of the demise of M&A, takeovers began ticking up again, chasing a bull market. And by 2015, new records were being set, *most deals fail* was packed away in storage, and the usual cyclical processes were turning like a watch mechanism on a time bomb: rising prices, larger premiums, greater size, a heightening of euphoria (mutterings of bubbles), with share prices dancing on each announcement. Bets were laid about how long it would take to blow up, and what would trigger it.

And what about governance? Little has changed since the '90s. There are more activists and buybacks, and institutional shareholders can now farm out their monitoring of companies to so-called proxy advisors, which make their judgments based on a rigid shareholder-centric catechism. But the overt hostility of the '80s has not reappeared. M&A had been routinized to such an extent that legal clashes are mostly technical and incremental, and developments that generate buzz—activist Bill Ackman of Pershing Square joining with Valeant Pharmaceuticals International, a classic asset-stripping, cost-cutting takeover vehicle with the economics of a '60s conglomerates, in 2014 to stalk Allergan, the maker of Botox (the effort failed)—were not as unprecedented as the media made them out to be. (And, predictably, Valeant rose and fell like so many classically over-leveraged conglomerates: in October 2015 its stock price collapsed amid allegations about its business practices, which included slashing R&D in acquired companies and jacking up drug prices.) The dominant ideal of governance continues to be, despite recent disasters, to align interests of top managers, boards, and shareholders. For all the surveys, consultants, lawyers, studies, conferences, and think tanks, latter-day governance is as rudimentary (and as dull) as squaring a board: align the interests, generate consensus. Kumbaya.

Still, despite a rising stock market, revived M&A, an economic recovery, and an improving jobs situation, not to say Apple's raft of nifty toys, few would describe the American economy as, well, youthfully buoyant. Labor participation lags, in part attributable to an aging population, but not completely. Productivity, despite the cost cutting, is mediocre. Growth sputters, particularly compared with China, which has its own issues. Inequality has been deepening since the early '80s. Rising M&A cycles often shadow bull markets. But that's cause and effect, what Keynes called animal spirits, not a judgment on the economic success or failure of high levels of M&A, whose consequences unfold in complex ways over long periods of time. The shell of the now "old" Wall Street remains, but encased in post-crisis regulation; beside it, a "new" relatively unregulated Wall Street has arisen, consisting of gargantuan, global, and growing former private-equity shops gone public—Blackstone, KKR, Apollo, Carlyle—aggressively investing in alternative assets like real estate and credit: complex amalgams of agent and principal, and so far a refutation of Jensen's dire warnings about the governance disaster of public ownership.[4] And yet, more broadly, the corporate world grows ever-more private, with buybacks, a private equity industry (which, as the market grows ever-more transactional and short term, now looks like long-term investing) steadily retiring more shares, and even tech start-ups like Uber, Snapchat, and Airbnb (taxis, texts, apartments) tapping private capital and postponing the old coming-out ball of the initial public offering: so-called unicorns. Some of this aversion to public status can be traced to uncertainties of running a public company, and the criticism that accompanies it, particularly over pay; some is the product of too much capital in search of gold. A growing herd of shareholder activists, including the ageless Icahn, cajole and threaten companies to meet shareholders' short-term desires; these hedge funds, not to say more traditional institutions, have agency and principal conflicts with their own investors, but when they get serious, they launch proxy contests, seeking board seats, not ownership. Directors retain the legal power to decide, and shoulder ever-greater burdens; senior manager pay, particularly in shares, inexorably rises as middle incomes stagnate. Meanwhile, the Berlean notion of stakeholdership appears as evanescent and elusive as Jensen and Erhard on integrity: a thicket of words, hiding—what? The corporation remains a realm of principals and agents, but the underlying conflict has less to do with managers and shareholders, and more to do with owners and workers, capital and labor—social divisions from the nineteenth century, and, reviving a very old issue, inequality, known to Marx and, for that matter, Plato.

Corporate governance sits uneasily within a larger politics, which is why so many managers want to go private. It is not, as many in the law and economics movement fervently wished, autonomous. Today, while shareholder governance represents orthodoxy, regular episodes of public outrage against Wall Street, executives, or corporations threaten to engulf it or, at least, envelope it in masses of new rules, which regulators cannot police and companies can never fully comply with.[5] Arguably, it's the worst of both worlds, inefficient *and* risky. Today, we live with a governance and takeover regime resembling in mood that of the early '60s: functional, seemingly inevitable, but not underpinned by deep and coherent belief. It is widely seen as requiring occasional adjustments, like an automobile tune-up, but it leaves a residue of cynicism behind. Regulatory oversight is quietly derided; Congress is feared, but not respected; voters are viewed as dangerously ignorant; power predominates. Key concepts like efficient markets or rational expectations, and the tendency to define success and efficiency in available, if straitjacketed terms—to, say, a stock price on any given day—have been discredited, but little has emerged to take their place. Ideological warfare over designated agents of corporate governance still simmers some forty years after Jensen and Meckling.[6] There's no visible road back to stakeholdership. Lipton's long defense of corporate management, as effective and brilliantly played as it has been, always had an anachronistic edge to it—a defense of an *ancien régime.*

Takeovers contain a powerful political contradiction. The M&A "game" at its '80s height (not in numbers, but in impact), as it was characterized by Wall Street and the media, was viewed as a winner-take-all adventure, a war, a struggle among smart guys, the apotheosis of risk-taking entrepreneurs and high-octane finance with the smell of arbitrage in the morning: a white-collar bloodsport. Everyone else, particularly workers and middle managers, each an agent theoretically prone to shirking and self-interest, could be handled contractually: they were not part of any governance equation, and the blood they shed occurred outside the frame. The result has been to abandon agents as expendable, unnecessary, unreliable, and potentially disloyal—a cost of doing business, like machinery or inventory. There was one problem with this view, however, besides the self-fulfilling nature of that belief in disloyalty and unfaithfulness: these folks silenced as voices in corporate governance make up the great mass of American voters, which in complex ways have been both drawn to and repelled by corporations and Wall Street. They possess great, if occasional, power. The nexus-of-contracts approach did not create the diminished sense of loyalty to the corporate enterprise—larger, cultural changes were afoot—but deepened it, particularly as senior executives swimming in stock options exchanged their agent status for the wondrous privileges of the principal—*ownership*—which, as part of the latter-day shareholder system, often implies power without responsibility. Today, this alignment of interests is celebrated as a panacea for the separation of ownership and control. But it also weakens and abandons ties between flesh-and-blood employees and the abstract conception they labor for called the corporation. It's a great irony that agency theory began with managers as the ultimate disloyal agents, with the most to gain or lose from pursuing their self-interest, and ended up with managers as members of a special class with special prerogatives and rewards who nearly always, one way or the other, walk away with those glittering tin trophies of American achievement—wealth, power, and worldly success.

ACKNOWLEDGMENTS

I met Bruce Wasserstein on an autumn day in 1998. I was working at *Institutional Investor,* in a slightly disheveled wedding cake of a building peering down on St. Patrick's Cathedral at 51st Street and Madison Avenue, once home to *Look* magazine and *Esquire.* Wasserstein Perella sat high in the reddish-hued Deutsche Bank building off Sixth Avenue, two blocks west, past 21 Club and the Museum of Broadcasting, next to the black slab of CBS. I had seen Wasserstein from across a room once, read about him though not deeply, but never met him. His office was a hangar stuffed with leather couches, Lucite deal tombstones, stacks of his recently published book, *Big Deal,* with a view east, toward Rockefeller Center: the skating rink was down there, a silver postage stamp. I was there because Wasserstein had this crazy idea to start a daily newspaper reporting on M&A, and he needed someone to run it. Well, it was his money; others, I learned, including some of his closest confederates, who were more proprietorial about how he spent his money than I was, were not fans. At the time, I was editor of *Institutional Investor,* a monthly magazine with a distinguished history—though (the irony was later apparent to me) I had received the top job in a battlefield promotion after the company had been sold over a year before. Commercially and journalistically, we had had a good year since the sale, but the Asian financial crisis had occurred and the shears of cost cutting were being audibly sharpened.

Besides, dot-com mania was in full bloom, with its frenzy of start-ups. Journalists, particularly the tech crowd, were getting rich, strange as that is to hear these days. The magazine business did not yet feel truly threatened, but it was coming, like winter.

Wasserstein was as advertised. His shirttail was out and his shoe-laces were untied; he was heavy; he pondered the ceiling. It was an easy interview. He talked. I listened. He sat in the chair and gently tapped his leg with what appeared to be a riding crop. He described his marvelous idea; later, I realized this was a variation of his "Dare to be great" speech. I can't recall the details, except it went on and on, and in the end I agreed to join his nascent enterprise. I was ready for something new, interested in the possibilities of working with a legend like Wasserstein.

And so for the next ten years, until his death, I worked for this man we referred to, out of his presence and with unearned familiarity, as "Bruce," or "Uncle Bruce" (and for his heirs for three more years, un-til they sold *The Deal*) covering transactions. It is an uneasy task to write about a figure you've worked for—listened to and observed at close range—and both liked and respected, without ever really know-ing him well. Contrary to his image, Wasserstein was a patient, long-term owner. He could be funny or remote; he was often opaque to the point of incomprehension; but he did not meddle in editorial matters; he did not yell and scream; he remained remarkably loyal. He was, in short, not your ordinary media owner. His idea was sort of crazy—and the notion of a daily national newspaper, *The Daily Deal,* was hair-raisingly expensive, particularly in the age of the Internet.

This book would never have been written had he not hired me to run *The Deal*'s editorial operation. I know there are parts of this book he might not agree with, particularly about events he was deeply in-volved with; he didn't necessarily approve of everything we wrote at *The Deal* either. But generally he was tolerant of differences, and his criticisms came after, not before, a story was published. For me, the years at *The Deal* turned into an immersion into the world of M&A, its trends and tendencies, its technical aspects and personalities, its scandals and myths. We spent a lot of time at *The Deal* pondering many of the themes that shape this account: from Delaware law to merger cycles, from private equity to post-merger integration to the nature of cycles. And when we had a chance, we got to consider larger questions like whether current levels of M&A were sustainable or whether M&A, broadly speaking, was good or bad—or something more ambiguous. I owe an enormous debt to the editors and reporters who labored at *The Deal*, day in and day out, through bubbles, recessions, terrorist attacks, budget cuts, layoffs, and financial crises.

There are far too many *Deal* people to thank individually, with two exceptions. I particularly spent many hours discussing, arguing, and debating legal and governance issues with *The Deal*'s Delaware maven and all-around raconteur, David Marcus, and with executive editor and acute observer of the media that swirled around dealmaking, Yvette Kantrow. Both read parts of the manuscript as well.

The longer I worked on this book the more I realized how long I had dwelled on certain matters, like the mechanism of corporate governance or the complexity of efficient markets or the role of institutional investors, that I had been writing about or thinking about well before that visit to Wasserstein. I was incredibly fortunate in 1990 to end up at a magazine, *Institutional Investor*, masterminded by the late Gilbert Kaplan, edited for many years by Peter Landau and David Cuduback, and shaped intellectually by Cary Reich, whose biography of André Meyer I quote promiscuously and gratefully. *Institutional Investor* was a monument to comprehensiveness made accessible, plus occasionally, as Kaplan wanted, broadly entertaining; it was a haven of long-form editing and writing lore of a kind now disappearing. The magazine allowed me to explore relatively arcane areas of politics, finance, and governance in the '90s that were really the foundations of *Bloodsport*.

I feel as if I've engaged in a kind of conversation over the years with my predecessors in financial journalism, if mostly as an often-dazzled reader. Chris Welles did some of his best work at *Institutional Investor*, and George Goodman—that is, "Adam Smith"—was the magazine's first editor. I was a neophyte at *Forbes* when Allan Sloan wrote his revelatory stories on LBOs and, with Howard Rudnitsky, the Milken network. I interviewed and wrote about the great John Brooks late in his career for the now-defunct *Financial World* and I profiled James Grant in my early days at *Institutional Investor,* the most fun I've ever had on a story. I commissioned and edited a review of *Barbarians at the Gate* for *II* when it was published, had a long, tortured but thought-provoking session with former Shearson CEO Peter Cohen about that best seller after I wrote a *II* profile of American Express's Jimmy Robinson III, and edited an *Institutional Investor* feature by Ida Picker about James Stewart's *Den of Thieves.* And at *The Deal* we always felt as if we were at least distantly related to the glories of Steven Brill's *The American Lawyer,* most directly through a newsletter we inherited that Brill had started in the '80s: *Corporate Control Alert.* A brief cup of coffee with Joe Nocera at the *New York Times* provoked me to move on this long-gestating project.

These were—and are—remarkable journalists, and their work reflected and shaped the history of that era. Like Wasserstein, they may not have always agreed with the liberties I've made of their work, and the context I've placed it in. But it was, by any measure, a glorious era for financial journalism and I hope I've done it justice.

I will always owe a debt to Steve Fraser, who edited my first two books, whose own work on Wall Street history is a challenge to anyone working that beat, and who reached out to help when I was just thinking about this project—when he was in the throes of his own book. I'm also happy to say I am one of many who have been able to tap Sarah Noble's fount of good sense and goodwill. The discussions I had with my agent Carol Franco were instrumental in making this book (I hope) more broadly accessible; and John Mahaney at Public Affairs did exactly what editors do too rarely these days: he made me cut, revise, and rethink. I have to thank Michael Peltz at *Institutional Investor* and Ed Finn and Phil Roosevelt at *Barron's* for providing steady work to subsidize this project. And I tip my hat to the redoubtable crew at *Barron's* copy desk, with whom I've spent many a lively Thursday and Friday over the past few years. I must add that Christine Arden's skilled copyediting on this manuscript was further proof why

I'm a fellow traveler, not a charter member, of the copyediting fellowship.

Last but hardly least: Camilla. A book project is rarely done alone. A book project sucks everyone around it into its turbulent wake, including the dog, two skeptical cats, and the itinerant children, Claire and Nick. Camilla understood what it meant when I started talking about doing another book; it's like letting a stranger move into your house, try on your shoes, and wander around in the middle of the night. (Actually, that fits the dog too.) Unlike M&A, only a fool would believe taking on a book project is driven by the maximization of wealth, which just happens to be a theme of this book. Camilla made room for this folly (hopefully in the architectural, or theatrical, sense) and its demands. I'm forever grateful for that and for so much else these many years.

NOTES

Introduction

1. David A. Hounshell and John Kenley Smith Jr., *Science and Corporate Strategy: DuPont R&D 1902–1980* (New York: Cambridge University Press, 1988), 1.

2. Ibid., 11.

3. For a discussion of Shapiro's restructuring of R&D and corporate strategy and Jefferson's stint as head of Central Research, see ibid., 588–589; for biographical details, see "Irving Shapiro, 85; Top DuPont Exec, Lawyer," *New York Times,* September 17, 2001.

4. Edward Graham Jefferson, "Biographical Memoirs," *Proceedings of the American Philosophical Association,* Vol. 153, No. 2, June 2008, 244.

5. Stuart Diamond, "Testing the Formula for a New Du Pont," *New York Times,* October 7, 1984.

6. Interview with Joseph Perella, *Institutional Investor,* June 1987, 412.

7. Lydia Chavez, "Du Pont's Unconvincing Merger," *New York Times,* November 14, 1982. Shareholder approval of the deal a year earlier was "punctuated alternately by sharp exchanges and warm applause," with Jefferson forced to defend the strategic logic of the deal and the presence of a Seagram representative on the board; see Kenneth B. Noble, "Takeover of Conoco Backed by Du Pont's Shareholders," *New York Times,* August 18, 1981.

Chapter One

1. Author's interview with Martin Lipton, October 13, 2013.

2. The biographical details on Adolf Berle come from Jordan A. Schwarz, *Liberal: Adolf A. Berle and the Vision of an American Era* (New York: Free Press, 1987).

3. As Schwarz recounts, in the 1930s Berle told his wife Beatrice that "his real ambition in life is to be the American Karl Marx—a social prophet" (ibid., 62).

4. Author's interview with Martin Lipton, October 13, 2013.

5. Adolf A. Berle and Gardiner Means, *The Modern Corporation and Private Property* (New Brunswick, NJ: Transaction Publishers, 2009).

6. Both the definitive chronology of Berle's intellectual shifts in the 1930s and the context of his debate with Merrick Dodd come from William W. Bratton and Michael Wachter, "Shareholder Primacy's Corporatist Origins: Adolf Berle and 'The Modern Corporation,'" *Journal of Corporation Law*, Vol. 34, 2008, 99.

7. Merrick Dodd, "For Whom Are Corporate Managers Trustees?" *Harvard Law Review* Vol. 45, 1932, 1145. Berle's reply came in "For Whom Corporate Managers Are Trustees: A Note," *Harvard Law Review*, Vol. 45, 1932, 1365.

8. Adolf A. Berle, "'Control' in Corporate Law," *Columbia Law Review*, Vol. 58, 1958, 1212.

9. Henry G. Manne, "Mergers and the Market for Corporate Control," *Journal of Political Economy*, April 1965, 110–120.

10. Ibid., 110.

11. Adolf A. Berle, "Modern Functions of the Corporate System," *Columbia Law Review*, Vol. 62, 1962, 433–449.

12. Ibid., 436–437.

13. Ibid., 445.

14. Berle, "Modern Functions of the Corporate System," 448. Berle elaborated on the subject of property rights in *Power Without Property* (New York: Harcourt Brace & Company, 1959). Berle argued that in a collective, corporatized society, the reality of private property had changed, and the shareholder ownership of the corporation "is no more private than a seat on a subway train" (p. 27).

15. Berle, "Modern Functions of the Corporate System," 448.

16. Ibid., 449.

17. Henry Hansmann and Reinier Kraakman, "The End of History for Corporate Law," the Center for Law, Economics and Business, Harvard Law School, Discussion Paper 280, March 2000.

Chapter Two

1. Adolf Berle, *Power Without Property* (New York: Harcourt Brace & Company, 1959), 63.

2. Harwell Wells, "'Corporate Law Is Dead': Heroic Managerialism, Legal Change, and the Puzzle of Corporation Law at the Height of the American Century," *University of Pennsylvania Journal of Business Law*, Vol. 15, 2013, 306. Wells's paper explores in depth the nature of mid-century corporate law and the context that Manning, among others, was reacting to.

3. Bayless Manning, "The Shareholders' Appraisal Remedy: An Essay for Frank Coker," *Yale Law Journal,* December 1962, 245.

4. Quoted in Abraham S. Goldstein, "Bayless Manning," *Stanford Law Review,* November 1971, vii–viii.

5. Stanley Reed, "Bayless Manning," *Stanford Law Review,* November 1971, vii.

6. Bayless Manning, review of *The American Stockholder* by J. A. Livingston, *Yale Law Review,* June 1958, 1477–1496.

7. Manning, "The Shareholders' Appraisal Remedy: An Essay for Frank Coker," December 1962, 223–265.

8. Ibid., 245.

9. Ibid.

10. Ibid.

11. Ibid., 245 (fn37).

12. Franklin C. Latcham, review of *Proxy Contests for Corporate Control* by Edward Aranow and Herbert Einhorn, *California Law Review,* May 1957, 225.

13. Abraham L. Pomerantz, review of *Proxy Contests for Corporate Control* by Edward Aranow and Herbert Einhorn, *University of Pennsylvania Law Review,* January 1969, 493.

14. Ibid., 497.

15. Much of this discussion of ethnicity in law firms comes from Eli Wald, "The Rise and Fall of the WASP and Jewish Law Firms," *Stanford Law Review,* April 2008, 101–165.

16. Wald, "Rise and Fall," 110.

17. Quoted in ibid., 132.

18. Wald, "Rise and Fall," 133.

19. Flom's biography is well known. But much of the information in this section comes from David Marcus's interview with Joe Flom, which appeared on page 30 of the July 19, 2010, issue of *The Deal* magazine. Other biographical details can be found in Lincoln Caplan's history of Skadden Arps, *Skadden: Power, Money and the Rise of a Legal Empire* (New York: Farrar, Strauss & Giroux, 1993).

20. Demas's basic biography is contained in his *New York Times* obituary, "George C. Demas, Expert on Corporate Takeovers," May 23, 1981.

21. "He's a Wall Street Superman," *Los Angeles Times,* April 11, 1967.

22. Demas quotes from ibid.

23. Pomerantz, review of *Proxy Contests for Corporate Control.*

24. David Marcus's interview with Joe Flom, *The Deal,* July 19, 2010, 30.

25. Arthur Long, quoted in Moira Johnston, *Takeover: The New Wall Street Warriors* (New York: Arbor House, 1986), 101.

26. Ibid., 100.

27. Quoted in Caplan, *Skadden,* 45.

28. Caplan, *Skadden,* 46.

29. Quoted in Caplan, *Skadden,* 153.

Chapter Three

1. Chris Welles, *The Last Days of the Club* (New York: E. P. Dutton, 1975).

2. Many of these details come from Felix Rohatyn, *Dealings: A Political and Financial Life* (New York: Simon & Schuster, 2010).

3. Ibid., 1–5.

4. The authority on Meyer is Cary Reich's *Financier: The Biography of André Meyer* (New York: John Wiley & Sons, 1983).

5. Ibid., 18.

6. Ibid.

7. Ibid., 19.

8. Author's interview with Felix Rohatyn, October 30, 2013; also see Rohatyn, *Dealings.*

9. Author's interview with Felix Rohatyn, October 30, 2013.

10. Jesse W. Markham, *A Financial History of the United States: Volume 2* (Armonk, NY: M. E. Sharpe, 2002), 288–290.

11. Reich, *Financier,* 21. Reich also devotes an entire chapter to Lazard and Avis (106–120).

12. Reich, *Financier,* 61.

13. Rohatyn, *Dealings,* 20.

14. Author's interview with Felix Rohatyn, October 30, 2013.

15. Reich, *Financier,* 226. Reich explores the complex triangle between Rohatyn, Geneen, and Meyer. Particularly in the early days of the relationship, Rohatyn would execute deals that Meyer had approved. Reich quotes one close observer: "Felix was the agent, but it was hard to separate Felix's contribution from André's." Rohatyn denied to Reich that this was the case.

16. Rohatyn, *Dealings,* 32.

17. John Brooks, *The Go-Go Years: The Drama and Crashing Finale of Wall Street's Bullish 60s* (New York: John Wiley & Sons, 1973), 153.

18. Rohatyn, *Dealings,* 31.

19. Ibid.

20. Ibid., 32..

21. Brooks, *Go-Go Years,* 179.

22. Rohatyn, *Dealings,* 36.

23. Ibid., 44.

24. This phrase originates with Paul M. Hirsch, "From Ambushes to Golden Parachutes: Corporate Takeovers as an Instance of Cultural Framing and Institutional Integration," *American Journal of Sociology,* January 1986, 800.

25. Fleischer was a major figure in mergers. He had written an early seminal piece on tender offers, later wrote a guide to the business, and advised on many major deals for decades. His stature was undoubtedly diminished by the dominance of Flom and Lipton.

26. David Marcus's interview with Joe Flom, *The Deal,* July 19, 2010, 30.

27. Rohatyn discusses the DLJ issue at the New York Stock Exchange in *Dealings*, 70–75.

28. Ibid., 74.

29. Ibid., 75.

Chapter Four

1. Lipton offered many biographical details about his early career in a 2013 interview with me, including his skepticism that anyone could predict the M&A market. In this chapter I cite other interviews as well, including one by the SEC Historical Society's Robert Colby on June 6, 2013, which focused on Lipton and corporate governance. Dan Slater wrote an insightful article on Lipton and his long ties to NYU, both the law school and the university, titled "Partner for Life," for the *NYU Law School Magazine*. And Lipton himself wrote a memoir, "My 60 Years at NYU," November 19, 2012, https://www.nyu.edu/content/dam/nyu/publicAffairs/documents/PDF/My60yearsAtNYU.pdf.

2. Author's interview with Martin Lipton, October 13, 2013.

3. Richard Phalon, *The Takeover Barons of Wall Street* (New York: G. P. Putnam's Sons, 1981), 175.

4. Steve Brill seems to have reported this story first, claiming seven sources. See "Two Tough Lawyers in the Tender-Offer Game," *New York Magazine*, June 21, 1976, 57.

5. Joseph Nocera, "It's Time to Make a Deal," *Texas Monthly*, October 1982, 57.

6. Author's interview with Martin Lipton, October 13, 2013.

7. William H. Starbuck, "Keeping a Butterfly and an Elephant in a House of Cards: The Elements of Entrepreneurial Success," *Journal of Management Studies*, Vol. 30, No. 9, 1993, 885–921.

8. Author's interview with Martin Lipton, October 13, 2013.

9. Ibid.

10. Ibid.

11. Ibid.

12. Chris Welles, *The Last Days of the Club* (New York: E. P. Dutton, 1975), 335–344.

13. Gilbert Kaplan's interview with Robert Baldwin, "Morgan Stanley's Race Against Itself," *Institutional Investor*, September 1980, 44.

14. David Marcus's interview with Joe Flom, *The Deal*, July 19, 2010, 30.

15. Welles, *Last Days of the Club*, 3.

16. Interview with Robert Greenhill, "The Way It Was: An Oral History," *Institutional Investor*, June 1987.

17. Julie Connelly, "The New Generation of Investment Bankers," *Institutional Investor*, September 1985, 165.

18. Author's interview with Martin Lipton, October 13, 2013.

19. Brill, "Two Tough Lawyers."

20. Ibid., 54.

21. Author's interview with Martin Lipton, October 13, 2013. On other occasions, Lipton has joked that he and Rohatyn became friends by sleeping together on that hallway couch during the crisis. Brill focuses on Garlock in "Two Tough Lawyers."

22. This quotation comes from Robert Slater, *The Titans of Takeovers* (New York: Prentice Hall, 1987), 9–10.

23. Nocera, "It's Time to Make a Deal," 57.

24. Brill, "Two Tough Lawyers," 56.

25. Herbert M. Wachtell, "Special Tender Offer Litigation Tactics," *The Business Lawyer,* May 1977, 1433.

26. These quotations come from my interview with Lipton on October 13, 2013.

Chapter Five

1. Brian R. Cheffins, "The History of Corporate Governance," paper presented at the annual meeting of the European Corporate Governance Institute, January 2012.

2. Arthur J. Goldberg, *New York Times,* "Debate on Outside Directors," October 29, 1972.

3. Frederick Andrews, "Management: The First Draft of a New Corporate Constitution," *New York Times,* April 22, 1977, 91.

4. Ralph Nader, Joel Seligman, and Mark J. Green, *The Taming of the Giant Corporation* (New York: Norton, 1976).

5. Harold Williams, "The Role of the Corporate Secretary in Promoting Corporate Accountability," paper presented at the annual meeting of the American Society of Corporate Secretaries, Boca Rotan, Florida, June 1, 1978.

6. There is a considerable literature on the travails of the American Law Institute's corporate governance project. See, for example, Jonathan R. Macey, "The Transformation of the American Law Institute," *George Washington University Law Review,* April 1993; Bayless Manning, "The Business Judgment Rule in Overview," *Ohio State Law Journal,* Vol. 45, 1985, 615–628; A. A. Sommer Jr., review of "A Guide to the American Law Institute Corporate Governance Project" by Charles Hansen, *The Business Lawyer,* August 1996; Kenneth Scott, "Corporate Law and the American Law Institute Corporate Governance Project," *Stanford Law Review,* May 1983; Cheffins, "The History of Corporate Governance," 6–10.

7. Robert Colby's interview with Joseph Grundfest, Securities and Exchange Commission Historical Society, June 20, 2013.

8. Ibid.

9. Louis Uchitelle, "Advocate of Paying Well Revises Thinking," *New York Times,* September 28, 2007.

10. Angus Burgin's *The Great Persuasion: Reinventing Free Markets Since the Depression* (Cambridge, MA: Harvard University Press, 2012) is an essential resource on the University of Chicago in the formative years of free-market economics, with a focus on Friedrich Hayek, Milton Friedman, John Maynard Keynes, and Lionel Robbins at the London School of Economics. Samuelson's quotation about Viner is on page 37. Also see R. H. Coase's memoir, "Law and Economics at Chicago," paper presented at the Henry C. Simon Memorial Lecture at the University of Chicago Law School, April 7, 1992.

11. The economics department at Chicago did not view itself, Burgin writes, as a "purposive group." On Viner's view of Knight, see Burgin, *The Great Persuasion,* 42.

12. Burgin, *The Great Persuasion,* 34.

13. Coase, "Law and Economics at Chicago."

14. The background of these market forecasters is effectively told in Walter A. Friedman, *Fortune Tellers: The Story of America's First Economic Forecasters* (Princeton, NJ: Princeton University Press, 2014).

15. See Peter Bernstein's *Capital Ideas: The Improbable Origins of Modern Wall Street* (New York: John Wiley & Sons, 1992).

16. Friedman, *Fortune Tellers,* p. 201. Peter Bernstein goes into greater technical detail on Cowles's study in *Capital Ideas,* 33–38.

17. Bernstein, *Capital Ideas;* see page 47 for the quotation about risk and page 53 for the quotation about an efficient portfolio.

18. Bernstein, *Capital Ideas,* 67.

19. See Athol Fitzgibbons, *Keynes's Vision: A New Political Economy* (Oxford: Clarendon Press, 1988).

20. George Stigler, "Henry Calvert Simons," *Journal of Law and Economics,* April 1975, 1.

21. Ibid., 3.

22. Coase discusses Simons in "Law and Economics at Chicago," 241. The "utopian" comment is on page 242.

23. Ibid., 241.

24. Quoted in Burgin, *The Great Persuasion,* 45.

25. The Chicago economists often wrote short memoirs and biographies. Director has his share, including the following: Edward Levi, "Aaron Director and the Study of Law and Economics," *Journal of Law and Economics,* September 1966, and Stephen Stigler, "Aaron Director Remembered," *Journal of Law and Economics,* October 2005. Both *The Great Persuasion* and Coase's memoir of Chicago's law and economics program include material on Director's key role at the university.

26. See Richard Posner, "The Chicago School of Antitrust Analysis," *University of Pennsylvania Law Review,* Vol. 127, 1979, 925–926.

27. Coase, "Law and Economics at Chicago," 244.

28. Ibid., 247.

29. Richard Posner, "Nobel Laureate Ronald Coase and Methodology," *Journal of Economic Perspectives,* Fall 1993, 204.

30. D. H. Robertson, quoted in Ronald Coase, "The Nature of the Firm," *Econometrica,* November 1937, 1.

31. Many of the details about Jensen's early years at Chicago come from Ralph Walkling's interview with Jensen at the Social Science Research Network; see "Pioneers in Finance: An Interview with Michael C. Jensen, Part I of II," December 20, 2011. All of the Jensen quotes in this chapter come from that interview.

32. Milton Friedman, "A Friedman Doctrine: The Social Responsibility of Business Is to Increase Its Profits," *New York Times Magazine,* September 13, 1970.

33. Michael C. Jensen and William Meckling, "Theory of the Firm: Managerial Behavior, Agency Costs, and Ownership Structure," *Journal of Financial Economics,* October 1976.

34. Ibid., 1.

35. William W. Bratton, "The 'Nexus of Contracts' Approach: A Critical Appraisal," *Cornell Law Review,* March 1989. That same year Bratton also wrote the related "The New Economic Theory of the Firm: Critical Perspectives from History," *Stanford Law Review,* July 1989.

36. Emanuel Derman, *Models. Behaving. Badly.* (New York: Free Press, 2011).

37. Ibid., 59.

38. Ibid.

39. Bratton, "The 'Nexus of Contracts' Approach," 415.

40. Ibid., 415–417. Bratton notes in passing that "characterized in the technical terms of social science methodology, the point [of agency theory] is a tautology—a statement true by definition" (p. 410).

41. Charles Perrow, *Complex Organizations: A Critical Essay* (New York: McGraw-Hill, 1986), 235.

42. Michael C. Jensen, "Toward a Theory of the Press," in Karl Brunner, ed., *Economic and Social Institutions* (Amsterdam: Martinus Nijhoff Publishers, 1979). This article is also available at the Social Science Research Network.

43. Ibid., 1.

44. Michael C. Jensen and William H. Meckling, "Between Freedom and Democracy," *The Banker,* October 1977.

Chapter Six

1. Richard Phalon, *The Takeover Barons of Wall Street: Inside the Billion-Dollar Merger Game* (New York: G. P. Putnam's Sons, 1981). Phalon's elegant, concise book is an invaluable look at a now-obscure transaction. It also represents one of the earliest entries into a genre that would soon boom.

2. Phalon, *Takeover Barons,* 25.

3. Ibid., 175–177.

4. Ibid., 179–180.

5. Phalon's anecdote about Liman and Sorenson are on pages 180–185 of *Takeover Barons.* The talking points are on page 180.

6. Phalon, *Takeover Barons,* 183.

7. Ibid., 232.

8. Jeff Madrick, *Taking America: How We Got from the First Hostile Takeover to Megamergers, Corporate Raiding and Scandals* (New York: Bantam Books, 1987), 173.

9. Martin Lipton, "Takeover Bids in the Target's Boardroom," *The Business Lawyer,* November 1979.

10. Ibid., 101.

11. Ibid., 101–102.

12. Ibid., 104.

13. Ibid.

14. Ibid.

15. Andrew Haldane, "The Race to Zero," speech to the International Economic Association, July 8, 2011.

16. Phalon, *Takeover Barons,* 208–209.

17. Lipton, "Takeover Bids," 105.

18. On *Dodge v. Ford,* see Lynn Stout, "Why We Should Stop Teaching *Dodge v. Ford,*" *Virginia Law & Business Review,* Spring 2008, and Jonathan R. Macey, "A Close Read of an Excellent Commentary on *Dodge v. Ford,*" *Virginia Law & Business Review,* Spring 2008.

19. Lipton, "Takeover Bids," 119.

20. Ibid., 113.

21. Ibid., 114.

22. Ibid., 115.

23. Frank H. Easterbrook and Daniel R. Fischel, "The Proper Role of a Target's Management in Responding to a Tender Offer," *Harvard Law Review,* April 1981.

24. Ibid., 1165.

25. Ibid., 1162.

26. Ronald Gilson, "A Structural Approach to Corporations: The Case Against Defensive Tactics in Tender Offers," *Stanford Law Review,* May 1981.

27. Easterbrook and Fischel, "Proper Role," 1169.

28. Ibid., 1173.

29. Ibid., 1182.

30. Ibid., 1183 (fn60).

31. Ibid., 1185.

Chapter Seven

1. Ronald Gilson, "Seeking Competitive Bids Versus Pure Passivity in Tender Offer Defenses," *Stanford Law Review,* November 1982; Lucian Bebchuk, "The Case

for Facilitating Competing Tender Offers," *Harvard Law Review,* Vol. 35, 1982. Easterbrook and Fischel entered the debate with "Auctions and Sunk Costs in Tender Offers," *Stanford Law Review,* Vol. 35, 1982. Gilson and Bebchuk then replied.

2. Jeff Madrick, *Taking America: How We Got from the First Hostile Takeover to Megamergers, Corporate Raiding and Scandals* (New York: Bantam Books, 1987), 194.

3. Susan C. Schneider and Roger M. Dunbar, "A Psychoanalytic Reading of Hostile Takeover Events," *Academy of Management Review,* July 1992, 537–567.

4. Icahn confessed to a genius for reductionism at a conference interview, "Delivering Alpha," *Institutional Investor* and CNBC, July 16, 2014.

5. Peter Drucker, *The Frontiers of Management* (Cambridge, MA: Harvard Business School Press, 2010), 235. The book was originally published in 1986.

6. Louis Lowenstein, "Pruning Deadwood in Hostile Takeovers: A Proposal for Legislation," *Columbia Law Review,* March 1983, 274.

7. Joseph Nocera, "It's Time to Make a Deal," *Texas Monthly,* October 1982, 4.

8. Robert Slater, *The Titans of Takeovers* (New York: Prentice Hall, 1987), 50.

9. Joel Seligman, *The Transformation of Wall Street* (New York: Houghton Mifflin, 1982), 431.

10. Ibid., 432. Seligman notes that Cohen promptly "disowned" the legislation: "Testifying in March 1969, he termed the Williams Act 'obsolete' and its use of disclosure to safeguard investors caught up in 'mid-twentieth-century industrial warfare' as 'inadequate.'"

11. Drucker, *Frontiers,* 242.

12. Ibid., 242.

13. Ronald Gilson, quoted in Lincoln Caplan, *Skadden: Power, Money and the Rise of a Legal Empire* (New York: Farrar, Strauss & Giroux, 1993), 140.

14. James Landis, *The Administrative Process* (New Haven, CT: Yale University Press, 1966).

15. Seligman, *The Transformation of Wall Street,* 416.

16. Ibid., 534–535.

17. See James J. McNider III, "What Is a Tender Offer?" *Washington & Lee Law Review,* June 1980; and Charlene Wendy Christofilis, "The Tender Offer: In Search of a Definition," *Washington & Lee Law Review,* June 1986.

18. Alan Brinkley, "The New Deal and the Idea of the State," in Steve Fraser and Gary Gerstle, eds., *The Rise and Fall of the New Deal Order, 1930–1980* (Princeton, NJ: Princeton University Press, 1989), 93.

19. Caplan, *Skadden,* 147.

20. John R. Evans, "Tender Offers: An SEC Perspective," address to the National Association of Corporate Directors, New York, June 22, 1979.

21. Ibid.

22. Edward F. Greene and James J. Junewicz, "A Reappraisal of Current Regulation of Mergers and Acquisitions," *University of Pennsylvania Law Review,* April 1984, 664.

23. Ibid., 665.

Chapter Eight

1. Paul Cowan, "The Merger Maestro," *Esquire,* May 1984, 62. The quote continues: "They're not trained to believe that thinking matters. People are used to letting the world define them instead of creating their own environments."

2. William D. Cohan, "Bruce Wasserstein's Last Surprise," *Vanity Fair,* May 2010.

3. Michael VerMeulen, "Yes, It's True What They Say About Bruce Wasserstein," *Institutional Investor,* April 1984, 142.

4. Jeff Madrick's line is from *Taking America: How We Got from the First Hostile Takeover to Megamergers, Corporate Raiding and Scandals* (New York: Bantam Books, 1987), 176. Cowan uses the movie reference in "The Merger Maestro," 58: "Wasserstein, who's more like a character in *The Big Chill* than *Chinatown,* uses Zen-like language to describe his mood in those high-pressure boardroom situations."

5. Photo in the *Michigan Daily,* October 14, 2009.

6. Bruce Wasserstein, *Big Deal: The Battle for Control of America's Leading Corporations* (New York: Warner Books, 1998).

7. Nicole Aber, "Bruce Wasserstein, University Alum and Finance Giant, Dies at 61," *Michigan Daily,* October 14, 2010. That classmate was Daniel Okrent, author, former Time Inc. journalist, and the first public editor of the *New York Times.*

8. VerMeulen, "Yes, It's True What They Say About Bruce Wasserstein," 140.

9. Interview with Joseph Perella, "The Way It Was: An Oral History," *Institutional Investor,* June 1987, 412.

10. Ibid., 413.

11. VerMeulen, "Yes, It's True What They Say About Bruce Wasserstein," 142.

12. Brett Cole, *M&A Titans* (Hoboken, NJ: John Wiley & Sons, 2008), 82. Cole interviewed Butler in 2006.

13. Interview with Bruce Wasserstein, "The Way It Was: An Oral History," *Institutional Investor,* June 1987, 414.

14. Cole, *M&A Titans,* 83. Cole interviewed Perella in 2007.

15. VerMeulen, "Yes, It's True What They Say About Bruce Wasserstein," 141.

16. Interview with Joseph Perella, "The Way It Was: An Oral History," *Institutional Investor,* June 1987, 414.

17. Quoted in Lincoln Caplan, *Skadden: Power, Money and the Rise of a Legal Empire* (New York: Farrar, Strauss & Giroux, 1993), 148.

18. VerMeulen, "Yes, It's True What They Say About Bruce Wasserstein," 147.

19. Cole, *M&A Titans,* 82. Cole interviewed Maher in 2007.

20. Ibid., 113. Cole interviewed Lovejoy in 2007.

21. Milton Friedman, "The Methodology of Positive Economics," in *Essays in Positive Economics* (Chicago: University of Chicago Press, 1966), 3.

Chapter Nine

1. Paul Cowan, "The Maestro of Mergers," *Esquire,* May 1984, 58.

2. Michael VerMeulen, "Yes, It's True What They Say About Bruce Wasserstein," *Institutional Investor,* April 1984.

3. Jeff Madrick, *Taking America: How We Got from the First Hostile Takeover to Megamergers, Corporate Raiding and Scandals* (New York: Bantam Books, 1987), 179–180.

4. Quoted in Robert Slater, *The Titans of Takeovers* (New York: Prentice Hall, 1987), 117. Slater cites *Forbes,* September 19, 1980.

5. Madrick, *Taking America,* p. 187.

6. Ibid., 182. Madrick quotes a single "participant" as saying that Flom seemed like the best investment banker around on the Pullman deal. Credit on these M&A deals is always difficult to target precisely, with ego, envy, competitive pressures, and questions of access making nearly every statement about who did what uncertain. Wasserstein, for all his "genius" (or so he was labeled), did not work alone; and Flom was a brilliant tactician.

7. Louis Lowenstein, "Pruning Deadwood in Hostile Takeovers: A Proposal for Legislation," *Columbia Law Review,* March 1983, 250.

8. Allan Sloan, *Three Plus One Equals Billions: The Bendix, Martin-Marietta War* (New York: Arbor House, 1983), 35.

9. Arthur Goldberg, "Regulation of Hostile Tender Offers: A Dissenting View and Recommended Reforms," *Maryland Law Review,* Vol. 43, No. 2, 1984.

10. Lowenstein, "Pruning Deadwood." Lowenstein focused on the Bendix, Martin-Marietta struggle. In this connection, he proposed that tender offers remain open for six months and that shareholders get to vote on any target response to a tender offer that entails so-called structural changes.

11. Robert Teitelman, "The Revolt Against Free-Market Economics," *Institutional Investor,* June 1992.

12. Lowenstein, "Pruning Deadwood," 253.

13. Ibid., 253.

14. Ibid., 256.

15. Martin Lipton, "Takeover Bids in the Target's Boardroom: An Update After One Year," *The Business Lawyer,* April 1981.

16. Author's interview with Martin Lipton, October 13, 2013.

17. Quoted in Cowan, "The Maestro of Mergers," 68.

18. Bruce Wasserstein, *Big Deal: The Battle for Control of America's Leading Corporations* (New York: Warner Books, 1998), 689.

19. Author's interview with Martin Lipton, October 13, 2013.

20. Author's telephone interview with Martin Lipton, July 17, 2014.

21. Ibid.

22. Wachtell Lipton memorandum on the Warrant Dividend Plan, September 1982.

23. Wasserstein, *Big Deal.* His discussion on the technical plusses and minuses of the poison pill, particularly in tender-offer defenses (pp. 689–700), is quite good.

Chapter Ten

1. Felix Rohatyn, *Dealings: A Political and Financial Life* (New York: Simon & Schuster, 2010), 159.

2. Ibid., 161.

3. "The Making of a Celebrity," *Institutional Investor,* December 1984.

4. See Cary Reich, *Financier: The Biography of André Meyer* (New York: John Wiley & Sons, 1983).

5. Rohatyn, *Dealings,* 161.

6. Ibid.

7. Ibid., 164.

8. Ibid., 164–165.

9. Ibid., 165.

10. Felix Rohatyn, *The Twenty-First Century: Essays on Economics and Public Finance* (New York: Random House, 1983).

11. Ibid., 10.

12. "Surge in Company Takeovers Causes Widespread Concern," *New York Times,* July 3, 1984.

13. Michael C. Jensen and Clifford W. Smith Jr., *The Modern Theory of Corporate Finance* (New York: McGraw-Hill, 1984).

14. Michael C. Jensen and Richard S. Ruback, "The Market for Corporate Control: The Scientific Evidence," *Journal of Financial Economics,* March 1983, 1.

15. Gershon Mandelker, "Risk and Return: The Case of Merging Firms," *Journal of Financial Economics,* December 1974, 303–335.

16. F. M. Scherer, "Corporate Takeovers: The Efficiency Arguments," *Journal of Economic Perspectives,* Winter 1988, 70.

17. Jensen and Ruback, "The Market for Corporate Control," 4–5.

18. Ibid., 2–3.

19. Michael C. Jensen, "Takeovers: Folklore and Science," *Harvard Business Review,* November 1984. Page numbers are based on the paper at the Social Science Research Network.

20. Ibid., 4.

21. Scherer, "Corporate Takeovers," 72.

22. Jensen, "Takeovers: Folklore and Science," 10.

23. Ibid., 13.

24. Council of Economic Advisors, *Economic Report to the President,* February 1985.

25. Ibid., 187.

26. Ibid., 189.

27. Ibid., 187–188.

28. Ibid., 188.

29. Ibid., 191.

30. Ibid., 192.

31. Ibid., 208. The report concludes: "Moreover, a rule that requires stockholders to sell their shares simply because a bid at a premium has been made would not be good public policy. . . . [I]f there is no market failure in the governance of publicly traded firms, then there is no principled basis on which to prevent stockholders in target firms from negotiating over a share of those gains" (p. 208).

32. Council of Economic Advisors, *Economic Report to the President,* 212.

Chapter Eleven

1. Adam Smith, *The Money Game* (New York: Vintage Books, 1976).

2. Ibid., 21.

3. Ibid., 22.

4. Ibid., 11.

5. Connie Bruck, *The Predator's Ball: The Inside Story of Drexel Burnham and the Rise of the Junk Bond Raiders* (New York: Penguin Books, 1988), 31.

6. D. Graham Burnett, "Tombstones and Toys," *Cabinet,* No. 54, Summer 2014, 21–26.

7. Bruce Wasserstein, *Big Deal: The Battle for Control of America's Leading Corporations* (New York: Warner Books, 1998), 84.

8. Bruck, *Predator's Ball,* 50.

9. Smith, *The Money Game,* 22.

10. James Stewart, *Den of Thieves* (New York: Simon & Schuster, 1991), 382.

11. James Grant, *Money of the Mind: Borrowing and Lending in America from the Civil War to Michael Milken* (New York: Farrar, Strauss & Giroux, 1994), 383.

12. Ibid., 376.

13. Allan Sloan in *Forbes* picked up on this in several of his mid-'80s stories on Milken. In "Mike Milken's Marvelous Money Machine," with Howard Rudnitsky, November 19, 1984: "Milken saw opportunity: a gaping market imperfection" (p. 207). That imperfection, Sloan and Rudnitsky noted, "has been partly closed" now that so much money had poured in (p. 222).

14. Bruck, *Predator's Ball,* 86.

15. Ibid., 86.

16. Ibid., 245.

17. Howard Rudnitsky, Allan Sloan, and Richard L. Stern with Matthew Heller, "A One-Man Revolution," *Forbes,* August 25, 1986, 35.

18. Cary Reich, "Milken the Magnificent," *Institutional Investor,* August 1986.

19. Bruck, *Predator's Ball,* 143.

20. Daniel Fischel, *Payback: The Conspiracy to Destroy Michael Milken and His Financial Revolution* (New York: HarperBusiness, 1995).

21. Wasserstein, *Big Deal,* 82.

22. Grant, *Money of the Mind,* 377.

23. Bruck, *Predator's Ball,* 62–66.

24. Ibid., 101.

25. Grant, *Money of the Mind,* 378.

26. Sloan followed his "The Clear and Present Dangers of LBOs" two weeks later with an analysis of the Metromedia LBO titled "The Magician," April 23, 1984, 32. On November 19, 1984, he and Howard Rudnitsky presented their dissection of Milken's network: "Mike Milken's Marvelous Money Machine," 207. "Corporate Takeovers—Is No One Safe?" followed on March 11, 1985, with a cover takeoff of Edvard Munch's *The Scream,* 138. "A One-Man Revolution" by Sloan, Rudnitsky, Richard Stern, and Matthew Heller ran on August 26, 1986, 34. And Sloan alone wrote "An Extra Slice of the Pie," February 9, 1987, 33, which takes apart a (secret) sweetheart deal that Drexel got for investing in Boesky's arbitrage fund.

27. Sloan, "The Clear and Present Danger in LBOs," 39.

28. Ibid.

29. Grant, *Money of the Mind,* 371–376.

30. Allan Sloan, "The Magician," *Forbes,* April 23, 1984, 32.

31. Allan Sloan and Howard Rudnitsky, "Mike Milken's Marvelous Money Machine."

32. Interview with Allan Sloan, November 10, 2015.

33. Stewart, *Den of Thieves,* 117.

34. Ibid., 118.

35. William Safire, "On Language; Beware the Junk-Bond Bust-Up Takeover," *New York Times,* January 27, 1985.

36. Fred R. Bleakley, "The Power and Peril of Junk Bonds," *New York Times,* April 14, 1985.

37. Nathaniel Nash, "Federal Reserve's Curb on Bonds Is Assailed by Administration," *New York Times,* December 24, 1985.

38. See Peter T. Kilborn, "The New Clash with Volcker," *New York Times,* December 26, 1985, and Robert D. Hershey Jr., "Fed Adopts 'Junk Bond' Curbs," *New York Times,* January 9, 1986.

39. Caroline Rand Harron and Michael Wright, "Fed Stands Firm; The Dow Plunges," *New York Times,* January 12, 1986.

Chapter Twelve

1. F. M. Scherer, "A New Retrospective on Mergers," *Review of Industrial Organization,* June 2006, 327–341.

2. F. M. Scherer, *Industry Structure, Strategy, and Public Policy* (New York: Harper-Collins College Publishers, 1996), 1.

3. Ibid.

4. Richard Posner, *Antitrust Law* (Chicago: University of Chicago Press, 1976). Posner later confessed that the first edition of the book was something of a jeremiad, replaced by a "profound, a revolutionary change in the law." Also see Robert Bork, *The Antitrust Paradox* (New York: Basic Books, 1978).

5. Richard Posner, "The Chicago School of Antitrust Analysis," *University of Pennsylvania Law Review,* Vol. 127, 1978, 931. Posner specifically attacked the Harvard school of industrial organization for its practice of doing competition studies in specific industries—and for not being "theoretical."

6. "Professor Emeritus Jesse W. Markham Dead at 93," Harvard Business School, July 8, 2009, http://www.hbs.edu/news/releases/Pages/jessemarkham.aspx.

7. Author's interview with F. M. Scherer, November 12, 2014.

8. Jesse W. Markham, *Conglomerate Enterprise and Public Policy* (Cambridge, MA: Division of Research, Graduate School of Business Administration, Harvard University, 1973).

9. Author's interview with F. M. Scherer, November 12, 2014.

10. Ibid.

11. David J. Ravenscraft and F. M. Scherer, *Mergers, Sell-Offs, and Economic Efficiency* (Washington, DC: Brookings Institute, 1987), 1.

12. Ibid., 1.

13. Details about the planning of the conference come from my interview with Susan Rose-Ackerman on January 19, 2015.

14. Author's interview with Susan Rose-Ackerman, January 19, 2015. In 1985, Rose-Ackerman was the director of Columbia Law School's law and economics center. She is now a professor of law at Yale.

15. Author's interview with Ellen Magenheim, January 19, 2015.

16. Much of the detail that follows from the conference is contained in a book: John C. Coffee, Jr., Louis Lowenstein, and Susan Rose-Ackerman, eds., *Knights, Raiders, and Targets: The Impact of the Hostile Takeover* (New York: Oxford University Press, 1988).

17. Quoted in Coffee, Lowenstein, and Rose-Ackerman, *Knights, Raiders, and Targets,* 208.

18. See Richard J. Evans, *Altered Pasts: Counter-factuals in History* (Waltham, MA: Brandeis University Press, 2013).

19. Quoted in Coffee, Lowenstein, and Rose-Ackerman, *Knights, Raiders, and Targets,* 208–209.

20. See Coffee, Lowenstein, and Rose-Ackerman, *Knights, Raiders, and Targets,* 253–259.

21. Quoted in ibid., 256.

22. Frank. H. Easterbrook and Gregg A. Jarrell, "Do Targets Gain from Defeating Tender Offers?" *New York University Law Review,* 1984, 284.

23. See Coffee, Lowenstein, and Rose-Ackerman, *Knights, Raiders, and Targets,* 314–354.

24. Quoted in ibid., 140.

25. See Coffee, Lowenstein, and Rose-Ackerman, *Knights, Raiders, and Targets,* 321–337.

26. Ibid., 336.

27. Quoted in ibid., 336.

28. See Peter J. Clark, *Beyond the Deal: Optimizing Merger and Acquisition Value* (New York: HarperBusiness, 1991). This 1991 book opens with the subhead "Most Deals Don't Work" and focuses attention on post-merger integration issues. Clark traces back consulting work on failed mergers to November 1984 as well as to a McKinsey & Co. study that noted that two-thirds of diversification programs failed to earn more than if they had used the money to invest in bank CDs. And in 1985, W. T. Grimm concluded that one in three mergers came unwound.

29. Scherer, "A New Retrospective on Mergers," 13–14. Scherer thought that the best research he did was in *Mergers, Sell-Offs, and Economic Efficiency* and that the finance academics deliberately ignored it, particularly its skepticism of event studies and efficiency. His experience in the polemics of the '80s, particularly with Jensen, eventually led him to give up the field. He notes that Brookings asked Jensen to read the book before publication as one of the peer reviews, but said he was too busy. Jensen, he says, in those years was beginning to alter his ideas about takeovers and market efficiency.

30. Scherer, "A New Retrospective on Mergers," 12.

31. Ibid., 13.

32. Ibid., 15.

33. Ibid., 16.

Chapter Thirteen

1. See Simeon E. Baldwin, "American Business Corporations Before 1789," *American Historical Review*, April 1903, 449–465; James Willard Hurst, *The Legitimacy of the Business Corporation Law of the United States, 1780–1970*, reviewed by William L. Cary, *Columbia Law Review*, November 1970; Alfred Chandler, "The Beginning of 'Big Business' in American Industry," *Business History Review*, Spring 1959; and Joel Seligman, "A Brief History of Delaware's General Corporation Law of 1899," *Delaware Journal of Corporate Law*, Vol. 1, No. 2, 1976, 249–287.

2. Alexis de Tocqueville, *Democracy in America*, ed. J. P. Mayer (New York: Doubleday, 1969), 693.

3. Seligman, "A Brief History," 265.

4. Ibid., 268.

5. Lincoln Steffens, "New Jersey: A Traitor State," *McClure's Magazine*, May 1905.

6. Quoted in Joseph Mahoney, "Backsliding Convert: Woodrow Wilson and the 'Seven Sisters,'" *American Quarterly*, Spring 1966, 71–80.

7. Lincoln Steffens, "Little Delaware Makes a Bid for the Organization of Trusts," *American Law Review*, No. 419, 1899, 419.

8. See Seligman, "A Brief History," 269. In footnote 102, he cites "State Laws: The Survival of the Unfit," *University of Pennsylvania Law Review*, No. 62, 1914, 509–510.

9. William L. Cary, "Federalism and Corporate Law," *Yale Law Journal,* March 1974, 666.

10. Gordon Moodie, "Forty Years of Charter Competition: A Race to Protect Directors from Liability?" John M. Olin Center for Economics and Business Fellows' Discussion Paper Series, Harvard University, September 2004, 14.

11. Ibid., 15. Moodie quotes Samuel Arsht and Walter K. Stapleton from "Delaware's New General Corporate Law: Substantive Changes," *Business Law,* November 1967. Arsht was in many ways the senior Delaware lawyer in the rewriting of the Delaware general corporate law; Stapleton was a younger associate, later a prominent federal judge. For an overview of the writing of the DGCL, see David Marcus, *The Deal,* May 19, 2008.

12. See Seligman, "A Brief History," 280.

13. Ibid., 282.

14. Lewis Black, "Why Corporations Choose Delaware," Delaware Department of State, Division of Corporations, 2007.

15. Elvin R. Latty, "Why Are Business Corporation Laws Largely Enabling?" *Cornell Law Review,* Summer 1965, 601.

16. Moodie, "Forty Years of Charter Competition," 19.

17. John Brooks, *The Go-Go Years: The Drama and Crashing Finale of Wall Street's Bullish 60s* (New York: John Wiley & Sons, 1973), 82.

18. Cary, "Federalism and Corporate Law."

19. Ibid., 663.

20. Ibid., 672.

21. Ibid., 673.

22. Ibid., 679.

23. Ibid., 684.

24. Ibid., 701.

25. Ibid., 705.

26. Ralph K. Winter, "State Law, Shareholder Protection and the Theory of the Corporation," *Journal of Legal Studies,* June 1977, 251–292.

27. Ibid., 254.

28. Ibid., 253.

29. See Roberta Romano, "The States as a Laboratory: Legal Innovation and State Competition for Corporate Charters," *Yale Journal on Regulation,* January 2006, 210–247, as well as her book praising the laboratory model of federalism, *The Genius of American Corporate Law* (Washington, DC: AEI Press, 1992). Ralph Winter wrote the Foreword.

30. John Coffee, "Symposium: The Next Century in Corporate Law," *Delaware Journal of Corporate Law,* Vol. 25, 2000, 88.

31. See Lucian Arye Bebchuk, "Federalism and the Corporation: The Desirable Limits on State Competition in Corporate Law," *Harvard Law Review,* Vol. 105, No.

7, 1992, 1443–1510; Ehud Kamar, "A Regulatory Competition Theory of Indeterminacy in Corporate Law," *Columbia Law Review,* Vol. 98, 1998; Marcel Kahan and Edward B. Rock, "Our Corporate Federalism and the Shape of Corporate Law," June 2004, faculty scholarship paper No. 46; Guhan Subramanian, "The Disappearing Delaware Effect," *Journal of Law, Economics & Organization,* April 2004, 32–59; Mark Roe, "Delaware's Politics," *Harvard Law Review,* August 2005, 2491–2543; Frank H. Easterbrook, "The Race for the Bottom in Corporate Governance," *Virginia Law Review,* Vol. 98, 2009, 685–706. Easterbrook declared Winter's paper "the most important contribution to the economic analysis of the corporate law since Ronald Coase's *The Nature of the Firm* in 1937"—and further commented that only Jensen and Meckling's agency theory paper is "a serious rival." This is just a sampling of the ongoing federalism-federalist debate.

32. Bayless Manning, "The Business Judgment Rule in Overview," *Ohio State Law Review,* Vol. 45, No. 3, 1985, 1.

33. *Cheff v. Mathes,* Delaware Supreme Court, 1964.

34. *Smith v. Van Gorkom,* Delaware Supreme Court, 1985. The case continues to be controversial. Stephen M. Bainbridge ("*Smith v. Van Gorkom,*" UCLA School of Law, Law and Economics Research Paper Series, May 2008) considers it the most important corporate law case of the twentieth century, and Jonathan Macey ("*Smith v. Van Gorkom:* Insights About CEOs, Corporate Law Rules, and the Jurisdictional Competition for Corporate Charters," *Northwestern University Law Review,* January 2002) argues that the case remains "intellectually frustrating" after fifteen years.

35. Bainbridge, in "*Smith v. Van Gorkom,*" lays out the payment of the damages on page 30.

36. In what was a rare outcome in Delaware, Justice McNeilly offered a blistering dissent to the majority opinion. McNeilly dismissed that opinion as an "advocate's closing address to a hostile jury" and "a comedy of errors." See http://wikisource.org/wiki/Smith_v._Van_Gorkom/Dissent_McNeilly.

37. Bayless Manning, "Reflections and Practical Tips on Life in the Boardroom After Van Gorkom," *The Business Lawyer,* January 1985, 1.

38. Daniel Fischel, "The Business Judgment Rule and the Trans Union Case," *The Business Lawyer,* August 1985, 1455.

39. See Moodie, "Forty Years of Charter Competition," 39. The legislature responded to the decision with section 102(b)(7) of the Delaware Code, allowing the indemnification of directors, which, Moodie notes, was "warmly welcomed by corporations and set off what was probably the largest migration of firms to Delaware in absolute terms in its history" (p. 41).

40. Manning, "Reflections and Practical Tips," 2.

41. Quoted in Macey, *Smith v. Van Gorkom,* 625.

42. *Unocal v. Mesa Petroleum,* Chancery, 1985.

43. Andrew G. T. Moore II, "The Birth of Unocal—A Brief History," *Delaware Journal of Corporate Law,* November 2006, 878.

44. This description comes from Moira Johnston, *Takeover: The New Wall Street Warriors: The Men, the Money, the Impact* (New York: Arbor House, 1986), 264. Johnston had particularly good access to the Pickens group, including the Skadden lawyers. Her depiction of the courtroom scenes is full of detail and captures the rich drama and tension of a number key mid-'80s cases.

45. Eric A. Chiappinelli, "The Life and Adventures of *Unocal*—Part 1: Moore the Marrier," *Delaware Journal of Corporate Law,* Vol. 23, 1998. Chiappinelli argues that Moore's desire to justify a flawed earlier decision in *Pogostin* led to the ambiguities of *Unocal,* years of needless litigation, and much of the subsequent takeover jurisprudence. Chiappinelli elaborates on this argument in an e-mail exchange dated February 3, 2015: "The Delaware court, especially the Supreme Court under Moore, did a serious disservice to corporate law with Unocal and Revlon. There's no reason I can think of why the BJR [business judgment rule] and the Entire Fairness tests couldn't have been slightly modified and tailored to M&A settings (whether friendly or hostile, one-bidder or multiple bidders) in ways that would have been clearer and more intellectually honest."

46. *Unocal v. Mesa Petroleum,* Delaware Supreme Court, June 10, 1985.

47. Moore, "The Birth of Unocal," 871 (fn19).

48. *Unocal v. Mesa Petroleum,* Delaware Supreme Court, 1985, 5–6.

49. Ibid., 1.

50. Ibid., 6.

51. Ronald Gilson and Reinier Kraakman, "Delaware's Intermediate Standard for Defensive Tactics," *The Business Lawyer,* February 1989, 254.

52. Lipton's influence on *Unocal* was both detailed and profound. See R. Franklin Balotti, Gregory V. Varallo, and Brock E. Czeschin, "UNOCAL Revisited: Lipton Influence on Bedrock Takeover Jurisprudence," *The Business Lawyer,* August 2005, 1399–1417.

53. *Unocal v. Mesa Petroleum,* Delaware Supreme Court, 1985, 7. The opinion argues: "It is now well recognized that such offers [two-tier bids] are a classic coercive measure designed to stampede shareholders to tender at the first tier, even at an inadequate price, out of fear of what they will receive at the back end of the transaction."

54. Moore, "The Birth of Unocal," 871 (fn19).

55. Michael Jensen, "When Unocal Won Over Pickens, Shareholders and Society Lost," *Financier,* November 1985, 50–52.

56. See David Margolick, "Law Review Is Caught in Corporate Crossfire," *New York Times,* September 24, 1984.

57. "Protecting Shareholders Against Partial and Two-Tiered Takeovers: The 'Poison Pill' Preferred," *Harvard Law Review,* June 1984, 1964–1983.

58. Ibid., 1983.

59. Margolick, "Law Review Caught in Corporate Crossfire."

60. Ibid.

61. Moore, "The Birth of Unocal," 884.

62. Johnston, *Takeover,* 268.

63. Robert Colby, "Interview with Joseph Grundfest," Securities and Exchange Commission Historical Society, June 30, 2013.

64. *Moran v. Household International, Inc.,* Delaware Supreme Court, November 20, 1985, 4.

65. Johnston, *Takeover,* 273. Johnston quotes Irving Shapiro on Moore: "It was a hot court. A lot of questions from the bench. But Justice Moore was climbing all over me with questions. I quickly interpreted that as saying, 'We'll show this guy that he's just another lawyer when he comes before this court.'"

66. *Moran v. Household,* 3.

67. Ibid., 7.

68. Moore, "The Birth of Unocal," 884.

69. Ibid., 885.

Chapter Fourteen

1. Michael Jensen, "Takeovers and the Business Judgment Rule," Proceedings of Corporate Governance: A Definitive Exploration of the Issues, UCLA, 1983, 1.

2. Ibid., 3–5.

3. Ibid., 5.

4. Ibid., 7.

5. Ibid., 11.

6. Ibid., 11.

7. *J. P. Stevens Shareholder Litigation,* Chancery, 1988.

8. *Guth v. Loft,* Delaware Supreme Court, 1939.

9. William T. Allen, Leo E. Strine, Jr., and Leonard P. Stark, "Judge 'the Game by the Rules': An Appreciation of the Judicial Philosophy of Walter K. Stapleton," *Delaware Law Review,* Vol. 6, 2003.

10. William T. Allen, "A Bicentennial Toast to the Delaware Court of Chancery 1792–1992," *The Business Lawyer,* November 1992, 365.

11. William T. Quillen and Michael Hanrahan, "A Short History of the Delaware Court of Chancery," *Delaware State Courts,* 1993, http://courts.delaware.gov /chancery/history.stm.

12. William T. Allen, "Our Schizophrenic Conception of the Business Corporation," *Cardozo Law Review,* 1992–1993, 1.

13. Ronald J. Gilson, "The Fine Art of Judging: William T. Allen," *Delaware Journal of Corporate Law,* Vol. 22, 1997, 914–916.

14. Quillen and Hanrahan, "A Short History of the Delaware Court of Chancery."

15. Donald F. Parsons, Jr., and Joseph R. Slights III, "The History of Delaware's Business Courts: Their Rise to Preeminence," *Business Law Today,* March/April 2008, 20–25.

16. Gilson, "The Fine Art of Judging," 916.

17. Allen, "Our Schizophrenic Conception," 278.

18. Quoted in Stephen J. Massey, "Chancellor Allen's Jurisprudence and the Theories of the Corporate Law," *Delaware Journal of Corporate Law,* Vol. 17, 1992, 687.

19. Willliam T. Allen, "Ambiguity in Corporate Law," *Delaware Journal of Corporate Law,* Vol. 22, 1997, 899.

20. William T. Allen, "The Pride and the Hope of Delaware Corporate Law," address published in the *Delaware Journal of Corporate Law,* Vol. 25, 2000, 70–78.

21. William Meyers, "Showdown in Delaware: The Battle to Shape Takeover Law," *Institutional Investor,* February 1989, 66.

22. Lawrence Cunningham and Charles M. Yablon, "Delaware Fiduciary Law After QVC and Technicolor: A Unified Standard (and the End of Revlon Duties)," *The Business Lawyer,* January 1994.

23. Meyers, "Showdown in Delaware," 71.

24. Ibid.

25. Ibid.

26. Andrew G. T. Moore II, "The 1980s—Did We Save the Stockholders While the Corporation Burned?" *Washington University at St. Louis Quarterly,* Vol. 70, 1992, 282.

27. Bayless Manning, "Reflections and Practical Tips on Life in the Boardroom after *Van Gorkom,*" *The Business Lawyer,* November 1985, 2.

28. Marcel Kahan, "Paramount or Paradox: The Delaware Supreme Court's Takeover Jurisprudence," *Iowa Journal of Corporate Law,* Vol. 19, 1994, 583.

29. Quoted in Quillen and Hanrahan, "A Short History of the Delaware Court of Chancery."

30. See footnote 5 on page 685 of Massey's massive review of Allen's jurisprudence, which focuses on Columbia Law School's John Coffee's repeated praise of Allen as "probably the country's most influential and respected judge on corporate law matters." Coffee also admitted that "law professors like [Allen] as a group." In footnote 6 on page 686, Massey did note that this view was not universal, either among law professors or in the press. *Newsday* writer John Riley presented his 1989 "Corporate Stalinism" award to Allen for his decision in *Time,* which a Wall Street chief echoed as "corporate Marxism."

31. Meyers, "Showdown in Delaware," 66.

32. Allen, "Ambiguity in Corporate Law," 895.

33. *Mercier v. Inter-Tel,* Chancery, August 2007.

34. Allen, "Ambiguity in Corporate Law," 898.

35. Ibid., 898.

36. Quoted in Massey, "Chancellor Allen's Jurisprudence," 691.

37. Allen, "Ambiguity in Corporate Law," 901.

38. Gilson, "The Fine Art of Judging," 914.

39. The classic modern formulation of this is Isaiah Berlin, "Two Concepts of Liberty," in *Four Essays on Liberty* (Oxford: Oxford University Press, 1969), 118–172.

40. Joseph Ellis, *The Quartet: Orchestrating the Second American Revolution* (New York: Knopf, 2015), 172. Ellis emphasizes how the compromises in the constitutional conventional between state and federal sovereignty not only were reflective of public opinion but also created an ambiguity that made it a "living" document.

41. Allen, "Our Schizophrenic Conception," 265.

42. Ibid.

43. Ibid., 273.

44. Ibid., 275.

45. Ibid., 280.

46. Ibid., 281.

Chapter Fifteen

1. Russell Baker, "Creature of *Fortune,*" *New York Times,* January 14, 1984.

2. Frank H. Easterbrook and Daniel R. Fischel, *The Economic Structure of the Corporate Law* (Cambridge, MA: Harvard University Press, 1991), 167.

3. "Ron Perelman: The Man Who Collects Companies," *Business Week,* September 10, 1995.

4. Connie Bruck, *The Predator's Ball: The Inside Story of Drexel Burnham and the Rise of the Junk Bond Raiders* (New York: Penguin Books, 1988), 201–240. Bruck provides a detailed narrative of the deal.

5. Clyde Haberman, "Arthur L. Liman, a Masterly Lawyer, Dies at 64," *New York Times,* July 18, 1997.

6. Ezra Zilkha, *From Baghdad to Boardrooms: My Family's Odyssey* (New York: E. K. Zilkha, 1999). The situation is discussed in John Close, *A Giant Cow-Tipping by Savages: Inside the Turbulent World of Mergers & Acquisitions* (New York: Palgrave Macmillan, 2013).

7. In *Predators' Ball,* Bruck notes that to incentivize Drapkin, Perelman insisted he be made a principal—that is, someone who has a financial stake in the deal. This was highly unusual for a partner at a major law firm.

8. Robert Cole, "A Victory by Revlon Seen Near," *New York Times,* August 28, 1985. The paper observed that Revlon was using a defense that CBS had successfully mounted to repel Ted Turner. "Revlon's gambit, analysts say, is to create so much debt that Pantry Pride's plan to raise money by selling Revlon-backed junk bonds would fail because investors would regard them as too risky."

9. Bruck, *Predators' Ball,* 223.

10. *MacAndrews & Forbes Holdings v. Revlon,* Chancery, October 24, 1985.

11. Anthony Ramirez, "Ron Perelman: Revlon's Striving Makeover Man," *Fortune,* January 5, 1986.

12. Quoted in John Brooks, *The Takeover Game* (New York: E. P. Dutton, 1987), 237. Bruck has a similar Rifkind quote in *Predator's Ball.* While looking out at St. Bartholomew's Church on Park Avenue from his office, Rifkind says, "If somebody could prove to you that the bricks of that cathedral [*sic*] could fetch a higher price in the market, would you dismantle it? I know, I know, today it is put 'em together and break 'em up—no cement anywhere."

13. Bruck, *Predators' Ball,* 222.

14. Ibid., 226–227.

15. *Revlon v. MacAndrews & Forbes Holdings,* Delaware Supreme Court, March 13, 1986.

16. See Ronald J. Gilson and Reinier Kraakman, "Delaware's Intermediate Standard for Defensive Tactics: Is There Substance to Proportionality Review?" *The Business Lawyer,* February 1989, 247–274.

17. Gordon Smith, "Chancellor Allen and the Fundamental Question," *Seattle University Law Review,* August 4, 1998, 585.

18. The quotation comes from Eric A. Chiappinelli, "The Life and Adventures of Unocal—Part 1: Moore the Marrier," *Delaware Journal of Corporate Law,* Vol. 23, 1998, 118. Also see Stephen J. Massey, "Chancellor Allen's Jurisprudence and the Theories of the Corporate Law," *Delaware Journal of Corporate Law,* Vol. 17, 1992; Smith, "Chancellor Allen and the Fundamental Question"; and Dennis Block, Stephen A. Radin, and Michael J. Maimone, "Chancellor Allen, the Business Judgment Rule, and the Shareholders' Right to Decide," *Delaware Journal of Corporate Law,* Vol. 17, 1992. The surveys by Massey and Block et al. were part of a 1992 issue of the *Delaware Journal of Corporate Law* dedicated to Allen's jurisprudence.

19. William T. Allen, "Independent Directors in MBO Transactions: Are They Fact or Fantasy?" *The Business Lawyer,* August 1990, 2056.

20. See Diana B. Henriques, *The Great White Shark of Wall Street: Thomas Mellon Evans and the Original Corporate Raiders* (New York: Scribner, 2000).

21. Many of the details on the developing Macmillan situation come from the Delaware court cases—namely, *Robert M. Bass Group v. Edward P. Evans et al.,* Chancery, July 18, 1988; *Macmillan v. Robert M. Bass Group,* Delaware Supreme Court, September 14, 1988; and *Mills Acquisition v. Macmillan,* Delaware Supreme Court, November 2, 1988.

22. *Mills Acquisition v. Macmillan,* Delaware Supreme Court, November 2, 1988.

23. Ibid.

24. *Mills Acquisition v. Macmillan,* Delaware Supreme Court, November 2, 1988. Also see William F. Johnson, "*Mills Acquisition Co. v. Macmillan, Inc.:* 'Corporate Auctions Now Require Sharper Supervision by Directors,' *American University Law Review,* Spring 1990.

25. *Mills Acquisition v. Macmillan,* Delaware Supreme Court, November 2, 1988.

26. Edward B. Rock, "Saints and Sinners: How Does Delaware Corporate Law Work?" *UCLA Law Review,* January 1997, 1048. Rock, nearly ten years after the Macmillan cases, still reflects on the raw impact of the *Macmillan* opinions: "When grouped together, the three opinions in *Macmillan* establish Evans and Reilly as among the villains of Delaware corporate law, with Wasserstein as an archetype of the unprincipled investment banker. The very language of the opinions proclaims its identity as morality play" (p. 1047).

27. Sarah Bartlett, "Delaware Gets Tough Toward Investment Bankers," *New York Times,* May 30, 1989.

28. Johnson, "*Mills Acquisition Co. v. Macmillan, Inc.:* 'Corporate Auctions Now Require Sharper Supervision by Directors,' 762.

29. "Edward P. Evans, Businessman and Top Va. Horse Breeder, Dies at 68," *Washington Post,* January 5, 2011.

30. Quoted in Bartlett, "Delaware Gets Tough."

31. Bruce Wasserstein, *Big Deal: The Battle for Control of America's Leading Corporations* (New York: Warner Books, 1998), 154.

32. William Meyers, "Showdown in Delaware: The Battle to Shape Takeover Law," *Institutional Investor,* February 1989, 72.

33. *City Capital Associates v. Interco Inc.,* Delaware Supreme Court, November 1, 1988, 7.

34. Andrew G. T. Moore II, "The 1980s—Did We Save the Stockholders While the Corporation Burned?" *Washington University at St. Louis Quarterly,* Vol. 70, 1992, 284.

Chapter Sixteen

1. *City Capital Associates v. Interco,* Chancery, November 1, 1988.

2. Carol Loomis, "The Inside Story of Time Warner," *Fortune,* November 20, 1989, 16.

3. *Paramount Communications v. Time,* Chancery, July 14, 1989.

4. Kathryn Harris, "Time Warner Caps Steve Ross' Big Comeback: With Huge Media Merger, He Lives Up to His Image of Financial Genius, Dreamer," *Los Angeles Times,* March 6, 1989.

5. Connie Bruck, *Master of the Game: Steve Ross and the Creation of Time Warner* (New York: Penguin Books, 1994), 246.

6. Ibid., 262.

7. Ibid., 263.

8. *Paramount Communications v. Time,* Delaware Supreme Court, February 26, 1990, 10.

9. The anecdote comes from Bruck, *Master of the Game,* 269.

10. *Paramount Communications Inc. v. Time,* Chancery, July 14, 1989, 7.

11. The anecdote comes from Loomis, "The Inside Story," 33.

12. Loomis, "The Inside Story," 18.

13. Richard W. Stevenson, "Not Just Another Charlie Bludhorn," *New York Times,* June 11, 1989.

14. "In Quotes," *New York Times,* July 2, 1989.

15. Paul Richter, "*Paramount vs. Time*: Delaware Showdown Set: Fate of a Media Giant Hangs in Balance as Court Rules on Unprecedented Case,*" Los Angeles Times,* July 10, 1989.

16. Floyd Norris, "Market Place: In Time Inc. Battle, Eyes Are on the Court," *New York Times,* June 15.

17. Richter, "*Paramount vs. Time*: Delaware Showdown Set."

18. Bruck, *Master of the Game,* 274. Bruck quotes an attorney who was worried that Moore might have felt there had been "corporate shenanigans."

19. *Blasius Industries v. Atlas,* Chancery, July 25, 1988.

20. William Meyers, "Showdown in Delaware: The Battle to Shape Takeover Law," *Institutional Investor,* February 1989, 75.

21. Ibid.

22. Stephen Labaton, "The Poison Pill Takes a Beating," *New York Times,* November 14, 1988.

23. Meyers, "Showdown in Delaware," 77.

24. Ibid.

25. *Paramount Communications Inc. v. Time,* Chancery, July 14, 1989. All quotes from Allen come from this opinion.

26. *Paramount Communications v. Time,* Delaware Supreme Court, February 26, 1990. Henry Horsey wrote this opinion.

27. Terry M. Hackett, "*Paramount Communications, Inc. v. Time Inc.:* Taking the Teeth Out of Proportionality Review," *Loyola University Chicago Law Review,* Fall 1990.

28. The opinion offered a baffling footnote that credited two academics, NYU's Ronald Gilson and Harvard's Reinier Kraakman, with noting a third threat: the well-known and noncontroversial opportunity loss. Horsey claimed the two believed that substantive coercion would buttress Unocal, despite the fact that he had already rejected its use. In a second footnote, Horsey got tangled up in efficient markets, arguing "that there may indeed be several market values for any corporation's stock. We have so held in another context," as if Delaware trumped the economists. Here, he again embraced Allen's conclusion, while ignoring his reasoning. What other context was he referring to? *Van Gorkom,* where Horsey scoffed at the significance of a 50 percent premium, then kicked the valuation problem back to Chancery to resolve. For Horsey, little had apparently changed.

29. Loomis, "The Inside Story," 3.

30. Eric A. Chiappinelli, "The Life and Adventures of Unocal—Part 1: Moore the Marrier," *Delaware Journal of Corporate Law,* Vol. 23, 1998, 140.

31. The issue of a Skadden "plot" was raised in a *New York Times* story by Diana B. Henriques, "Top Business Court Under Fire; Critics Say Politics is Hurting Delaware Judiciary," May 23, 1995. The case involved a suit by a Technicolor shareholder, Cinerama, claiming that shareholders had gotten too little in the buyout engineered by Perelman. The case dragged on for two decades in Delaware—UCLA law professor Stephen Bainbridge calls it "corporate law's *Jarndyce v. Jarndyce*" on his blog (http://www.professorbainbridge.com/professorbainbridgecom/2004/03/cinerama-v -technicolor-the-anticlimax.html)—and involved five remands from the Delaware Supreme Court to Chancery, two full trials, and a flock of opinions. Both Moore and Allen handled aspects of the case; Skadden defended Perelman, who in the end lost, paying Cinerama $5.6 million in damages. Bainbridge describes one Supreme Court decision in this series, *Cede & Co. v. Technicolor,* as one of "the worst Delaware Supreme Court decisions in history." The *Times* seemed to be suggesting that Perelman, or his lawyers at Skadden, tried to bring down Moore, who had twice joined unanimous decisions against the Revlon chief. The evidence offered was a $1,200 campaign contribution to Governor Tom Carper from Revlon. The fact that Skadden had an office in Wilmington, and that Leo Strine, a Carper aide and soon-to-be-named Chancery vice-chancellor, had once worked at Skadden, provided the ammunition. But in the end this Skadden plot as well as the partisan charges stretch credulity, particularly given the fact that Moore had so clearly made enemies during his tenure.

32. Henriques, "Top Business Court Under Fire; Critics Say Politics Is Hurting Delaware Judiciary."

33. Andrew G. T. Moore II, "The 1980s—Did We Save the Stockholders While the Corporation Burned?" *Washington University at St. Louis Quarterly,* Vol. 70, 1992, 287. On the Paramount case, Moore defended the logic of the Supreme Court opinion. Time never planned to sell and there was no breakup envisioned, so *Time* should be judged by *Unocal* rather than by *Revlon*. Moore seemed to agree that "shareholder would tender into Paramount's cash offer in ignorance of the strategic benefit that Time's combination with Warner might produce." In short, with a strategic plan, nearly any defensive action of a board is "reasonable." Moore added: "We did establish the rules by which the battles were fought."

Chapter Seventeen

1. John Brooks, *The Takeover Game: The Men, the Moves, and the Wall Street Money Behind Today's Nationwide Merger Wars* (New York: E. P. Dutton, 1987).

2. Connie Bruck, *The Predator's Ball: The Inside Story of Drexel Burnham and the Rise of the Junk Bond Raiders* (New York: Penguin Books, 1988), 205.

3. Carol Loomis, "The Biggest, Looniest Deal Ever," *Fortune,* June 18, 1990. Loomis says that the deal brought the "excessive Eighties to an absurdly fitting end." In fact, more absurdity and destruction were to come.

4. "Robert Campeau's Special Genius," *New York Times,* January 17, 1990.

5. See Steve Fraser, *Every Man a Speculator: A History of Wall Street in American Life* (New York: Harper-Collins, 2005). Fraser covers a lot more than the 1980s, but he captures in great detail the ambiguity of Americans toward Wall Street—the dreams and the nightmares. He's quite good on the allure of the '80s: "The after-hour social life of Wall Street's newest moguls had a narcotic effect on journalists." That imagery continues to captivate. See John Close, *A Giant Cow-Tipping by Savages: Inside the Turbulent World of Mergers and Acquisitions* (New York: Palgrave Macmillan, 2013).

6. Jensen's statement to the House Ways and Means Committee was published as "Active Investors, LBOs and the Privatization of Bankruptcy," in the *Journal of Applied Corporate Finance* (Spring 1998), and in a book, *Theory of the Firm: Governance, Residual Claims and Organizational Forms* (Cambridge, MA: Harvard University Press, 2000).

7. Jensen, "Active Investors," 36.

8. Ibid., 36.

9. Ibid., 37.

10. Ibid., 37–39. Few major LBO firms even in that early period employed only ten people. Moreover, while the LBO firms did often reduce the size of their corporate headquarters (though not always), they could not eliminate certain centralized functions, including senior managers, who were often paid well above the remuneration levels of public companies.

11. Jensen, "Active Investors," 39–40. Jensen was testifying just as LBOs were about to crash in a historic recession. Jensen's source for much of his performance data, former Harvard grad student Steven Kaplan (later at the University of Chicago), continued to study LBO performance for the next several decades. Kaplan and others have shown persistent above-market returns—so-called alpha—particularly for top-quartile firms. See Robert Teitelman, "Private Equity Giants Take an Alternative Route," *Institutional Investor,* April 2003.

12. Jensen, "Active Investors," 41–44.

13. Felix G. Rohatyn, "The Debt Addiction," *New York Review of Books,* April 13, 1989.

14. Felix G. Rohatyn, "The Blight on Wall Street," *New York Review of Books,* March 12, 1987.

15. Ibid., 2.

16. Ibid., 5.

17. Ibid., 6.

18. Ibid., 7–9.

19. Ibid., 9.

20. Rohatyn, "The Debt Addiction." Rohatyn proposed that a blue-ribbon committee be formed "to undertake an objective review of these matters for the Congress and the administration, and make recommendations." He proposed a two-year deadline. Rohatyn does not explain how such an omnibus bill could be enacted when basic tender-offer changes remained stalled. He also proposed that the United States needed to shift from consumption to investment.

21. Ibid., 9.

22. See James Stewart, *Den of Thieves* (New York: Simon & Schuster, 1991), 457. In his acknowledgments, Stewart thanks his parents: "At their hands, I learned the moral lessons of this book long before I knew anything about the riches and power of Wall Street."

23. Rohatyn, "The Debt Addiction," 1–2.

24. Rohatyn, "The Blight," 2.

25. "King Henry: Why KKR's Kravis May Be Headed for a Fall—Even If He Wins the Battle for RJR Nabisco," *Business Week,* November 14, 1989.

26. Bryan Burrough and John Helyar, *Barbarians at the Gate: The Fall of RJR Nabisco* (New York: Harper & Row, 1990), 354.

27. Hope Lampert, *True Greed: What Really Happened in the Battle for RJR Nabisco* (New York: NAL Books, 1990). Lampert was also the author of *Till Death Do Us Part: Bendix vs. Martin Marietta.* The KKR books include Sarah Bartlett, *Money Machine: How KKR Manufactured Power and Profits* (New York: Warner Books, 1991), and George Anders, *Merchants of Debt: KKR and the Mortgaging of America's Business* (New York: Basic Books, 1992). Bartlett's book is more gossipy, personal, and critical; Anders's focuses more on the transactions and is the best history of the firm to date.

28. "Book Discussion on *Barbarians at the Gate,*" C-Span, November 19, 2008. All of the Burrough and Helyar quotations come from this video.

29. Felix Rohatyn, *Dealings: A Political and Financial Life* (New York: Simon & Schuster, 2010), 203.

30. Ibid.

31. "Book Discussion on *Barbarians at the Gate.*"

32. Burrough and Helyar, *Barbarians,* 73.

33. Ibid., 94.

34. Ibid., 497–498.

35. *In Re RJR Nabisco, Inc. Shareholder Litigation,* Chancery, February 8, 1990.

36. Bryan Burrough, "Top Deal Maker Leaves a Trail of Deception in Wall Street Rise," *Wall Street Journal,* January 22, 1990, 1.

37. Anthony Bianco, *Rainmaker: The Saga of Jeff Beck, Wall Street's Mad Dog* (New York: Random House, 1991). This book is a fascinating look at 1980s dealmaking, despite the fact that Bianco's role as a friend and chronicler of Beck is a classic confusion of journalistic roles. Bianco appeared miffed when Burrough beat him to the Beck tale he had been sitting on.

Chapter Eighteen

1. Charles Hansen, "The Duty of Care, the Business Judgment Rule, and the American Law Institute Corporate Governance Project," *The Business Lawyer,* August 1998, 1355–1376; A. A. Sommer's review of Charles Hansen's "A Guide to the American Law Institute Corporate Governance Project," *The Business Lawyer,* August 1996, 1331–1338.

2. Francis Fukuyama, *The End of History and the Last Man* (New York: Free Press, 1992).

3. Henry Hansmann and Reinier Kraakman, "The End of History for Corporate Law," The Harvard John M. Olin Discussion Paper, March 2000, http://www.law. harvard.edu/programs/olin_center/papers/pdf/280.pdf.

4. Ibid., 1.

5. Ibid., 4.

6. Citations and downloads have become a kind of best-seller list in the social sciences. In 2001, Kraakman and Hansmann were No. 5 on the list of most-cited corporate law papers; see Fred Shapiro and Michelle Pearse, "The Most Cited Law Review Articles of All Time," *Michigan Law Review,* 2012. The list overall is led by William Cary on Delaware, with Easterbrook and Fischel on "The Proper Role" at No. 2, Ralph Winter on state law at No. 4, and Lipton's "Takeover Bids" at No. 10. Kraakman's paper on efficient market mechanisms appears on that list with Ronald Gilson at No. 4. On the Social Science Research Network, which Michael Jensen has long been involved in, Kraakman's paper with Meckling on agency theory comes in at No. 2 for the most downloads. No. 1 is "'I've Got Nothing to Hide' and Other Misunderstandings of Privacy," by David J. Sovlove. No. 5 is a paper titled "Fuck," by Christopher M. Fairman.

7. Marcel Kahan and Edward B. Rock, "How I Learned to Stop Worrying and Love the Pill: Adaptive Responses to Takeover Law," *University of Chicago Law Review,* June 2002.

8. Reinier Kraakman, "The Best of All Possible Worlds (or Pretty Darn Close)," *University of Chicago Law Review,* June 2002.

9. Andrei Shliefer and Robert Vishny, "The Limits of Arbitrage," *Journal of Finance,* March 1997, 35–55.

10. An enormous amount has been written about the AOL, Time Warner merger, so much so that's it's become a cliché. Perhaps the best treatment of it as a deal, not a soap opera, is Robert F. Bruner, *Deals from Hell: M&A Lessons That Rise Above the Ashes* (Hoboken, NJ: Wiley & Sons), 2004. Bruner is the dean of the University of Virginia's Darden School of Business and has written extensively about the craft of M&A.

11. See William B. Chandler III and Leo E. Strine Jr., "The New Federalism of the American Corporate Governance System: Preliminary Reflections of Two Residents of One Small State," *University of Pennsylvania Law Review,* Vol. 152, 2003. Chandler was Allen's successor as chancellor of the Court of Chancery, and Strine was a

vice-chancellor. Strine eventually succeeded Chandler as chancellor and is now chief justice of the Delaware Supreme Court.

12. Kahan and Rock, "How I Learned to Stop Worrying and Love the Pill," 901.

13. Richard Posner, *The Crisis of Capitalist Democracy* (Cambridge, MA: Harvard University Press, 2010). Posner's dissection of the 2008 financial crisis involved some serious questioning of what had once been Chicago verities, including the strong form of efficient markets, mark-to-market accounting, and the reality of bubbles. Posner also analyzed the alignment of interests between executives and shareholders: "The two aims—better aligning executives' incentives with those of shareholders, and reducing the riskiness of executives' compensation—are inconsistent. Shareholders in a publicly held corporation are generally less risk-averse than executives, because they have a smaller stake in the enterprise, so they can diversify away any risk. . . . Top executives have much more to lose, in reputation and future earnings prospects, from the collapse of their company" (pp. 183–184).

14. Brian R. Cheffins, "The History of Corporate Governance," European Corporate Governance Institute, Working Paper No. 184/2012, January 2012, examines Jensen's view of corporate governance and public corporations in 1992. Cheffins quotes Jensen in his presidential address to the American Finance Association in 1992: "[S]ubstantial data support the proposition that the internal control systems of publicly held corporations have generally failed to cause managers to maximize efficiency and value." Jensen blames the shutdown of the capital markets in the early '90s "as an effective mechanism for motivating change, renewal and exit." Cheffins sees this as the "economics scholars" gradually adopting "corporate governance in their lexicon."

15. Michael C. Jensen, "The Eclipse of the Public Corporation," *Harvard Business Review,* September–October 1989.

16. Michael C. Jensen with Donald H. Chew, "U.S. Corporate Governance: Lessons from the '80s," in Peter L. Bernstein, ed., *The Portable MBA in Investment* (Hoboken, NJ: John Wiley & Sons, 1995).

17. Ibid., 3.

18. Ibid., 6.

19. Ibid., 9–11.

20. Michael C. Jensen, "Value Maximization, Stakeholder Theory, and the Corporate Objective Function," *Journal of Applied Corporate Finance,* Fall 2001.

21. Ibid.

22. Joseph Fuller and Michael C. Jensen, "Just Say No to Wall Street," *Journal of Applied Corporate Finance,* Winter 2002. Fuller was the CEO of the Monitor Group, a consulting firm Jensen worked with.

23. Acceptance speech for the European Financial Management Readers' Choice Best Paper, 2004, for "The Agency Cost of Overvalued Equity and the State of Corporate Finance."

24. Ibid.

25. Michael C. Jensen and Kevin J. Murphy, *CEO Pay and What to Do About It: Restoring Integrity to Executive Compensation and Capital-Market Relations* (Cambridge, MA: Harvard Business Review Press, 2008).

26. Michael C. Jensen and William Meckling, "The Nature of Man," *Journal of Applied Corporate Finance,* Summer 1994. Jensen also published the essay in a book: *Foundations of Organizational Strategy* (Cambridge, MA: Harvard University Press, 1998).

27. See Warner Erhard and Michael C. Jensen, "Putting Integrity into Finance," Harvard Business School Negotiation, Organizations and Markets Research Papers, September 2014.

28. "Michael C. Jensen," *The Journal of Finance,* April 2010, vi–ix.

Chapter Nineteen

1. Louis Lowenstein, *Sense and Nonsense in Corporate Finance* (New York: Addison-Wesley, 1991), 145.

2. Ibid., 147.

3. See Robert Teitelman, "Merge or Die: Slow Economy Sheds New Light on M&A," *Institutional Investor,* January 2014.

4. Robert Teitelman, "Private Equity Giants Take an Alternative Route," *Institutional Investor,* April 2003.

5. See Stephen Bainbridge, *Corporate Governance After the Financial Crisis* (Oxford: Oxford University Press, 2012), particularly his discussion of "quack corporate governance regulations." Bainbridge notes that the resurgence of federal regulation has constrained Delaware. Martin Lipton arrives at roughly the same place from a very different path in "Will a New Paradigm for Corporate Governance Bring Peace?" Harvard Law School Forum on Corporate Governance and Financial Regulation,, October 5, 2015, http://corpgov.law.harvard.edu/2015/10/05/will-a-new-paradigm-for-corporate-governance-bring-peace/. Lipton points to the rise of proxy advisors and particularly activist investors, which he argues have been encouraged by the Securities and Exchange Commission. "Over the past thirty years," he writes, "the net effect of legislative and regulatory actions has been to create an environment in which the corporate governance of public companies is highly regulated and there is little or no restraint on the tactics employed by activist hedge funds."

6. See Leo E. Strine Jr., "Can We Do Better by Ordinary Investors? A Pragmatic Reaction to the Dueling Ideological Mythologists of Corporate Law," *Columbia Law Review,* Vol. 114, 2014, 449–502. Strine, the current chief justice of the Delaware Supreme Court, particularly aims his ire at Harvard Law's Lucian Bebchuk, who, he writes, would label anyone in favor of a limitation on shareholder direct democracy as an "insulation advocate."

INDEX

ALEX HALPIN

Robert Teitelman was the founding editor-in-chief of *The Deal* and the longtime author of the magazine's opening column, "Transactions." Prior to *The Deal* he was a writer for *Forbes* and the editor of *Institutional Investor* magazine.

PublicAffairs is a publishing house founded in 1997. It is a tribute to the standards, values, and flair of three persons who have served as mentors to countless reporters, writers, editors, and book people of all kinds, including me.

I. F. Stone, proprietor of *I. F. Stone's Weekly*, combined a commitment to the First Amendment with entrepreneurial zeal and reporting skill and became one of the great independent journalists in American history. At the age of eighty, Izzy published *The Trial of Socrates*, which was a national bestseller. He wrote the book after he taught himself ancient Greek.

Benjamin C. Bradlee was for nearly thirty years the charismatic editorial leader of *The Washington Post*. It was Ben who gave the *Post* the range and courage to pursue such historic issues as Watergate. He supported his reporters with a tenacity that made them fearless and it is no accident that so many became authors of influential, best-selling books.

Robert L. Bernstein, the chief executive of Random House for more than a quarter century, guided one of the nation's premier publishing houses. Bob was personally responsible for many books of political dissent and argument that challenged tyranny around the globe. He is also the founder and longtime chair of Human Rights Watch, one of the most respected human rights organizations in the world.

•   •   •

For fifty years, the banner of Public Affairs Press was carried by its owner Morris B. Schnapper, who published Gandhi, Nasser, Toynbee, Truman, and about 1,500 other authors. In 1983, Schnapper was described by *The Washington Post* as "a redoubtable gadfly." His legacy will endure in the books to come.

Peter Osnos, *Founder and Editor-at-Large*